Race and Manifest Destiny

RACE
AND MANIFEST DESTINY

The Origins of American
Racial Anglo-Saxonism

Reginald Horsman

Harvard University Press
Cambridge, Massachusetts
and London, England

Copyright © 1981 by the President and Fellows
of Harvard College
All rights reserved
Printed in the United States of America

This book has been digitally reprinted. The content remains identical to that of previous printings.

Library of Congress Cataloging in Publication Data

Horsman, Reginald.
    Race and manifest destiny.
    The origins of American racial Anglo-Saxonism
    Includes bibliographical references and index.
    1. United States—Territorial expansion.   2. Racism—United States.   3. Racism—Great Britain.   I. Title.   II. Title: Anglo-saxonism.
E179.5H69   305.8'00973   81-4293
ISBN 0-674-74572-8 (cloth)   AACR2
ISBN 0-674-94805-X (paper)

For
John, Janine, and Mara

Acknowledgments

I wish to thank the College of Letters and Science and the Graduate School of the University of Wisconsin-Milwaukee for helping to support the research which led to this book.

Chapter 4 originally appeared in somewhat different form in the *Journal of the History of Ideas* 37 (July–Sept. 1976): 387–410; part of chapter 6 is from a paper delivered in February 1975 at a Newberry Library Conference on the American Revolution and will form part of the published proceedings of that conference; some material in chapters 7 and 8 originally appeared in the *American Quarterly* 27 (May 1975): 152–168 (Copyright, 1975, American Studies Association).

Reginald Horsman

University of Wisconsin-Milwaukee

Contents

	Introduction	1
I	**EUROPEAN AND COLONIAL ORIGINS**	7
1	Liberty and the Anglo-Saxons	9
2	Aryans Follow the Sun	25
3	Science and Inequality	43
4	Racial Anglo-Saxonism in England	62
II	**AMERICAN DESTINY**	79
5	Providential Nation	81
6	The Other Americans	98
7	Superior and Inferior Races	116
8	The Dissemination of Scientific Racialism	139
9	Romantic Racial Nationalism	158
III	**AN ANGLO-SAXON POLITICAL IDEOLOGY**	187
10	Racial Destiny and the Indians	189
11	Anglo-Saxons and Mexicans	208
12	Race, Expansion, and the Mexican War	229
13	A Confused Minority	249
14	Expansion and World Mission	272
	Conclusion	298
	Notes	305
	Index	357

Race and Manifest Destiny

Introduction

By 1850 American expansion was viewed in the United States less as a victory for the principles of free democratic republicanism than as evidence of the innate superiority of the American Anglo-Saxon branch of the Caucasian race. In the middle of the nineteenth century a sense of racial destiny permeated discussions of American progress and of future American world destiny. Many think of rampant doctrines of Caucasian, Aryan, or Anglo-Saxon destiny as typical of the late years of the nineteenth century, but they flourished in the United States in the era of the Mexican War.

The contrast in expansionist rhetoric between 1800 and 1850 is striking. The debates and speeches of the early nineteenth century reveal a pervasive sense of the future destiny of the United States, but they do not have the jarring note of rampant racialism that permeates the debates of mid-century.[1] By 1850 the emphasis was on the American Anglo-Saxons as a separate, innately superior people who were destined to bring good government, commercial prosperity, and Christianity to the American continents and to the world. This was a superior race, and inferior races were doomed to subordinate status or extinction. This new racial arrogance did not pass unnoticed at the time. A minority frequently asked why the American Anglo-Saxons could so easily read God's intentions for mankind, and some, unkindly but accurately, pointed out that there was no "Anglo-Saxon race"; England clearly contained a mixture of peoples, and the white population of the United States was even less homogenous. The religious orthodox had the additional problem of reconciling the idea of a superior separate race with the biblical notion of one human species descended in just a few thousand years from Adam and Eve through Noah. But the logical inconsistencies and contradictions were ignored. Even the critics of the new assumptions of peculiar racial destiny acknowledged that the idea had caught the political and popular imagination, and even the opponents of a vigorously expansionist foreign policy cast their arguments in racial terms.

The origins of this American rejection of other peoples have to be sought both in Europe and the United States. In one respect the new assumptions stemmed logically from a whole trend toward racialist thinking in Western thought in the first half of the nineteenth century. The ideas of superior and inferior races that permeated American thinking about continental and world mission also often permeated the thinking of the English and of western Europeans in general by the mid-nineteenth century. When Gobineau published his work on the inequality of the human races in 1854, he was summarizing and amplifying more than half a century of ideas on race rather than inaugurating a new era. It is impossible to understand why the United States viewed its international role racially by 1850 without understanding why the European nations had also come to think of themselves in racial as well as political terms.

But the United States had a history that gave a particularly fervent and unique quality to the arguments of special racial destiny and accentuated the rate at which a racial explanation of world power was accepted. Since the seventeenth century the idea of the Americans as a "chosen people" had permeated first Puritan and then American thought. It is not uncommon for a people to think of themselves as chosen, but it is much rarer for a people to be given apparent abundant empirical proof of God's choice. God's intentions were first revealed in the survival and prosperity of the tiny colonies, elaborated by the miracle of a successful revolution against the might of Great Britain, and confirmed by a growth that amazed the world in the sixty years after that conflict. When religious fervor assumed a less central role in America, it was succeeded by the political fervor of a successful revolution.

If the continent had been empty and colonized only by white Europeans, the remarkable success of the United States would have still made it a rich breeding ground for the new racial thought of the nineteenth century; but it was neither empty nor exclusively white. In the first half of the nineteenth century many in the United States were anxious to justify the enslavement of the blacks and the expulsion and possible extermination of the Indians. The American intellectual community did not merely absorb European ideas, it also fed European racial appetites with scientific theories stemming from the supposed knowledge and observation of blacks and Indians. In this era the popular periodicals, the press, and many American politicians eagerly sought scientific proof for racial distinctions and for the prevailing American and world order; the intellectual community provided the evidence they needed.

The success of the Puritan settlement, the triumph of republicanism in the Revolution, the extensive material prosperity, the rapid territorial growth, and the presence of blacks and Indians all gave a special quality to the manner in which the United States received and developed the racial thought of Western Europe. Yet American racial thought was also peculiarly English. As English colonials, the new Americans fell heir to a long Anglo-Saxon-Teutonic tradition. In the seventeenth and eighteenth centuries, long before a specifically racialist Anglo-Saxon concept emerged, the Americans shared with the English a belief in the political and individual freedoms of the Anglo-Saxon period. Americans of the Revolutionary generation believed they were helping to recreate freedoms enjoyed in England more than seven hundred years before.

The term "Anglo-Saxon" has had a long history of misuse. In reality there was never a specific Anglo-Saxon people in England. A number of tribes from northern Germany began to settle in England in large numbers in the fifth century; they were not an homogenous group of "Anglo-Saxons," and they did not completely replace the Celtic tribes already living in England. Later the Viking invasions resulted in the settlement of other groups from northern Europe, and the Normans were added to the mix by the Conquest. When in the nineteenth century the English began writing "Anglo-Saxon" in a racial sense, they used it to describe the people living within the bounds of England, but, at times, they also used it to describe a vague brotherhood of English-speaking peoples throughout the British Isles and the world.

In the United States in the nineteenth century the term "Anglo-Saxon" became even less precise. It was often used by the 1840s to describe the white people of the United States in contrast to blacks, Indians, Mexicans, Spaniards, or Asiatics, although it was frequently acknowledged that the United States already contained a variety of European strains. Yet even those who liked to talk of a distinct "American" race, composed of the best Caucasian strains, drew heavily on the arguments developed to elevate the Anglo-Saxons. It was repeatedly emphasized that it was the descendants of Anglo-Saxons who had successfully settled the eastern seaboard and established free government by means of a Revolution. An Irishman might be described as a lazy, ragged, dirty Celt when he landed in New York, but if his children settled in California they might well be praised as part of the vanguard of the energetic Anglo-Saxon people poised for the plunge into Asia.

The process by which the long-held beliefs in the superiority of early Anglo-Saxon political institutions became a belief in the innate superiority of the Anglo-Saxon branch of the Caucasian race was directly linked to the new scientific interest in racial classification. But in a more general sense it involved the whole surging Romantic interest in uniqueness, in language, and in national and racial origins. Both directly from Germany and by transmission through England, the Americans were inspired to link their Anglo-Saxon past to its more distant Teutonic or Aryan roots. Even in colonial America the ancient idea of the westward movement of civilization had brought dreams of a great new empire on the North American continent, but as German philologists linked language to race and wrote of tribes spreading westward from central Asia following the path of the sun, the Americans were able to see new meaning in their drive to the Pacific and Asia. They could and did conceive of themselves as the most vital and energetic of those Aryan peoples who had spilled westward, "revitalized" the Roman Empire, spread throughout Europe to England, and crossed the Atlantic in their relentless westward drive. Americans had long believed they were a chosen people, but by the mid-nineteenth century they also believed that they were a chosen people with an impeccable ancestry.

By 1850 a clear pattern was emerging. From their own successful past as Puritan colonists, Revolutionary patriots, conquerors of a wilderness, and creators of an immense material prosperity, the Americans had evidence plain before them that they were a chosen people; from the English they had learned that the Anglo-Saxons had always been peculiarly gifted in the arts of government; from the scientists and ethnologists they were learning that they were of a distinct Caucasian race, innately endowed with abilities that placed them above other races; from the philologists, often through literary sources, they were learning that they were the descendants of those Aryans who followed the sun to carry civilization to the whole world.

The new ideas fell on fertile ground in the 1830s and 1840s. In a time of rapid growth and change, with its accompanying insecurities and dislocations, many Americans found comfort in the strength and status of a distinguished racial heritage. The new racial ideology could be used to force new immigrants to conform to the prevailing political, economic, and social system, and it could also be used to justify the sufferings or deaths of blacks, Indians, or Mexicans. Feelings of guilt could be assuaged by assumptions of historical and scientific inevitability.

In the 1840s and 1850s there were obviously specific reasons why particular Americans desired Texas, Oregon, California, Cuba, Canada, and large parts of Mexico and central America, and why many urged the commercial penetration of Asia. Agrarian and commercial desires and the search for national and personal wealth and security were at the heart of mid-nineteenth-century expansion, but the racial ideology that accompanied and permeated these drives helped determine the nature of America's specific relationships with other peoples encountered in the surge to world power. By the 1850s it was generally believed in the United States that a superior American race was destined to shape the destiny of much of the world. It was also believed that in their outward thrust Americans were encountering a variety of inferior races incapable of sharing in America's republican system and doomed to permanent subordination or extinction.

My interest in this book is in suggesting how and why by the mid-nineteenth century many Americans were less concerned with the liberation of other peoples by the spreading of republicanism than with the limitless expansion of a superior American Anglo-Saxon race. My concern is not with the history of science, of language, or of ideas in themselves, but in how the ideas of various sections of the intellectual community both reflected and influenced popular and political attitudes. My interest is in the origins of the new racial ideology and in how it affected the course of American expansion rather than in ways in which the ideology was used internally in an attempt to protect the interests of various classes and groups within American society. To me the Americans of 1850, when talking or writing of their world mission, have always made a lot less sense than the Americans of the Revolutionary generation, and I have written this book in an attempt to find out why.

I

EUROPEAN AND COLONIAL ORIGINS

1

Liberty and the Anglo-Saxons

> Has not every restitution of the antient Saxon laws had happy effects? Is it not better now that we return at once into that happy system of our ancestors, the wisest and most perfect ever yet devised by the wit of man, as it stood before the 8th century?
>
> Thomas Jefferson, August 13, 1776

Although the concept of a distinct, superior Anglo-Saxon race, with innate endowments enabling it to achieve a perfection of governmental institutions and world dominance, was a product of the first half of the nineteenth century, the roots of these ideas stretch back at least to the sixteenth and seventeenth centuries. Those Englishmen who settled in America at the beginning of the seventeenth century brought as part of their historical and religious heritage a clearly delineated religious myth of a pure English Anglo-Saxon church, and in the seventeenth and eighteenth centuries they shared with their fellow Englishmen an elaborately developed secular myth of the free nature of Anglo-Saxon political institutions. By the time of the American Revolution Americans were convinced that Anglo-Saxon England before the Norman Conquest had enjoyed freedoms unknown since that date. The emphasis was on institutions rather than race, but since the sixteenth century, both on the European continent and in England, the Anglo-Saxons had also been firmly linked to the Germanic tribes described by Tacitus.

The first enthusiastic English interest in Anglo-Saxon England was a product of the English Reformation. As early as the 1530s the Saxon church was studied to provide propaganda to justify Henry VIII's break with Rome. The main object of the research was to show that the English church was returning to the purer practices of the period before 1066. Supposed Anglo-Saxon precedents were used to support the argument that England had cleansed the Roman Catholic Church of the abuses introduced through the centuries by papal power.[1]

The key figure in establishing a historical base for the new Anglican church that emerged under Elizabeth was Archbishop Matthew Parker. To justify the Elizabethan church settlement, Parker became a major patron of Anglo-Saxon scholarship, collecting manuscripts, encouraging the study of the Anglo-Saxon language, and publishing texts. Depending heavily on the help of his secretary, John Joscelyn, Parker effectively initiated the serious study of pre-Norman England.[2] Although the object of Parker's group was to establish the antiquity of the customs of the new English church, his efforts also stimulated an interest and pride in general English history in the Anglo-Saxon period. John Foxe, in his *Acts and Monuments* (1563), emphasized the early development of English church practices, but he also stressed the uniqueness of the English and their nature as "a chosen people," with a church lineage stretching back to Joseph of Arimathea and his supposed visit to England, and with John Wyclif as the true originator of the Reformation.[3] The religious propagandists of the late sixteenth century defended a church that was peculiarly English in its inspiration. Whatever the errors of the rest of Europe, it was believed that the English had cleansed of corruption a church whose roots stretched back to shortly after the time of Christ.

The interest in Anglo-Saxon religious sources, which helped to justify the break with Rome, also eventually helped overturn the Arthurian legends, which had dominated medieval accounts of the origins of the English people. Rather than the traditional story of the settlement of England by Brutus, his Trojans, and Britons, which had been given its greatest elaboration by Geoffrey of Monmouth, emphasis now shifted to the Germanic tribes as colonizers of Anglo-Saxon England.[4] In emphasizing the Germanic origins of the English, antiquarians of the early seventeenth century linked the English arguments to the general Germanic movement in Europe and ultimately to Tacitus.

Lauding the peculiar qualities of the Germanic people had been common on the Continent since the early years of the Reformation; German reformers drew an analogy between the earlier "Germanic" or "Gothic" destruction of the universal Roman Empire and the new destruction of the universal Roman Church.[5] Theories were advanced which foreshadowed the ultra-Teutonism of the nineteenth and twentieth centuries. In 1580 Goropius Becamus, a Flemish physician, argued that German was the first of all languages and had been spoken in the Garden of Eden by Adam. This argument was too outlandish even for most Teutons, but Goropius's emphasis on the great antiquity and excellence of the German language gained many followers in England as well as on the Continent. Throughout the seventeenth century Continental arguments in praise of the Germanic heritage were cited in English works on the origins and institutions of the Anglo-Saxons.[6]

The linking of superior institutions to a particular people was given a major impetus in England by the writings of Richard Verstegen and William Camden. In 1605 Verstegen dedicated his *Restitution of Decayed Intelligence* to James I, "descended of the chiefest blood royall of our ancient English-Saxon Kings." Verstegen wrote with passion of England's Germanic and Anglo-Saxon past, the Germanic roots of the English language, and, surprisingly for this early date, the common racial origin of the Saxons, Danes, and Normans. Using Tacitus as his source, he described the courage and high principles of the Germanic tribes, and he emphasized that the English, like the Germans, were an unmixed race; the great invasions of England by Danes and Normans merely reunited old brethren.[7] Discussions of the English as a perfect blend of the great northern peoples was not common until the nineteenth century, and Verstegen foreshadowed later racial interpretations of the German and Saxon past.

William Camden did not espouse the Germanic cause with the same vigor and consistency as Verstegen, but in his *Britannia* he helped to overturn medieval accounts of the English past by his attack on the theory of descent from Brutus and his Trojans. Later, in his *Remaines concerning Britaine*, he argued that the English were descended from a great German people, and he saw God's hand in the guiding of the Angles and Saxons to England. Both Verstegen and Camden were interested in the special characteristics of the English as a people as well as in the institutions of the Anglo-Saxon period.[8]

The emphasis on the Anglo-Saxons as a vigorous branch of the sturdy Germanic tree continued as one thread in the political arguments of the seventeenth century. As yet, not all agreed that political liberty had been brought to England by the Anglo-Saxons (Sir Edward Coke traced English liberties back long before that time), but the emphasis on Anglo-Saxons as particularly able Germans now became a commonplace in writings on English history.[9] The primary source for Germanic characteristics was Tacitus's *Germania*, which was constantly used over the following centuries to defend the idea of the Germans as a freedom-loving, noble race. "In the peoples of Germany," wrote Tacitus, "there has been given to the world a race untainted by intermarriage with other races, a peculiar people and pure, like no one but themselves." This "pure" race, he argued, had a high moral code and a profound love of freedom and individual rights; important decisions were made by the whole community. These ideas were woven into seventeenth-century discussions of Anglo-Saxon political institutions; "some have sent us to Tacitus and as far as Germany to learn our English constitution" was the comment of an English pamphleteer.[10]

In the first half of the seventeenth century the political and legal history of the Anglo-Saxons became a central issue in the growing rift between Parliament and the Crown. Parliamentarians found in the supposed antiquity of Parliament and of English common law a rationale for opposition to royal pretensions. The scholarly basis for the opposition to the king was often provided by the research of men associated with the Society of Antiquaries. Deeply involved in the basic work of the society were Sir Robert Cotton, John Selden, and Sir Henry Spelman: Cotton blamed the loss of the legal privileges of the Saxon period on the Norman Conquest; Selden praised Anglo-Saxon law in contrast to the later development of royal absolutism; and Spelman emphasized the oppression of post-Conquest feudal tenures and became an ardent advocate of the Anglo-Saxon language.[11]

As royal pretensions increased in the first decades of the seventeenth century, the parliamentarians defended English rights as rooted in immemorial law and custom. Anglo-Saxon history was corrupted to provide a defense for parliamentary arguments. Two famous documents—the *Modus Tenendi Parliamentum* and the *Mirror of Justices*—whose true origins were late medieval were used to bolster the claims that King Alfred had instituted annual sessions of Parliament and universal male suffrage, and that the House of Lords had been a part of the English Constitution since the time of Edward the Confessor.[12]

The most famous of the parliamentarians who used and developed a historical myth to resist the king was Sir Edward Coke. Coke stressed the antiquity of the common law, the common law courts, and the House of Commons, but he was not in the tradition of those like Verstegen who saw a Germanic origin for much that was best in England. Coke was more peculiarly English in his arguments; he traced the history of the common law of England back before the coming of the Anglo-Saxons to time immemorial.

Ultimately, sharp differences developed among those who opposed royal power. Coke believed that the common law had survived unscathed from the most distant times and should at all costs be protected; but the Levellers thought that the common law had been corrupted by post-Conquest tyranny, and that it should be swept away. The arguments of the Levellers and their successors were ultimately to be of more importance to the American colonists than those of Coke, though Coke did much to popularize the idea of the supreme abilities of the Anglo-Saxons. Like the later colonial revolutionaries, the Levellers believed that the excellent government which had existed before the Norman Conquest had to be restored by abolishing all the abuses that had crept into English law and government since that time. But, whatever the arguments as to the state of England prior to the Anglo-Saxons and on the condition of England after the Norman Conquest, there was general agreement that the England of the Anglo-Saxons had been a country in which the citizens were protected by good laws and in which representative institutions and trial by jury flourished. The myth of a pure Anglo-Saxon church, developed in the sixteenth century, was in the seventeenth century joined by a more powerful myth of a free Anglo-Saxon government.[13]

When in England the violence and turmoil of a half century subsided in the aftermath of the Glorious Revolution of 1688, there emerged a classic "Whig" view of the past. In this view a golden age of good government had existed in England prior to the Norman Conquest. The Conquest had eroded English liberties, but had been followed by a long struggle for the restoration of good government, of which the foundation had been the Magna Carta and the capstone the seventeenth-century victories over the usurpations of the Stuarts. As a result of these victories England was a nation with a continuity of law and institutions stretching back more than a thousand years, a nation inhabited by Anglo-Saxons who had always been freedom-loving, and who had always exhibited an outstanding capacity for good government.

Not all Englishmen accepted the classic Whig view. There were anti-Whigs, like Thomas Hobbes, who saw Anglo-Saxon society in a truer light, and there were also the "Real Whigs" or "Commonwealthmen," who believed that the struggles of the seventeenth century had failed to restore to England the liberties that had existed before the Norman Conquest. The Real Whigs were often more enthusiastic about the Anglo-Saxons than those who accepted the more general Whig interpretation of the past, for they were anxious to contrast the Anglo-Saxon government with the government accepted by modern Englishmen. The Real Whigs also wrote of the Germanic peoples from whom the Anglo-Saxons had sprung. Particularly influential was Robert Molesworth's *Account of Denmark*, published in the 1690s, which praised "the northern nations" for introducing the arts of good government and foreshadowed the eighteenth-century interest in the Scandinavian peoples as part of a dominant Germanic family.[14]

In the seventy years after 1660 the myth of Anglo-Saxon England flourished in English politics, and fascination with the period was heightened by a flowering of Anglo-Saxon scholarship, particularly at Oxford. In these years the study of the Anglo-Saxon language and sources was advanced by a whole group of prominent scholars, including Francis Junius, Edward Thwaites, George Hickes, and Humphrey Wanley. These scholars did nothing to correct the prevailing myths concerning Anglo-Saxon freedom, and their linguistic studies did much to expand the interest in links between the Anglo-Saxons and other Germanic peoples.[15] The eighteenth-century English view of the Anglo-Saxons was a mythical one produced by two centuries of religious and political conflict and reinforced by the image of the Germanic peoples that originated with Tacitus and was elaborated by a whole series of post-Reformation Continental writers.

As colonial Englishmen the settlers in America fully absorbed the mythical view of the English past developed between 1530 and 1730. They perceived the Anglo-Saxons only through the distortions of sixteenth- and seventeenth-century religious and political controversy and through its supporting scholarship. They imbibed the general Whig theory of history, but where they differed most sharply from the majority of Englishmen was in eventually accepting the minority English viewpoint that the English constitution had not been cleansed of the religious and political abuses that had emerged since the Conquest. In the mid-eighteenth century it was the English radicals, the Real Whigs, who appealed most strongly to Americans dissatisfied with their relationship to the English political establishment. For a time the colonials, like the English, were proud of their constitution as settled by the Glorious Revolution, but by the time of the American Revolution they wholeheartedly welcomed the views of those English radicals who were asking for a reform of the English system in order to restore its pristine Anglo-Saxon vigor.[16]

The books which established and defended the Whig view of English history were readily available and popular in colonial America. Law, the training ground for so many Revolutionary politicians, was the most traveled route to Anglo-Saxon England. Colonial law students were weaned on the *Institutes* of Sir Edward Coke, particularly "Coke on Littleton," the standard first law text in the colonies. Jefferson admired "old Cooke" all his life, and shortly before he died expressed the view that while Coke had made good Whigs of American lawyers, the shift to Blackstone (whose first volume was published in England in 1765) had helped to produce Tories in America as well as in England.[17] The pamphlets of the Revolutionary era are filled with citations from Coke, yet Blackstone also believed in the freedom of the Anglo-Saxon period and stressed the merits of Tacitus's depiction of the early Germanic tribes.[18]

American lawyers also learned of the supposed freedoms of pre-Conquest England from a variety of other texts on English land tenure. At the heart of the Whig writings on feudalism was the belief that the feudal system was introduced into England only at the time of the Norman Conquest. Anglo-Saxon England, according to this view, was a land of yeoman farmers. To many Americans the sweeping away of entail and primogeniture after the Revolution eliminated the last remnants of the feudal system and restored the freedoms of the period before 1066. The works of Sir Henry Spelman and Sir John Dalrymple, which were well known in the colonies, depicted Anglo-Saxon England as a land free from the burdens of feudalism.[19]

The colonists believed fully that the Anglo-Saxons were a particularly successful branch of the freedom-loving Germanic peoples described by Tacitus. Tacitus's *Germania* was readily available in colonial America, often in translation, and was enjoyed by many, including John Adams and Thomas Jefferson. Tacitus's ideas also reached the colonists through a variety of other books. When Montesquieu, in *L'Esprit des lois*, used Tacitus for his explanation of the influence of the Germanic peoples, he was following a trend rather than breaking new ground. Montesquieu's popularity, however, helped confirm the view that the British political system could be traced to the woods of Germany.[20]

More generally read than Montesquieu was Paul de Rapin-Thoyras's *Histoire d'Angleterre*, which was translated into English in 1726. Rapin was very popular in the colonies. He presented a thoroughly Whig view of English history, emphasizing that the Anglo-Saxons were Tacitus's Germans, creating the basis of English parliamentary government in a new homeland. The effect of Rapin's work was enhanced in the colonies on the eve of the Revolution by the publication of the English radical Catherine Macaulay's *History of England*. Again liberty was depicted as traveling with the Anglo-Saxons from the woods of Germany across the sea to England.[21]

The flow of works across the Atlantic was particularly strong on the eve of the Revolution. A pamphlet which was subsequently woven into the very fabric of Revolutionary constitutional argument was the *Historical Essay on the English Constitution*, published in London in 1771. This radical publication achieved considerable popularity in both England and the United States. It carried praise of Anglo-Saxon institutions to the extreme in discussing the origins of the English constitution. The Anglo-Saxon England described here was a democratic country of united local communities, meeting in an annual parliament and enjoying trial by jury: "if ever God Almighty did concern himself about forming a government for mankind to live happily under, it was that which was established in England by our Saxon forefathers." The Normans, the pamphleteer argued, had brought political and religious oppression to England and had inaugurated a long, continual struggle between Saxon freedom and Norman tyranny.[22]

When in the early summer of 1776 Pennsylvania representatives were preparing to meet to draft their influential new constitution, an anonymous author in Philadelphia summarized the arguments of the *Historical Essay*, with his own comments, to guide the Pennsylvanians in their constitution-making. This pamphlet by "Demophilus" was entitled *The Genuine Principles of the Ancient Saxon, or English Constitution*. It was issued just after the printing of the Declaration of Independence, and the author included that document at the end of his own work. The Pennsylvanians, he argued, should need little convincing that "this ancient and justly admired pattern, the old Saxon form of government, will be the best model, that human wisdom, improved by experience, has left them to copy."[23]

The extensive pamphlet and protest literature of the 1760s and 1770s revealed the extent to which the colonists had learned the lessons taught by the Whig interpreters of English history and, in particular, by the eighteenth-century Real Whigs. The revolutionaries drew their precedents and principles from a wide variety of historical and contemporary sources, but whatever their various inspirations there was a strong, general belief that they were acting as Englishmen — Englishmen contending for principles of popular government, freedom, and liberty introduced into England more than a thousand years before by the high-minded, freedom-loving Anglo-Saxons from the woods of Germany. The various ingredients in the myth of Anglo-Saxon England, clearly delineated in a host of seventeenth- and eighteenth-century works, now appear again in American protests: Josiah Quincy, Jr. wrote of the popular nature of the Anglo-Saxon militia; Sam Adams stressed the old English freedoms defended in the Magna Carta; Benjamin Franklin emphasized the freedom the Anglo-Saxons had enjoyed in emigrating to England; Charles Carroll depicted Saxon liberties torn away by William the Conqueror; and Richard Bland argued that the English constitution and parliament stemmed from the Saxon period.[24] Patrick Henry was reputed to have been licensed to practice law after a month or two studying "Coke on Littleton" and a digest of the Virginia Acts, and he wrote his resolution against the Stamp Act on the fly leaf of Coke's famous work. George Washington admired the pro-Saxon history of Catherine Macaulay, and she visited him at Mount Vernon after the Revolution.[25]

The vision of heroic, freedom-loving Anglo-Saxon England permeates the arguments of the Revolutionary generation, but it is in the writings of Thomas Jefferson that the theme appears most strongly, and he best reveals the form in which the myth was transmitted to future generations. Although Jefferson read deeply in the works of the classic parliamentary propagandists of the seventeenth century, his predeliction was not for standard Whig interpretations of the period after 1688, but for those radical Real Whigs who argued that many of the corruptions introduced into the English constitution after the Norman Conquest still existed in the eighteenth century. The Anglo-Saxons, thought Jefferson, had lived under laws based on the natural rights of man; after 1066 these rights had been eroded by the impositions of kings, clerics, lawyers, and by the whole system of feudalism.[26]

Jefferson never lost the admiration for Anglo-Saxon England that he had gained studying law and politics in the 1760s and early 1770s. Throughout his life he was fascinated by the Anglo-Saxon language, and he wrote a simplified grammar in the hope of making it more accessible to American students. He included Anglo-Saxon as part of his curriculum for the University of Virginia because, he wrote, "As the histories and laws left us in that type and dialect, must be the text-books of the reading of the learners, they will imbibe with the language their free principles of government." Jefferson's interest in the language continued throughout his life. As late as 1825, when he was eighty-one, he commented that the study of Anglo-Saxon "is a hobby which too often runs away with me."[27]

The depth of Jefferson's reading can be seen not only from his later arguments and the cast of his mind, but from the overt evidence of his *Commonplace Book*. In these collections of quotations and extracts Jefferson goes beyond the English legal historians to display a fascination with the history of the northern nations in the years before the Anglo-Saxon settlement of England. This interest in the Teutonic peoples generally, which was becoming of increasing importance in England and on the Continent in the late eighteenth century, was eventually to be an important factor in transforming an emphasis on Anglo-Saxon society and institutions into an emphasis on the racial group to which the Anglo-Saxons supposedly belonged. Later in his life Jefferson referred to Tacitus as "the first writer in the world without a single exception," but Jefferson also delved deeply into Simon Pelloutier's *Histoire des Celtes*, Robert Molesworth's *An Account of Denmark*, and Paul Henri Mallet's *Histoire de Dannemarc*.[28]

Jefferson was particularly intrigued by the problem of the actual location in Germany of the tribes that had invaded England, and he copied large sections from those authors who had attempted to describe specific homelands on the European mainland. When he read of the original Saxon homeland in the Cimbric Chersonesus of Jutland and Schleswig-Holstein, this was no idle reading and copying. Later, in 1784, when he proposed an ordinance to create new states in the Mississippi Valley, he suggested the name Cherronesus for the Denmark-like area between Lakes Huron and Michigan — not a name of the new America but an echo of a name of the old Germanic tribes.[29] In the time of the later Roman Empire, Jefferson believed, northern Europe was inhabited by tribes who lived close to nature and had a form of government that reflected the natural rights of man. Some of these tribes, generally known as the Anglo-Saxons, left northern Europe in the middle of the fifth century and established in England a form of government based on popular sovereignty. In his stress on the attributes of the particular peoples involved in creating Saxon free institutions, Jefferson was foreshadowing the later interest in the racial origin of Anglo-Saxon accomplishments.[30]

Jefferson argued not for wholesale innovation but for a return to the principles of English government in the Anglo-Saxon period. He rejected Coke's view that the common law had survived unscathed and free since Anglo-Saxon times and maintained that the law itself had been corrupted by the Norman Conquest. The Conquest and subsequent oppression led to the curtailing of the natural rights that had once been protected by Anglo-Saxon law and institutions. Jefferson concluded that in a variety of areas, ranging from land tenures to political democracy, the English had failed in their efforts since 1066 to restore the freedoms that had existed before that date. His sources for this information were many and varied. Few of the main Whig and Real Whig accounts of the seventeenth and eighteenth centuries escaped his attention. To the end of his life he believed Rapin's history of England was the best, and he also thought highly of Catherine Macaulay. From Scottish jurist Lord Kames, Jefferson imbibed the broad principles of a natural rights philosophy, and from Kames's *British Antiquities* he obtained yet another view of the nature of Anglo-Saxon democracy. This ideal view of Anglo-Saxon political democracy was reinforced and broadened by his reading of the works of Henry Care, Anthony Ellis, James Burgh, and a variety of other writers. Jefferson also readily accepted the arguments of Sir Henry Spelman and Sir John Dalrymple that feudalism came into England only with the Norman Conquest. To Jefferson this was of particular importance, for he came to believe that Anglo-Saxon freedom had been based on land held by innumerable farmers in fee simple. Nothing gave him more pleasure in Revolutionary Virginia than his work for the abolition of primogeniture and entail.[31]

The ideal Anglo-Saxon England that Jefferson believed in was a land of small political units and a land in which local rule prevailed in most concerns. In its early form there was an elective king, annual parliaments, a system of trial by jury, and land held in fee simple. Even the clergy did not batten themselves upon society until a later date. Near the end of his life, in 1825, Jefferson contrasted the Saxon and the Norman conquests of England, "the former exhibiting the genuine form and political principles of the people constituting the nation, and founded in the rights of man; the latter built on conquest and physical force, not at all affecting moral rights, nor even assented to by the free will of the vanquished. The battle of Hastings, indeed, was lost, but the natural rights of the nation were not staked on the events of a single battle. Their will to recover the Saxon constitution continued unabated."[32] This view of Anglo-Saxon England was in its way as unreal as those writings which depicted Arthur's England as a Camelot of brave knights, fair ladies, and magic swords, but it persisted in English and American thinking long after Jefferson's death.

Anglo-Saxon studies represented no abstract academic exercise for Jefferson. When in the years from 1773 to 1776 he established first an American and then a European reputation, his arguments impressed upon his contemporaries the extent to which he believed that the Saxon government and way of life should become a model for the new America. His *Summary View of the Rights of British America*, published in 1774, suggested that the king should be reminded that in coming to America the emigrants from England had exercised the same natural right under which "their Saxon ancestors" had left the woods of northern Europe and settled in England. Their mother country had exerted no claim on them in Britain, and there was nothing to distinguish the emigration of Englishmen to North America from that of the Saxons to England. Even the land in America was not held from the king. Land in America, like land in Saxon England, should be completely free from feudalism.[33]

It should come as no surprise that a large section of Jefferson's Declaration of Independence echoed the old seventeenth-century argument that a usurping king had taken away immemorial liberties, and in the months following the Declaration Jefferson clearly revealed the historically based Revolution that he had in mind. In August 1776 John Adams told his wife about the work of the committee which was suggesting inscriptions for the Great Seal of the United States: "Mr. Jefferson," he wrote, "proposed the children of Israel in the wilderness, led by a cloud by day and pillar of fire by night; and on the other side, Hengist and Horsa, the Saxon chiefs from whom we claim the honor of being descended, and whose political principles and form of government we have assumed." On the previous day Jefferson had written: "Has not every restitution of the antient Saxon laws had happy effects? Is it not better now that we return at once into that happy system of our ancestors, the wisest and most perfect ever yet devised by the wit of man, as it stood before the 8th century?"[34]

When in the summer of 1776 Jefferson returned to Virginia, he wanted to sweep away the vestiges of a feudal land system, establish religious freedom, set up a general system of education, and revise the entire legal structure. Here was Jefferson at his happiest, combing the law books of a thousand years to restore a system he thought had made men happier and freer. For Jefferson the abolition of entail and primogeniture was a sweeping away of Norman tyranny. Even in his bill for religious freedom in Virginia, he thought he was helping to restore the purity of Anglo-Saxon England before 1066, for with William the Conqueror had come the priests who added religious to political tyranny.[35]

Late in his life, Jefferson wrote to thank English radical Major John Cartwright for his book on the English constitution. Cartwright, he said, had deduced the constitution from "its rightful root, the Anglo-Saxon." That constitution "was violated and set at naught by Norman force." Jefferson told Cartwright that he hoped Virginia would divide its counties into wards of about six miles square, for these "would answer to the hundreds of your Saxon Alfred." In each of these wards Jefferson wanted an elementary school, a militia company, a justice of the peace, a constable, responsibility for the poor and roads, local police, an election of jurors, and a "folk-house" for elections. "Each ward," wrote Jefferson, "would thus be a small republic within itself." His Anglo-Saxon dream stayed with him until the end of his life. In 1825 he wrote to an English member of Parliament regarding England and the United States that "these two nations holding cordially together, have nothing to fear from the united world. They will be the models for regenerating the condition of man, the sources from which representative government is to flow over the whole earth."[36]

In the very act of revolution the Revolutionary generation believed they were reinforcing their links with their Anglo-Saxon ancestors while separating from the government of Great Britain. Jefferson was exceptional in the depth of his scholarly interest and belief in a free Anglo-Saxon past, but a belief in the free Anglo-Saxons was part of the common currency of political and constitutional arguments in these years. In this regard, as in so many others, Jefferson was able to distill in memorable language the essence of the general beliefs of his contemporaries.

When in 1790 James Wilson of Pennsylvania delivered a famous series of law lectures in Philadelphia, he revealed the extent to which the Anglo-Saxon myth had permeated American thought. Wilson was no ardent Saxonist like Jefferson. He believed that the common law had diverse origins—Greek, Roman, British, Saxon, Norman—but there was no escaping the Saxon interpretation of America's roots. His conclusion was that the original general frame of the British constitution, much altered in contemporary England, but "bearing . . . a degree of resemblance" to some of the constitutions lately formed in the

United States, was "of Saxon architecture." All the respected contemporary scholarship in England and the United States supported this argument. American common law, he argued, more resembled that of Anglo-Saxon England than that of the Normans.[37] American lawyer-politicians, a numerous and dominant breed, ensured that in the early years of the new nation the general historical belief in the free Anglo-Saxon past would be reinforced by numerous examples drawn from the roots of English and American law.

The religious and political struggles and the historical rewriting of over two hundred years had given the English and the Americans a historical perspective that left them particularly susceptible to racial explanations of the course of history. Both the English and the Americans believed that their ancestors had devised free political institutions over a thousand years before in England, and that even earlier a spirit of freedom had existed in the woods of Germany among the peoples from whom the Anglo-Saxons were descended. In explaining this phenomenon Jefferson and his contemporaries were restricted by an Enlightenment view of a general human capacity for progress. They admired the Anglo-Saxons, but they generally avoided making unfavorable comparisons with other peoples. Yet by the time of the American Revolution, a variety of new tendencies in European thought were preparing the ground for a whole new explanation of what appeared to be a remarkable persistence of free, democratic government among the Anglo-Saxons. The earlier explanations of the Germanic origin of the supposed Saxon love of freedom were now to receive extensive elaboration. The old Anglo-Saxon myth was ultimately to appear innocuous alongside an overpowering Aryan myth which helped transform respect for Anglo-Saxon institutions into a new racial interpretation of English and American success. The way for this new myth was being prepared in the second half of the eighteenth century; in the nineteenth century the Americans were to share in the discovery that the secret of Saxon success lay not in the institutions but in the blood.

2
Aryans Follow the Sun

> *Ex oriente lux:* the march of culture, in its general lines,
> has always followed the sun's course.
>
> August Friedrich Pott, 1833

The seeds of a new racial Anglo-Saxonism were sown on the continent of Europe and in England in the last decades of the eighteenth and the first decades of the nineteenth century. A variety of influences that contributed to the growth of a European Romantic movement helped to change the emphasis from a continuity of institutions to the continuity of innate racial strengths. Conversely, the emphasis on superior racial characteristics as a reason for strong institutions led to an emphasis on inferior racial characteristics as a reason for weak institutions. Of central importance was the Romantic emphasis on the uniqueness, the peculiar qualities, of individuals and peoples. This became a focal point of German Romantic thinking in the last decades of the eighteenth century. The idea of a nation's possessing its own *Volkgeist*, its own special national spirit, fell on fertile ground among English-speaking peoples who had long traced their institutions to a glorious Anglo-Saxon past and were seeking to explain their success in the modern era. Also, the Romantic emphasis on emotion, imagination, and feeling rather than on dispassionate, calm analysis eventually helped create and maintain a fuzziness of thought that was useful to the wilder manifestations of racial Anglo-Saxonism.[1] Whatever the intentions of the founders of the German Romantic movement, many of their followers throughout Europe, and eventually America, were to jumble race, nation, and language into a hodgepodge of rampant, racial nationalism.

Two movements—a burst of nationalism specifically German and a swelling interest in the Germanic peoples that was European in scope—helped to fire the English and the Americans with a vision of the Anglo-Saxons as a superior people creating nations capable of ruling the world. The quickening German nationalism of the late eighteenth century, with its emphasis on the continuity of the German language and the German people, had peculiar relevance to English and American peoples who could trace their origins to the same Germanic roots. In writing of the historic greatness of the German people, German nationalists were able to build on assumptions that had been present since Tacitus and amplified since the Reformation. The cult of a special people and an ideal German national type had been present in Germany for over three hundred years. In the early sixteenth century Ulrich von Hutten had lauded the Germans as a masculine people, and even in the centuries when racial arguments were ill-formed and inconsistent, specific Teutonic themes had never been absent from European thought.[2] But it was only in the eighteenth century that recurring themes began to be shaped into a consistent ideology.

In stressing the glories of the Germanic past, the early German Romantics and their precursors were in some measure influenced and given sustenance by the very Anglo-Saxon myth that they were to help transform into a racial doctrine. The Anglo-Saxons were praised as Germans who had taken an instinctive love for freedom and shaped it into an effective government and nation. The most prominent of the eighteenth-century German historians who admired England was Justus

Möser. Möser absorbed the myth of the free Anglo-Saxons and the Norman yoke and was anxious that Germany herself should develop a specific nationality from the same ingredients that had proved so successful in England.[3]

Ironically, the great precursor of German Romanticism, Johann Gottfried von Herder, while defending the unity of mankind, eventually helped open a Pandora's box of virulent racial theories with his stress on language as the basis of nationality and his emphasis on the common past of a people. Of key importance was his replacing the idea of the nation as a political unit with that of a nation as a cultural community. The *Volk* was a nation formed from a tribal community and as such had a distinct individuality. When he praised the history of the Germans, Herder warned that it would be dangerous to consider them as a chosen people, but his warnings were ignored.[4] After Herder the ideas of the German Romantics intertwined with those of the political nationalists of the early nineteenth century to bring a new fervor to the exaltation of the Germanic past. Confronting the French Revolution and Napoleon, German patriots threw off the universal ideas of the Enlightenment and accelerated the trend toward particularism. The ambivalence of Herder was succeeded by an unquestioned assertion of the values of the German language and the strengths of the German race. Fichte, Schleiermacher, and eventually Hegel exalted the state, the language, and the German people and helped destroy the eighteenth-century vision of mankind as one. The exaltation of the state as an instrument of divine purpose, although intended primarily to stimulate the growth of a German nation, fell on receptive ears in England and the United States.[5]

Yet while the image of the nation as a living entity eventually inspired nationalists in both England and America, of more immediate importance were those arguments which depicted the Germanic peoples as a constantly expanding and diffuse force in European and world history. Teutonism had been European in scope since the sixteenth and seventeenth centuries. The integration of Tacitus and the history of the Germanic tribes into the English Anglo-Saxon myth in the seventeenth and eighteenth centuries had been paralleled in France by those who had used

Tacitus to exalt the Germanic over the Gallo-Roman influence. François Hotman, in his *Francogallia*, published in the 1570s, praised the first generations of Frankish rule when there was supposedly a free constitution and an elective king.[6] From that time forward the Germanic argument and rebuttals were never absent from discussions of early French history. In the early eighteenth century Count Henri de Boulainvilliers, using Tacitus as a main source, emphasized the primitive freedom of the German forests and the excellence of the Frankish peoples who emerged to settle France. He contrasted these ideas of freedom with the Roman ideals of empire and power. As well as giving impetus to the Germanic movement in France, he provided additional arguments for the English Germanists.[7]

By far the best known of the French eighteenth-century Germanists was Montesquieu, and his writings spread, on both sides of the Atlantic, the idea of the noble, free simplicity of the tribes of the German forests. Writing in a pre-Romantic context, Montesquieu had no firm idea of racial distinctions. He believed that mankind in general had an innate instinct for liberty, and that this instinct could be realized. His main emphasis was on climatic environment, not on innate racial characteristics. Yet he had a special admiration for the Germans and their political instincts. He pointed out that the Franks were Germans, drew heavily on Tacitus for his description of German characteristics, and stressed the Germanic origins of the English government, arguing that this "beautiful system was invented first in the woods." To Montesquieu ideas of liberty were intimately linked to the Germanic peoples: "The German nations that conquered the Roman Empire were certainly a free people."[8]

Until well past the middle of the eighteenth century, the oft-repeated admiration for the Germanic people was beset with a confusion which reveals a lack of specific racial thinking. As yet the peoples and tribes of early European history had not been firmly linked to Germanic or non-Germanic roots in view of their supposed accomplishments or failures. The Germanic tribes were extensively praised, but no great efforts had been made to thrust particular western European peoples outside the Germanic orbit. Germans and Celts were often confused. Cluverius in the early seventeenth century had divided the primitive peoples of Europe into Celts (including Gauls, Britons, Germans, Saxons, and others) and Sarmatians (the Slavs). This confusion was continued by Pelloutier as late as 1750, and in the 1760s Gibbon described the *Edda* as the sacred book of the ancient Celts.[9] This uncertainty was ended by two interrelated movements: on the one hand, the burgeoning Romantic interest in the distant past gained particular sustenance from a general European fascination with the history and mythology of "the northern nations," and linked the Saxons to a heroic age of German-Scandinavian peoples; on the other, German philologists linked language to race and nation and traced Anglo-Saxon roots deep into a prehistoric Indo-Germanic past.

The linking of the Germanic to a general Norse tradition had been foreshadowed in England as far back as the beginning of the seventeenth century in the work of Richard Verstegen and more specifically argued near the end of the century in Robert Molesworth's *An Account of Denmark*; but interest was now to go far beyond government and law to mythology, language, and race.[10] The most influential work in expanding Saxon-Germanic interests into the whole Norse tradition was Paul Henri Mallet's *L'Introduction à l'histoire de Dannemarc*, which was originally intended to counter some of Molesworth's views on the course of later Danish history. Mallet idealized the Scandinavians as Tacitus had idealized the Germanic tribes. The book first appeared in Copenhagen in 1775, but it was soon translated into German and English and helped stimulate Norse and Germanic studies throughout Europe. Mallet incorporated the still frequent confusion on race by failing to separate the Scandinavians from the Celts, but the whole tendency of his work was to praise the northern nations of Europe as the upholders of liberty. Ancient Scandinavia, like ancient Germany, was the home of free institutions. While reinforcing and extending existing views of primitive Germanic freedom, Mallet was of seminal importance in creating an interest in Scandinavian mythology and poetry. Throughout Europe a fresh literary dimension was quickly added to the existing emphasis on government and law among the primitive Germanic and Norse peoples.[11]

Mallet's confusing the Scandinavians with the Celts was corrected by Thomas Percy in 1770 when he published his English translation of Mallet's work under the title *Northern Antiquities*. Percy indicated that the Gothic or Teutonic peoples were distinct from the Celtic and that descended from the former were the Germans, the Saxons, and the Scandinavians. He also argued that the Celts lacked that peculiar love of liberty which characterized the Gothic peoples. In Gaul, for example, "the inferior people were little better than in a state of slavery; Whereas . . . the meanest German was independent and free." The shift from merely praising Germans or Saxons to attacking other peoples was vital in transforming the whole Anglo-Saxon movement into a matter of innate racial distinctions.[12]

Percy's influence was particularly strong because of his earlier publication of the *Reliques of Ancient English Poetry*, a work which stirred pride and interest in English national origins, and which greatly influenced the English Romantics, especially Sir Walter Scott. Even the Germans read Percy, and Herder was inspired by the *Reliques* to collect Lithuanian folk songs.[13] In his brief essays accompanying the poems Percy praised the Gothic nations, and he stressed that the Viking invasions of England had merely reunited the Germanic people. The "ideas of chivalry," wrote Percy, "prevailed long before in all the Gothic nations, and may be discovered as in embrio in the customs, manners, and opinions of every branch of that people. That fondness in going in quest of adventures, that spirit of challenging to single combat, and that respectful complaisance shewn to the fair sex (so different from the manners of the Greeks and Romans), all are of Gothic origin, and may be traced up to the earliest times among all the Northern nations."[14] A new Romantic image of the past was beginning to emerge, and the idea of the Anglo-Saxons as adventurous, brave, and respectful toward women took its place alongside that of the Anglo-Saxons as originators of trial by jury and parliamentary institutions. Romanticism enhanced the image of the Anglo-Saxons by making them of concern to novelists and poets as well as to lawyers and politicians.

The quickening Romantic interest in the primitive peoples of

Europe helped to stimulate rich praise of ancient Celts as well as of the Germanic peoples, but it quickly became apparent that many of the proponents of the Germanic peoples were not content with general praise of the population of early Europe. Rather they found in the deepening myths about primitive tribes with pure characteristics and a love of freedom a way to link the old praise of Germanic freedoms and Anglo-Saxon institutions to specific racial characteristics, to exalt the Teutonic or Norse peoples and debase the rest.[15]

In Great Britain the clear separation of Celt and Teuton and the emphasis on the importance of race took a marked step forward in 1787 with the publication of John Pinkerton's *Dissertation on the Origin of the Scythians or Goths*. Pinkerton, who possessed a striking polemic style, argued that the Celts were an inferior people, who had been driven out of much of Europe by the Goths—a term which included Greeks and Romans as well as Germans and Scandinavians. Foreshadowing the Teutonism that was to come out of Germany in following decades, Pinkerton argued that the Goths (the ancient Scythians) spread northward from Persia to give birth to all the great peoples of history.[16]

Pinkerton had firm views on race. Although they differed from those of most of his contemporaries, they were to become a commonplace in nineteenth-century scientific and popular writing. "A Tartar, a Negro, an American [Indian] &c &c differ as much from a German, as a bull-dog, or lap-dog, or shepherd's cur, from a pointer," wrote Pinkerton. "The differences are radical; and such as no climate or chance could produce: and it may be expected that as science advances, able writers will give us a complete system of the many different races of men."[17] In the nineteenth century scientists who argued for marked innate differences between races delighted in comparing the human to the canine species.

Pinkerton was unusual in that he did not merely praise Germanic characteristics, but also made comparative racial judgments. He wrote of the Celts who "have been savages since the world began, and will be for ever savages while a separate people; that is, while themselves, and of unmixt blood."[18] By violently attacking contemporary Scots and the Welsh, Pinkerton assured wide publicity for his work as well as inspiring bitter rebuttals. Many disagreed with him, but he was not ignored. An interest in the northern nations, their history, and their mythology flourished in England and on the Continent in the last decades of the eighteenth century. This interest gave the Anglo-Saxons a fuller historical past, and it also made possible a new sense of national unity in England and America. The Viking invasions and even the Norman Conquest could be viewed as making possible the reunification of the ancient Germanic-Norse peoples. As the older Saxon myth persisted in English thinking, it meant that in the first half of the nineteenth century old interpretations of the free Saxons and the imposition of the Norman yoke existed vigorously side by side with newer ideas of an overriding Germanic-Norse mystique.

While the Saxonists in Great Britain gained general sustenance from German nationalism and from the European-wide fascination with a Germanic-Norse past, the aspect of European scholarship that ultimately most directly fired the English and American imagination was the detailed work on the origins of the German language and race. The philological researches into the Indo-European language family from which the German and English languages were descended became of particular use to Saxonists who envisaged an expansion of Anglo-Saxons over the whole world. Efforts to determine the origin of the Indo-European language group assumed strong racial overtones. The fundamental error was the assumption that affinity of language proved affinity of race. This led to a search for an original homeland of the Indo-European people. Long before what later became known as Aryanism dominated a new German nation, it influenced, in less virulent form, England and the United States.

There had long been arguments that the human race had originated in the region between the Indus and the Ganges. Herder had adopted this view with enthusiasm, and his fascination with India and its ideas helped to give an oriental cast to the early German Romantic movement.[19] The philologists of the early nineteenth century were, however, to give a whole new racial cast to the fascination with the roots of mankind. They were to conjure up an image of a specific, gifted people—the Indo-Europeans—who spilled out from the mountains of central Asia to press westward following the sun, bringing civilization, heroism, and the principles of freedom to a succession of empires. When in the first half of the nineteenth century this idea became dominant, it paralleled in scientific writing the development of a clearly delineated notion of a superior Caucasian race. Eventually, sections of the original Indo-European racial stock were depicted as a Caucasian elite.

Although most of the work on the original homeland came from German scholars, the linguistic basis for this theory had its origin in the writings of the distinguished British orientalist and philologist Sir William Jones. Jones went to India as a judge in the 1780s and there founded the "Asiatick Society." The journal *Asiatic Researches* began to appear in the late 1780s and quickly had a major impact on European scholars. Jones was led by his interest in Hindu law to a study of Sanskrit, and in February 1786 he read a seminal paper in which he argued that Sanskrit, Greek, and Latin must have sprung from the same original language, and that it was likely that Gothic (German), Celtic, and old Persian belonged to the same family. His paper appeared in *Asiatic Researches* and created a considerable stir, particularly in Germany. Hegel called it the discovery of a new world.[20]

The philological work inspired by Jones soon became inextricably entangled with the older idea of an Asiatic origin for the human race and the idea of the spreading westward of this primitive population. Not all agreed with Jones, nor did the different theorists agree with one another, but the general tendency was to look to Asia, and particularly to the mountainous regions north of India, for the origin of a particularly gifted people. The study of language was soon seen as the key to understanding the relationships of ancient peoples. In Germany the whole idea of the eastern homeland was disseminated by Johann Christoph Adelung in the first decade of the nineteenth century. He disagreed with Jones's linguistic theories but he placed the origin of the whole human race in the vale of Kashmir.[21]

More significant ultimately than the grafting of the philological research onto the old belief that the origin of the human race was in Asia was its grafting onto the belief in the excellence of the primitive Germans; the idea was developed that a primitive German people had come from the steppes of Asia to stand firm against Roman decadence.[22] The study of a language group that actually involved most of the languages of Europe was given a distinctive Germanic cast by German scholars. The key figure in Germanizing the ideas of Sir William Jones was Friedrich von Schlegel.

Schlegel falsely believed that Sanskrit was the common source of what were later called the Indo-European languages, but vital for his successors was his assumption that the existence of an original language presupposed the existence of an original race. He wrote of a specific, gifted people who had moved out of the region of India in the distant past and had carried their language westward. This vigorous people had saved civilization by revitalizing a degenerate Roman Empire and providing for the eventual triumph of Christianity. There was to be no complete agreement either on the site of the original homeland or on the common source of the Indo-European language family, but the confusion of language and race was generally accepted.[23] In the first half of the nineteenth century the terms *Indo-European* and *Indo-Germanic* were most commonly used to describe the language group; the term *Aryan* did not achieve general popularity until used by Max Müller later in the century. That Indo-Germanic could be used to describe the origin of a variety of languages, including the Celtic, is an indication of the extent to which philological study was linked to the general history of the Germanic peoples.

The full flowering of the arguments about the original homeland and a people of superior qualities came in the years between 1820 and 1850. H. F. Link, writing in the early 1820s, thought that the languages had descended from Zend through Sanskrit, and that the Armenia-Georgia-Media region was the original home of the pure, primitive race, but Franz Bopp established in the 1830s in his *Comparative Grammar* that all the languages involved, including Zend and Sanskrit, stemmed from some common ancestor. Although Bopp showed the common origin of practically all the existing languages of Europe, he used the term Indo-Germanic to describe this general family.[24]

The usefulness of this basic research was obscured by romantic dreams of a special racial group, an *Urfolk*, which had advanced westward out of Asia to revitalize the West. Scholars generally began to accept the suggestion made by J. G. Rhode in 1820 that this people had originally lived on the plateau of central Asia, around the sources of the Oxus and the Jaxartes. Rhode imagined that a sudden drop in temperature on the Asian plateau had dispersed this primitive people throughout Europe.[25] The work of Franz Bopp and Julius von Klaproth generally advanced Rhode's theories of a central Asiatic homeland, but it was August Friedrich Pott who, in the years from 1833 to 1840, painted the most vivid scenes of a people arising from the valleys of the Oxus and the Jaxartes and the slopes of the Hindu Kush to press relentlessly westward. Pott imagined these tribesmen as having been pulled west by an all-pervasive impulse as they followed the course of the sun; their route became the route of civilization, and *ex oriente lux* became a reality. "The march of culture, in its general lines," wrote Pott, "has always followed the sun's course. The people of Europe at first nestled in the bosom of Asia."[26]

By the 1840s the vision of vigorous peoples sweeping westward out of Asia had been widely disseminated by German scholars. The identity of race and language was taken for granted, and race was exalted as the basis of a nation. Friedrich List, in his work on political economy, published in 1841, divided Europe into three races—the Slavic, the Germanic, and the Latin—based on three major linguistic groups. He asserted that it could hardly be doubted "that providence has by preference dedicated the Germanic races by means of their nature and character, to the solution of the great task of leading world-affairs, civilizing wild and barbaric countries and populating those that are still uninhabited."[27] In the 1840s Christian Lassen, A. Kuhn, and Jakob Grimm all helped to reinforce the earlier ideas of language, race, and the westward movement of civilization, and helped to complete the idea that only the Germanic peoples had continued the task begun so long ago by vigorous tribesmen pressing westward across Europe. Grimm was particularly influential, and in his history of the German language, published in 1848, he wrote of it as proven that the people who had founded the nations of Europe had originally emigrated from Asia, pulled westward by an irresistible impulse. The further a race had penetrated, the earlier it must have started on its course and the greater its imprint on world history.[28]

In little more than fifty years a whole scholarly base had been created for the idea of affinity between language and race, and what was best in Europe and the world was increasingly ascribed to that people, soon generally to be called Aryan, who had pressed westward out of central Asia to revitalize the Roman Empire and eventually dominate Europe and the world. The original language spoken by this people might have spawned a variety of European languages, but its best racial characteristics had been passed on in dominant form through the Germanic peoples. The German philologists laid the foundation for the modern study of language and also traced the Germanic-Norse myth deep into prehistory by inventing an heroic race to speak the original Indo-European language.

The fascination of the German philologists with Asia, the original homeland, and the diffusion of an energetic people westward quickly spread into other European countries. In France Jules Michelet fell under the sway of the German Romantics and German scholarship. "Follow the migrations of mankind from East to West along the sun's course and along the tracks of the world's magnetic currents," he wrote in 1831; "observe its long voyage from Asia to Europe, from India to France . . . At its starting point in India, the birth place of races and of religions, *the womb of the world.*"[29]

In England the whole matter had attracted enough interest by 1830 for the *Edinburgh Review* to devote a review article to the subject. The author was doubtful about the religious implications of the new ideas and somewhat confused in general and his whole discussion was concerned more with peoples and races than with languages. It was generally agreed, he said, both in England and on the Continent, that the origin of language had to be sought in the region which was the cradle of the human race. He thought that "the most remarkable" theory advanced was that of Adelung, but he admitted that this had now "been pretty generally received on the Continent, particularly by the scholars of Germany." He summarized this theory as being that Middle or Central Asia had formed the mighty reservoir from which streams of population had poured into Europe and India. What perturbed him most about this theory were the implications for the Mosaic account of Creation, and he could not accept the "extravagance" of Klaproth, who placed the dispersion of "the Indo-Germanic" race before the flood, and who argued that this race had deteriorated in India by mixing with dark-skinned aborigines. Yet after reiterating his faith in Genesis and stressing that the Indo-Germanic theory appeared to be inconsistent with Moses, the author admitted that the only possible explanation seemed to be that Sanskrit, Greek, Latin, and German were derived from a common source, and that there were "some probabilities" in favor of the Indo-Germanic theory.[30]

In the 1830s the British began making their own contributions to the new German philology. In 1831 James C. Prichard, the famous ethnologist and philologist, published *The Eastern Origin of the Celtic Nations*. This work established beyond a doubt that Celtic was related to Sanskrit, Greek, Latin, and German. Prichard was famous in these years as the best-known British defender of the unity of mankind, but he accepted the special characteristics of the Germanic peoples.[31] Within a few years German philology had its own school in England, inspired by the work of Benjamin Thorpe and John M. Kemble. Thorpe had worked in Copenhagen under Rasmus Kristian Rask, and Kemble had intimate ties with Germany; he had studied there and became a friend of the Grimms. Thorpe and Kemble delved anew into Anglo-Saxon manuscripts and were able to integrate their work into the mainstream of Indo-European scholarship.[32]

The English had long ago formed a firm link between their "free Anglo-Saxons" and the Germanic tribes of the declining years of the Roman Empire, but now their strong roots were seen to penetrate even deeper into the past. In the middle decades of the nineteenth century the English adopted this new extension of their history and made their past even more glorious by tracing a continuous chain from a homeland in central

Asia, through the forests of Germany, to the shores of England. And the Americans were able to take pride in a westward advance which had passed beyond England across the Atlantic to press on relentlessly across the American Continent, eventually to complete the grand trek by bringing civilization back to the Asian homeland.

While the English were delighted to trace their ancestry back for thousands of years, they were less willing to accept the idea of an all-pervasive Germanic-Norse mystique. Although aspects of this argument were widely disseminated in the writings of Thomas Carlyle in the 1830s and 1840s, they never achieved total acceptance in England. A major obstacle in England to the linking of Germans, Saxons, Danes, and Normans as one great race was that the English thought of themselves as the supremely successful group within the Germanic tradition. Also, the long-established myth of free Anglo-Saxons resisting a Norman yoke was far too deeply engrained in English thinking. The English never forgot their earlier Saxonism, which depicted the Normans as brutal, tyrannical oppressors, and they were never content to accept a theory which submerged the Saxons into a greater European mass. They used the new ideas to give the Saxons a still more distant and glorious past, but they also continued to elevate the Saxons above all others who supposedly shared a common Germanic and Indo-European heritage. The Saxons became the elite of an elite.

The tendency to keep the Anglo-Saxons as a separate, superior people within a larger Germanic race was also increased by the early emphases of English Romanticism. In the first decades of the nineteenth century, before the new scholarship from the Continent had any major impact on England, the idea of free Anglo-Saxons gained a fresh dimension under the impact of a burgeoning medievalism, a medievalism which had its immediate origins in the late eighteenth century. The main arguments were along traditional lines, but a new Romanticism was present — an emphasis on personal, individual traits rather than on abstract institutional excellence. This approach is seen at its most marked in the novels and poems of Sir Walter Scott and is also marked in the historical writing of the Frenchman Augustin

Thierry. Both helped to bridge the gap between the older idealization of Anglo-Saxon institutions and the mid-century emphasis on the Germanic Anglo-Saxon race, and both of them gained some of their inspiration from Sharon Turner's classic *History of the Anglo-Saxons*, which was published between 1799 and 1805. Turner was a transitional figure. He amplified and refined the scholarship of the previous two hundred years while laying the foundation for Saxon studies in the first decades of the nineteenth century. The work was for the most part traditional in its use of the Anglo-Saxon myth, but it was also touched by new Romantic ideas of the medieval past.

Turner believed that the English "language, our government, and our laws, display our Gothic ancestors in every part." He stressed the love of liberty among the Anglo-Saxons and the early origin of parliamentary institutions, but he was realistic in his depiction of the ferocity of his English ancestors in their uncivilized state. He also specifically defended the idea of a single human species (this would have been unnecessary fifty years before), and though he praised Thomas Percy for his clear analysis of the distinction between the Celts and the Goths, he attacked Pinkerton for his virulent abuse of the Celtic people. Turner did, however, use a frequent nineteenth-century argument when he contended that the conquest of the Roman Empire by the Germanic nations was a healthy recasting of human society rather than a barbarization. Turner's work greatly stimulated Saxon studies in the first decades of the nineteenth century, but his personal affinities were more with the scholars of the seventeenth and eighteenth centuries than with the nineteenth-century adherents of frenetic racial and linguistic theories.[33]

The impact of the new Romantic tendencies is muted in Turner's history, but it reaches full realization in the novels of Sir Walter Scott, who acknowledged his debt to both Turner and Percy. Scott's impact on his contemporaries — novelists, historians, poets, painters — was decisive. In creating in mature form the Romantic historical novel, Scott achieved an unparalleled influence and success throughout Europe and the United States. Suddenly there was a new, personal, dramatic way of perceiving the past, and this not only thrilled his general audiience, but also inspired historians to achieve a new richness of personal and social description. "These Historical Novels," wrote Carlyle, "have taught all men this truth, which looks like a truism, and yet was as good as unknown to writers of history and others, till so taught: that the bygone ages of the world were actually filled by living men, not by protocols, state-papers, controversies and abstractions of men."[34] This shift from the institutional to the personal, from the general to the particular, was at the heart of the Romantic creed and helped to transform the image of nations and races as well as individuals.

Scott's influence went far beyond the English-speaking countries. Augustin Thierry remembered that he "saluted the appearance of 'Ivanhoe' with transports of enthusiasm."[35] Even Leopold von Ranke, who was offended by the inaccuracies in Scott's work, admitted that "the romantic historical works of Sir Walter Scott, which were well known in all languages and to all nations, played a principal part in awakening sympathy for the actions and passions of past ages. On me too they exercised their spell and I read his works more than once with the most lively interest."[36] That Scott in subdued form echoed the views of those Romantics striving to use the past to laud the spirit of particular nations or races is perhaps best revealed in Heine's comment on the novels: "Their theme . . . is the mighty sorrow for the loss of national peculiarities swallowed up in the universality of the newer culture — a sorrow which is now throbbing in the hearts of all peoples. For national memories lie deeper in the human breast than is generally thought."[37] Though this tells us more about Heine than about Scott, it indicates the extent to which Scott filled a need for the whole Romantic generation. And if he filled needs in France and Germany, how much more did readers in England and the United States thrill to his tales of their heroic ancestors and his simplified romantic vision of the past.

For the Anglo-Saxon, *Ivanhoe* was the supreme work. In this book Scott inspired a whole generation with a vision of Saxon freedom and honesty. As a novelist he was able to depict these attributes as a matter of individual and racial traits rather than institutional excellence. This was no dry-as-dust account of

Anglo-Saxon charters and land tenures, but a story of virtuous flaxen-haired Saxon maidens and sturdy, blue-eyed Saxon yeomen. He wrote in the first chapter of *Ivanhoe* that four generations had not been enough to blend the hostile blood of the Normans and the Anglo-Saxons, and throughout the novel he constantly praised the homely, blunt, simple, honest qualities of his Saxon heroes. The Anglo-Saxon language was "far more manly and expressive" than French, and Cedric's "homely diet, eaten in peace and liberty" far better than "the luxurious dainties" of a foreign conqueror.[38]

Scott's most immediate impact was in France, where art entwined with reality as Augustin Thierry, profoundly influenced by the novelist, in 1825 published his *Histoire de la conquête de l'Angleterre*. Thierry believed that the history of England for centuries after the Norman Conquest could be explained as a racial struggle. Subordinating political and religious considerations to those of race, he made even Beckett and Henry II contend as Saxon and Norman.[39]

The emphasis was clearly moving from institutions to individuals and races, but it was only in the twenty years after the publication of *Ivanhoe* that the new pride in the whole Germanic-Norse tradition began to mingle freely with the older English Saxonism. Even then the tradition of the Norman yoke survived in vigorous form. Consistency was no virtue for the Romantics, and they were quite capable of pitting Saxon against Norman while believing that the Norman Conquest ultimately represented a reuniting of the northern peoples.

The Romantics in the early nineteenth century increasingly looked for ways in which individuals and peoples differed rather than for the qualities common to all human beings. Individuals, nations, races were all endowed with a personal spirit which distinguished them from all others. This emphasis on the distinctiveness of human beings ultimately presented a challenge—both to a religion which viewed mankind as descended from common ancestors and to a science which classified human beings as belonging to one species with one set of innate characteristics. In the first half of the nineteenth century, as historians, philosophers, novelists, and poets sang the praises of individual achievement — of individual men, of individual nations, and of individual races — science itself presented them with reasons for wide differences in human progress and gave them ample evidence to explain individual and national failure as well as success.

3

Science and Inequality

> Of the great influence of Race in the production of National Character, no reasonable inquirer can now doubt.
>
> *Edinburgh Review,* January, 1844

The flowering of the new science of man in the first half of the nineteenth century was ultimately decisive in giving a racial cast to Anglo-Saxonism. Scientists, by mid-century, had provided an abundance of "proofs" by which English and American Anglo-Saxons could explain their power, progress, governmental stability, and freedom. Rather than the eighteenth-century emphasis on the human race, its problems, and its progress, there was in the following century a feverish interest in distinctly endowed human races—races with innately unequal abilities, which could lead either to success and world power or to total subordination and extinction. In western Europe and America the Caucasian race became generally recognized as the race clearly superior to all others; the Germanic was recognized as the most talented branch of the Caucasians; and the Anglo-Saxons, in England and the United States, and often even in

Germany, were recognized as the most gifted descendants of the Germans. The scientific study of man provided supposedly empirical proofs for the assertions of propagandists and patriots.

Whatever the specific methods used — and works on race ranged from impressionistic studies based on cultural differences to those of supposed exact scientific measurement — there was in the first half of the nineteenth century a sharp increase in the number of racial theorists who were prepared to defend inherent, unchangeable differences between races. The roots of this change lay in eighteenth-century developments in scientific classification, but clearly many of the nineteenth-century writers on race were also responding to that interest in national identity, uniqueness, and separateness that was coming to dominate European thought. The subject of racial classification was of general popular interest by the middle of the nineteenth century, and works based on supposedly exact cranial measurements were reviewed side by side with impressionistic studies by enthusiastic amateurs.

Rather than merely praising Anglo-Saxons or Germanic tribes for their accomplishments, those interested in the science of man were able by comparative methods to establish reasons for superiority and inferiority; an essential shift in emphasis occurred when arguments about the inferiority of other "races" assumed an importance as great or even greater than arguments about the excellence of Caucasians or elite groups within the Caucasian race. The Anglo-Saxons had already been firmly linked to their Germanic ancestors; they were in the process of being linked to the linguistic racial group from which they were descended. Now scientists were to place them firmly within a superior Caucasian race and ultimately were to give them special characteristics even within that race. The Anglo-Saxons were to become the final product of a long line of superior beings who stretched back through an Indo-Germanic cradle to Creation itself.

Those who in the nineteenth century began to think in terms of inherent racial superiority and inferiority had to cope both with the orthodox Christian view of the unity of man and with the eighteenth-century natural philosophers, who saw mankind as capable of indefinite improvement. The Christian view stemmed directly from the account in Genesis. God had created Adam and Eve and from this pair, through Noah and his sons, Shem, Ham, and Japheth, had descended all mankind: "These three were the sons of Noah; and from these the whole earth was peopled." Additional complications had been added by those biblical scholars who had devised a chronology for the time since Creation. In England and the United States the generally accepted date for the Creation was that of Archbishop Ussher, who in the seventeenth century had fixed the date at 4004 B.C. If all the varieties of mankind had descended from one pair in less than six thousand years, then it was difficult to write of inherent, wide gulfs separating different races.[1]

Although the religious view of the unity of mankind had not been shattered by the Renaissance, the travels of Europeans from the fifteenth to the nineteenth centuries eventually did much to erode an orthodox position. The discovery of America and its Indian inhabitants was only one step in a process which climaxed in the eighteenth century with Cook's voyage to Australia and the penetration of the Pacific. Could all these isolated "savages" have sprung from one pair in the Garden of Eden less than six thousand years before? If this was true, how had they reached such distant lands, and why was there such an apparent gulf in accomplishment between the Europeans and the diverse peoples they encountered? Even in the early sixteenth century Paracelsus and Giordano Bruno had suggested a polygenetic explanation, and the idea that there had been more than one original pair was given greater elaboration in the seventeenth century by Frenchman Isaac de la Peyrère.[2] In the following centuries many Europeans were reluctant to accept Australian aborigines and South African Hottentots as long-lost relatives.

The early polygenetic arguments were crushed by the prevailing Christian monogenetic view, but the necessity of explaining the reasons for wide gulfs in accomplishment remained. Dramatic European advances in science and technology widened the gap that separated Europeans from the newly discovered peoples in the rest of the world. In the eighteenth century the prevailing explanation of the differences in accomplishment was still optimistic about the future. The traditional attitude toward non-European peoples had been to view them as tribes which had degenerated, but philosophers of the Enlightenment suggested the possibility of indefinite progress. Europeans were the high point in a steady advance from a state of savagery—an advance which was still continuing, and one that was available to "savages" as well as to Europeans. The prevailing Enlightenment view of a hierarchy of all Creation with Europeans on the highest rung, and with differences the product not of inherent characteristics but of environment, dominated thinking in England and the United States in the eighteenth century. All peoples were capable of change and improvement.[3]

Yet, though Enlightenment thinkers stressed the unity and general improvability of mankind, they also accelerated the process of secularization of thinking which had begun in the age of discovery and in the scientific advances of the sixteenth and seventeenth centuries. Enlightenment philosophers defended the unity of mankind on non-Christian grounds and often challenged the traditional churches. By separating science from theology they opened the way for science to reach entirely different answers from those of the orthodox. Also, in their search for knowledge, the natural scientists strove to observe and classify. Detailed physical comparison, often used in the eighteenth century to demonstrate the ultimate unity of the world and its inhabitants, was in the nineteenth century used to demonstrate fundamental human differences. Comparative anatomists and craniologists were ultimately to prove quite capable of seeing what the society at large wanted them to see.[4]

The generally accepted classifications of human beings from the seventeenth to the early nineteenth century all assumed the unity of the human species. When François Bernier in the late seventeenth century made the first significant classification of the races of mankind, he reached the conclusion that there were at least four main races within the human species: European, African, Asiatic, and Lapp. His classification was based on physical characteristics, mainly color. This tentative beginning reached a different level of development in the work of Carolus Linnaeus in the 1730s. In his *Systema Naturae* Linnaeus classified mankind as part of the whole animal creation, and he divided the human species into four varieties: European (albus), American (rubescus), Asiatic (fuscus), and African (niger). To Linnaeus species were unchangeable; the same species were in existence as had been created by God. Linnaeus did not clash with orthodox religion, and within twenty years the unity of mankind was given further support by the influential definition of species propounded by the Comte de Buffon. He argued that two animals were of the same species if they could perpetuate themselves by interbreeding; if they could not breed, or if their offspring were sterile, then they were of different species. Buffon believed that the varieties of mankind stemmed primarily from differences in climate, food, and manners, with the last two depending in essence on the first. His definition of species quickly became standard.[5]

Like Linnaeus and Buffon, Johann Friedrich Blumenbach believed in the unity of mankind, and he denied the inherent inferiority of any race. Yet, like them, he was influential in taking the study of mankind out of the realm of the theologians and in making it a matter of physical comparison. Beginning in the 1770s with a fourfold division of mankind, Blumenbach eventually settled on the fivefold division which was the basic classification inherited by writers in the first half of the nineteenth century. Blumenbach argued for one human species containing five varieties—Caucasian, Mongolian, American, Ethiopian, and Malay. He introduced the name *Caucasian* to describe the variety of mankind—the Georgian—that had originated on the southern slopes of Mount Caucasus. This, to Blumenbach, was the most beautiful race, and he said it must be "considered as the primary or intermediate of these five principal races."[6] Other races represented a degeneration from the original type. Although Blumenbach defended the concept of a single human species, he also emphasized the ways—shape of skull, face, hair, color—in which the different varieties could be physically classified. Georges Cuvier in the early nineteenth century suggested a threefold division of the human species—Caucasian, Mongolian, and Negro—which became of great importance, but Blumenbach's fivefold division formed the basis of the work of most influential writers on race in the first half of the nineteenth century.[7]

While the most important eighteenth-century naturalists defended monogenesis and generally agreed that human differences arose from environmental factors, polygenetic arguments occurred with more frequency as the dangers of heresy lessened. Defenders of polygenesis sharply increased the tendency, which was already present in monogenetic racial classifications, of exalting all white races at the expense of the colored. At the heart of the polygenetic position was a refusal to believe that other people who appeared in every way "savage" and physically different could have sprung from the same ancestors. This was particularly the case when Europeans compared themselves to Africans. English physician John Atkins wrote in the 1730s that "I am persuaded the black and white Race have, *ab origine*, sprung from different-coloured first Parents."[8] Influential nonspecialists were willing to endorse a polygenetic position as early as the mid-eighteenth century. Voltaire consistently attacked the idea that mankind was descended from a single pair, and David Hume, while not taking a specifically polygenetic position, defended the concept of the inherent inequality of races. "I am apt to suspect the negroes," he wrote, "and in general all the other species of men (for there are four or five different kinds) to be naturally inferior to the whites. There was never a civilized nation of any other complexion than white, nor any individual eminent either in action or speculation."[9]

The best-known defenders of polygenesis in the last decades of the eighteenth century were Christoph Meiners and Georg Foster in Germany, Jean-Joseph Virey in France, and John Pinkerton, Lord Kames, and Charles White in Great Britain. Also influential in England and the United States was Bernard Romans, who wrote a much-read description of Florida. Throughout this era commentators on race came from a variety of intellectual backgrounds. Historians, philosophers, and lawyers, as well as physicians, comparative anatomists, and craniologists were willing to make pronouncements about racial differences, and society at large ultimately drew support for its racial judgments from a broad base of scientific and amateur opinion.

The exaltation of the whites can be found in its most obvious form in the work of the German philosopher Christoph Meiners, who, like Blumenbach, taught at the University of Göttingen. He divided mankind into the white and the beautiful, and the black and the ugly. Only the first had true courage and love of liberty; the second had character defects leading to a lack of the gentler feelings. Unlike many of his contemporaries in Germany, however, Meiners was enthusiastic in his praise of Celtic peoples.[10] The Frenchman Jean-Joseph Virey was considerably influenced by Meiners, and he accepted the division of mankind into the white and beautiful, and the black and ugly. In his writings he used language that was to become common in the next half-century: "The European, called by his high destiny to rule the world, which he knows how to illumine with his intelligence and subdue with his courage, is the highest expression of man and at the head of the human race. The others, a wretched horde of barbarians, are, so to say, no more than its embryo." Virey was particularly virulent on the subject of blacks, reaching the conclusion that they were not true men but were connected more closely to the apes.[11] Virey's work was praised and used in the American South in the 1830s.

Great Britain, with its strong outward thrust among a variety of peoples in America, Africa, and the Pacific, was a fertile field for the theories of racial differentiation in the late eighteenth century. John Pinkerton, in attacking the Celts and praising the Goths, did not hesitate to challenge the environmental view of racial difference, asserting that science would soon provide "a complete system of the many different races of men."[12] Pinkerton was unusual in that he vigorously stressed inherent racial differences in writing of European peoples. This was to be a commonplace by the mid-nineteenth century, but was extremely rare in the eighteenth. More common was the desire to be separated from the nonwhite savages of the world, particularly the blacks.

Edward Long, in his popular history of Jamaica, argued strongly for the theory that blacks were "a different species of the same *genus*." He disagreed with Buffon's argument that climate was the cause of observable differences, pointing out that for this to be the case the world would have to be much older than was generally believed. Long stressed supposedly unchangeable physical differences: the black color, the presence of wool – not hair – the infesting of black bodies by black lice, and the bestial smell. Long was frequently cited by other writers and, like Virey, was used by the American Southerners in the 1830s when they defended slavery through a depiction of innate black inferiority.[13]

The arguments of the English surgeon Charles White, in his *Account of the Regular Gradation in Man*, published in 1799, were similar to those of Edward Long. Like Long, White argued that the blacks were of a different species. White contended that "there exist material differences in the organization and constitution of various tribes of the human species; and not only so, but that those differences, generally, mark a regular gradation, from the white European down through the human species to the brute creation." Also, White argued, "the opinion that all people descended from one pair at first cannot be maintained, unless we find some other causes of the diversity of colour besides those which have been usually assigned to it." White's argument was that the different species were originally created with the distinctive marks they still retained, and that the worst specimens of the human race lived in Africa. At the top was "the white European; who being most removed from the brute creation, may, on that account, be considered as the most beautiful of the human race. No one will doubt his superiority in intellectual powers; and I believe it will be found that his capacity is naturally superior to that of every other man." White was obviously still influenced by the idea of the chain of being, but he was forcing the links apart.

Finally, by writing a paean to the white European, White demonstrated the way in which dispassionate scientific analysis was so often to be thrown aside in the next fifty years:

Where shall we find, unless in the European, that nobly arched head, containing such a quantity of brain, and supported by a hollow conical pillow, entering its centre? Where the perpendicular face, the prominent nose, and round projecting chin? Where that variety of features, and fulness of expression; those long, flowing, graceful ringlets; that majestic beard, those rosy cheeks and coral lips? Where that erect posture of the body and noble gait? In what other quarter of the globe shall we find the blush that overspreads the soft features of the beautiful women of Europe, that emblem of modesty, of delicate feelings, and of sense? What nice expression of the amiable and softer passions in the countenance; and that general elegance of features and complexion? Where, except on the bosom of the European woman, two such plump and snowy white hemispheres, tipt with vermillion?

White's style was more that of a bad novelist than a good surgeon, but the whole passage has a touch of the more dangerous tone of later exaltations of Teutonic womanhood.[14]

Blacks were always central to early English and American racial classifications, but the isolation of the American Indians also convinced some, as it had since the sixteenth century, that the only reasonable explanation for their presence in the Americas was a separate Creation. Scottish philosopher Lord Kames, while arguing that no race was innately inferior to any other, also argued that there were wide differences between races: "A mastiff differs not more from a spaniel, than a white man from a negro, or a Laplander from a Dane." Kames tried to reconcile himself with the religious orthodox by arguing that the different species arose after the original Creation, and that in the dispersion of mankind different groups were modified to fit different climates.[15] His conclusion regarding the American Indians was that it was "highly improbable that they are of the same race," and he asserted it is "beyond any rational doubt, that there are different races or kinds of men, and that these races or kinds are naturally fitted for different climates: whence we have reason to conclude that originally each kind was placed in its proper climate, whatever changes may have happened in later times by war or commerce."[16] Here Kames stood the environmental argument on its head by asserting that races were originally made different to fit the varied climates rather than the varied climates producing temporary changes in humans.

Less reluctant than Kames to write of inequality and polygenesis was Bernard Romans in his description of Florida. Romans wrote of the Indians as "a people not only rude and uncultivated, but incapable of civilization." The Indians, he argued, drew their origin from a different source than that of other people "or any other species of the human genus, of which i think there are many species." God, Romans argued, had created an original man and woman in the New World, and "there were as many *Adams* and *Eves* (every body knows these names to have an allegorical sense) as we find different species of the human genus."[17] "Every body" knew nothing of the sort, for such direct challenges to Genesis were to provoke strong rebuttals from the religious orthodox until well past the middle of the nineteenth century.

For all their vigor in argument, those who defended polygenesis were not in the main line of ethnological thought in the last years of the eighteenth century. Linnaeus, Buffon, and Blumenbach towered above those who defended a polygenetic position. But the way had been prepared for the idea of distinct races with unequal inherent capabilities. The arguments for polygenesis eventually grew much stronger, especially in America, and in the nineteenth century the main monogenetic view also came to embrace the idea of permanently different varieties or races within the human species. Many were willing to accept and defend the idea of inherent inequality while attempting to maintain their religious orthodoxy. One could either argue for divine intervention at some time after the original Creation, or simply assert that subsequent to the Creation separate races had developed permanently inherited characteristics.

By far the most influential ethnologist in England in the first half of the nineteenth century was James Cowles Prichard. He was a firm believer in monogenesis. Prichard's most important ethnological work was his *Researches into the Physical History of Man*, first published in one volume in 1813, and reaching its final state in the five-volume edition published between 1836 and 1847.[18]

Throughout his writings Prichard defended the concept of one human species and theoretically refused to believe in the inherent inferiority of any race. Yet, as his editions progressed, his concessions grew. By the 1840s Prichard had so defined "permanent variety" as to make it in practical terms little different from the "race" of the believers in polygenesis. Prichard wrote that permanent varieties were very like species in that they displayed characteristic peculiarities that were permanently transmitted. They differed from species, however, in that such deviations had not been present from the time of the creation of the group.[19] If traits were permanently transmitted it made little difference, except of course to the religious orthodox, that they had not always been there. Prichard was also willing to make judgments based on observed cultural traits, and he developed a very high opinion of the Germanic tribes: "In moral energy the German race was superior to the rest of mankind." He added that "the Goths were a people susceptible of civilisation, remarkable for the soundness of their understanding, and for intellectual qualities of the highest kind."[20] Prichard was cautious and moderate compared to the American ethnologists of the 1840s, but he generally enforced the belief in the special abilities of the white, Germanic variety of the human species.

Prichard attempted to maintain an orthodox view, but the establishing of racial hierarchies proceeded rapidly in a host of scientific and amateur writings. In the first decades of the nineteenth century, scientists and others studying the varieties of the human race reflected to a marked degree the general shift in thought from the universal to the particular, from an interest in what nations and people had in common to an interest in what made them unique. Frequently, the supposedly careful comparisons of cranial capacities and angles, and a variety of other detailed physical features, resulted in an endorsement of what was being said by patriots, poets, and novelists. As there was no general agreement on what constituted a proper scientific study of races, all types of evidence were brought forward to support the general idea of inherent differences. Some were to be discounted as "nonscientific" sooner than others, but all helped the prevailing rush to racial differentiation. Even those views which were widely attacked as irreligous were given wide dissemination.

Englishman William Lawrence's *Lectures on . . . the Natural History of Man*, first published in 1819, went through numerous editions by the 1840s and was widely cited by American writers on race. Lawrence accepted the fivefold classification of Blumenbach and argued that the Caucasians were clearly a superior race: "In stating the moral and intellectual inferiority of the native Americans to the white races, I speak of an inferiority common to them with the other dark-coloured people of the globe." Even in the least advanced stages of civilization, wrote Lawrence, the superiority of the white races could be distinguished—one had only to compare the ancient Germans with the Hottentots or a tribe of American Indians. Lawrence was able to argue for all this while still maintaining that these races were but one variety of the human species.[21]

The precision with which scientists distinguished between different racial groups was enhanced in these years by the increased fascination with anthropometry—anatomical measurement. This took a variety of forms, but of particular importance were those comparative methods relating to the features, the skull, and the head: physiogonomy, craniology, and phrenology. Craniology attained great scientific respectability by the 1840s, although its specific conclusions were later to be overturned. Phrenology, which reached conclusions similar to those of craniology, had a good deal of scientific support through the 1830s, but was to lose respectability by the middle of the century. Even then, however, it continued as a potent popular system for the dissemination of racial ideas. Anthropometry in general made possible a variety of supposedly empirically based generalizations about differences between various Caucasian races as well as between the white and colored races of the world. The foundations of anthropometry were laid in the eighteenth century in the work of Johann Kaspar Lavater, Pieter Camper, and Blumenbach, but it was only in the nineteenth century that the new detailed physical comparisons became a means of distinguishing a variety of supposedly superior and inferior races.

In the last decades of the eighteenth century, the Swiss-born minister Lavater attempted to define character by a detailed study of the head and face. He was impressionistic in his methods, but he stirred a wide interest in this type of physical comparison. Pieter Camper made a more direct contribution to the physical separation of the races by his arguments for the importance of the facial angle. This was the angle formed by two intersecting lines — one drawn horizontally from the ears to the nostrils, the other a line formed by the shape of the face from the forehead to the front teeth; the sharper the angle, it was argued, the less the intelligence. At 70 degrees was the Negro, usually illustrated in later works as just above the orangutan or ape; at the apex was "the Grecian antique" with an angle of 100 degrees. This simple device of the facial angle was used in a variety of illustrations in the early nineteenth century to illustrate differences in human intelligence.[22]

Although Blumenbach did not agree with the simple calculations of Camper's facial angle, he laid great stress on a more sophisticated comparison of skulls, hair, color, and bodily structure, and he wrote of the particular beauty of the Caucasians as demonstrated by their skulls. Blumenbach gave respectability to craniology as a scientific study. His influence, as well as that exerted by the less authoritative statements of Lavater and Camper, helped ensure that comparisons of skull, head, and face would play a vital part in nineteenth-century racial classifications.[23]

The greater sophistication of later studies did not bring scientific caution, but rather reinforcement for those who wished to defend inherent racial difference. In 1829 the Englishman William F. Edwards, who lived in France and later founded "the Societé Ethnologique de Paris," used physical comparison of the head rather than color as a means of separating races in *Des caractères physiologique des races humaines*. Edwards's main interest was in the racial history of France, and he emphasized that within a basic race as defined by Blumenbach other races could be identified by comparing the proportions of their heads. He argued that two separate races existed historically in France — the roundheaded Gaels and the longheaded Cymri. Edwards's work was much praised on the continent of Europe, and he was influential in both England and the United States.[24]

In the 1830s Belgian astronomer Jacques Quetelet extended the process of comparing human types by using a whole series of measurements whose average gave the type of a particular group. But he also leaned heavily on the facial angle as a means of comparing intelligence. The Swede Anders Retzius in the 1840s took the classification a step further by ascertaining the ratio of the length and the breadth of the cranium. From this he was able to divide human beings into two main groups — the roundheaded Brachycephalics and the longheaded Dolichocephalics — and to make further distinctions by analyzing prognathous and orthognathous characteristics. Shape remained important, but some stressed skull size or capacity as an indication of brain-power. The German Friedrich Tiedemann (as well as the American Samuel George Morton) used millet seed and shot to demonstrate the differences or similarities between the skull capacities of the different races. From this, brain size and intelligence were deduced.[25] Although not all reached the conclusion that there were innately different races, the variety of detailed measurements in the first half of the nineteenth century gave a new certainty to those who wished to argue for inherent differences between races.

The course of a new science — phrenology — is revealing of the manner in which science and popular opinion intertwined to confirm the rapidly growing belief in wide divergencies between peoples of the world. Until the 1840s phrenology was treated with seriousness by the scientific community, and it continued to influence the general population long after that date. One medical historian asserts that "phrenology . . . was certainly at least as influential in the first half of the nineteenth century as psychoanalysis was in the first half of the twentieth."[26] In its early scientific phase phrenology provided inherent, physical reasons for racial differences, and in its later popularization it provided a channel through which such ideas could be disseminated among the general population.

Phrenology originated in the work of Franz Joseph Gall and Johann Gaspar Spurzheim in the first decades of the nineteenth century. Their interest was scientific, and their most important publication was on the anatomy and physiology of the nervous system. Gall originally argued, and his work was supplemented by Spurzheim, that the brain was divided into separate faculties, each of which dealt with a specific emotion, sentiment, or power of reasoning. In general the size of a particular part of the brain indicated the extent of power, and the size of the individual faculties could be ascertained by an examination of the head or skull. After the work of Gall and Spurzheim, it was generally accepted by phrenologists and their supporters that there were thirty-five distinct faculties or organs which made up the brain; later, in the 1830s and 1840s, additions and changes were made in the original divisions. Phrenologists were able to reach conclusions from either skulls or heads. In the case of a living subject they also stressed the four "temperaments" — sanguine, bilious, nervous, and lymphatic. An individual could fit into one of these categories or into a combination of two, and after reaching a conclusion on temperament a phrenologist found it easier to comment on specific phrenological characteristics.[27]

Phrenology spread rapidly in Europe and the United States in the 1820s and 1830s. The leading phrenologist after Spurzheim's death in 1832 was the Scotsman George Combe. Combe's interest in the power and reputation of Great Britain ensured that some of the most influential writings on phrenology would take on a distinctly Anglo-Saxon cast. George Combe and his brother Andrew did a great deal to popularize phrenology in Great Britain and the United States, and the *Phrenological Journal*, founded in Edinburgh in 1823, became the main organ of the movement.[28]

Most of the phrenological writing was permeated with optimism regarding possibilities for individual improvement. It was laid down as axiomatic that the size of a particular organ or faculty in the brain could be developed by exercise, that is, by the use and encouragement of the particular ability. Such exercise was said to be particularly important in childhood and youth when the maximum change could be effected. Confident as they were of the possibility of individual improvement, phrenologists were equally convinced that the degree of improvability of a particular race was strictly controlled by the original cerebral organization. Anxious to broaden their appeal and to avoid religious controversy, the phrenologists usually avoided polygenetic arguments as an explanation for racial difference. They based their arguments on the observable cranial differences between the races of mankind and on the permanence of original distinctions between skull types.[29]

George Combe, who was the most influential phrenologist in the United States as well as Great Britain, stressed the importance of genetic inheritance. Even in *The Constitution of Man*, which was in general remarkably optimistic regarding the future of mankind and less concerned with race than his later works, Combe stressed racial differentiation. He argued that the "cerebral development" of different peoples was dissimilar, and that "each Hindoo, Chinese, New Hollander, Negro, and Charib, obviously inherits from his parents a certain general type of head; and so does each European."[30] The physical structure of the head explained all. Individuals and nations that were distinguished for moral and intellectual force of mind had large brains—one could, for example, compare the Teutonic race with the Hindu.[31] Mental constitution, not climate or terrain, was the vital factor. "When we regard the different quarters of the globe," Combe wrote in 1843, "we are struck with the extreme dissimilarity in the attainments of the varieties of men who inhabit them. If we glance over the history of Europe, Asia, Africa, and America, we shall find distinct and permanent features of character, which strongly indicate natural differences in their mental constitutions."[32]

Praise for the Caucasian race was universal among the phrenologists. The broadest distinction established was that between whites and nonwhites, but most writers were also prepared to make distinctions on both sides of that unbridgeable gulf. George Combe commented that the Celtic race was "far behind the Teutonic,"[33] and the belief was common that the Anglo-Saxons had the most perfect cerebral organization, an organization that placed them above other Caucasians as well as far above the non-Caucasians of the world. In commenting on the English settlement and westward advance in America, Combe said at the end of the 1830s that "the existing races of native American Indians show skulls inferior in their moral and intellectual development to those of the Anglo-Saxon race, and that, morally and intellectually, these Indians are inferior to their Anglo-Saxon invaders, and have receded before them."[34] Combe also commented upon looking at the skull of a Hindu that one could understand, with the aid of phrenology, why "one hundred millions of them are at this moment kept in subjection by forty or fifty thousand Englishmen."[35] The simple statement in an 1846 article in the *Phrenological Journal* was that "we conclude that among nations, as among individuals, force of character is determined by the average size of head; and that the larger-headed nations manifest their superior power, by subjecting and ruling their smaller-headed brethren — as the British in Asia, for example."[36]

From the 1840s on the phrenologists wrote for a popular audience, not for scientists, and they disseminated their racial classifications and assumptions widely. Their method of dividing the brain to analyze individual mental characteristics was now dismissed by respectable scientists, but many of their general assumptions regarding cranial size and shape as a means of comparing the innate mental capacities of different races remained unchallenged. After the phrenologists lost scientific respectability, many researchers with impeccable scientific reputations continued to use varieties of cranial comparison to categorize the various races by innate mental capacity.

By the 1840s it was common for writers on race to emphasize wide gulfs between different peoples, and many argued that these gulfs were unbridgeable. Such views were not hidden away in obscure publications, for the study of man and his racial divisions was becoming a passion. When in 1844 Robert Chambers published his *Vestiges of the Natural History of Creation* anonymously and propounded an evolutionary theory of man's advancing through stages to emerge finally as the superior Caucasian, his book was attacked as godless, but there were four editions in seven months. The *Edinburgh Review* commented that "he believes that the human family may be (or ought to be) of many species, and all sprung from apes." The book sold 24,000 copies by 1860.[37] Those who believed that the whole of prehistory had been explained and placed chronologically by the Bible were suffering severe shocks in the middle decades of the century. Although there was still reluctance on the part of most scientists to challenge the account of the origin of the human species given in Genesis, geologists had shattered traditional views of the age of the earth. The publication of Sir Charles Lyell's *Principles of Geology* in 1830 made it quite clear that the history of the earth had to be counted in millions, not thousands of years. This did not result in the immediate overturning of Genesis, anymore than had the earlier astronomical discoveries, but it certainly made it possible for early ethnologists to begin to cut their science loose from the account of the origin of mankind given in the Bible.[38]

By the middle years of the nineteenth century the science of man was being pursued vigorously across a variety of disciplines, and the whole trend was toward ever more elaborate physical classifications of the reasons for the basic differences between the various human races. Writers on race were rapidly abandoning the idea that mankind was one and that human capacity was everywhere the same. The polygenetic argument highlighted the enthusiasm with which some sought different ancestors for people they were condemning to permanent inferiority, but, whether or not they believed in polygenesis, writers on race were ready to assign physical rather than environmental causes for differences in human attainment. The biblical account of Creation had its staunch and influential scientific defenders throughout the first half of the nineteenth century, but by 1850 there were very few scientists prepared to defend the inherent equality of the different races of the world.

The importance of race, of "blood," was assumed in a manner quite unlike that of one hundred years before. In reviewing Michelet's *History of France* the *Edinburgh Review* commented in 1844 that "of the great influence of Race in the production of National Character, no reasonable inquirer can now doubt." There was a similarity in national character between the French and the Irish, the reviewer asserted, and this could be ascribed to "their Gaelic blood."[39] In less than fifty years the emphasis in studying human beings had shifted dramatically from the general to the particular, from what was universal to what was unique. Such attitudes permeated all aspects of scholarly and creative endeavor. Scientists in their study of man were not aloof from the nationalistic and parochial tendencies of the age. Rather they found the necessary empirical evidence to confirm views that had become increasingly common among intellectuals generally since the last decades of the eighteenth century.

4
Racial Anglo-Saxonism in England

> A Saxon race, protected by an insular position, has stamped its diligent and methodic character on the century. And when a superior race, with a superior idea to work and order, advances, its state will be progressive . . . All is race; there is no other truth.
>
> Benjamin Disraeli, *Tancred* (1847)

The myth of the Anglo-Saxons was transformed in the years from 1815 to 1850. Until the end of the eighteenth century the main use of the myth had been internal: in England to resist royal absolutism and to defend the broadening of political rights; in America to justify a revolution and the ending of a supposed royal domination. Anglo-Saxon institutions had been held up as a free, even democratic, model deserving modern emulation. But in the first decades of the nineteenth century Englishmen and Americans increasingly compared the Anglo-Saxon peoples to others and concluded that blood, not environment or accident, had led to their success. England and the United States had separated their institutions, but both countries were surging forward to positions of unprecedented power and prosperity. It was now argued that the explanation lay not in the institutions but in the innate characteristics of the race.

The world was falling under the sway of the English and their American brethren because nature herself had decreed it.

In England the image of the free Anglo-Saxons that had persisted since at least the sixteenth century continued, but it was also melded with ideas of Teutonic greatness and destiny developed by the comparative philologists and German nationalists and with the concept of inherent Caucasian superiority developed by those interested in the science of man. Some, of course, resisted the headlong rush toward a racial explanation of history, but many were swept away in an emotional tide of racial theory. Year by year the Anglo-Saxon doctrines that were being shaped were fed by the increasing power of Great Britain and the United States. This was an age in which the English language, English law, and English institutions seemed ready to dominate the entire world. The new racial ideas rapidly began to permeate English and American publications and found articulate and able spokesmen. A variety of threads were now woven into a new Anglo-Saxon racial tapestry.[1]

Thomas Carlyle was the first great British writer to view Saxon triumphs as being clearly a product of racial superiority. This lowland Scot had little sympathy for the Celts, stressed the Norse origins of Scotland's population, and described Robert Burns as "one of the most considerable Saxon men of the Eighteenth century"; he was "a piece of the right Saxon stuff." For Carlyle Scotland fell within the great Norse complex of peoples. "From the Humber upwards," he wrote, "the Speech of the common people is still in a singular degree Icelandic; its Germanism has still a peculiar Norse tinge."[2] Carlyle's inspiration was Germany, and among his mentors were Herder, Fichte, Goethe, Kant, Friedrich von Schlegel, and Novalis, but the passion of his arguments was peculiarly his own. He was imbued with a sense not only of the power of the individual hero, but also of the power of the individual race—the Teutonic. He saw in the vigor of that race a transforming power in the world. Individual men and individual races were created unequal.[3]

To Carlyle the Teutonic people were the whole amalgam of Germans, Norsemen, and Anglo-Saxons, including the English, who had colonized throughout the world. Race was more important to him than any religious division: "at bottom, Danish and Norse and Saxon have no distinction, except a superficial one, — as of Heathen and Christian, or the like." Odin was "the Type Norseman; the finest Teuton whom that race has yet produced." The old Norse sea kings were the "progenitors of our own Blakes and Nelsons!"[4] Teutonism had revivified a Europe dominated by Rome, and now "once more, as at the end of the Roman Empire, a most confused epoch and yet one of the greatest, the Teutonic countries find themselves too full . . . And yet, if this small rim of Europe is overpeopled, does not everywhere else a whole vacant Earth as it were, call to us, Come and till me, come and reap me!"[5] To Carlyle the earth was "empty" until settled, farmed, and governed by the Anglo-Saxons, as to many Americans the American Continent was "empty" until made productive by the expansion of the American people.

England and the Saxons, argued Carlyle, had been assigned two great tasks in world history: the industrial task of conquering "some half or more" of the planet "for the use of man" and the constitutional task of sharing the fruits of conquest "and showing all people how it might be done." The tribe of Saxons, "fashioned in the depths of Time, 'on the shores of Black Sea' or elsewhere, 'out of Hartzgebirge rock' " still had this great work of conquest to accomplish: "No property is eternal but God the Maker's: whom Heaven permits to take possession, his is the right; Heaven's sanction *is* such permission." Carlyle would not accept the idea of a post-Conquest racial split between Saxons and Normans: the "Normans were Saxons who learned to speak French." For Carlyle the supreme destiny belonged to the race and its individual great men, not simply to the nation. "Of a truth," he wrote, "whomsoever had, with the bodily eye, seen Hengst and Horsa mooring on the mud-beach of Thanet, on that spring morning of the year 449; and then, with the spiritual eye, looked forward to New York, Calcutta, Sidney Cove, across the ages and the oceans; and thought what Wellingtons, Washingtons, Shakspeares, Miltons, Watts, Arkwrights, William Pitts and Davie Crocketts had to issue from that business, and do their several taskworks so, — *he* would have said, those leatherboats of Hengst's had a kind of cargo in them!"[6]

To Emerson, Carlyle wrote that he believed the great "Wen" of London might for some centuries be the meeting place for "all the Saxons," but after centuries "if Boston, if New York, have become the most convenient *'All Saxondom,'* we will right cheerfully go thither to hold such festival, and leave the Wen."[7] The Saxons were a race destined for greatness and accomplishment; other races could be viewed as obstacles to progress. In his famous "Occasional Discourse on the Nigger Question" Carlyle wrote of the whole black population of the West Indies as "equalling almost in number of heads one of the Ridings of Yorkshire, and in *worth* (in quantity of intellect, faculty, docility, energy, and available human valour and value) perhaps one of the streets of Seven Dials." The West Indies now grew tropical fruits and spices; Carlyle hoped that they would one day grow "beautiful Heroic human Lives too, which is surely the ultimate object they were made for: beautiful souls and brave; sages, poets, what not; making the Earth nobler round them, as their kindred from of old have been doing; true 'splinters of the old Harz Rock'; heroic white men, worthy to be called old Saxons."[8] Carlyle's popularity, both in England and the United States, did much to disseminate the idea of a superior Anglo-Saxon race with a world mission to fulfill.

Those who saw race as the key to historical explanation, and as the basis of English and American nineteenth-century power, did not all agree on the details of their racial explanation. They selected those parts of the various hypotheses that were attractive to them, and they discarded the rest. Both Carlyle and Thomas Arnold in large part paid little heed to ethnological theories regarding the Caucasian race and placed their strongest emphasis on the Teutonic heritage. Thomas Arnold, who in his inaugural lecture at Oxford in 1841 lauded the Germanic roots of the English nation, expressed uncertainty about the question of the inherent superiority of some races over others, but he leaned in the direction of an imbalance of inherent qualities: "If there be, as perhaps there are, some physical and moral qualities enjoyed by some nations in a higher degree than by others, and this, so far as we can see, constitutionally, yet the superiority is not so great but that a little over presumption and carelessness on one side, or a little increased activity or more careful discipline on the other, and still more any remarkable individual genius in the generals or in the government, may easily restore the balance, or even turn it the other way."[9] Arnold would have agreed with Kipling that the Anglo-Saxons should not forget their human fallibility.

The dangers of arrogance troubled Arnold, but he had no doubts about the heritage, the power, and the destiny of the English race. He emphasized that while the English owed a great deal to Greece and Rome in ideas, they owed nothing to them in race: "Our English race is the German race; for though our Norman forefathers had learnt to speak a stranger's language, yet in blood, as we know, they were the Saxons' brethren: both alike belonged to the Teutonic or German stock." The key to medieval and modern history was the impact of the German races on the Roman Empire. Rome of the fourth century possessed Christianity and the intellectual and political legacies of Greece and Rome: "What was not there, was simply the German race, and the peculiar qualities which characterize it." The English race and language, he argued, were now overrunning the earth, and, together with the Germanic peoples, had dominated the world; "half of Europe, and all America and Australia, are German more or less completely, in race, in language, or in institutions, or in all."[10]

Arnold's views became best known in the 1840s, when they greatly influenced the next generation of Saxonists, including E. A. Freeman, but they were clearly emerging when he was young. In the late 1820s when he first saw the valley of the Rhine, he rhapsodized, "before us lay the land of our Saxon and Teutonic forefathers — the land uncorrupted by Roman or any other mixture; the birthplace of the most moral races of men the world has yet seen — of the soundest laws — the least violent passions, and the fairest domestic and civil virtues. I thought of that memorable defeat of Varus and his three legions, which for ever confined the Romans to the western side of the Rhine, and preserved the Teutonic nation — the regenerating element in modern Europe — safe and free."[11]

By the early 1840s in England the position of the Anglo-Saxons within a general racial framework was well established. When in 1845 Samuel Laing wrote a passionate defense of the Scandinavians as the supreme Teutons, the *Edinburgh Review* redressed the balance with a discussion of the whole Teutonic position. The reviewer pointed out that the researches of living antiquaries had finally shown that "the different tribes of Teutonic blood" — Germans, Anglo-Saxons, Scandinavians — were similar in the main elements of their national life. This unity began with language: some centuries before the Christian era "a single Teutonic language must have existed, from which, as from a common centre, all the existing dialects of that name have radiated and diverged." Also, throughout the Teutonic nations, "the same political and judicial system universally prevailed" — all of them embodied the principles "of popular freedom and popular influence." Finally, before the Christian era, all the Teutonic nations had the same system of religious worship. Present differences among the Teutonic nations could largely be accounted for by the different times at which Christianity had been introduced.[12] Rather than wanting to disparage the Scandinavians in opposition to Laing's views, the *Edinburgh Review* argued for a common cause: "We would wish indeed that all the tribes of Teutonic kindred, embracing, we believe, a hundred millions of mankind, should look on each other with a kindly partiality . . . glorying with a national pride in the common honours of their Teutonic ancestry. Of none of the children of the house, whether Goth or Frank, Saxon or Scandinavian, have the others any reason to be ashamed. All have earned the gratitude and admiration of the world."[13] In his impartial feeling for Teutons, this reviewer went further than most Englishmen of the 1840s toward granting others parity with the Anglo-Saxons.

When in 1847 a new edition of Percy's translation of Mallet's *Northern Antiquities* was issued, I. A. Blackwell in his introduction developed similar themes of Teutonic supremacy, while making passing reference to the divisions of the ethnologists. After commenting that "the Caucasian Variety is unquestionably the highest" in the human scale, Blackwell went on to discuss the Teutonic regeneration of mankind—a mankind which had stagnated under Roman imperial despotism: "But the hardy tribes of the Teutonic race then issued from the forests of Germania," Blackwell wrote, "and after the long period of desolation and slaughter, regenerated the Romanized nations of Europe, by infusing into them, along with their Teutonic blood, a portion of that spirit of personal independence which appears to be the peculiar characteristic of the Teutonic race." The Germans in the nineteenth century, Blackwell continued, had arrived at the highest point ever "of human intellectuality," while Britain, formed by a blending of Saxon and Scandinavian tribes, had reached an unparalleled peak of commercial prosperity and greatness. "The civilization that germinated on the plains of the Ganges some forty centuries ago, has been transmitted from race to race, until we now find it in the north-west of Europe, with the Germans in the possession of the more intellectual, and the English of the more practical, elements that constitute its essence."[14] The *Edinburgh Review* in 1851 placed the homeland a little differently, but reached essentially the same conclusion: "the Arian nations . . . carried the germs of civilisation from a common centre on one side into India, and, on the other side, into Asia Minor, Greece, Italy, and the rest of Europe."[15]

John M. Kemble was cautious in his racial judgments compared to many of his contemporaries, but his *Saxons in England*, published in 1849, placed English-German kinship on a firm scholarly base. His main focus was institutional, and he stressed land division and the mark, but he also emphasized the common blood of the Anglo-Saxons and the Teutons and the destiny of the Germanic tribes: "dimly through the twilight in which the sun of Rome was to set for ever, loomed the Colossus of the German race, gigantic, terrible, inexplicable."[16] The *Edinburgh Review*, in praising Kemble's work, pointed out that great advances in Anglo-Saxon studies and philology had thrown new light on the whole earlier period, and the reviewer drew conclusions that were based on more than Kemble: "the true mission of the Germanic peoples was to renovate and reorganize the western world. In the heart of the forest, amid the silences of unbroken plains, the Teuton recognised a law and fulfilled duties, of which the sanctity if not the memory, was nearly extinct among races who deemed and called him a *barbarian*. He felt and he reverenced the ties of family life, chastity in women, fealty in man to his neighbour and his chief, the obligation of oaths, and the impartial supremacy of the laws. And it is the portraiture of the Teuton doing his appointed work, in re-infusing life and vigour and the sanctions of a lofty morality into the effete and marrowless institutions of the Roman world, which is drawn in the volumes before us."[17]

While links with Aryan and Germanic tribesmen carrying the seeds of civilization and freedom gave a noble heritage to most Englishmen, this could not satisfy the young Disraeli. Carlyle and Arnold above all else wanted the Anglo-Saxons to be Teutons; the young Disraeli above all else wanted them to be Caucasians. He needed a link between the tribes of the German forests and the tribes of the eastern Mediterranean; he found it in the Caucasian race of the ethnologists. Disraeli's novels of the 1840s popularized the word *Caucasian* while exalting the Jews.[18] Most Englishmen were to reject what he had to say about Jewish supremacy, but many were to accept his contention that the influence of race on human action was "the key to history." "Progress and reaction," wrote Disraeli in 1852, "are but words to mystify the millions. They mean nothing, they are nothing, they are phrases and not facts. All is race. In the structure, the decay, and the development of the various families of man, the vicissitudes of history will find their main solution."[19] Although Disraeli was given to extravagant statements which he had no intention of living by, he was consistent in his espousal of the idea that race lay at the heart of human affairs.

Disraeli accepted Blumenbach's division of the human species into five varieties. The Caucasian, he believed, was "the superior class," and among the Caucasians the Jews "could claim a distinction which the Saxon and the Greek and the rest of the Caucasian nations, have forfeited. The Hebrew is an unmixed race." The Caucasians in general were granted an original "firstrate organisation," and the Jews had retained their original structure in an "unpolluted" form. The Jews had survived their centuries of persecution because "you cannot destroy a pure race of the Caucasian organisation."[20] The adulation of the Jews as the purest of the pure was the dominant racial theme in Disraeli's works, but throughout his novels he also paid homage to his country as well as his ancestors. Most of what the Romantics had to offer was of supreme appeal to Disraeli the novelist; he lauded passion over reason, the medieval over the modern, imagination over intellect, and race as an enduring, unconquerable thread.

When in *Tancred* (1847) Coningsby as a "Saxon" protests that he also comes from Caucasus, the Jew Sidonia's answer is that "your race is sufficiently pure. You come from the shores of the Northern Sea, land of the blue eye, and the golden hair, and the frank brow: 'tis a famous breed, with whom we Arabs have contended long; from whom we have suffered much: but these Goths, and Saxons, and Normans were doubtless great men."[21] Although *Tancred* was a long hymn in praise of the Jewish race, Disraeli also explained the greatness of England: "It is her inhabitants that have done this; it is an affair of race. A Saxon race, protected by an insular position, has stamped its diligent and methodic character on the century. And when a superior race, with a superior idea to work and order, advances, its state will be progressive . . . All is race; there is no other truth."[22]

Disraeli's commitment to theories of the supreme importance of race and Caucasian superiority reveal a dilemma for the Anglo-Saxonists. Although many were happy to accept scientific theories maintaining that a nation's power and prosperity stemmed from inherent physical and mental differences between races, they were less enthusiastic about accepting racial categories which lumped Anglo-Saxons together with Jews and other groups considered undesirable. In a similar manner even the philological theories regarding the original Indo-European people, theories which gave the Anglo-Saxons a long and distinguished history, also meant accepting a kinship with a variety of peoples, including Indians. Throughout the 1840s praise of the Teutons was a stronger theme in England than praise of the Caucasians, and by 1850 two well-known efforts were made to place the Anglo-Saxon-Teutonic strain into a more exclusive category: one, that of R. G. Latham, although controversial, was in the mainstream of scholarly research; the other, that of Robert Knox, although influential in England and America, was an impassioned racial diatribe.

Latham, a philologist, suggested a tripartite division of the human species: the Mongolidae of Asia, Polynesia, and America; the Atlantidae of Africa; and the Iapetidae of Europe. The original "Caucasians" (that is, the Circassians and Georgians) were placed not with the Europeans but with the Mongolidae. He objected to the classification, which had been used "in more than one celebrated work of fiction," that had lumped together under the Caucasian name "Jews, Greeks, Circassians, Scotchmen, ancient Romans, and other heterogeneous elements." Of the three divisions, the influence of the Atlantidae on the history of the world had been "inconsiderable," that of the Mongolidae "material rather than moral," but that of the Iapetidae "moral as well as material."[23] A logical extension of Latham's views came in the following year when he argued against the theory of an Asiatic origin of the Aryans and instead proposed a European homeland. This idea was taken up with more enthusiasm later in the century.[24]

A more sensational attack on the broad depiction of the Caucasians and a passionate espousal of racial doctrines came in Robert Knox's *Races of Men*, published in 1850. The anatomist who had been responsible for buying the hardly cold bodies provided by the murderers Burke and Hare in the Edinburgh of the 1820s could hardly be expected to be squeamish in racial matters, and Knox preached a frenetic racial doctrine. From 1846 on Knox spread his ideas in lectures throughout England.[25] He contemptuously dismissed earlier writers, even the greatest. Blumenbach and Prichard, according to Knox, had failed to understand basic racial divisions and antagonism, and Thomas Arnold had confused a variety of races under the name *Teutonic*. "Race is everything," wrote Knox, "literature, science, art — in a word, civilization depends on it."[26] In this he agreed with Disraeli, but he agreed with little else. The fivefold division of Blumenbach made no sense to Knox. There was no such thing as a Caucasian race; instead there were numerous unmixable races even within Europe itself. Since the earliest historic times man had been divided into distinct races, races which had remained unchanged and were unchangeable. Races could not successfully intermingle; when they interbred they gradually died out, overwhelmed by pure races. Strangely, along with this absolute racialism, came a revival of old environmentalism, in a new guise. Races could not live successfully in all climates — without the influx of new blood, Europeans could not survive in tropical countries.[27]

Knox's preference was to use *Scandinavian* where others had used *Germanic* or *Teutonic*. The Scandinavian was about to become the dominant race of the earth; a subgroup of that race, the Anglo-Saxon, "had for nearly a century been all-powerful on the ocean." The race had always enjoyed noble qualities, and the Romans had at no period conquered "the Saxon or true German, that is, Scandinavian race." This Scandinavian race provided the only democrats on earth, "the only race which truly comprehends the meaning of the word liberty." Free government was the special talent of the Anglo-Saxons: "their laws, manners, institutions, they brought with them from the woods of Germany, and they have tranferred them to the woods of America."[28]

Except for the overriding theme of the supreme importance of race, Knox had little coherence of thought, and there was hardly any logical progress in his arguments. In spite of the supposed talents of the Saxons for freedom, Knox argued that England still suffered from a Norman yoke in its government, and he failed to explain why the Normans failed to have his "Scandinavian" genius for government. He also had a harsh, at times realistic, view of the Anglo-Saxons. He painted them as a vigorous, acquisitive, aggressive race, natural democrats, but lacking men of artistic genius or abstract thought. They were a race "of all others the most outrageously boasting, arrogant, self-sufficient beyond endurance, holding in utter contempt all other races and all other men." What is more, although no race perhaps exceeded them in a sense of justice and fair play, this was shown *"only to Saxons."* They did not extend their love of justice to other races.[29]

For the non-Scandinavian-Saxon races of men Knox had little respect or hope. He thought the theories stressing a broad Caucasian category could not be right, because Jews and Gypsies were included in that grouping. Disraeli's ideas on the supremacy of the Jewish race he dismissed as idle romance, and the Celts also felt Knox's lash. The Celtic character was an amalgam of "furious fanaticism; a love of war and disorder; a hatred for order and patient industry; no accumulative habits; restless, treacherous, uncertain: look at Ireland." Although Ireland had suffered from *Norman* rule, "the source of all evil lies in *the race*, the Celtic race of Ireland." Wales and Scotland had the same racial fault, and the Celtic race should be forced from the soil, "by fair means, if possible; still they must leave. England's safety requires it. I speak not of the justice of the cause; nations must ever act as Machiavelli advised: look to yourself."[30]

The "dark races" of the earth, according to Knox, could never be taught true civilization: "Destined by the nature of their race to run, like all other animals, a certain limited course of existence, it matters little how their extinction is brought about." The inferiority of the dark races (and here Knox included a great variety of peoples, including the Chinese) stemmed from "specific characters in the quality of the brain itself." If they were to survive, it would be in the tropical regions, unsuitable for the Anglo-Saxons, where the blacks might hold out.[31] Although Robert Knox had a wild irrational streak and formed theories peculiarly his own, much of what he wrote, however illogically put together, represents a selection from various theories put forward in the previous half century or more. He was a peculiar example of what a confused, and perhaps dangerous, mind could make of what had often been put forward as precise scholarship into linguistic origins, history, race, and mythology. The overturning of Enlightenment thought had in the area of the study of man and race produced a sad deterioration in human understanding and hopes.

The dog-eat-dog philosophy of Knox was at one extreme of the Anglo-Saxonism that was flourishing in England by midcentury. At the other were the pious, vague platitudes filling the justly short-lived magazine *The Anglo-Saxon*, published in London in 1849 and 1850. Its tone was set by the emblem on the front cover—Pope Gregory I looking at a group of cherubic children, accompanied by the motto *Non Angli sed Angeli*. The magazine quoted Knox, yet also referred to his "erratic and frequently . . . unsteady pen."[32] Whereas Knox dealt with the cruel realities of power, the *Anglo-Saxon* stressed the Christian mission of the Anglo-Saxon race.

At the center of the magazine's philosophy was a familiar Saxonism—the race had an innate love of liberty, equal laws, and free institutions. Although the "arts and sciences of Greece and Rome" were grafted "on the native stock of Saxon genius," not foreign enlightenment but "the inborn spirit of the race produced the germs which have unfolded into a civilization more noble and grand than ever flourished in the capitals of Athens or of Rome." The Saxons were also firmly linked to their Teutonic ancestry. Anglo-Saxon readers (and it is difficult to imagine many others) were asked to "be proud that we belong to the great Teutonic stock," which "appears destined to people and rule the East as well as the West." These Teutons had peculiar abilities which were permanent, and which had existed from the beginning of the race. The Anglo-Saxon branch was now rapidly taking over the world.[33]

Although criticism was leveled at the Celts, the *Anglo-Saxon* was prepared to include them in its vague concept of family, for a mystical faith was placed in the English language. The spreading of the English language would somehow enable the Anglo-Saxons to absorb and transform those Celts who spoke English. As the Anglo-Saxons spread they would afford "shelter, and protection, and support to other families and less favoured races of mankind." A great stress was laid on "the *Destiny*, the *Mission*, of the Anglo-Saxons," and above all else this was a Christian mission: "The whole Earth may be called the *Fatherland* of the Anglo-Saxon. He is a native of every clime—a messenger of heaven to every corner of this Planet."[34] It was even maintained that when a community began to speak the English language it was "half Saxonised" even if there were no Anglo-Saxons there. The magazine emphasized that pride of race was not pride of nation or conquest, but in effect it was more confident than Knox that the Anglo-Saxon race would rule the world: "Feebly dwindling day by day / All other races are fading away." In practical terms the magazine praised Rajah Brooke's bloody expeditions into Sarawak, omitting the violent aspects of those endeavors, and depicting him as an agent of Saxon destiny.[35] By equating the success of the Anglo-Saxons with world progress, the theorists of Anglo-Saxonism could justify any means to accomplish the desired end.

By the time the young E. A. Freeman was taking his degree at Oxford in the 1840s, the ingredients for the new racial interpretation of Anglo-Saxon destiny were all present. By the end of the 1840s Freeman was already writing of "Teutonic greatness" and was able to compare those seeds planted in the "German forest or on . . . Scandinavian rock" with all the legacy of Greece and Rome and to decide clearly in favor of the former. This was the impact of the German search for racial roots, not the gentle, Romantic medievalism of Scott. "I cannot conceive," wrote Freeman in 1850, "that the external history of the days of Crecy and Agincourt, with all their tinsel frippery of chivalry, can ever be brought into real comparison with those of true and unmixed Teutonic greatness."[36] Freeman's main work, however, lay in the future, and it is Charles Kingsley who best represents the impact of the new ideas in England by the middle years of the century. Although one does not have to accept the suggestion of one biographer that Kingsley typifies the Victorian man as Queen Victoria typifies the Victorian woman,[37] Kingsley did reach a whole middle-class audience that shunned more esoteric explanations of England's past. In racial matters he absorbed and transmitted in simplistic form a whole host of themes that permeated the first half of the nineteenth century. That Kingsley was able to blend Anglo-Saxon racial theory into his defense of Christianity, home, family, womanhood, monarchy, and empire is an indication of the pervasiveness of the new Anglo-Saxonism.

From the late 1840s until his death in 1875, Kingsley expounded the virtues of the English branch of the Teutonic race and its role in world history. His religion had a curious pagan tinge: "I say that the Church of England is wonderfully and mysteriously fitted for the souls of a free Norse-Saxon race," he wrote to his wife in 1851, "for men whose ancestors fought by the side of Odin, over whom a descendant of Odin now rules."[38] Kingsley was particularly influenced by the concept of a strong Norse element in Teutonism and Anglo-Saxonism. When in 1849 he gave up lecturing at Queen's College, he described to his successor what his next lecture would have been. The essence of it was that in the late Anglo-Saxon period the system was rotting for lack of original thinking—the "Anglo-Saxon, (a female race) required impregnation by the great male race,—the Norse introduction of Northmen by Edward paving the way for the Conquest, &c." He asked his successor to give the students a lecture "on the rise of our Norse forefathers—give them something from the Voluspa and Edda."[39]

Yet for all his Norse emphasis, Kingsley gave what had become a common interpretation of the overrunning of the Roman Empire: the regeneration of the degenerate peoples of Europe by vigorous Teutons. According to Kingsley not only the future Europe but also the Church needed this infusion. Kingsley fully developed these ideas in his strange, impressionistic Cambridge lectures of 1860-61, but he had suggested them much earlier. In his preface to *Hypatia* in the early 1850s he had pointed out that "the *mens sana* must have a *corpus sanum* to inhabit." This was provided by the Teutonic or Gothic nations. Into a world drained by the influence of Rome came the "infusion of new and healthier blood." The Teutonic nations brought with them "comparative purity of morals; sacred respect for women, for family life, law, equal justice, individual freedom, and, above all, for honesty in word and deed."[40] Later, in his Cambridge lectures, Kingsley argued that God had fitted the Teutonic race to become the ruling race of the world, indeed "the welfare of the Teutonic race is the welfare of the world." Although those tribes that swept over the Roman Empire had no supreme general on earth, they may have had "a general in Heaven."[41]

For all his sense of Christian destiny, Kingsley could be as ruthless as Robert Knox in describing the fate of other races. He believed that degenerate races, including the North American

Indians, were better off dead. Like the *Anglo-Saxon* magazine, Kingsley admired Rajah Brooke (he dedicated *Westward Ho* to him), and he was Brooke's defender when many criticized his attacks on the Sarawak "pirates." "The truest benevolence," wrote Kingsley in 1849, "is occasional severity. It *is* expedient that one man die for the people. One tribe exterminated, if need be, to save a whole continent. 'Sacrifice of human life?' Prove that it is *human* life." Kingsley was confident that the Anglo-Saxons were spreading the virtues of the Teutonic race throughout the world and in doing so extending God's kingdom: "Because Christ's kingdom is a kingdom of peace; because the meek alone shall inherit the earth, therefore, you Malays and Dyaks of Sarawak, you are also enemies to peace . . . you are beasts, all the more dangerous, because you have a semi-human cunning."[42] The reign of world peace, order, and morality was to be established by the Anglo-Saxon Teutonic Christians and if necessary was to be founded on the bodies of inferior races.

By the middle years of the nineteenth century the simple praise of Anglo-Saxon institutions and freedom, which had assumed such importance in the sixteenth and seventeenth centuries, had undergone a profound change in England. Rather than emphasizing earlier freedom as a basis for internal reform, the new theorists were envisaging a world shaped to the desires of a supposedly innately superior Anglo-Saxon race. There was a firm and increasing belief that what was good for the Anglo-Saxons was good for the world. In Germany in the early nineteenth century ideas of historic Teutonic greatness were used most frequently to strengthen demands for nationhood. But the English were attracted to the idea of their race as a regenerating force for the whole world, for in Great Britain, throughout her colonies, and in the United States the Anglo-Saxons were apparently completing that march begun in the dawn of history by Aryan tribesmen. It was this aspect of the new Teutonism that also found most fertile ground on the other side of the Atlantic, in the United States. There, ideas and dreams indigenous to American history melded with a variety of themes from Europe to transform Revolutionary idealism for human progress into an ideology of continental, hemispheric, and even world racial destiny for a particular chosen people.

II

AMERICAN DESTINY

5

Providential Nation

> The sun never shone on a cause of greater worth. 'Tis not the affair of a city, a country, a province, or a kingdom; but of a continent — of at least one eighth part of the habitable globe.
>
> Thomas Paine, *Common Sense* (1776)

The American colonists of the seventeenth and eighteenth centuries inherited in full measure the myth of a free Anglo-Saxon past. The Revolutionary generation even gave this myth a new vigor by freely using it to justify their exceptional actions in breaking away from Great Britain and reshaping their government. Americans were throwing off their allegiance to what they perceived to be a corrupt, unjust system, not disavowing their ancestry, and it was possible to admire the English while hating the British government. Many Americans continued to distrust and fear Great Britain throughout the nineteenth century, and some hated the English, but many of America's leaders believed that, with the exception of the United States, England was the happiest and most democratic country under the sun. The belief that the Americans were the most distinguished descendants of the Anglo-Saxons grew rather than diminished in the decades after the Revolution.

As colonial Englishmen the leaders of the Revolutionary generation looked back to a distant past of free government, but as Americans they looked forward to a world reshaped by a successful American republic. Like American Anglo-Saxonism, the sense of unique national destiny and purpose that pervaded the Revolutionary generation had its roots deep in colonial America and in Europe. The most direct and strongest influences on America's leaders came from the Enlightenment, but since the seventeenth century Americans had often thought of themselves as a special people with a providential role in world history. America's sense of mission, even when conceived in religious terms, had always embodied a strong outward thrust. In the seventeenth century American beliefs had been intimately entwined with the Protestant Reformation in England and with militant Puritanism.[1] The English theorists and publicists who defended the creation of the Puritan Commonwealth thought of their country as an expanding republic with a mission to fulfill. James Harrington wrote in his *Oceana* of Puritan England as a "Commonwealth for increase" and said such a commonwealth was not for itself alone, but was "given as a Magistrate of God unto mankinde for the vindication of common Right, and the law of Nature."[2] John Milton, somewhat disillusioned by the course of events in the mid-seventeenth century, asked "Where is this goodly tower of a commonwealth, which the English boasted they would build to overshadow kings, and be another Rome in the west? "[3]

After the Restoration the idea of the English nation as the crusading agent of God's will faded, and republican ideas became a less important thread in English thought, but the Americans never lost the belief that they were a special, chosen people, a people destined to change the world for the better. From the beginning New Englanders thought of their settlements as an example to other nations and believed they had an obligation to take the word to other peoples.[4] Peter Bulkeley stated the former idea succinctly in the middle of the seventeenth century when he told the Puritans that "the Lord looks for more from thee, then [sic] from other people . . . Thou shouldst be a special people, an onely people, none like thee in all the earth."[5] As American settlements advanced outward, the Puritans not only saw God's kingdom moving to the West, but also thought of America as the place from which the renovation of the world would begin. In the 1740s Jonathan Edwards saw the regeneration of the Old World as a major mission of America.[6]

While Puritan ideas contributed to a belief that in some special way the people on the American continent would influence the world, more fundamental myths of human progress gave a particular significance to the advance of pioneers across the American continent. In moving west American pioneers were perceived, both in Europe and America, as continuing a movement of civilization that had been continuous since the earliest times. Throughout European history the West was thought of as the region in which lay the land of eternal youth and happiness and as an arena for the destiny of nations.[7] These ideas were already ancient when Bishop Berkeley wrote his oft-quoted line that "westward the course of empire takes its way" and suggested that "time's noblest offspring is the last."[8] The whole idea of America as the "noblest offspring" had been strengthened in England and the American colonies by the obvious prosperity and progress of the transatlantic settlements. Civilization appeared to be passing from Asia Minor to Greece, to Rome, to England, and across the Atlantic to the New World.

In less favorable circumstances the Americans could have become one of those many groups of people who have believed themselves favored by Providence, but who eventually have been chastened by disappointment. What was unique in the American experience was overwhelming success on the bountiful North American continent and the remarkable events that dominated its history from the seventeenth to the mid-nineteenth centuries. The American continent was the most desirable, accessible, and usable of all those areas settled and exploited by Europeans from the fifteenth to the nineteenth centuries. The sheer richness of America was a constant amazement to the Europeans: the endless land, the dense forest, the abundant game, the great savannahs. Within a hundred years of English settlement, America was a populous land of rich farms, bustling cities, and crowded ports; on all sides were the overt signs of progress.

While Europeans had to measure progress within an already complex civilization, and could perceive decline as well as advance, Americans had only to leave the coast to measure a tangible progress. Jefferson expressed it best in 1825, near the end of his life. A traveler coming eastward from the Rockies, he wrote, would see the equivalent of a survey in time "of the progress of man from the infancy of creation to the present day." Living in the first range of mountains in the interior of the country, Jefferson said, "I have observed this march of civilization advancing from the seacoast, passing over us like a cloud of light, increasing our knowledge and improving our condition, insomuch as that we are at this time more advanced in civilization here than the seaports were when I was a boy. And where this progress will stop no one can say. Barbarism has, in the meantime, been receding before the steady step of amelioration, and will in time, I trust, disappear from the earth."[9]

The Enlightenment idea of progress gave a whole new impetus to the image of America as an arena for the betterment of mankind, and in America itself the idea of progress was never totally divorced from the belief in actual expansion and geographic destiny. Although this involved the literal transformation of the land, it also involved the idea of the West as a place of future greatness and perfection. In this last sense the idea of the West existed long before it was given a racial meaning by the image of superior Aryan tribesmen carrying civilization westward along the path of the sun. In taming the North American continent Americans could create a new society and new institutions, throwing off the corruptions and despotisms of Europe while beginning the establishment of a better world order. Englishman Andrew Burnaby, who visited America at the end of the 1750s, later commented that "an idea, strange as it is visionary, has entered into the minds of the generality of mankind, that empire is travelling westward; and every one is looking forward with eager and impatient expectation to that destined moment when America is to give law to the rest of the world."[10]

The successful American Revolution provided for the American people a powerful, overt sign that Providence had indeed marked them for great deeds. In a direct way the new republic experiment was equated with universal freedom and progress. On the North American continent mankind was at last working out its destiny with institutions that made possible the protection of man's natural rights and allowed him full self-realization. As American prosperity increased so did American confidence that Providence was working through the American people and American nation to achieve a new life for mankind. The reshaping of the world was to be achieved both by example and by American physical expansion. Americans spreading across the North American continent would be a visible sign of the success of free republican institutions, a success which would inspire other peoples to throw off their shackles and establish similar institutions based on the natural rights of man. Although there was pride both in special American accomplishments and in a distinguished historical heritage, this pride was tempered by a belief that other peoples, if given the opportunity, could build free institutions. At the core of the sense of the continental and world mission in the early years of the republic was a profound optimism. There was confidence in the special abilities of the American people, but there was also hope that most other peoples would be liberated and transformed rather than dominated or destroyed.

In the decades spanning the American Revolution the belief that expansion was an integral part of American destiny permeated American thinking. Some feared its effect on American republicanism, but few doubted that American pioneers would continue to press westward: Franklin envisioned American pioneers spreading across the Mississippi Valley and outnumbering the people of England; the young poet Philip Freneau spoke of the time when this new population would "spread Dominion to the north and south and west / Far from th'Atlantic to Pacific shores"; Hugh H. Brackenridge wrote, with Shakespearean echoes, of America as "the seat of empire, the abode of kings"; and Thomas Paine in his *Common Sense* had no doubts that the coming war for independence involved far more than thirteen colonies along the eastern seaboard. "The sun never shone on a cause of greater worth," he said, "'Tis not the affair of a city, a county, a province, or a kingdom; but of a continent — of at least one eighth part of the habitable globe."[11] The continent, however, was only the beginning. Timothy Dwight conjured up a future in which America would give law to the world:

> Hail Land of light and joy! Thy power shall grow
> Far as the seas, which round thy regions flow;
> Through earth's wide realms thy glory shall extend,
> And savage nations at thy scepter bend.
> Around the frozen shores thy sons shall sail
> Or stretch their canvas to the ASIAN gale.[12]

Even the problems of the 1780s did not quench the bubbling confidence in a future continental destiny. In 1785 John Adams declared that the United States was "destined beyond a doubt to be the greatest power on earth." In the next year Thomas Jefferson wrote that "our Confederacy must be viewed as the nest from which all America, North and South, is to be peopled."[13] At the end of the tumultuous, dangerous decade American geographer Jedidiah Morse wrote that "it is well known that empire has been travelling from east to west. Probably her last and broadest seat will be America . . . the largest empire that ever existed . . . we cannot but anticipate the period, as not far distant, when the AMERICAN EMPIRE will comprehend millions of souls, west of the Mississippi."[14] This idea of the westward movement of empire was firmly fixed in American thinking in the post-Revolutionary years. "There is nothing, in my little reading," wrote John Adams in 1807, "more ancient in my memory than the observation that arts, sciences, and empire had travelled westward; and in conversation it was always added since I was a child, that their next leap would be over the Atlantic into America."[15]

Continental expansion was thought inevitable because it was decreed by Providence. In the debates preceding the War of 1812 John A. Harper of New Hampshire told Congress that "it appears that the Author of Nature has marked our limits in the south, by the Gulf of Mexico; and on the north, by the regions of eternal frost."[16] Richard M. Johnson of Kentucky pointed out that the "waters of the St. Lawrence and the Mississippi interlock in a number of places, and the great Disposer of Human Events intended those two rivers should belong to the same people."[17] America's natural frontiers were conceived of in the broadest terms.

While American leaders believed that the American people would span the continent and carry American institutions with them, there were different theories about the political structure that would result from this expansion. Jefferson suggested that though there would be a compatibility of peoples and political systems in the Americas, size would necessitate sister republics rather than one huge nation. He told John Jacob Astor that he viewed Astoria at the mouth of the Columbia "as the germ of a great, free and independent empire on that side of our continent, and that liberty and self-government spreading from that as well as this side, will insure their complete establishment over the whole."[18] As late as the 1820s both James Monroe and Thomas Hart Benton thought that the region west of the Rockies would be independent, and Henry Clay saw no reason for hurrying American settlements in that region.[19]

Continental unity was suggested as a possibility, however, even in the earliest days of the republic. A judge in the isolated, danger-ridden state of Franklin wrote in 1786: "Is not the continent of America one day to become one consolidated government of United States?"[20] John Quincy Adams was willing as early as 1811 not only to support expansion to the Pacific Coast, but also to urge political unity across the whole breadth of America. "The whole continent of North America," he wrote to his father, "appears to be *destined by Divine Providence* to be peopled by one *nation*, speaking one language, professing one general system of religious and political principles, and accustomed to one general tenor of social usages and customs. For the common happiness of them all, for their peace and prosperity, I believe it is indispensable that they should be associated in one federal Union."[21]

The capacity of other peoples to benefit from the American example and American help was asserted frequently in the years before 1830. When Henry Clay in 1818 urged support for South

American revolutionaries he said the United States should "desire the redemption of the minds and bodies of unborn millions, from the brutifying effects of a system whose tendency is to stifle the faculties of the soul, and to degrade them to the level of beasts. I would invoke the spirits of our departed fathers. Was it for yourselves only that you nobly fought?" The idea of sacrifice for others was to become rare by the late 1840s. Similarly in 1819, when Clay attacked the actions of Andrew Jackson in Florida, he urged Congress not to allow liberty to fail in the United States: "We are fighting a great moral battle, for the benefit not only of our country, but of all mankind. The eyes of the whole world are in fixed attention upon us."[22]

James Barbour of Virginia, a Jeffersonian to his core, expressed joy in 1818 that the African slave trade was apparently coming to an end. Africa, freed from all the disastrous effects of the trade, "may, under the benign influence of peace, reason and religion, indulge a hope, that in the fulness of time she may participate in the blessings of civilization, with all its beneficent effects."[23] Expansion could be conceived not as the survival of the fittest but as a boon for all mankind. Edward Everett in 1824 characterized the westward advance in America as "the human family, led out by Providence to possess its broad patrimony."[24] Major General Edmund Pendleton Gaines told Governor George M. Troup of Georgia in 1825 that he approached the state authorities "as brethren of one great political family, whose fair fame has attracted the admiration of every civilized country, and whose example has led to the establishment of liberty in South America, and promises to aid in its final extension and permanent establishment throughout every portion of the world."[25] For David Trimble of Kentucky in 1827 the American continent was "the chosen land of liberty — vineyard of the God of peace; and we, its husbandmen, selected by the unseen will of Providence to till the soil, and feed the famished nations with the food of independence." The Americans consistently believed that they were a chosen people, but at its best this concept involved being chosen for special duties, not simply for special privileges.[26]

Even at the end of the 1820s, when a shift in emphasis was

gaining momentum, the drive for Oregon was interpreted as the planting of the seeds of improvement and progress for all mankind. Joseph Richardson of Massachusetts supported American occupation of the area. He argued that it was part of the duty owed by the government toward their successors, the children of the old states, "destined by Providence to carry westward, to the utmost bounds, the blessings of civilization and liberty." Richardson saw no weakening of the Union through expansion: it was a moral duty, for expansion involved salvation and freedom for millions of human beings. "The principles of self-government are capable of universality," argued Richardson. "They are in concert with the laws of the moral universe, and are applicable to communities on the broadest scale." For millions of Europeans, he said, America offered the only hope of recovering the freedom and happiness designed for man by God and nature. American occupation of Oregon would mean "an extension of the blessings of civilization, of freedom, and happiness, to the human race."[27]

That strange New Englander, Hall J. Kelley, who devoted his life to the promotion of the Oregon settlement, never abandoned his objectives of supporting democracy and Christianity on the shores of the Pacific. Until the end of his life he believed he had helped to accomplish what he had asked for in his 1830 pamphlet on Oregon. "The most enlightened nation on earth," he wrote, "will not be insensible to the best means of national prosperity. Convinced of the utility and happy consequences of establishing the Oregon colony, the American Republic will found, protect and cherish it, and thus enlarge the sphere of human felicity, and extend the peculiar blessings of civil polity, and of the Christian religion, to distant and destitute nations."[28] Although Kelley also frequently listed the many commercial advantages that would flow from his proposed colony, a strong sense of Christian mission permeated his arguments. He combined commercial advantage with human improvement, not commercial advantage with racial destiny.

The most fervent advocate of America's role in the westward thrust of civilization was Thomas Hart Benton. Benton, who was to have a distinguished though idiosyncratic career as a senator and Democratic party leader, clearly revealed in his writings and speeches the changing perceptions of the meaning of American expansion and the manner in which racial exclusiveness ultimately replaced hopes for the whole of humanity. In 1818-1819 Benton wrote a series of articles for a St. Louis newspaper; the articles were subsequently published as a pamphlet. Benton's main theme was the glorious prospects for Asiatic trade which would be opened up by the possession of the mouth of the Columbia River and the way in which this trade would cause St. Louis to blossom as one of the great cities of the world. His whole argument was based on a mind-boggling underestimation of the difficulties of carrying on a trade from the mouth of the Columbia, across the Rockies, and down the Missouri to St. Louis. Even the Pacific itself was viewed by Benton as "comparatively narrow, and almost free from the perils of the sea."[29] Although Benton argued that the development of this route would engross for the United States the trade of India and most of Asia, he was able in his youth to conceive of the implications of this plan in universal terms.

The movement of civilization toward the West was characterized by Benton as "the disposition which 'the children of Adam' have always shown 'to follow the sun.' " This disposition, he argued, had never before been stronger, for Europeans were now pouring into America, and Americans were streaming into the interior of the continent: "All obey the same impulse — *that of going to the West*; which, from the beginning of time has been the course of heavenly bodies, of the human race, and of science, civilization, and national power following in their train." Benton continued with an image which, with significant modifications, was to capture the imagination of Americans in the 1840s and 1850s: "In a few years the Rocky Mountains will be passed, and 'the children of Adam' will have completed the circumambulation of the globe, by marching to the west until they arrive at the Pacific ocean, in sight of the eastern shore of that Asia in which their first parents were originally planted."[30] More than a quarter of a century later, Senator Benton celebrated the accomplishment of his dream, but on that day in the Senate he lauded "the arrival of the van of the Caucasian race" at the Pacific as one of the greatest events in the history of the world, and in his speech he carefully graded the five races of mankind.[31] For Benton, as for so many others, "the children of Adam" were to become "the van of the Caucasian race" between 1819 and 1846.

Although Benton in these early years was expansionist, he always held out hope to general humanity. A war with Spain, he said, "would be the most happy event for ourselves and for the human race that could now take place." The Floridas and Cuba would be obtained for the United States, the New World would be freed from the Old, and a corridor of republics would be created across North and South America. Even his dream of an American road to India, although chiefly cast in the most grandiose commercial terms, envisioned the spreading of republican ideas. He foresaw happy effects on the people of India, because close association with the people of the United States would ameliorate their condition "by making them familiar with the doctrines of Christianity, and the liberal principles of free and popular governments."[32]

Republicanism was at the crux of Benton's arguments as a young man. He believed a great future for the United States lay in encouraging the creation of an independent republic west of the Rockies: "a new republic, composed of her children, speaking her language, inheriting her principles, devoted to liberty and equality, and ready to stand by her side against the combined Powers of the old world." Benton thought in Revolutionary terms of new free republics contending with the monarchies and tyrannies of Europe. A republic on the Pacific shore of North America would have "great and wonderful benefits" for the people of eastern Asia. "Science, liberal principles in government, and the true religion, might cast their lights across the intervening sea. The valley of the Columbia might become the granary of China and Japan, and an outlet to their imprisoned and exuberant population. The inhabitants of the oldest and the newest, the most despotic and the freest Governments, would become the neighbors, and, peradventure, the friends of each other." Benton went on to envision the United States' seeking connections with Asiatic powers against their common enemies of freedom in Europe.[33] Benton, of course, was frequently carried away by his own bombast (John Quincy Adams called him "a liar of magnitude beyond the reach of Ferdinand Mendez Pinto"),[34] but the Benton of the 1820s did not yet see the Americans as simply the vanguard of Caucasian supremacy. He was vitally interested in trade and in prosperity, but beyond that he was more interested in republics than in race. As a senator, Benton never abandoned his dream of either a vast, rich trade across the Pacific or of America's bringing hope to the peoples of Asia, but never again after the 1820s was he able to conceive of cooperation with non-white peoples in the same sanguine terms.

Representative John Floyd of Virginia, who devoted so much of the 1820s to his unsuccessful campaign for United States occupation of the mouth of the Columbia River, and who was, like Benton, dazzled by the commercial prospects of such an endeavor, suggested in 1821 that Chinese immigrants might be attracted to the area: "they [the Chinese] would willingly, nay, gladly, embrace the opportunity of a home in America, where they have no prejudice, no fears, no restraint in opinion, labor, or religion."[35] Such dreams were to be possible for only a few more years.

For all the optimism regarding the regeneration of other peoples, most enthusiasm was reserved for the idea of populating the North American continent with a homogenous American people. This would bring into being a vast nation, or sister republics, peopled by white Americans with one language, one culture, and identical political institutions. And even at a time when elaborate Indian policies were being shaped with the avowed intention of preserving the Indians, there was a disturbing tendency to think of the North American continent as completely empty. Jefferson even managed to think of the South American continent without its people when, in the 1780s, he wrote of the republic as being the nest from which both North and South America would be peopled. He repeated his thought in 1801 when he opposed the colonization of blacks in the West. He looked forward to distant times "when our rapid multiplication will expand itself . . . and cover the whole northern, if not the southern continent, with a people speaking the same language, governed in similar forms, and by similar laws; nor can we contemplate with satisfaction either blot or mixture on that surface."[36] Jefferson, like so many in the next generation, skipped lightly over the question of what would happen to the numerous peoples in North and South America if there was to be no "blot or mixture" in that vast area.

The emphasis on the special abilities of the people who were destined to settle the North American continent was also strong, even in these early years. Henry Clay, who urged the United States to help the inhabitants of South America share in the benefits of republican freedom, still had no doubt that the available areas of North America should be peopled by Americans from the United States. Providence had decreed, he said in 1820, that the whole of this continent, including Texas, was to be settled (to Clay, as to most other Americans, Indian occupancy was not settlement). The only question that remained was "by whose race shall it be peopled?" Far better that it be settled by American freemen than by those under despotism, for then, even if areas broke away, they would end "with a race partaking of all our qualities."[37] James Monroe also believed that the citizens of the United States had more wisdom and energy than the inhabitants of other parts of the Americas, although he was less interested in the Americans as descendants of Englishmen than as citizens of a republic.[38]

Those Americans who were to settle throughout the American continents were usually thought of by their fellow countrymen as essentially English in ancestry. Crèvecoeur's view of the American as a new man proved appealing to some nationalists and to Irish-American politicians who hated the English, but for the most part American leaders thought of themselves as the most gifted children of Anglo-Saxon forbears. They believed not simply in the careless usage which would refer to anyone from Great Britain as "English," but rather in the stricter sense of feeling distinct from the Scots, Irish, and Welsh. Jefferson thought of the Anglo-Saxons as his ancestors, although family tradition placed his roots close to Mount Snowden in Wales,[39] and, in spite of a large immigration of Scots-Irish and Germans in the eighteenth century, most Americans did not think of themselves as an amalgam. Still less, of course, did they include the Afro-Americans in any calculation of themselves as a distinct people. The language and dominant customs of America were English, and non-English groups were expected to conform to English culture.

When Jedidiah Morse in 1789 discussed the American people in his geography, he pointed out that "the greater part . . . are descended from the English; and, for the sake of distinction, are called Anglo-Americans." He went on to say that intermingled with the Anglo-Americans were the Dutch, Scotch, Irish, French, Germans, Swedes, and Jews, but clearly he did not believe that this intermingling changed the basic character of the Anglo-American population.[40] The blacks and Indians were, of course, simply excluded from his considerations when describing the American people.

For the most part, before 1815, the term Anglo-Saxon was not used to characterize the American population in any racial sense. The term was well known and often appeared, but it was used to describe those inhabitants of England before 1066 from whom the Americans claimed descent and whose institutions many Americans thought they were emulating. One problem with using Anglo-Saxon to link Americans and Englishmen before 1815 was the reluctance to praise the English in a contemporary sense in the direct aftermath of the Revolution and in a time of badly strained relations and ultimately a second war. The feeling of "racial" unity with the English was already present, however, if muted, and when John Randolph, in December 1811, attacked the policies which were leading to war against England, he spoke of antipathies against those "whose blood runs in our veins; in common with whom we claim Shakespeare, and Newton, and Chatham, for our countrymen; whose form of government is the freest on earth, our own only excepted; from whom every valuable principle of our own institutions has been borrowed—representation, jury trial, voting the supplies, writs of habeas corpus—our whole civil and criminal jurisprudence—against our fellow Protestants identified in blood, in language, in religion with ourselves." In early 1815 he made the link even clearer when he wrote that Napoleon could pride himself on success in "that the seeds of eternal discord are sown between the two great families of the Anglo-Saxon race."[41] To think of belonging to one of the "two great families of the Anglo-Saxon race" was a commonplace among American politicians by 1850; it was, however, still rare in 1815.

It was later asserted that Randolph had been a key figure in popularizing Anglo-Saxon as a term of current usage, and throughout his life he thought of the Anglo-Saxons as a distinct people with a long and distinguished history, flourishing in the early nineteenth century on both sides of the Atlantic. When some representatives in Congress in 1824 flirted with the idea of aid for Greek revolutionaries, Randolph told them that "along with some most excellent attributes and qualities—the love of liberty, jury trial, the writ of habeas corpus, and all the blessings of free government, that we have derived from our Anglo-Saxon ancestors, we have got not a little of their John Bull, or rather John Bull Dog spirit—their readiness to fight for anybody, and on any occasion."[42]

With the easing of British-American difficulties after 1815, there was a renewed interest in attributes shared by English and American Anglo-Saxons, but it was still common to combine pride in an English heritage with hope for the improvement of the entire human race. New Englander Edward Everett was extremely proud of his English heritage, but he avoided asserting the innate inferiority of other peoples. His eloquent defense of the English and their accomplishments was later to be used very differently by those who had lost his faith in general human improvability. Speaking at Plymouth in December 1824, he recounted the history of a unified human race, but he also emphasized that "our forefathers . . . sprang from the country and the stock, the best adapted to furnish the habits and principles essential to the great undertaking" in America, and said that "I may presume that there is not one who hears me, that does not regard it as a matter of congratulation and joy, that our fathers were Englishmen." England, to Everett, was the only European country where constitutional liberty had enjoyed a stable existence. At Worcester on July 4, 1833, he spoke of the ties that bound America to "the land of our fathers." England was a nation "of common blood," and there the doctrine of American independence was learned. It germinated in "the hereditary love of liberty of the Anglo-Saxon race." At Lexington in 1835 he said that those Americans who had fallen there "stood on the solid rock of the old liberties of England."[43]

Everett, though no more a militant expansionist than a believer in strict racial categories, also believed fully in America's continental mission and in its leadership role for the world. As early as 1824 he spoke of the importance of extending "one government, one language, and, substantially, one character, over so vast a space as the United States." If the American Union survived, the continent would eventually "be filled up with the mightiest kindred people known in history."[44] A believer in one human race under God, Everett represented in the 1820s and 1830s what was best in the American sense of mission. His pride in his own people, descended from the English, at times touched on the racial and could be used in that way, but he did not condemn others to extinction or permanent inferiority, and his idea of progress embraced the people of the entire world.

James Barbour of Virginia similarly believed in America's destiny and in the special qualities of its system and its people, but perhaps even more than Everett he also believed in the capabilities of others to share in his dream of progress. Unlike Everett he feared the effect of unlimited expansion, even if peaceful, on America's republican institutions. Barbour in 1825 regretted what he thought was inevitable expansion to Oregon. Fifty years earlier, he said, the valley of the Mississippi had been like Oregon; now it was teeming "with a mighty population — a free and happy people. Their march onward, therefore, to the country of the setting sun, is irresistible." Even if the American people in the Far West eventually became independent, the United States could console itself "that all the parts of the great whole will have been peopled by our kindred, carrying with them the same language, habits, and unextinguishable devotion to liberty and republican institutions."[45]

Everett and Barbour are transitional figures. They praised the American people as being particularly gifted in the arts of government, and Everett was happy to embrace English and Americans in one great Anglo-Saxon family; yet in their view of the rest of the world, they owed more to the thought of the eighteenth than of the nineteenth century. They still believed that republicanism, good government, and education would transform other peoples, and both men emphasized America's duties more than America's wants.

Yet while some Americans in the years after the Revolution talked and wrote easily of how they would share with other peoples the freedoms that had been so happily bestowed on them, this dream was already being challenged not only by pride in a peculiarly English heritage, but also by the reality of black slavery and warfare with the Indians. Proponents of expansion in the early years after the American Revolution found it far simpler to think of improving other peoples in abstract rather than in practical terms. They wrote and spoke most confidently of Americans' advancing into supposedly empty areas and transforming them into bastions of American republicanism. When presented with an opportunity to spread republican ideas, they tended to react as Senator Thomas B. Reed of Mississippi had done in opposing participation in the Panama Congress, if that body "is to have the power of giving Hayti equal rank with communities of men composed of the descendants of the Saxons, the Franks, and ancient Germans."[46] Abstract dreams of universal improvement and cooperation were threatened by practical problems inherent in relations between white Europeans and other peoples and by what at times appeared to be an unbridgeable gap between the two. The whole of European and transatlantic thought was affected by this, but in America the dramatic proximity of different peoples gave immediacy to what was a general problem of European culture in the first half of the nineteenth century.

6

The Other Americans

> I consider men who are unacquainted with the savages, like
> young women who have read romances, and have as
> improper an idea of the Indian character in the one case,
> as the female mind has of real life in the other.
> The philosopher, weary of the vices of refined life,
> thinks to find perfect virtue in the simplicity
> of the unimproved state.
>
> Hugh Henry Brackenridge, *National Gazette*, February 6, 1792

In the late eighteenth and the early nineteenth centuries there was in America a struggle between a theoretical view of mankind and race provided by Enlightenment thought and a practical view stimulated by overt contacts between white Americans and blacks or Indians on the North American continent. Linnaeus and Blumenbach were as much a part of American thought as they were of European. Jefferson and his circle inherited the Enlightenment view that all mankind was of one species, and that mankind in general was capable of indefinite improvement. Before 1815 the prevailing intellectual view in America as well as in Europe was that environment, not innate racial differences, accounted for the marked gaps in achievement between different peoples and different nations. This was the point of view inherited by the Revolutionary generation, and it was the view supported by American intellectuals in the early years of the nineteenth century.[1]

The first major American work on racial differences was Samuel Stanhope Smith's *An Essay on the Causes of the Variety of Complexion and Figure in the Human Species.* This was first published in 1787 and issued in enlarged form in 1810. Smith defended the unity of the human species and argued strongly that racial differences, including color, could be accounted for by environment. Smith was by far the most influential writer on race in the American scientific community, and he took issue with those few writers who in the last decades of the eighteenth century had defended polygenesis as an explanation of variety among different peoples; he was particularly intent on refuting the arguments of Lord Kames and Charles White. Smith's views dominated the scholarly discussion on race in this post-Revolutionary generation.[2] Even John Drayton, governor of South Carolina, wrote in his 1802 *A View of South-Carolina* that he agreed with Smith "that all mankind have originally descended from one pair; and that a difference of complexion is only produced by change of situation, and a combination of other circumstances."[3] Hugh Williamson, in his *Observations*, in 1811 defended essentially the same point of view and argued that "the earth has been peopled by a single race of men." Men became black in a hot climate because that was the color best fitted to a high temperature: "All the changes that have been made in the human species; all the differences in colour, shape, and feature . . . may doubtless be produced by climate, food, and education or habits."[4]

Through the early years of the nineteenth century both religion and science confirmed Americans in the view that mankind consisted of one human species, that the obvious physical differences were the result of environment, and that the vast differences in the human condition and accomplishments stemmed from the same cause. This view was to change radically by 1850. That it did was partially the result of a general change in western European and transatlantic thought, but the change also came about because of the peculiarities of the American experience. New racial ideas which influenced the whole of Western society in the first half of the nineteenth century fell on especially fertile ground in the United States. Ideas flowed both ways across the Atlantic in the formative years of the new ethnology. The American experience and American conclusions drawn from this experience helped to shape western European attitudes. Racial differences were dramatized in the United States, for white, black, and red were thrust together from the earliest settlements. While blacks, of course, were central to the general development of American thought on race, Indians were of particular importance in the development of American racial thought in the context of an expanding and aggressive nation. In dealing with the Indians the United States began to formulate a rationale of expansion which was readily adaptable to the needs of an advance over other peoples and to a world role.

Although eighteenth-century intellectual opinion in both Europe and the United States maintained a belief in one human species and in the capacity for improvement of all varieties of that species, there is ample evidence to show that the relegation of American blacks to a fixed and lower racial category was no simple product of the new scientific ethnology. Long before scientists and others developed an intellectual rationale to justify the permanent inferiority of nonwhites, the process of debasing blacks had been carried out in the daily life of America, and, whatever the theory, blacks in practice were not regarded merely as men and women of a different complexion. Winthrop Jordan has shown that Englishmen from the very beginning of their contact with blacks conceived of them in some measure as a distinct people with particularly strong ties to the animal kingdom. To Englishmen blacks were heathen, savage, and "beastly." Blacks were not simply regarded as debased because they were slaves: they were also enslaved because of what was regarded as their different and debased nature. There is considerable evidence that by the end of the colonial era the Enlightenment view of innate human equality was being challenged on a practical level in the American colonies. Whites, by the very laws they passed and the attitudes they assumed, placed blacks on a different human level.[5]

The development of practical racial attitudes in regard to blacks was temporarily obscured in America in the late eighteenth century, both by the prevailing transatlantic Enlightenment philosophy and by the course of the American Revolution. Many saw the inconsistency in demanding freedom while holding men in slavery, and the vigorous antislavery movement of the last decades of the eighteenth century defended the natural rights of Negroes. There was also a vigorous defense of their natural abilities. The accepted intellectual view was that the lack of accomplishment among the Negroes could be accounted for by their original environment and their slave status, much as their color could be accounted for by climatic factors.[6]

While the Revolution helped to stir some to an attack on slavery, the necessity of justifying the institution in what was now regarded as the freest country in the world, under a government theoretically based on the natural equality of mankind, eventually helped produce a specific, intellectual condemnation of the Negro race as separate and inferior. If slavery was to continue then it became essential to demonstrate that the fault lay with the blacks, not with the whites. As early as 1784-1785 attacks on the institution of slavery produced proslavery petitions signed by over a thousand Virginians.[7] The intellectual-scientific climate of the Revolutionary generation favored the public espousal of a doctrine of innate equality, but there was a persistent undercurrent of doubt.

In publicly questioning whether or not Negroes had the same inherent mental capacities as whites, Jefferson was a rarity among American intellectuals of his generation. But in his doubts he better expressed the American attitudes embodied in the laws and policies of the colonial era than did his fellow intellectuals in their repetition of standard Enlightenment environmental doctrines. In his *Notes on the State of Virginia* Jefferson advanced "as a suspicion only, that the blacks, whether originally a distinct race, or made distinct by time and circumstances, are inferior to the whites in the endowments both of body and mind. It is not against experience to suppose, that the different species of the same genus, or varieties of the same species, may possess different qualifications." To Jefferson it was impossible for the blacks to be incorporated into white society.[8]

While the orthodox intellectual position was not favorable to Jefferson's viewpoint, there are indications that here, as in so many other matters, Jefferson was publicly reflecting what many others believed. When Virginian St. George Tucker in 1798 issued a plea for the ending of slavery, he conceded that Virginians in general thought that the Negroes were mentally inferior. He also argued that the blacks, once freed, could not be incorporated into Virginian society. Jefferson, he said, had made it clear in his *Notes on the State of Virginia* why this was impossible. "If it is true, as Mr. Jefferson seems to suppose," wrote Tucker, "that the Africans are really an inferior race of mankind, will not sound policy advise their exclusion from a society in which they have not yet been admitted to participate in civil rights; and even to guard against such admission, at any future period, since it may eventually depreciate the whole national character?" Tucker thus advocated both gradual emancipation and the exclusion of blacks from civil rights. "Though I am opposed to the banishment of Negroes," he wrote, "I wish not to encourage their future residence among us."[9] Attacks on slavery, or even confident assertions that the ways in which blacks differed from whites stemmed merely from environment and circumstance, did not in the Revolutionary generation lead to arguments that the blacks should be incorporated into white society. Since the seventeenth century Americans had proceeded in law and custom as though the blacks were essentially different. The presence of large numbers of blacks in the debased condition of slavery and the grassroots white antipathies toward these blacks clearly made many Americans extremely receptive to theories of inherent racial difference; indeed it helped create a scientific attitude of mind that was willing, even anxious, to develop such theories.

The American school of ethnology that gradually developed in the years to mid-century, and ultimately advanced arguments for polygenesis and for superior and inferior races, was participating in a general shift of Western culture toward racialist thinking, but the vigor with which it espoused the new ideas stemmed also from its presence in an existing multiracial and unequal society. Since at least the sixteenth century the English had been a confident, arrogant people. This confidence had been fed by success. In America it was also fed by the prospects of an apparently limitless potential on a boundless continent. In the seventeenth and early eighteenth centuries the blacks were merely a useful form of labor—a form of labor which caused embarrassment and unease only by stirring in whites atavistic fears of blackness and bestiality. In an age of natural rights and Revolution America's black slaves became a far greater embarrassment, for they marred the republican perfection of the new nation. But antislavery thought never grew strong enough to overcome slavery in areas with large black populations. The foreign slave trade could be abolished, because while appeasing moral qualms and giving a victory to those who vigorously supported the antislavery cause, it also helped to keep blacks from coming to America. Soon, however, many Americans eagerly grasped at new racial theories which placed the onus of black slavery on the blacks themselves; they were slaves because their innate ability best fitted them to be slaves.

While the presence of large numbers of blacks made Americans particularly receptive to arguments defending innate differences between races, the American Indian was of more direct relevance for the development of an ideology of American expansion. If the Americans were a providential people destined to regenerate the other peoples of the world, then the American Indians became the first test. They occupied the land which Jefferson intended to transform into an empire for liberty.

From the beginning of English settlement in America, there had been a dual image of the North American Indians. There had always been both an admiration for the supposed simple life as well as hatred for "savage" violence. The Puritans at first had high hopes of saving souls in North America and at first thought in terms of Indian acculturation. Their position was, of course, completely ethnocentric. They believed the Indians would readily give up their way of life and gladly accept the God and the civilization that was being offered to them. A rapid disillusionment set in as the Indians protected their way of life and land by warfare. Throughout the colonies the Indians came to be viewed as a stumbling block to civilization, and in New England they were viewed with particular hatred as agents of the devil. In general the Indians by the latter years of the seventeenth century were despised because they had tried to remain

Indian and had shown little desire to become Christian gentlemen. The Indians could therefore be thrown off the land, mistreated, or slaughtered, because in rejecting the opportunities offered to them they had shown that they were sunk deep in irredeemable savagery. In practice, like the blacks, they were regarded as different human beings even when there was no general rationale to explain any racial differences.[10]

In the eighteenth century, attitudes toward the Indian were modified both because of the changing nature of American society and because of the impact of European ideas. In America in the eighteenth century the frontier began to move away from the eastern seaboard. Some areas were now completely free from Indian attack or even contact, and some colonials began to appreciate the Indians from a distance, developing an interest in the Indian way of life and praising aspects of Indian culture. This greater detachment of those on the eastern seaboard blended in with the developing view of mankind emerging in the eighteenth century from the European Enlightenment. By the mid-eighteenth century the prevailing intellectual view of the Indian in both Europe and America was an optimistic one. At the basis of this optimism was the Enlightenment view that all mankind was of one species, and that mankind in general was capable of indefinite improvement. If the Indians had the same innate capacity as the Europeans, then their "savage" state could be regarded as temporary. Those observers, such as Bernard Romans, who were prepared to argue that the Indians were a separate species were not in the main line of learned opinion in either Europe or the United States.[11]

Some were prepared to argue not merely that the Indians were capable of improvement, but that the state in which they were existing was an especially felicitous one. This idea had existed in some form since the time of the first contacts, but in the eighteenth century the idea of the Indian as a noble savage, revealing in his splendid simplicity the weaknesses and vices of an effete Europe, became a major theme of European creative writers. The image also permeated a variety of other works, even those of many travelers and observers who purported to be giving an accurate description of Indian life.[12] In practical terms, however, the image of the Indian as a noble savage to be admired and even emulated, although influential in American literature into the mid-nineteenth century, was less important for the actual shaping of an ideology of expansion than the ideas of those who saw the Indian as an improvable being who could and should be taught the virtues of the American way of life. American intellectuals of the eastern seaboard accepted this Enlightenment view of the Indian and were sensitive to any European attacks on the Indian which denigrated the New World as a whole. When Buffon and De Pauw wrote of the degeneracy of animal life in the New World and of the Indian as an inferior form of mankind, they were vigorously rebutted by the Americans, most notably Jefferson, who thought of America as an arena for the general improvement of mankind, not its debasement. Because the attack on the Indian by the European believers in degeneracy was part of a general attack on the New World, it had to be rebutted by patriotic Americans anxious to defend their continent and their new country.[13]

In shaping an Indian policy the Americans of the Revolutionary generation had their first experience of discovering what the creation of an American empire for liberty meant to other peoples. A great new nation was to rise up on the North American continent. What was to be the place of the Indians within this nation? From the time of the Revolution it was apparent that the attitude of America's leaders on the eastern seaboard was not the attitude of the actual empire builders, and ultimately the attitudes of the empire builders, not the leaders of the Revolutionary generation, were to prevail.

For the leaders of the new America the ideas of progress inherent in the Enlightenment took on a peculiarly powerful form. American leaders argued that they could offer the Indians a cleansed version of European civilization. The impact of Enlightenment ideas was of particular importance because so many of the early American governmental leaders were fully aware of, and even contributed to, the most important eighteenth-century transatlantic intellectual currents. Men who were intellectuals as well as politicians were decisive in the formulation of the theoretical basis of early American Indian policy.

Those Americans who lived on the eastern seaboard and thought in Atlantic and universal terms were able to separate the practical horrors and violence of border warfare from the theoretical problems of Indian relations. They often had a sense of perspective which enabled them to see the violence and faults of American frontiersmen and to observe that the Indians were fighting to protect their lands and families. American leaders, of course, did not want to stop the expansion westward, but in the post-Revolutionary years they wished to work out policies that by saving and transforming the Indians would show to the world that America was carrying out its announced mission. The leaders of the early seventeenth century had seen the Indians as souls to be saved; the leaders of the post-Revolutionary generation saw the Indians as fellow human beings who could and would be raised on the scale of human society. Enlightenment theory was to be carried out in practice in America. Above all else America's leaders wanted a prosperous, powerful, expanding America, for this they believed would be for the good of the world. But it was an America in which they could envisage transformed Indians, Indians who would be indistinguishable in their way of life from the farmers who surrounded them. The leadership of the United States until 1829 came from the eastern seaboard and conceived of mankind in eighteenth-century terms. As they viewed the illimitable regions of the West they could see no reason why the advance of white settlers across the continent could not be compatible with the presence of Indians who had been transformed from "savages" to civilized beings. And it was in thinking of a future America where there would be transformed Indians that the eastern intellectual and political elite differed most sharply from those hundreds of thousands of Americans who were engaged in carving new states out of the North American continent, and who were to play an increasingly large part in American politics and diplomacy in the forty years after the Revolution.

In adopting the idea that to civilize the Indians would be the first American triumph in transforming mankind, the leaders of the United States made it clear that they felt the eyes of the world were upon them. Henry Knox, secretary of war under

Washington, wrote in 1793 that "if our modes of population and War destroy the tribes the disinterested part of mankind and posterity will be apt to class the effects of our Conduct and that of the Spaniards in Mexico and Peru together —." When he resigned at the end of the following year, Knox showed a sensitivity not only to contemporary opinion but also to posterity. "A future historian," he wrote, "may mark the causes of this destruction of the human race in sable colors."[14]

From the late 1780s on Knox, in his public utterances and in his speeches and letters to the Indians, said that the national policy of the United States was to civilize the Indian tribes. This civilization policy meant, of course, making the Indians into Americans. The ideal was that of an American agrarian society. Ignoring the extensive agricultural development among the Indian tribes with which the United States was in contact, Knox and other national leaders of the period placed the whole confrontation in the simple context of a primitive hunting society, on a lower stage of human evolution, encountering an American agrarian society at the highest stage of human development. The Indians were to be civilized by the adoption of private property, by the men's farming in the American manner, by the women's learning to spin and weave, and by the introduction of a Christian education. Knox asserted in 1792 that the United States wanted the opportunity to impart to the Indians "all the blessings of civilized life, of teaching you to cultivate the earth, and raise corn; to raise oxen, sheep, and other domestic animals; to build comfortable houses, and to educate your children, so as ever to dwell upon the land."[15]

The full expression of this philosophy of an expansion that would transform the Indians came with the presidency of Thomas Jefferson. Whatever the practical doubts Jefferson had regarding the black slaves surrounding him, he allowed his theoretical view of mankind full reign in regard to the more distant Indians. His was the classic Enlightenment position, and he wrote in the 1780s that "proofs of genius given by the Indians of N. America, place them on a level with Whites in the same uncultivated state." Like Knox, Jefferson ignored the agricultural aspects of Indian society and preached the adoption of agriculture and private property as the path to civilization. "Let me entreat you therefore," he told a delegation of Indians in 1808, "on the lands now given you to begin to give every man a farm, let him enclose it, cultivate it, build a warm house on it, and when he dies let it belong to his wife and children after him."[16]

Where Jefferson differed from Knox and from most of his contemporaries was in the enthusiasm with which he favored the bringing of civilization, and in the manner in which he pushed the theory to its logical conclusion by arguing for the physical absorption of the Indians within the American population. After telling the Indians to adopt farming and private property, he asserted "you will become one people with us; your blood will mix with ours: and will spread with ours over this great island." Jefferson told the Delaware, Mohicans, and Munsees: "You will unite yourselves with us, and we shall all be Americans." Jefferson's secretary of war, Henry Dearborn, generally echoed his president's doctrines. He believed that the progress of civilization among the Indians before 1803 was proof of the practicability of destroying all distinctions between Indians and "civilized people."[17]

The philosophy argued for so eloquently by Jefferson remained the official hope of the United States until the mid-1820s, and for some the hope persisted throughout the nineteenth century. Secretary of War William Harris Crawford reported to the Senate in 1816 that it was the desire of the government "to draw its savage neighbors within the pale of civilization." A similar attitude was expressed in 1818 by Representative Henry Southard. "In the present state of our country," he wrote, "one of two things seems to be necessary, either that those sons of the forest should be moralized or exterminated. Humanity would rejoice at the former, but shrink with horror from the latter."[18]

While America's leaders of the post-Revolutionary generation incorporated the Enlightenment view of mankind as an integral objective of their Indian policy, there is ample evidence that this view was being rejected in America by those who were actually encountering the Indians. Long before science provided a rationale for rejecting the Indians as equal human beings, America's empire builders regarded the Indians as "violent savages" and as much less than inherently equal members of the human species. As Southerners had come to accept the idea of blacks as inherently "different," in spite of the assertions of an intellectual elite, Westerners built their own image of the Indian, which contrasted sharply with the eighteenth-century intellectual transatlantic view. The practical groundwork for the rejection of ideas defending the inherent equality of all human beings had been firmly laid in the United States by the end of the eighteenth century. American science after 1815 was to confirm for many Americans beliefs they already held. The practical rejection of the Enlightenment view of mankind at an early date is obscured by the eagerness with which an American intellectual elite accepted it.[19]

The greater detachment of many eastern leaders had been made possible by the advance of settlement out of the coastal plain into the piedmont and ultimately into and across the Appalachians. In the eighteenth century a new and nonfrontier America developed along the eastern seaboard. As Indian dangers disappeared a settled way of live developed, and intellectuals were given the leisure and detachment to comment on and participate in the views of the European theorists. Yet by the middle of the eighteenth century, a renewed Indian struggle to protect their lands developed on a frontier which had now become detached from the eastern centers of population. The Anglo-French struggles of the mid-1740s to 1760 were deeply entwined in Indian warfare, Pontiac's uprising renewed it in 1763, and from Dunmore's War in 1774 to Wayne's victory at Fallen Timbers in 1794 there were constant and bloody border struggles. In the West the conflicts of the Revolution continued unabated after the achievement of independence. As American pioneers pushed farther from the eastern centers of population, they felt increasingly neglected by the eastern elite. Scots-Irish in Pennsylvania attacked the pacifism of Quaker leaders, frontiersmen in the valleys of east Tennessee saw little merit in a North Carolina government that neglected their defense, and Kentuckians were to take matters into their own hands as they despaired of help from Virginia.

The border warfare of the Revolutionary era both fascinated and horrified the pioneers and their descendants. The heroes and villains of this struggle were to fill the popular literature and pioneer histories of the next hundred years. The horrors of the Wyoming Valley, the heroes of Boonesborough, the disaster at Blue Licks became a vital part of the history and mythology of the next generations. Essential to this legacy was a deep hatred of the Indians with whom the frontiersmen had contended. When in 1794 the new territorial assembly of Tennessee petitioned Congress for a declaration of war on the Creeks and the Cherokees, they stated that there was scarcely "a man of this body, but can recount a dear wife or child, an aged parent or near relation, massacred by the hands of these blood-thirsty nations, in their houses or fields." The assembly reminded Congress that "citizens who live in poverty on the extreme frontiers, were as entitled to be protected in their lives, their families and little property, as those who were in luxury, ease and affluence in the great and opulent eastern cities."[20] These men scoffed at Enlightenment ideas of Indian equality and improvability.

Hatred of the Indians and an avid desire for their lands were common sentiments in the frontier regions. Arthur St. Clair, later to be governor of the Northwest Territory, commented in 1774 from western Pennsylvania that "it is the most astonishing thing in the world the disposition of the common people of this country; actuated by the most savage cruelty, they wantonly perpetrate crimes that are a disgrace to humanity." Fourteen years later he still despaired of peace with the Indians. "Our settlements are extending themselves so fast on every quarter where they can be extended; our pretensions to the country they inhabit have been made known to them in so unequivocal a manner, and the consequences are so certain and so dreadful to them, that there is little probability of there ever being any cordiality between us."[21]

Even Revolutionary dangers did not slow the avid desire for land and the disregard of Indian humanity. In 1777, when Congress was particularly anxious to keep peace on the borders, Colonel George Morgan wrote to John Hancock that parties of settlers had gathered to massacre even friendly Indians at their hunting grounds, and that it was "not uncommon to hear even those who ought to know better, express an ardent desire for an Indian war, on account of the fine lands those poor people possess."[22] In 1791, at the time George Washington and Henry Knox were beginning to shape an Indian policy based on ideas of national honor and the spreading of civilization, it was reported from Fort Pitt that a party of volunteer militia had killed four friendly Indians—three men and a woman. "Although this action appears very much like deliberate murder," wrote Isaac Craig, "yet it is approved of, I believe, by a majority of people on the Ohio."[23]

The Kentuckians, who had suffered greatly from Indian attacks during the Revolution, hated the Indians with a passion. When in 1786 Colonel Benjamin Logan led an expedition northward across the Ohio to attack Indian villages, the friendly Shawnee chief Moluntha was murdered although he came forward carrying the American flag and holding out the articles of the United States-Shawnee treaty signed earlier that year.[24] Major John Hamtramck's comment in 1790 was that even if a treaty could be signed that spring "the people of our frontier will certainly be the first to break it. The people of Kentucky will carry on private expeditions against the Indians and kill them whenever they meet them, and I do not believe there is a jury in all Kentucky who would punish a man for it . . . the thirst of war is the dearest inheritance an Indian receives from his parents, and vengeance that of the Kentuckians, hostility must then be the result on both sides."[25]

The Kentucky attitudes were echoed throughout Tennessee. John Sevier in 1785 wrote to the governor of North Carolina to defend the murderer of an Indian. "I can't pretend to say what he might have done," wrote Sevier, "but must believe, that had any other person met with the same insult from one of those bloody savages, who have so frequently murdered the wives and children of the people of this country for many years past, I say had they been possessed of that manly and soldierly spirit that becomes an American, they must have acted like Hubbard."[26] A basic motive for the attempt to create the independent state of Franklin in the mid-1780s was the feeling that the inhabitants of eastern Tennessee had been deserted by the North Carolinians, who did not understand the perils of frontier life. One resident defended the separation movement with the comment that the Franklinites "say that North-Carolina has not treated us like a parent, but like a step-dame. She means to sacrifice us to the Indian savages."[27]

Those Americans who had been exposed to Indian attacks endorsed the views attributed to the whole population by British observer John Smyth: "The white Americans also have the most rancorous antipathy to the whole race of Indians, and nothing is more common than to hear them talk of extirpating them totally from the face of the earth, men, women, and children." The French soldier Chastellux expressed a similar opinion when he said that the reason the inhabitants of New York had taken up arms and displayed courage was that they were "animated by an inveterate hatred against the Indians, whom the English always sent ahead of their own armies."[28]

Significantly, the first prominent literary figure of the trans-Appalachian West, Hugh Henry Brackenridge, reflected in his writings popular frontier hatred of the Indians rather than the more benign view of the Indians presented by the Enlightenment tradition. His novel *Modern Chivalry* achieved great popularity beyond the mountains, although it never won a comparable reputation along the eastern seaboard. Brackenridge was raised in York County, Pennsylvania, and educated at Princeton, but the major part of his career was spent in Pittsburgh. It has been suggested that some of his anti-Indian prejudice possibly stemmed from witnessing Indian attacks in York County; certainly his experiences in Pittsburgh after 1781 confirmed his prejudices.[29] Even before he moved to Pittsburgh he attacked the idea that the Indians should have a right "to a soil which they have never cultivated" and wrote of the Indians "as sunk beneath the dignity of human nature," though they "bear resemblance and are seen in the shape of men." His attacks took on a particular virulence, however, after he moved west.[30]

The incident that confirmed Brackenridge in unremitting hostility toward the Indians was the death by torture of Colonel William Crawford in 1782. This episode epitomized for many frontiersmen all the horrors of Indian war and captivity. Crawford, a prominent figure in western Pennsylvania, in 1782 led an expedition against the Indian towns at Sandusky in what is now northern Ohio. His expedition was routed, Crawford was captured, and was tortured to death by fire over several hours. This, of course, had happened to others, but Crawford was well known, and two who escaped from the Indians gave detailed accounts, including a vivid description of his death. It was this description which transformed Simon Girty, who was present at the torture scene and taunted Crawford, from being one of a number of frontier renegades into the supreme frontier villain of the Revolutionary era.

Brackenridge arranged for the publication of the two accounts. In his letter transmitting the narratives for publication he made a once-famous remark that he was also adding some observations on "the animals vulgarly called Indians . . . having an opportunity to know something of the character of this race of men, from the deeds they perpetrate daily round me."[31] The introduction to the book form of the narratives stated that they might be useful in inducing the government to take some steps to chastise and suppress the Indians, "and from hence they will see that the nature of an Indian is fierce and cruel, and that an extirpation of them would be useful to the world, and honorable to those who can effect it."[32]

When in 1786 Congress appointed a superintendent for the Indians north of the Ohio, Brackenridge commented that he doubted the Indian savages could be restrained by the giving of presents: "It would be for the good of the country," he wrote, "if, when the blankets and leggins come, the superintendent would give them to some of the poor women and children whose husbands and fathers have been murdered in the war."[33] Brackenridge in the early 1790s was prepared to take issue with those who wrote in praise of the Indians. "I consider men who are unacquainted with the savages, like young women who have read romances, and have as improper an idea of the Indian character in the one case, as the female mind has of real life in the other. The philosopher, weary of the vices of refined life, thinks to find perfect virtue in the simplicity of the unimproved state." At about the same time Brackenridge was urging the conquest of Canada in order to cut off British support for the Indians.[34]

Brackenridge's indictment of the philosophical attitude was echoed in 1808 by the editor of a collection of captivity and atrocity stories: "The philosopher who speaks with delight, of the original simplicity, and primitive innocence of mankind, may here learn, that man, uncivilized and barbarous, is even worse than the most ferocious wolf or panther of the forest. That men of philosophic minds, feeling in themselves the impulse of humanity entertain such mistaken notions of the Indians, is evident from the writings of many."[35] Although the Indian policy of Washington, Jefferson, and Monroe was based on ideas of improvability stemming from the eighteenth-century Enlightenment, eventually it was reshaped by the resistance and pressure of the frontier states and their inhabitants.

In the states that confronted the Indian in the last decades of the eighteenth century, the Indian was often regarded as an expendable, inferior savage. The rhetoric of improvability and assimilation did not convince the Georgians or the Tennesseans. They did not want a government civilization policy that perpetuated Indians on their lands. They wanted to expel Indians, not transform them.

When after 1789 American leaders, influenced by Enlightenment thought, increasingly turned to a policy that tried to combine expansion with permanent occupancy by transformed Indians, they were thwarted by an American population greedy for land. Those Americans who pressed forward rapidly into new areas believed the Indians unworthy to retain land they did not use in the European manner. And as the Indians desperately fought to preserve the lands they lived on from white encroachment, their "savage" actions were used to condemn them. The white failure to temper greed with morality was transferred to the Indians, and frontiersmen urged the government to remove or eliminate the "savage," "beastlike" Indians who resisted their advance.

The official Indian policy espoused by Washington and Jefferson failed. It soon became apparent that even Jefferson himself believed the rapid move westward of white Americans to be far more important than the attempt to civilize Indians. Jefferson convinced himself that reducing Indian landholdings as rapidly as possible was the quickest way to force the tribes to assume white culture. Throughout his two administrations he ignored the reality of Indian degradation under ever more rapid white pressure and wrote and talked of a success in "civilizing" the Indians that was based more on his abstract dreams than it was on the practical realities of Indian relations in the period of William Henry Harrison and Tecumseh.

While Enlightenment hopes were collapsing in the West in bloody border battles and hatreds, they were foundering in the South on the rock of the widespread presence of blacks. In the West violence engendered by the white advance was used to condemn the Indians who had been provoked to resist; in the South the degradation engendered by slavery was used as a justification for continuing the enslavement. As yet these grass-roots beliefs did not have their own intellectual rationale, but they were to get one in the generation after 1815. The supposed lessons of the American experience hastened the collapse of Enlightenment theory and helped produce scientific theories of black and Indian inferiority. Along with this debasement of other races was to come an enhancement of the white race as superior, in particular an enhancement of the American Anglo-Saxon "race." For a moment in the heat of Revolutionary enthusiasm, it appeared that the American mission was to be a mission for all mankind, but the practical realities of both slavery and expansion soon made it apparent that the mission was more parochial, and that nationalistic and personal desires were to overwhelm universal hopes.

7

Superior and Inferior Races

> History and observation both teach that . . . the Mongol, the Malay, the Indian, and the Negro, are now and have been in all ages and places inferior to the Caucasian.
>
> Josiah C. Nott, *Two Lectures* (1844)

Although American intellectuals in 1815 generally accepted the environmental view of racial differences which they had inherited from the European Enlightenment, there were already signs that informed American opinion was ready to provide a scientific rationale for what was believed by many of those in direct contact with blacks and Indians. In providing this rationale American scientists were clearly participating in a general interest in racial differences that dominated western thought by the 1850s; but they were also responding to needs within American society itself. By the 1840s the American theorists on race were providing a mass of material defending innate differences between races; these ideas were sweeping all before them in America and were being used in Europe by those who were challenging the long-established views on the unity of the human race.

As early as 1808 Dr. John Augustine Smith attacked Samuel

Stanhope Smith's environmentalism in college lectures in New York city,[1] but the first well-publicized onslaught was that of Dr. Charles Caldwell. Caldwell was an opinionated and argumentative physician, who from 1811 to the middle of the century consistently and loudly defended the cause of innate racial differences. He published a great deal on a variety of subjects and lectured extensively throughout the country. A North Carolinian who had received his medical education at the University of Pennsylvania, Caldwell was professor of natural history at that university before moving to Kentucky in 1819. There he became a prominent member of the medical profession, first at Transylvania University and from 1837 on at a new medical school he founded in Louisville.[2]

Caldwell first attacked Smith's views in 1811 and was unrelenting in his onslaught on environmentalism. He later called Smith's *Essay* "one of the most fallacious productions I have ever perused." The crux of Caldwell's objection was that races could not be altered by environment, and he quickly found himself the center of controversy as the religious orthodox claimed he was attacking the idea of the original unity of the human race, which meant, of course, a challenge to Genesis. In later articles Caldwell denied attacking religion, simply stating that climate could not account for the distinction between races; divine involvement had been needed.[3] During the next forty years most American scientists who argued for innate, irreversible differences between races tried to avoid a direct attack on the Bible. Often they argued that because God had originally created Adam and Eve he could also have interposed at a later date to create racial diversity. This usually did not satisfy the religious orthodox, who correctly surmised that any attack on the unity of the human race would ultimately bring a direct challenge to Genesis. Many of Samuel Stanhope Smith's friends and supporters never forgave Caldwell for his attack on the environmental theory, for they connected Smith's death in 1819 with his distress at the attack.[4]

After Caldwell moved to Transylvania University, he renewed his advocacy of innate differences between races, both continuing in the manner of his original attack and appearing as an enthusiastic supporter of the new science of phrenology. Caldwell went to Paris in 1821 to buy books and apparatus for the Transylvania medical school. There he met Gall and Spurzheim, attended Spurzheim's lectures, and became an ardent convert to their doctrines. When he came back to America he quickly began to spread phrenological theories. He inaugurated a series of lectures on phrenology in the Transylvania medical school, traveled extensively throughout the United States to deliver lectures, and also published both on phrenology and on general racial matters. By the end of the 1830s he was the best-known American phrenologist, and Scotsman George Combe, the leading European phrenologist, traveled to Louisville to meet him on his tour of the United States. Other American physicians, such as Dr. John Bell and Dr. B. H. Coates, helped to popularize phrenology in America in these early years, but it was Caldwell who did the most to generate interest in the subject and used it to advance supposedly empirical proofs of the innate differences between races.[5]

By 1830 Caldwell was well known for his pronouncements on race in both his phrenological and in his general scientific writings. In the late 1820s he examined the heads of parties of Indians, compared them to Indian skulls found in western mounds, and reached the conclusion that "when the wolf, the buffalo and the panther shall have been completely domesticated, like the dog, the cow, and the household cat, then, and not before, may we expect to see the *full-blooded* Indian civilized, like the white man." Advances among Indians, he argued, had been among half-breeds and the more white blood, the more civilization. "The only efficient scheme to civilize the Indians," argued Caldwell, "is to *cross the breed. Attempt any other and you will extinguish the race.*"[6]

When in 1830 Caldwell published his *Thoughts on the Original Unity of the Human Race*, he tried to reach a broader audience by making it a general work on racial differences rather than an analysis based on phrenological principles. His intent, he confidently announced, was to refute Prichard's *Researches into the Physical History of Man*, the most important contemporary work on the unity of the human species. Caldwell now felt confident enough to make a direct challenge to those who defended the origin of mankind as depicted in Genesis. He argued that God had created not one but four original species — Caucasian, Mongolian, Indian, and African — and that he had made them superior and inferior. This, he said, should not encourage injustice between races: "The Caucasians are not justified in either enslaving the Africans or destroying the Indians, merely because their superiority in intellect and war enables them to do so."[7] In the course of his book, however, Caldwell made it very clear that he assumed innate inferiority led inevitably to these results.

At the heart of Caldwell's argument was the assertion that the accepted biblical chronology was incompatible with what historical research was demonstrating about the antiquity of racial differences. This chronological problem was to be used many times in the next twenty-five years by those who attacked the original unity of mankind and often by those like Samuel G. Morton and Josiah C. Nott who had a far higher standing in the scientific community than Caldwell. Caldwell pointed out that according to the chronology accepted by the orthodox, Noah and his family had come out of the ark 4179 years ago (he added, modestly, "they are believed to be Caucasian"). It could also be shown by the Egyptologists that 3445 years ago a nation of Ethiopians had existed near Egypt. Thus since the very earliest times the races of mankind had been distinct.[8] The problem was to be formulated more elaborately, but again and again during the next decades the same basic question was to be asked of the religious orthodox: How could whites and blacks have become so distinct in less than two thousand years after the supposed date of the Creation?

The Caucasian, Caldwell argued, must at one time have been as "uninstructed" as the African or the Indian. He had outstripped the others because he was "superior to them in native intellectual faculties." The African and the Indian were "inferiorly organized and endowed." In discussing the Africans he used the centuries-old white argument that there was a close link between the blacks and the apes, asserting that in the genital organs the black "resembles the ape fully as much as he does the

Caucasian."[9] Efforts to civilize the Indian were a waste of time: "The years of his race are not only numbered; they are comparatively few." When improvements among the Indians occurred, it was to be ascribed chiefly to racial interbreeding. The Indians as Indians were doomed; "Civilization is destined to exterminate them, in common with the wild animals."[10] This view of the Indians had long been that of much of the general population throughout the western region in which Caldwell now taught.

For Caldwell the Caucasian race was without any question innately superior: nature had been "less bounteous" not only to the Africans and the Indians, but also to the Mongolians and Malays. "To the Caucasian race," he wrote, "is the world indebted for all the great and important discoveries, inventions, and improvements, that have been made in science and the arts."[11] Caldwell's open defense of polygenesis and his vigorous discussion of superior and inferior races was new in America in 1830. It was to become commonplace by 1850, and Caldwell's words were to be echoed in a variety of ways by scientists and popular writers who claimed to be basing their arguments on far more extensive and different scientific evidence.

The most influential American scientific writing defending innate racial differences was not to appear until after 1839, but public assertions of the existence of superior and inferior races increased rapidly in the 1830s. At first the main scientific evidence was advanced by those interested in phrenology, which in the 1830s had an intellectual as well as popular vogue in the United States. When Spurzheim traveled to the United States in 1832, he was received enthusiastically by many of the eastern intellectual elite, and when the visit ended in his unexpected death, his Boston funeral was a major public occasion. The intellectual interest continued until the extensive American lecture tour of George Combe at the end of the decade. Only in the 1840s did scholarly opinion begin to move away from phrenology as the "practical phrenologists" emphasized the commercial and fortune-telling aspects of the readings of heads and "bumps."[12]

Like their European contemporaries, the American phrenologists were optimistic about the possibilities of improvement for those who had a sound basic structure of the brain; but they also argued that nonwhite races had structures that were fundamentally deficient, and that they could not be developed to the level of the white brain. Most phrenologists ignored the problem of the original unity or multiplicity of races and simply asserted that physical comparison of the head or skull of the different races revealed basic differences. In the 1820s and 1830s the phrenologists were in the vanguard of those who perceived innate physical differences between the races, and although their specific analysis of the brain was eventually rejected by American scientists, they at first exerted considerable influence by their supposed empirical comparison of physical structure. Until the 1840s many Americans of impeccable scientific reputation thought that phrenology was a valid approach to the physical comparison of individuals and races.

One of the first general American works of phrenology was that of George Calvert in 1832. Calvert carefully listed thirty-five faculties, represented in different parts of the brain, that controlled a variety of human thoughts, desires, and emotions. He emphasized that the general phrenological doctrine was that a small brain could not manifest a powerful mind; the mind could be developed by education, but its effects were limited by the original organization: "No skill or education or control of outward circumstances could ever enlarge to excellence the intellectual capacity of an individual with a brain like that of the New Hollander; nor depress to inferiority that of an individual with one like Göthe."[13] The accusation of inferior basic "organization" was typical of the analyses of the phrenologists and affected writings that were not specifically phrenological in type. In a general work on the connection between religion and health, Amariah Brigham pointed out in 1835 that "the dark colored races" (he included the American Indian) had been unreceptive to the missionaries because their "physical organization" was unsuitable. A basic element in this deficient organization was *"the organ of the mind."* In the dark races of man, the anterior and superior portions of the head were depressed. Accordingly, although improvement, and even great improvement, was possible, this would take generations and even centuries.[14]

It was neither circumstances nor environment but specific, inherent physical differences that accounted for the failure of the non-Caucasian races to achieve Christianity and civilization. Phrenologists helped convince many other scientists as well as laymen that there were specific differences between races.

The intellectual defense of innate racial differences received a further boost in the 1830s by the widespread southern defense of slavery. Southern apologists of the institution developed an array of arguments to demonstrate specific and permanent Negro inferiority. The tacit assumptions of Negro "difference" and inferiority which had permeated the colonial period now for the first time were shaped into a coherent racial theory. It is a commonplace to point out that the catalyst for this southern defense of its institution was the launching of a northern abolitionist attack in the 1830s, and this certainly stimulated vigorous southern rebuttals; but in a larger sense the Southerners were sharing in, and taking advantage of, the general shift toward racialist thinking in Europe and the United States. This racialist thinking was used to justify far more than the southern institution of slavery. It served to defend the subordination or even extermination of non-European peoples throughout the world and was believed by Europeans to explain the ever-increasing gulf in power and progress that separated them from the peoples they were overrunning. The overt intellectual argument for innate black inferiority was being developed in America before the full surge of abolitionism, it was not restricted to the South in the 1830s and 1840s, and it was not peculiar to those who wished to defend slavery.[15]

As early as 1826 Dr. Thomas Cooper of South Carolina College had written privately that "I do not say the blacks are a distinct race: but I have not the slightest doubt of their being an inferior variety of the human species and not capable of the same improvement as the whites." He believed that "the inferiority of natural intellect among the blacks cannot be denied . . . They are not capable of much mental improvement, or of literary or scientific acquirement.[16]

The full flowering of southern attacks on the idea of innate black equality came, however, only after the Virginia debates on the gradual emancipation of slaves in 1831 and 1832. The idea that there were those in Virginia still willing to urge the abolition of slavery aroused sharp fears among Southerners. One speaker in the Virginia legislature seized on the old comparison with dogs to attack the absurdity of emancipation and equality. "Nor do I believe in that Fan-faronade about the natural equality of man," said William H. Roane. "I do not believe that all men are *by nature* equal, or that it was in the power of human art to make them so. I no more believe that the flat-nosed, woolly-headed black native of the deserts of *Africa*, is equal to the straight-haired white man of Europe, than I believe the stupid, scentless greyhound is equal to the noble generous dog of *Newfoundland*."[17] From 1832 on a steady stream of southern works defended slavery, and many of them contributed to the idea of the innate inequality of all races. In condemning blacks southern propagandists helped stimulate other racial categorizations.

The most influential pamphlet to be inspired by the Virginia debates was Thomas R. Dew's *Review of the Debate*. Dew's work was more cautious on the racial issue than Caldwell's earlier *Thoughts*. Dew's main contention was that to end slavery would be a disaster, for there was no way of colonizing the blacks, and the freed slaves would have to remain in Virginia. Like Jefferson nearly fifty years before, Dew thought that the presence of large numbers of free blacks in Virginia would be disastrous to both races. Slaves, he said, were *"utterly unfit for a state of freedom among the whites."* Blackness, not slavery, was the essential cause of the Negro condition, for "the emancipated black carries a mark which no time can erase; he forever wears the indelible symbol of his inferior condition; the *Ethiopian cannot change his skin, nor the leopard his spots.*"[18] Dew avoided the species question, but his general theme was clear: blacks could not be free to participate in white society, for all men and all races were not created equal.

As Southerners in the 1830s became increasingly sensitive on the subject of slavery, they were able to take comfort in the variety of writings in both Europe and the United States that were challenging the belief in innate human equality. When in 1833

Richard H. Colfax put out a pamphlet to combat the views of the abolitionists, he went to a number of European authorities—including Lord Kames, Voltaire, and Sir William Lawrence—who had emphasized the sharp differences among the races of mankind, and he expressed his disagreement with both Blumenbach and Dr. Samuel Stanhope Smith. The essence of Colfax's argument was that as the Negroes were of a distinct species no change in their circumstances could make them equal to the whites. "There never existed a tribe of whites," he wrote, "who were characterized by as much grossness of intellect, listless apathy, sluggishness, and want of national and personal pride, as even the most refined Africans."[19] European racial arguments attracted considerable interest in the South, and in 1837 J. H. Guenebault of South Carolina selected those portions of J. J. Virey's *Histoire naturelle* that related to blacks and reissued them as the *Natural History of the Negro Race*.[20]

While many found Genesis to be an insuperable obstacle to the argument for a separate origin of human races, arguments defending the idea of superior and inferior races filled the pamphlets of these years. In 1835 J. J. Flournoy was willing to accept the Negroes as members of one human species descended from Adam and Eve, but he argued that divine intervention had made them into an inferior race. Flournoy made his peace with the religious by using the old argument that the curse of Cain had been revived in Ham and his descendants. The blacks were essentially different from the rest of mankind because they were twice fallen. Flournoy argued that he disagreed not only with Dr. Samuel Smith and his environmentalism but with Thomas Dew and his position that the blacks could not be colonized. He thought that every possible effort should be made to send the Negroes away, as the whole race had a predilection for "violence and carnage."[21]

Southerners, whether believing in one or in several human species, were willing to state overtly in the 1830s that the innate differences between blacks and whites could be overcome neither by education nor by environment. The blacks were doomed to permanent inferiority. What had long been implicit in southern thinking had, by the end of the decade, become explicit. By the mid-1840s ex-Governor James Hammond of South Carolina was able to write that he repudiated "as ridiculously absurd, that much lauded but nowhere accredited dogma of Mr. Jefferson, that 'all men are born equal.'" The Jefferson of the Declaration of Independence was now under constant attack in the South, but the ideas of black inequality he had tentatively suggested in his *Notes on the State of Virginia* had now been expanded into a whole southern ideology.[22]

In expounding their views of racial inequality, the Southerners had no need to think of themselves as an embattled minority. What they had to combat was the attack on the institution of slavery, not arguments for racial equality. For the South the sad irony of the years from the mid-1830s to the Civil War was that, as the northern attack on slavery increased in intensity, northern racial theorists generally agreed with the South that the colored races were unfit to mix with the whites on any equal basis. The authoritative foundation for this conclusion was laid in the twenty years after 1839 by an American school of ethnology, a school that included the most important racial theorists. These ethnologists first argued that there were irreversible differences between races and eventually defended polygenesis. The center of the school was in Philadelphia.[23]

The seminal publication of the new American ethnology was Samuel George Morton's *Crania Americana*, issued in 1839. Morton was no Southerner defending slavery, but a Philadelphia physician engaged in basic research. He established in Philadelphia the world's largest scientific collection of human skulls. Louis Agassiz said in 1846 that "this collection alone is worth a journey to America." Comparing cranial size, capacity, and structure Morton emphasized the basic physical differences between races. By the end of the 1840s he contended that there had been various Creations of human beings in different parts of the world. Morton's research, though controversial, was regarded as basic to an understanding of human racial origins until Darwin shattered the work of the American school. Morton was at the core of this group, which included English-born Egyptologist George R. Gliddon, southern physician Josiah C. Nott, and archaeologist Ephraim G. Squier.[24]

Although Morton based his conclusions on physical comparisons, he was also deeply impressed by historic Caucasian achievements and by the evidence of separate human races three thousand years before in Egypt. Morton pointed out that the Caucasian and the Negro were as distinct in ancient Egypt as they were in the nineteenth century, and like Caldwell in his *Thoughts* he said that the accepted biblical chronology meant that the differentiation into races would have to have taken place in little more than a thousand years. Morton regarded this as quite impossible. From this evidence the only conclusion was that biblical chronology was wrong or that distinct races had existed from the time of Creation.[25]

In *Crania Americana* Morton examined the crania of Indian tribes of North and South America and strove to place his work within the broad stream of research on man. This scientific caution was to give his work all the more weight. In his introduction, before proceeding to the detailed cranial comparison of Indians, he gave his general views on race, pointing out that since the earliest times races had possessed the same distinctive qualities. He did not challenge religion directly (Morton was always cautious in this regard), but he did challenge the environmental explanation of racial differences, suggesting that the same God who had created mankind could also have created racial differences. By leaving moot the question of when God had done this, he avoided the question of whether the Mosaic account of Creation, with only one original pair, was scientifically false.[26]

Morton believed Blumenbach's division of the human family into five races was inadequate, but he accepted it as a working hypothesis. Within these races Morton found twenty-two families, which he said were really "groups of nations." Morton was clearly concerned with observed cultural traits as well as with physical differences based on cranial research. He characterized the Caucasian race as "distinguished for the facility with which it attains the highest intellectual endowments." He acknowledged that what were called "the English or Anglo-Saxons" were a blend of Belgae ("a branch of the Teutonic stock"), Saxons, and Normans, but he did not enter into any extensive discussion of these or other component groups. The Anglo-Saxon family, he wrote, is "inferior to no one of the Caucasian families in intellectual endowments, and possessed of indomitable courage and unbounded enterprise, it has spread its colonies widely over Asia, Africa and America; and, the mother of the Anglo-American family, it has already peopled the world with a race in no respect inferior to the parent stock."[27]

The American Indians were the main subject of Morton's work, and his conclusion was that "the intellectual faculties of this great family appear to be of a decidedly inferior cast when compared with those of the Caucasian or Mongolian races." While contending that the inaptitude of the Indian for civilization had been clearly demonstrated by experience, Morton showed his usual caution by admitting that it was not possible to tell how near the Indian could approach the Caucasian if a single family were educated for several generations. The Indians, Morton argued, were a separate race, distinct even from the Mongolian, and divided into two families—the American and the Toltecan.[28]

Although Morton himself was no phrenologist, and he was to move clearly away from phrenology during its popularization in the 1840s, he still treated the subject with great seriousness in the late 1830s. Phrenologist George Combe and Morton corresponded, Combe visited Morton and inspected his collection of skulls, and as a result of their conversations Combe wrote an essay on the principles of phrenology as an appendix to *Crania Americana*.[29] Thus the work that Benjamin Silliman's journal described as "the most extensive and valuable contribution to the natural history of man" which had yet appeared on the American continent included a section on the principles of phrenology.[30]

In his phrenological essay Combe emphasized that the size of the brain was indicated by the dimensions of the skull, and that nationalities as well as individuals could be differentiated by the size of their brains. He was particularly scathing in his discussion of the American Indians. In Africa, he argued, some of the inhabitants had at least advanced beyond "the savage condition" to create "cities, rude manufactures, agriculture, commerce, government and laws; and in these respects they greatly excel several of the tribes of native Americans, who have continued wandering savages from the beginning to the end of their existence." Though there were some exceptions, he said of the Indians, "speaking of the race, we do not exaggerate in saying, that they remain to the present hour enveloped in all their primitive savageness and that they have profited extremely little from the introduction amongst them of arts, sciences and philosophy."[31]

American phrenologists were, of course, delighted with Morton's book and with Combe's involvement in this major scientific publication. Benjamin Silliman's favorable review was reprinted in the *American Phrenological Journal*, but this review was a model of scientific caution compared to that written by racial theorist and phrenologist Dr. Charles Caldwell. Caldwell argued that Morton's measurements had shown decisively the superiority of the Caucasian brain over that of other races, and he went on to add his own comments on the peculiar excellence of the Anglo-Saxons. Here Caldwell simply threw all scientific caution to the winds and wrote what he felt. Great Britain he said, was peopled chiefly by Anglo-Saxons, "the most endowed variety of the Caucasian race. Their brains are superior in size, and more perfect in figure, than the brains of any other variety." Their brains were also the most powerful and "hence the surpassing strength and grandeur at home, and the influence and sway over the other nations of the earth, of those who possess them. The vast and astonishing productions of art in Great Britain, her boundless resources of comfort and enjoyment in peace, and her unequalled means of defence and annoyance in war, are as literally the growth of the brains of her inhabitants, as her oaks, and elms, and ash trees are of her soil. We shall only add, that the inhabitants of the United States, being also of the best Caucasian stock . . . promise to be even more than the Britons of future ages."[32] Morton had at least based his assertions on what he believed to be accurate scientific measurements; Caldwell was simply asserting that Anglo-Saxon brains were better than other Caucasian brains.

Caldwell was a minor figure in the 1840s, but Morton and his supporters were at the very heart of American ethnological research. Their confidence in defending innate racial differences grew throughout the decade. In 1842 Morton read to the Boston Society of Natural History a paper which advanced the argument that all the American nations except the Eskimos were of one race, a race "peculiar, and distinct from all others," and inferior to the Mongolian. Morton, still concerned not to challenge religion directly, shunned specific arguments for separate Creations, merely pointing out that distinct races had existed in the most distant past.[33]

In spite of Morton's efforts to avoid religious controversy, his work brought opposition from the religious orthodox while gaining an extremely wide circulation in the South, particularly after publication in 1844 of his second major work—the *Crania Ægyptica*. In this work Morton devoted much of his argument to showing that the Egyptians, with their great civilization, were Caucasian, not a Negro race as had been suggested by others. "Negroes," he said, "were numerous in Egypt, but their social position in ancient times was the same that it now is, that of servants and slaves." This conclusion by the scholarly Philadelphian was exactly what most Southerners wanted to hear, although southern ministers were disturbed by his additional assertion that "the physical or organic characters which distinguish the several races of men, are as old as the oldest records of our species."[34] Southern ministers were usually delighted to accept scientific arguments for black inferiority; they objected only to the assertion that such inferiority could be traced to multiple Adams and Eves.

Morton's follower, Dr. Josiah C. Nott of Mobile, was far more willing than Morton to resort to polemics and to use his scientific conclusions to comment on the contemporary racial scene. Also, in spite of frequent denials, he delighted in presenting evidence that would embarrass ministers attempting to defend the literal truth of Genesis. One of the South's leading surgeons and a defender of polygenesis, slavery, and inherent black inferiority, Nott, between 1844 and the Civil War, achieved an international scientific reputation by writing on race.[35] He confidently reached the conclusion that the "Almighty in his wisdom has peopled our vast planet from many distant centres, instead of one, and with races or species originally and radically distinct."[36]

In his first major contribution to the racial argument, published in 1844, Nott proclaimed: "History and observation both teach that . . . the Mongol, the Malay, the Indian, and the Negro, are now and have been in all ages and places inferior to the Caucasian." The human race, he argued, was descended from several or many original pairs, placed by God in climates best suited to their organization. Racial interbreeding was a disaster, for it led to hybrids less fertile than their parents, to deterioration, and ultimately to disappearance. Since the time of Buffon the production of sterile offspring had been accepted as proof that the interbreeding animals belonged to separate species. By asserting that mulattoes were less fertile than either the whites or blacks who had produced them, Nott was able to suggest that here was additional evidence that blacks and whites were separate species. If a hundred white men and a hundred black women were put on a desert island and cut off from communication with the rest of the world, Nott argued, they would ultimately become extinct (Nott avoided the sexual implications of merely saying one hundred whites and one hundred blacks). When the Caucasians mixed with other races, there were disastrous effects: "This adulteration of blood is the reason why Egypt and the Barbary States never can again rise, until the present races are exterminated and the Caucasian substituted." To keep Caucasian blood pure was to ensure the continuation of civilization and progress: "Wherever in the history of the world the inferior races have been conquered and mixed in with the Caucasian, the latter have sunk into barbarism." Civilization was to be found only among the various branches of the Caucasian race.[37]

Although Nott was intent on defending the necessity of slavery, he was as contemptuous of the American Indians as he was of the blacks. Unlike Morton, Nott saw no reason for distinguishing between the Indian families of Central America, responsible for the great monuments, and the "wandering" tribes of the northern part of the continent. Cortez had shown, argued Nott, that five hundred "Caucasian arms and heads were worth more than millions of these miserable creatures." The beaver and the bee, he contended, displayed the same type of skill in construction as the Mexican: "every thing in the history of the Bee shows a reasoning power little short of that of a Mexican." Nott believed that the full-blooded North American Indians were unimprovable. The boasted civilization of the Cherokees and Chickasaws meant nothing: "Whatever improvement exists in their condition is attributable to a mixture of races."[38] The Indians, he argued, could not survive the advance of civilization.

This was all much wilder than the conclusions drawn by Morton from his cranial researches, yet Morton wrote to Nott encouraging him in his work and particularly praising his remarks on hybrids—the mulattoes. Nott hardly needed encouragement. He delighted in the furor his writings created, and he engaged in spirited public debates with those who took exception to what they considered his irreligious beliefs. Nott's later summary of what he had perceived in Morton's writings demonstrates well the conclusions that could be drawn from the work of the American school of ethnology: "Dr. S. G. Morton," he wrote in 1849, "by a long series of well-conceived experiments, has established the fact, that the capacity of the crania of the Mongol, Indian, and Negro, and all dark-skinned races, is smaller than that of the pure white man. And this deficiency seems to be especially well-marked in those parts of the brain which have been assigned to the moral and intellectual faculties." Thus Morton's cranial measurements and other general phrenological ideas intertwined to give Nott some of the "proof" he required. In this same pamphlet Nott endorsed what was becoming much more common in the last years of the 1840s: the drawing of distinctions even among the varieties of the supreme Caucasian race. "The ancient German," he wrote, "may be regarded as the parent stock from which the highest modern civilization has sprung. The best blood of France and England is German; the ruling caste in Russia is German; and look at the United States, and contrast our people with the dark-skinned Spaniards. It is clear that the dark-skinned Celts are fading away before the superior race, and that they must eventually be absorbed."[39]

By the mid-1840s Morton's work had given a whole new respectability to the idea of distinct races with different innate capacities. His efforts helped both to inspire more fervent assertions of racial differences, such as those of Josiah Nott, and to convince some of the most eminent scientific figures in America that races were inherently different. When Louis Agassiz emigrated to America in 1846 he quickly expressed a desire to meet Morton and was taken by Asa Gray to Philadelphia. Later he also corresponded with Josiah Nott, and Nott collected specimens for him along the Gulf. In the four years after his arrival in the United States, Agassiz moved to the position of endorsing the idea of separate Creations for different human races. This fitted neatly into his earlier advocacy of separate centers for the nonanimal kingdom. His reaction was emotional as well as scientific. After first seeing Negroes he wrote to his mother that "the more pity I felt at the sight of this degraded and degenerate race, the more . . . impossible it becomes for me to repress the feeling that they are not of the same blood as we are."[40] He soon found the scientific evidence to support his feeling.

By 1850, while still arguing for man's spiritual and moral unity under God, Agassiz maintained that there were essentially different human races. Genesis, he argued, merely described the origin of one race; it gave an account of "the branches of the white race." Agassiz insisted in his writings that scientists had the right to consider questions of racial origin without reference to politics or religion, and he made it quite clear that he believed his scientific research had practical applicability. Scientists, he said, had an obligation "to settle the relative rank among these races, the relative value of the characters peculiar to each, in a scientific point of view." To Agassiz realism meant acknowledging that there were superior and inferior races: "it seems to us to be mock-philanthropy and mock-philosophy to assume that all races have the same abilities, enjoy the same powers, and show the same natural dispositions, and that in consequence of this equality they are entitled to the same position in human society." History, he said, demonstrated that different races were not naturally equal. Educational programs for "the inferior races," argued Agassiz, should be based on the recognition of the inequality of human races.[41]

When it became clear that Agassiz had openly endorsed polygenesis, Nott was delighted. In a letter to Morton he commented that "with Agassiz in the war the battle is ours. This was an immense accession for we shall not only have his name, but the timid will come out from their hiding places."[42] Nott was right, for with Agassiz convinced, the doctrine of polygenesis achieved general scientific respectability in America. What is equally clear is that Agassiz had endorsed the innate inequality of human races as well as their separate origin.

By the late 1840s the racial question was at the heart of scholarly discussion in the United States, and a variety of writers tried their hand at reconciling racial diversity and religion. The concept of racial inequality had clearly carried the day, but some scholars and many clergymen and laymen were still anxious that the new theories should somehow be reconciled with the account in Genesis. The most general disagreement with Nott and Morton was not that they had divided the world into superior and inferior races, but that in adopting polygenesis as the original reason for racial differences, they had challenged the Mosaic account of Creation. When Charleston minister and naturalist John Bachman presented a comprehensive defense of the unity of the human species in the early 1850s, he had no intention of arguing for Negro equality; he simply maintained that the obvious differences between the races had been brought about by a process of variation that had become permanent.[43]

Bachman turned verbal somersaults to reconcile Genesis, racial variation, fixity of species, and Negro inferiority, but he was a scholar and a fine naturalist. Others who took sides in the scientific racial argument were simply amateurs, yet they were often given as much weight as those who claimed to be engaged in empirical research. New York lawyer William Frederick Van Amringe, in a long, diffuse book published in 1848, argued that while all men sprang from Adam and Eve, God had made four distinct species soon after the flood. In reaching his conclusions Van Amringe depended on instinct and observation, not on scientific measurement. Distinct races had existed for nearly four thousand years, and only among the "Shemetic" species (essentially Caucasian) did the elements of civilization exist. By "the special favor of the Creator," said Van Amringe, this Shemetic species "is more highly favored in constitution than others." While other species were not as well endowed, it was the duty of the Shemetic species to help them as much as possible: "it must go on conquering and to conquer, until every species of man shall have been brought to the highest degree of perfection of which the nature of each is susceptible." Van Amringe did not even suggest that he was trying to base his work on any empirical research, but he was taken seriously and his views disseminated widely through the politically influential *Democratic Review*.[44]

When in 1852 Dr. S. Kneeland wrote an introduction to the American edition of an English work on race, he commented that the English author supported the position of diversity of races which had been maintained by Agassiz, Van Amringe, and Morton. Kneeland saw nothing strange in lumping together the conclusions of two of the most eminent men of science in America with the amateur meanderings of a lawyer. Kneeland said the key question was not whether a race could be improved, but whether all had the same capacity for being improved. "History need not be very deeply consulted," he wrote, "to convince one that the white races, without an exception, have attained a considerable degree of civilization and refinement; and that the dark races have always stopped at a considerably lower level. There must have been a time when the Caucasian was as ignorant and uncivilized as the American [Indian] or the African; all were once simple children of Nature . . . the former have advanced, the latter have degenerated from the original type of their species." All the evidence, wrote Kneeland, led to the conclusion "that the dark races are inferiorly organized, and cannot, to the same extent as the white races, understand the laws of Nature."[45]

By the early 1850s the inherent inequality of races was simply accepted as a scientific fact in America, and most of the discussion now concerned either the religious problem of accepting polygenesis as an explanation of racial differences or the problem of exactly defining the different races. The general tendency was for greater and greater refinement of racial divisions, both among the white and the colored races, but some, in their zeal to debase the nonwhites, were willing to accept the Caucasians as a unified group. In an extremely popular work on Negroes and slavery published in 1853, New York physician John H. Van Evrie erased all racial, national, and class distinctions among Caucasians in order utterly to condemn the blacks. Van Evrie said of the Caucasian that "the flowing beard, projecting forehead, oval features, erect posture and lordly presence, stamp him the master man wherever found." The colored races, he argued, were capable of only limited development, and he suggested that perhaps Confucius, and many other ancient Chinese, were Caucasian.[46]

Morton's death in 1851 was a severe blow to the American school, but its work reached a climax in 1854 when Josiah C. Nott collaborated with Egyptologist and professional lecturer George R. Gliddon to produce the ponderous *Types of Mankind*. The book was an attempt to present all the evidence which had been advanced to prove that distinct races had existed from the beginning of time, and that they had been created separately, with different intellectual, moral, and physical capabilities. Gliddon was a good friend of Nott's and Morton's and he was constantly involved in what he hoped would be money-making projects. Even more than Nott he lacked caution, and he delighted in riling the religious. After Morton's death in 1851 he had written to E. G. Squier that together with Nott he could carry on "the great cause." If they could all agree on some publication, he wrote, "I will cooperate in giving their 'Reverence' a d---d deal of trouble!"[47]

The patchwork *Types*, with long separate sections by Nott and by Gliddon, also had the prestige of containing an essay by Agassiz; it began with a biographical memoir of Morton by Dr. Henry S. Patterson of Philadelphia. Although expensive it sold thirty-five hundred copies in four months and went through ten editions by 1871. Gliddon was intensely concerned with puffing it in the press, and he wrote some of his own reviews.[48] The book's tone was set in Patterson's biographical memoir on Morton. While writing it, in December 1853, Patterson heard of the death of a young friend, Richard H. Kern, who had been killed by Indians while with a surveying party in the Great Basin of the Rockies. Patterson cried out in a footnote that Kern needed to be avenged: "We have had too much of sentimentalism about the Red-man. It is time that cant was stopped now. Not all the cinnamon-colored vermin west of the Mississippi are worth one drop of that noble-heart's blood. The busy brain, the artist's eye, the fine taste, the hand so ready with either pen or pencil, — could these be restored to us again, they would be cheaply purchased back if it cost the extermination of every miserable Pah-Utah under heaven!" Subsequent editions retained this outburst.[49]

With Nott and Gliddon bearing the main burden of the writing, the work had a dogmatic tone. They argued that "beyond dispute" all the nations and tribes mentioned in the Pentateuch were Caucasians. The diversity of races was a scientific fact. There had been many original pairs in different zones of the world. The races were different, and the differences were permanent. In four thousand years, the authors argued, the Negroes had not advanced a single step from their savage state. All history and scientific observation "seem to render fugacious all probability of a brighter future for these organically inferior types, however sad the thought may be." The American Indian was as irredeemable as the Negro: "It is a clear as the sun at noon-day, that in a few generations more the last of these Red men will be numbered with the dead . . . a civilized *full-blooded* Indian does not exist among them." Nott, who had seen the remnants of Indian tribes in the vicinity of Mobile, claimed direct expertise: "To one who has lived among American Indians, it is vain to talk of civilizing them. You might as well attempt to change the nature of the buffalo."[50]

The Caucasian, according to *Types*, was not one race, but a group of related races which were the sole standard-bearers of civilization: "The Creator has implanted in this group of races an instinct that, in spite of themselves, drives them through all difficulties, to carry out their great mission of civilizing the earth. It is not reason, or philanthropy, which urges them on; but it is destiny." By expanding outward, covering the earth, and "supplanting inferior types," the Caucasian races were "fulfilling a law of nature." This was no peaceful mission, for the inferior races were doomed: "Nations and races, like individuals, have each an especial destiny: some are born to rule, and others to be ruled . . . No two distinctly-marked races can dwell together on equal terms. Some races, moreover, appear destined to live and prosper for a time, until the destroying race comes, which is to exterminate and supplant them." The mission preached in Nott's and Gliddon's *Types* was that of a superior race or races making the world a better place by overwhelming and exterminating those inferior races that stood in their path. The best and fittest would survive to create a better world: "human progress has arisen mainly from the war of the races. All the great impulses which have been given to it from time to time have been the results of conquests and colonizations."[51] The polygenetic arguments of *Types* were soon to be overturned, but its racial message reflected well the dog-eat-dog philosophy of white world mission that had ended Enlightenment dreams of general human improvement.

Those who hated slavery at times found hope for black improvability, and friends of the Indian still hoped that through education the Indians would become indistinguishable from the Americans; but the idea of distinct races with innately different capabilities was firmly engrained in American scientific thinking by the middle of the century. Polygenesis remained controversial, though the most important American ethnologists accepted it; but the idea of a hierarchy of races, with the Caucasians clearly and permanently at the top, was generally accepted. American science provided Americans with a confident explanation of why blacks were enslaved, why Indians were exterminated, and why white Americans were expanding their settlements rapidly over adjacent lands. These ideas did not exist in scholarly isolation. Racial differences were a vital issue for Americans. The slavery question was at the center of American politics, the dilemmas of Indian relations constantly erupted to disturb the central government as well as the western states, and by the 1830s and 1840s involvement in the Southwest and California thrust the Mexicans into American racial discussions. By mid-century the science of man was a practical, not an abstract, subject, and Americans eagerly read popular discussions of the new scientific theories.

8
The Dissemination of Scientific Racialism

> The antagonism of races is working itself out in every instance where two races are put in collision by the quicker or slower extinction of the inferior and feebler race.
>
> *De Bow's Review*, February 1854

By the mid-nineteenth century even those New England journals which were most reluctant to accept the new ideas readily admitted that race had become a topic of general intellectual and popular interest. The *American Whig Review* commented in 1849 that "ethnology is the . . . science of the age," and in the following year that "the scientific study of humanity, from being for a century back the theme of a few speculative philosophers, is become at last a topic of general and even popular interest." The *Massachusetts Quarterly Review* commented that "a decided impulse to the study of Ethnology has manifested itself in every scientific circle."[1]

This interest was not based simply on concern with slavery or the fate of the Indians. There was also a widespread fascination with the general question of whether mankind was divided into superior and inferior races and with the explosive issue of whether Genesis accurately described the origin of all human beings. This interest was reflected both in the amount of space devoted to such issues in the major periodicals and by the way in which the assumptions and the very phrases of the new scientific defenders of innate racial differences appeared in the mouths of the politicians. Americans were reminded constantly that the observable differences between races could be shown scientifically to be based on physical and mental factors which had remained the same throughout history and against which environment and education were helpless. The theory of polygenesis, with its direct challenge to the Bible and organized religion, was often played down or even ignored, but arguments for innate mental and physical differences between races enjoyed wide acceptance in the publications of the 1840s and 1850s.

In the South the new ideas permeated all types of periodicals—literary, political, agricultural—at the earliest date and assumed the strongest form. The eagerness with which the South wished to justify its slave system by proving that the Negroes were innately incapable of benefiting from freedom helped the theories about general racial distinctions gain wide acceptance. Proslavery pamphlets helped to disseminate the same material, and these pamphlets, along with a variety of other articles on the same subject, were often first printed in southern periodicals. These periodicals printed numerous articles advancing supposedly scientific reasons for black inferiority.

From the mid-1830s on it became common to assert that the Negroes were at least a permanently inferior variety, if not a completely separate, species. In 1834 a physician who said he had practised in Africa argued in the *Farmer's Register*, published in Virginia, that the stomach and skeleton of Negroes, particularly their spine, differed fundamentally from those of the whites. "That they are a distinct race," he said, "I think is evident from these, and other peculiarities."[2] In the following year Thomas Cooper defended slavery in the *Southern Literary Journal* and took issue with those who argued that Negroes were equal in intellectual capacity to the whites: "The blacks may be of the same species, for the mixed progeny will breed. But they are an inferior variety of the animal, man. I appeal to the facial angle of Cowper [sic], Blumenback, White, and Lawrence. I appeal to the more accurate observations of the Phrenologists and Organoligists . . . Ignorant and superficial people may laugh at Phrenology. I am not writing for such. The whole multitude of Physiologists are with me, in Europe and here."[3] As early as 1838 Robert G. Harper indicated the rapidity with which the new arguments were gaining acceptance in the South: "That the African negro is an inferior variety of the human race, is, I think, now generally admitted."[4] W. G. Ramsay of South Carolina, in two articles in the *Southern Agriculturalist* in 1839, argued that environment had not produced the essential difference between blacks and whites. The blood of the parents, he said, not climate, brought about the essential difference in moral and intellectual qualities: "We are almost tempted to believe that there must have been more Adams' than one, each variety of colour having its own original parent." Even with the same advantages, he added, blacks could not attain the same eminence as whites.[5]

If whites generally were considered innately superior, it was perfectly logical to assume innate differences between other races of the human species. A Washington physician argued in the *Southern Literary Messenger* in 1839 that there were differences in innate capacity between the five basic human stocks: "How else can we account for the fact, that from the earliest periods of which history presents any record, to the present day, the Caucasian variety has invariably held the same undisputed and enviable superiority over all the other races?" The whites, he said, had always held sway over "the four inferior varieties." The dark races were capable of some improvement, but could never equal the white.[6]

In the early 1840s an increased emphasis was placed on the scientific basis of black inferiority. "The knife of the anatomist has demonstrated," it was stated of the blacks in October 1842, "that the brain proper, is smaller in them than in other races of men."[7] In the following month, in the short-lived *Magnolia*, the condemnation of the Negro was linked to the problem of the origin of mankind and general racial hierarchies. The author accepted the account of Creation as given in Genesis, but argued for later divine intervention to create races with different capacities. He accepted Blumenbach's "beautiful and accurate system" of division into five races, and he also laid great stress on the evidence that could be adduced from the facial angles originally described by Pieter Camper. Distinctions between races were innate and did not depend on climate: "the African race is, and has ever been, far inferior, in natural powers of intellect, to the white man." The size and shape of the skull in the Negro, he said, approximated that of the orangutan: "These peculiarities are permanent and universal." Two years before Morton produced his major scientific treatise to prove it, this author confidently asserted that the Egyptians were not black. His conclusion was that "there are broad natural distinctions between the several races of men . . . the Ethiopian, or Negro race, is inferior to the others, especially the Caucassian, or white, in that peculiar physical organization which alone accompanies high intellectual power." Earlier in the same year a writer in *Magnolia* had mentioned "these grown children, the Negro Race, of whose absolute, permanent and hopeless inferiority, no philosopher can now entertain a question."[8]

In the nation at large theories of innate racial differences were somewhat slower to achieve overt acceptance than in the South, but in the 1840s the new ideas infiltrated every section of the country. When in December 1850 the *American Whig Review* surveyed the history of racial theories, it said of the five divisions of the human species made famous by Blumenbach that "these have been too trivialized by our phrenological hornbooks to need repetition in this place. Who has not heard of the Caucasian, Ethiopian, Mongolian, Malayan, and American races?"[9] Although this quotation gives too much weight to the phrenologists (for there were many other influences), they had done much to spread on a national level that interest in the physical basis of racial differences that for a time had most immediate attraction for Southerners. "Practical" phrenology became a fad among all classes of society in the 1840s. Although phrenology later lost its intellectual support, those interested in the commercial aspects of the subject widely disseminated the arguments regarding innate differences between races that had been common in American phrenological writing since 1830.

When George Combe visited the United States at the end of the 1830s, he noted in his journal that the practical phrenologists were numerous, and that in Philadelphia, New York, and Boston phrenological establishments sold casts and gave readings for set fees. In the 1840s and 1850s individuals traveled from village to village, carrying charts, casts of heads, and phrenological handbooks, prepared to give an introductory lecture, and even prepared to read a head for a set fee. The oracles of practical phrenology in the United States were the Fowler brothers, Orson and Lorenzo. Together with their sister Charlotte, her husband, and Lorenzo's wife, they established a large-scale business in New York. They published books, ran a museum, sold equipment to practical phrenologists, read heads, and branched out into the fields of mesmerism, hydrotherapy, hygiene, marriage guidance, and temperance. By the late 1840s there was a considerable popular interest in phrenology; phrenological handbooks (often given away free with a reading) had a mass circulation, and phrenological references were abundant in the general literature of the period. Books, charts, and popular lectures made phrenological terms common currency in the mid-nineteenth century.[10]

The Fowler books on phrenology reached every corner of the country, and the message they carried on racial matters was that developed by Combe, Caldwell, and other scientific phrenologists: Caucasians were for the most part capable of indefinite improvement, while other races were irredeemably limited by the deficiencies of their original cerebral organization. All-important were the frontal and coronal portions of the head and brain which contained the intellectual and the moral organs. "The European race (including their descendants in America)," wrote the Fowlers, "possess a much larger endowment of these organs, and also of their corresponding faculties, than any other portion of the human species. Hence their intellectual and moral superiority over all other races of men." The frontal, coronal parts of the head were extremely prominent in some great men such as Daniel Webster, while "men of ordinary talent, possess a respectable endowment of these organs. The Hindoos, Chinese, American Indians, and the African race, still less, but much more than the lower order of animals."[11]

In regard to blacks and American Indians, the Fowlers generally followed Combe in giving an assessment more common among the phrenologists than among the other writers on race, an assessment in which the usual role of blacks and Indians was reversed to put the blacks on top. Although Combe wavered in his later writings, most of his arguments on race placed the Negro above the American Indian in inherent capacity. He argued that "in the Negro brain the moral and Reflecting organs are of larger size, in proportion to the organs of the animal propensities . . . than in that of the Indian. The Negro, is, therefore, naturally more submissive, docile, intelligent, patient, trustworthy, and susceptible of kindly emotions, and less cruel, cunning, and vindictive, than the other race." Combe's emphasis on black docility suited well his opinion that slavery could safely be abolished. Yet in placing the black above the Indian, Combe condemned both: "The one is like the wolf or the fox, the other like the dog. In both, the brain is inferior in size, particularly in the moral and intellectual regions, to that of the Anglo-Saxon race, and hence the foundation of the natural superiority of the latter over both."[12]

The Fowlers asserted that in Negroes there was a striking correspondence between their present character and their phrenological development, although they held out some hope for Negroes with education and cultivation. Their general prognosis, however, was unfavorable, for Negroes possessed a "large, or very large tune, which inspires them with melody," but they had smaller reasoning organs. These "smaller reasoning organs," the Fowlers said, "would give them but little depth of intellect, and a feeble judgment, with very little talent for contriving and planning."[13] The phrenologists generally classified the Negro as harmless and stupid.

The Fowlers were as pessimistic regarding the future of the American Indians as were most other phrenologists; little or no hope was held out for the success of the Indian civilization policies. "Their small amount of brain in the coronal region of the head," wrote the Fowlers, "when compared with their immense development of the animal passions and selfish feelings, would bring them chiefly under the dominion of the animal nature of man, and render them little susceptible of becoming civilized, humanized, and educated." The Fowlers claimed that civilization among the Cherokee had been possible because members of that tribe had a different cerebral organization from that of other Indians. The animal portion of their brain was smaller, the Fowlers claimed, and the human reasoning portion larger. To the Fowlers the Cherokee were an exception.[14]

From the first interest in phrenology among the intellectuals in the 1820s to its popularization in the middle of the century, the phrenologists defended the idea of inherent racial differences and the concept of inferior and superior races. They found in skulls and heads what they wanted to find: a physical confirmation of supposedly observed cultural traits. Whites were inventive, creative, powerful; blacks were docile and ignorant; Indians were savage and intractable. But the phrenologists also made a basic a priori assumption. Although the whites varied in the conformation of their heads and thus of their brains, they were in general capable of vast improvement. Non-Caucasian races were assumed to have an inherent physical organization that sharply limited the extent of improvement that could be expected. Environment, circumstance, and education could only modify the non-Caucasian; they could not effect a transformation.

With the publication of Morton's *Crania Americana* in 1839 and the burgeoning national scientific interest in the new racial questions, the popularization of racial ideas soon spread far beyond the southern and the phrenological journals. Also, far more attention was paid to polygenesis as a reason for innate differences between races. By August 1842 theories of polygenesis had had enough impact to elicit an article in the politically influential *Democratic Review*, published in New York, defending the common descent of all races from Adam and Eve. While acknowledging the inferiority of other races to the Caucasian and laying great stress on skull and brain structure, the author would not concede the impossibility of improvement.[15] Later in the same year a reviewer of one of Morton's pamphlets rejected his contention that the Indians were a separate and inferior race. Yet even so, the author concluded that the Indians were doomed to extinction.[16]

Views of the nature of the Indian in the periodical literature of the early 1840s showed a somewhat inconsistent mixture of the new racial theories and an older tone of literary regret. More consistent was the assumption that the Indians were, in any event, becoming extinct. The *Democratic Review* from its inception in the 1830s questioned literary idealization of the Indian and asked for a more "realistic" attitude. A reviewer in 1838 objected to the "sickly sentimentality" that was wasted on savage tribes. The Indians had suffered from white contact, he admitted, but "they have suffered, because of their own inherent vices of character and condition" rather than from white faults. A few years later a reviewer praised a work of George Catlin's on the Indians, except for its "over-enthusiasm for savage life," and thought the reader left the book almost convinced that the savages were humane and worthy of consideration. Soon, however, "our own race is restored in our minds to its elevated position."[17]

In the early 1840s some writers in the *Southern Quarterly Review* were still writing of the Indians in the "noble savage" tradition, but a harsher portrait soon dominated. In 1843 an author attacked those writers who had tried to maintain that all the races of the world were equally capable of improvement: "this they do in utter defiance of history, which unanswerably disproves the fallacy. The Zingalee or Gypsies, the North American Indians, the negroes of St. Domingo, have shown themselves wholly incapable of civilization."[18] In the following year another writer in the review concluded that the civilization of a barbarous race could be effected "only genetically, or by intermarriage." With no prospect of intermarriage, the Indian was doomed: "The snow melts not more certainly before the meridian sun, than the savage races of the earth before the advancing tides of civilization."[19]

In the second half of the 1840s, as the work of the American school of ethnology became far more widely known, the racial debate was of constant interest in the periodicals, both northern and southern. The *Democratic Review* now rapidly succumbed to the new ideas. A writer discussing slavery in 1846 pointed out that not one of the black nations in Africa from which the slaves had been drawn "ever possessed any literature, or even an alphabet, however rude; and the spoken languages are miserably poor. This is, and probably always will be, the case in Africa." The author decided that, in some mysterious way, the blacks, like the Indians, would eventually disappear from the United States. The time would come, he said, when the expensive labor of slaves would no longer be profitable: "When the blacks shall have been thrown upon their own resources, the increase in their numbers will stop, and ultimately they must become extinct as a race on this continent."[20] The vague assertion that other races would simply fade away under the pressure of white Americans became increasingly common by mid-century.

By 1850 the *Democratic Review* was prepared to print that "few or none now seriously adhere to the theory of the *unity* of races." Not Morton, or Nott, or Agassiz, but the New York lawyer Van Amringe was acknowledged as the writer who had shattered the remaining doubts. The magazine simply maintained that there was no conflict with religion: "The whole state of the science at this moment, seems to indicate that there are several distinct races of men on the face of the earth, with entirely different capacities, physical and mental, that these races are known to have existed for at least five thousand years entirely distinct, and to have been as much so at that remote period as they are at this moment, retaining their specific characteristics through every variety of circumstance, climate and condition; yet, nevertheless, the origin of all these distinct races was from Adam through Noah."[21] This statement represented a grafting of Genesis onto the arguments evolved by the American school to defend their theories of separate Creation.

Those who attempted to argue that the unity of the human race was necessary to maintain the truth of the Scriptures were attacked in the pages of the *Democratic Review*. The Reverend Thomas Smyth was taken to task for trying to demonstrate, "in spite of all the evidence of our senses to the contrary," that the different human races were one. The reviewer was not prepared to accept "the brutal and soul-degrading theory that the white species are on a level with the incapable blacks."[22] Not content with a simple review, the *Democratic Review* three times in little more than a year devoted articles to a discussion of Smyth's work. What really interested the journal was not the controversy over Genesis but rather those theories of innate racial differences that could be used to defend existing American circumstances and policies. If necessary, it was said in an article in September 1850, it could be conceded that all men are descended from Adam and Noah. The key matter was the existing differences between races—these were "radical and inconvertible."[23] Racial differences could not be altered by circumstances, philanthropy, or education: "The fact that the dark races are utterly incapable of attaining to that intellectual superiority which marks the white race is too evident to be disputed."[24] When John Bigelow, in his *Jamaica in 1850*, argued that Jamaican blacks would eventually create a prosperous state, the *Democratic Review* vigorously disagreed. The blacks, it was argued, could not benefit properly from schools, churches, and a productive environment. By his own description of Jamaica, the reviewer argued, Bigelow condemned the black race: "He shows its complete inferiority to the white race, and its utter incapacity to maintain by itself the state of civilization, to which it had been advanced by white aid."[25]

By the early 1850s the *Democratic Review* simply assumed that it had been scientifically proven that other races were incapable of reaching the level of the white race. Although polygenesis was not considered essential to this conclusion, multiple Creations were often suggested or implied. "The unity of the human race was not long since regarded as a thing fixed according to Mosaic history," wrote a reviewer in December 1851. "It is now demonstrated that the origin of man was diverse, and that races have, since all time, been what they are now."[26] Religious qualms seldom concerned the journal.

The new racial views received their coldest reception among the intellectual establishment of New England. Consistently rejected in this region were those explanations of inequality that directly challenged the Mosaic account of Creation. Writers in both the *North American Review* and the *American Whig Review* attacked those who were undermining the Bible through their scientific theories. When the *American Whig Review* discussed Robert Chambers's *Vestiges of Creation*, the pre-Darwinian evolutionary work that shocked most of its reviewers, the author protested that the book possesses "in a supereminent degree, all those traits of impudence, arrogance, and profound ignorance of Revelation, that characterize the whole genus."[27] The same journal also took exception to one of Josiah C. Nott's pamphlets, arguing that "the author does not treat the historical character of Scripture with the respect usually given it by the most learned and valuable authorities."[28] Unlike the *Democratic Review*, the *American Whig Review* commended to its readers Thomas Smyth's work on the unity of human races.[29] The *New Englander* was particularly disturbed by Louis Agassiz's espousal of polygenesis and by his argument that the account in Genesis referred only to the origin of the white race. Obviously worried by "the high authority" of Agassiz, the reviewer regretted that "science" appeared to be saying that the rest of the population of the world could not be improved and given a true Christian civilization.[30]

At the heart of the religious trepidation was a fear best expressed not in a New England periodical, where it was most common, but in a southern journal. In the *Southern Literary Messenger* William Archer Cocke attacked those theorists who said the events in the Bible applied to only one branch of human beings. "If there are distinct species of Man," he said, "then the Bible is untrue; if there are other races than the descendants of Adam, they are free from the penalty 'of man's first disobedience' and the tragic scene of Calvary but a mockery and a delusion." Most did not take their fears this far, but the religious orthodox tried to shun any arguments that endorsed multiple original Creations.[31]

Yet while New England journals placed a heavy emphasis on the defense of Scripture from theories which challenged the literal truth of Genesis, they increasingly found themselves on the defensive or even succumbing to the beliefs in inherent racial inequality. In 1849, in a long article on American ethnology, an author in the *American Whig Review* quoted Morton on the inferiority of the Indian race and Prichard's praise of Morton's work, before he eventually chose to come down on the side of the Indian capacity for improvement: "It has not yet been satisfactorily shown that the American race is deficient in intellect, or that there is that wide difference in their 'moral nature, their affections and consciences' which some have asserted." If the Indians still showed no improvement after being treated as human beings and in accordance with an enlightened policy, it would then be time to say they were inferior.[32] In the following year the review retreated still further. After discussing the general scholarly and popular interest in the study of race, the author surveyed the whole history of racial theories. Although he followed the general tone of the magazine in being careful to avoid wild assertions of superiority and inferiority, he leaned toward a theory of multiple races.[33]

Although New England periodicals generally had a more cautious tone than those of other regions, the new racial ideas were given a wide circulation there, and the elevation of the Caucasian over other races was challenged only by a minority. A belief in monogenesis in no way precluded a belief in innate differences within races as they existed in the mid-nineteenth century. A review article on Prescott's *Conquest of Mexico* in an 1849 issue of the *Massachusetts Quarterly Review* was critical of Prichard's idea of the unity of races, stressed the "inferior organization" of the Indians, and lauded the Anglo-Saxon. The Anglo-Saxon, it was argued, was "eminently Caucasian." He would not mix "his proud blood, in stable wedlock with another race. There seems to be a natural antipathy to such unions with the black, or even the red, or yellow races of men — an antipathy almost peculiar to this remarkable tribe, the exterminator of other races."[34]

In the *New Englander* the distinctions were made a little more gently. The most perfect type of the human race, a reviewer pointed out in 1850, was found in the Caucasus: "From the peculiar characteristics of this type, the others all depart, in different degrees, towards those which are inferior — the hue of the complexion becomes less varied and beautiful, the symmetry of the form less elegant, and the development of intellectual, and even of physical vigor, inferior; till in the extreme varieties man seems almost of a different species." This writer leaned toward original unity, but he emphasized the nineteenth-century racial mission of the United States. The Puritan should evangelize and elevate other races: "Then shall each inferior race learn according to its measure, whatever is valuable in the freedom and piety which bless this land."[35] Even when condemning other races to permanent inferiority, many New Englanders longed to elevate them to the limit of their potential.

By the middle of the century the writings of the American school of ethnology were receiving their widest circulation in the South. It was also in the South that the school's emphasis on the original separation of races was used most strongly to elevate the white race and condemn all others to inferiority or even extinction. The most important single figure in disseminating the new racial theories in extreme form was Josiah C. Nott. His books, his pamphlets, his articles in professional journals all spread the new ideas in a most strident manner, but he also reached a wider public through his impact on the *Southern Quarterly Review* and on *De Bow's Review*, both journals of considerable influence in the South. Nott's ideas were debated vigorously in the pages of the former and given considerable support in the latter through the efforts of his friend, James De Bow.

The *Southern Quarterly Review* was obsessed with racial matters from the mid-1840s to the mid-1850s. It addressed the question directly in 1845 by publishing an article that took issue with Nott's attack on monogenesis. The journal gave him space for a reply and in the following years was happy to publish his articles.[36] Nott used the journal both to defend the idea of the innate inequality of races and to advance his arguments for separate Creations. His regular theme was that an irreconcilable gulf existed between the different races, and that nonwhite races could not be raised to the white level through education or changed circumstance. Blacks, of course, were dismissed as unimprovable, but Nott ranged far to attack other races. "Their wants would seem to be few, their capacity limited, and incapable of development," he wrote of the American Indians in 1846. The Indians, he suggested, belonged to a different species.[37]

Nott was an ardent advocate of polygenesis and did not fear to challenge the Bible. "A powerful argument against their Adamic origin," he said of the Indians, "is the impossibility of civilizing or christianizing them."[38] In two articles in 1850 Nott took racial inequality as acknowledged and simply devoted most of his space to arguments for original diversity.[39] In the first he used the history of the Jews to argue that a race stayed the same throughout time; in the second he used the work of the Egyptologists to show the antiquity of the white, black, and other races and to demonstrate the limitations of the biblical account of the origin of man. "The physical history of mankind, as wrought out in the last few years," he said, "is, to our minds, wholly irreconcilable with the account given in the Book of Genesis."[40]

In the early 1850s the *Southern Quarterly Review* eagerly discussed all the main books on race and accepted without question the idea of innate inequality, but tried to maintain a balance between the polygenesis and the monogenesis positions.[41] When Nott and Gliddon's *Types of Mankind* appeared in 1854, the reviewer in the *Quarterly* objected to its flippant tone toward the Bible, but he agreed with the authors' contention that distinct races had existed throughout recorded history: "Either there were separate creations of different types of mankind, or man must have existed on earth for Chiliads of years. Both of these propositions may be true — one of them must be true."[42] Either proposition contradicted the biblical account. In the following year the editor partially offset the stream of articles which either explicitly or implicitly endorsed polygenesis by printing an article defending unity.[43] This concession to the religious orthodox in no way affected the arguments for the innate inferiority of some races. The general arguments printed in the journal supported the contention that blacks were slaves to the Caucasians "because of natural, unalterable, and eternal inferiority."[44] It did not matter if man arose from one pair or three thousand pairs, it was argued; races in the mid-nineteenth century were essentially different.[45] "Without entering into the vexed question of the origin of races," another author said, "we take the generally undisputed admission, that the races, as they now exist, are characterized by essential differences in their moral and mental constitution — that these differences are so deeply rooted, that education can do little more than modify them in individuals."[46] Infinite progress was now possible only to the Caucasians, and some thought even the branches of the Caucasians were unequal.

De Bow's Review, which was founded in Charleston in 1846 but immediately moved to New Orleans, welcomed the new racial views. From its first issues it combined a rampant racialism with its general purpose as a magazine devoted to commercial matters. De Bow was a great admirer and friend of Nott's, and the magazine became a major forum for Nott's views and, in exaggerated form, the views of the whole American school of ethnology. The scientific opinions were used in a direct and practical manner to defend the perpetual enslavement of the Negro, the extermination of the Indian, and the maintenance and enlargement of the American Caucasian dominion. By 1854 even polygenesis was accepted without question: "The doctrine of the Unity of Race, so long believed by the world, is ascertained to be false. We are not all descended from one pair of human beings. The fact is now as well established in the scientific world as that a horse cannot produce a cat or a lion a mouse. The negro till the end of time will still be a negro, and the Indian still an Indian. Cultivation and association with the superior race produce only injury to the inferior one. Their part in this mysterious world-drama has been played, and, like the Individual, the race must cease to exist."[47] Nott's and Gliddon's *Types* was welcomed by *De Bow's Review* as the definitive word on the subject of racial diversity.[48]

Blacks and Indians fared equally badly with De Bow, partly because of the influence of Nott's views, and the journal regularly advanced evidence to defend the institution of slavery. All the old arguments for black inferiority were repeated, with a firmer reliance on supposed scientific facts. Dr. Samuel A. Cartwright of New Orleans, whose views received wide attention in the South in the 1850s, placed great emphasis on the supposed physical peculiarities of the Negro race. His conclusion was that the Negro was a "slave by nature" because of specific physical limitations: "his blood is blacker than the white man's"; "his brain is a ninth or tenth less than other races of man, his facial angle smaller"; "deficiency of red blood in the pulmonary and arterial systems" caused indolence and apathy.[49] Southern physicians, who theoretically were in the best position to comment on the essential physical unity of the human species, were in the vanguard of those "discovering" basic physical differences.

Nott often used *De Bow's Review* to expound his views on the importance of racial purity. If the superior race was not kept pure, then it would not maintain the necessary talents to rule and control lesser races. In an effort to make his ideas of separate races conform to Buffon's definition of species, he continued to stress that "hybrids" produced by the crossing of races tended toward infertility. That the different races of mankind could, in fact, easily interbreed and produce fertile offspring was a major stumbling block to those who wished to make the different races separate species. Morton had dealt with this problem by simply questioning the whole hybridity argument as a basis for defining species and had clashed with John Bachman on this point. Nott, however, simply created the evidence he wanted. He argued that the offspring of whites and blacks was less fertile, and that such a mixture, if not replenished by further interbreeding, would in the course of time die out. Nott also used this argument as a means of further exalting the Teutonic branch of the white race. Southern Europeans, and in general those of somewhat darker skins, he argued, were more successful than the purer white races in producing fertile offspring by interbreeding with blacks: "our observations have led us to the opinion," he wrote in 1851, "that the cross of the pure white stock (by which we mean the descendants of the ancient Germans) and the negro, does not, when kept separate, produce an indefinitely prolific variety, at least in the Atlantic and North Western States, at a distance from the tropics or native latitude of the negro."[50] Any racial mixture weakened the superior stock.

"A great aim of philanthropy," Nott argued, "should be to keep the ruling races of the world as pure and as wise as possible, for it is only through them that the others can be made prosperous and happy."[51] The difficulty with this self-serving suggestion was that in much of his writing Nott made it quite clear that prosperity and happiness were not to be the lot of the non-Caucasian races. He often suggested that the white race, and particularly the Germanic branch of the white race, was destined to replace other races in large parts of the world. For Nott the Indian was a useful model for depicting the results of a clash between a superior and an inferior race. The Indian, Nott wrote in 1847, "is an untamable, carnivorous animal, which is fading away before civilization . . . the race must soon be extinct—even the pure blood Mexicans, who I have no question are a different race from the aboriginal savage, are going down in darkness to their long home."[52] The theme of inevitable extinction was constantly reiterated, and the final judgment was that missionary and civilization efforts were useless: "Do what we will, the Indian remains the Indian still. He is not a creature susceptible of civilization; and all contact of him with the white race is death. He dwindles before them—imbibing all their vices, and none of their virtues. He can no more be civilized than the leopard can change his spots. His race is run, and probably he has performed his earthly mission. He is now gradually disappearing, to give place to a higher order of beings. The order of nature must have its course."[53]

The wild, ruthless views of Scotsman Robert Knox's *Races of Men* were compatible with the arguments being propounded in *De Bow's Review*, and in 1852 Knox's ideas were openly acknowledged as the inspiration for an article in the journal. It was argued that God had given the whites, for their own preservation and purity, a strong feeling of racial antagonism. When superior and inferior races met, the only hope for the latter was serfdom or slavery. To clash was fatal for the inferior race: "The antagonism of races is working itself out in every instance where two races are put in collision by the quicker or slower extinction of the inferior and feebler race." Some races would simply be exterminated, others engulfed. A writer in the *Southern Quarterly Review* said that within a century or two the Indians in America would be extinct and the Spanish, French, and German settlements "swallowed up in the Anglo-Saxon tongue and type."[54]

The idea of inferior races simply disappearing under Caucasian pressure was given major impetus among American writers on race by the contrast of what was happening to the Indian tribes and what was happening to southern blacks. The Indians had tried to resist the will of the whites and were being exterminated; the blacks had been kept in slavery and were increasing in numbers. The fate of the Indian awaited those who did not yield to the all-encompassing Caucasian civilization, and this fate was made inevitable by the irreversible physical basis of their inferiority. One author managed in a remarkable analogy to extend the experience of the American Indians to China: "The extinction of the red race upon this continent may be said to be almost consummated; and China, which by a sort of instinct, excluded the whites for thousands of years, is now open to a similar influence, and a crisis is reached in the history of the dark species of man." The ultimate world predominance of the white race was apparently certain, the author argued, for the dark species had always receded and died out when encountering the whites.[55] A reviewer in the *Southern Quarterly Review* said he found Robert Knox's book on race a "startling work" and too extreme, but he quoted from it in his own attempt to justify slavery on the basis of the diversity of races. He reiterated Knox's point that "slavery . . . or extermination, seems to be the fate of the dark races, when invaded by or otherwise brought into juxtaposition with the white."[56] Although Knox's wild ramblings were extreme, his arguments fitted neatly into the American pattern of black slavery and Indian disappearance.

The transformation in scientific racial thinking was striking between 1815 and 1850, but equally striking was the manner in which the new ideas became a topic of popular discussion. By 1850 the natural inequality of races was a scientific fact which was published widely. One did not have to read obscure books to know that the Caucasians were innately superior, and that they were responsible for civilization in the world, or to know that inferior races were destined to be overwhelmed or even to disappear. These ideas permeated the main American periodicals and in the second half of the century formed part of the accepted truth of America's schoolbooks.[57]

The differentiation into superior and inferior races had gone so far that by 1850 practically all of the most important writers on race in America believed that there had been separate Creations of the different races, and though many periodicals tried to straddle the fence on the issue, practically all gave wide publicity to polygenetic views. When *Putnam's* reviewed Nott's and Gliddon's *Types*, the reviewer pointed out that the "American school" had flatly denied the old, established theory of human unity, and he went on to say that "the preponderance of evidence is on the side of fixed and primordial distinctions among the races, and of a multiple or national, rather than an individual or dual origination in history."[58] Even those who clung to the idea of one human species generally believed that a permanent inequality of races had arisen since the original Creation of Adam and Eve.

Although the United States shared in a general Western movement toward racialist thinking, American writers in the years from 1830 to 1850 led Europeans in expounding views of innate racial differences. Many Americans had long felt that an immense gulf existed between themselves and the other races of the American continent. They had developed policies based on tacit assumptions of innate racial differences long before there was any scientific base for what was occurring. American intellectuals had now provided the proofs that the society desired. The new theories of innate racial differences were for the most part grasped with enthusiasm; only the arguments for polygenesis caused qualms. By 1850 the science of man was of vital interest throughout America, scientific proofs of racial separation were widely disseminated, and the future of the American continents and the world was thought of in terms of white domination and the subordination or disappearance of other races.

9

Romantic Racial Nationalism

> One is tempted to imagine that the Anglo-Norman race has received from Divine Providence a fee-simple conveyance of this planet, with the appurtenances thereunto belonging.
>
> J. D. Nourse, *Remarks on the Past* (1847)

While racial thought common to the whole of Europe gained a particular virulence among scientific writers in America by mid-century, those themes of Romantic particularism, nationalism, and emotion which had transformed European attitudes since the end of the eighteenth century also deeply permeated a variety of other areas in American thinking. American Romanticism, like its European counterpart, emerged in a variety of forms; American writers adopted literary themes and styles of European Romanticism; New England intellectuals developed their own optimistic transcendentalism under the influence of German and English mentors; American historians delved into the striking themes and great ideas which had inspired past nations; and American nationalists wove a variety of threads into a fervent cry for a greater America. Even in their call for a distinctive American literature, American writers gained strength from those German Romantics who saw literature and language as embodying the soul of a nation. Whatever the particular form taken by American Romanticism, it clearly represented a rejection of eighteenth-century reason and universalism in favor of intuition and particularism. The American Romantics were less interested in the features uniting mankind and nations than in the features separating them. Like the scientists, who shared many of their preconceptions, they looked for what was special and different, not what was general and alike.

The growth and acceptance of the Romantic movement in American literature parallels in time the growth and acceptance of the new scientific racialism. The watershed in both was the period from 1815 to 1830; after 1830 the new ideas quickly swept to success. In one sense, with all their emphasis on scientific measurement and physical comparison, the new scientific racial theorists were themselves responding to the changes in thought embodied in the general concept of Romanticism. Many of their scientific measurements in effect reinforced intuitive beliefs about racial peculiarities and uniqueness. There was never any sharp separation between a precise scientific racialism and literary racial nationalism, for scientists discussed culture and national attitudes in the most general and impressionistic of terms, while some nonscientific writers became interested in the physical basis of racial differentiation. By the 1840s the leading American periodicals often blended ideas on race from a variety of different sources: scientific treatises, monographs on history and philosophy, novels, and poems. Science provided a solid basis for the new assumptions, but the creative writers often gave dramatic expression to new beliefs of racial superiority and destiny even before the scientists provided specific proofs for what had been assumed.

The scientists for the most part emphasized the broad divisions within the human species and particularly enhanced the status of Caucasians at the expense of others. The creative writers and historians emphasized the special achievements of individual peoples, nations, and languages and were able to exalt the Anglo-Saxons over all other members of the Caucasian race. Also, the two groups were mutually reinforcing, for the scientists used the historical and cultural descriptions of the Teutonic and Anglo-Saxon peoples as evidence to bolster their generalizations regarding inferior and superior races, while creative writers grew more confident in their assumptions when scientists gave physical reasons why some races had talents far above others.

In confusing nation, language, and race, American writers leaned heavily on European inspiration. While some French writers—particularly Madame de Staël, Michelet, and Thierry—were influential in transmitting European ideas across the Atlantic and in helping to create in the United States a sense of national racial destiny, by far the greatest influence was exerted by English and German writers. And even the German ideas were far more often known through English sources than directly from the German authors. The American attitude toward English writers remained ambivalent in the first half of the nineteenth century. American authors called for a distinctive American culture and for an end to the simple aping of European models, but they also emphasized a common Anglo-Saxon past, the virtues of the English language, and pride in a race which appeared to be winning control of much of the world. Politically the ambivalence was partially resolved by attacking the aristocratic English government while praising the innate qualities of the English people; but in the literary world English authors were read avidly throughout the United States and emulated by American writers, even while the movement for distinctiveness in American art forms grew in strength. The main British periodicals—particularly the *Edinburgh Review* and the *Quarterly Review*—were well known and read in the most influential American circles and probably exerted as much influence as the main American periodicals in the early decades of the nineteenth century.[1]

All of the important English writers were read in America, but the two of particular importance in creating a sense of racial unity and destiny were Sir Walter Scott and Thomas Carlyle. Scott was by far the most popular of the English Romantics in America and, as in England, Scott did more than any other writer to bring the idea of the sturdy Anglo-Saxon past into the popular consciousness. In the South some emphasized a kinship with the aristocratic Normans, particularly in the years immediately prior to the Civil War, but Scott's impact generally was to bind Americans firmly to their English roots and to reinforce them in the idea that America, a country which in reality increasingly consisted of a blending of races, was the new bastion of an old and successful English people.[2]

Beginning with the publication of *Waverley* in 1814, Scott's novels swept through America. Already known for his poems, Scott achieved his true popularity only by the publication of the Waverley novels, particularly *Ivanhoe*. Unprotected by copyright Scott's novels proved a lucrative source of income for American publishers. By 1823 some five hundred thousand volumes of Scott had been printed in the United States. At the end of the century John Hay commented that "I have heard from my father—a pioneer of Kentucky—that in the early days of this century men would saddle their horses and ride from all the neighboring counties to the principal post-town of the region when a new novel by the Author of *Waverley* was expected."[3]

Although Scott was popular throughout America, the South received him with particular enthusiasm. Touring the South in 1829 Edward Everett found that Scott's characters were memorialized in the names of steamboats, barges, and stagecoaches, and that the small library on his Mississippi steamboat consisted mostly of Scott's novels.[4] When the Waverley Hotel opened in Mobile in 1839 a local editor wondered what Sir Walter would have said and wished it the success "*its* namesake obtained from, and holds upon the world."[5] Scott's "Southron" was a term quickly appropriated by American Southerners. When Willie P. Mangum was elected to the United States Senate in 1830, a writer commented that "he is a genuine & unblenching *Southron* in feeling & principle."[6] Scott may well have helped inculcate Southerners with chivalric ideals, but he also helped convince them that they had a glorious racial lineage in a historical English past. Well into the middle years of the century Scott's novels continued to have great popularity, and even the most widely read new novelists were measured against him.

Carlyle and Coleridge were both influential in spreading the ideas of the German Romantics in the United States. Coleridge was of particular importance in New England where the transcendentalists were led to German sources through his writings, but Carlyle was read for his own sake throughout the country.[7] Carlyle was influential in helping to introduce the Americans to the broadening of Saxonism into the whole Germanic-Norse tradition. He was read in America from the 1820s on, and by the late 1830s American politician and diplomat Nicholas P. Trist was able to write to a friend that "I have become Germanized (not in the language unhappily, but in Carlyle's English). It has been natural for me to think of Goethe — and then of your New Orleans office, and Goethe's picture there and of your Germany trip, etc. Sartor Resartus you have read of course."[8]

Carlyle's reputation grew rapidly in America in the 1840s. The *Democratic Review* referred to him in 1840 as "one of the most extraordinary writers of the age," and after listing his works the reviewer flattered his readers by saying that he presumed they were already too well acquainted with them to require an account of their contents. The *North American Review* suggested in 1846 that the "great reason why Carlyle is welcomed so generally in this country by those who dislike his style and do not admire his ways of thinking is, that he manifests a strong friendship for his race." The *Southern Quarterly Review* began an article on Carlyle's works in 1848 with the comment that "the spirit of Thomas Carlyle is abroad in the land. The strong thinker, the earnest soul, is making an impress wherever the Saxon tongue and Saxon blood prevail."[9] In exalting Norse-Germanic roots and the brotherhood of all Saxons, Carlyle found a ready audience in the United States.

The ideas of the German Romantics also reached the United States in a more direct fashion. Although there had been some interest in German literature even in colonial America, it was the generation of American students who attended German universities after 1815 that first brought direct knowledge to swell the interest aroused by English and French authors. The Northerners Edward Everett, George Bancroft, John L. Motley, George Ticknor, and Longfellow, and Southerners such as

Thomas C. Reynolds, George Henry Calvert, and Philip Tidyman brought back from their German studies a new appreciation of the special national qualities of German literature and a new knowledge of the German language. As early as 1816 George Ticknor commented on the difficulties of a stranger understanding German literature because it "is a peculiar national literature, which . . . has sprung directly from their own soil, and is so intimately connected with their character," and in the following year George Bancroft discussed the new German spirit in a general article for the *North American Review*. Opportunities for Americans to become acquainted with German thought increased steadily after that time.[10]

German émigrés, such as Carl Follen, who was the first to teach German at Harvard (in 1825), and Francis Lieber, who had a long and distinguished career in the South, helped in the dissemination of German ideas, and even as early as the 1820s it was possible to speak of a "German craze" in the Boston area. By the 1830s Theodore Parker, George Perkins Marsh, and Longfellow were delving deep into German sources and northern languages, expanding their interests from German literary theory and philosophy to the whole area of language and philology. In the South too German literature and philosophy were discussed in the leading periodicals, particularly in the *Southern Literary Messenger*. Although German studies never enjoyed the overwhelming attention devoted to English culture, the combination of direct German influence and the extensive adoption of German ideas by English writers ensured a wide dissemination of German thought in the years after 1815.[11]

The philosophical and literary themes of European Romanticism were gaining general currency throughout the United States in the first three decades of the nineteenth century, but their reception varied in the different American regions. It was not simply a matter of the Americans aping Europe; it was more a question of the Americans selecting from a multitude of transatlantic ideas those that best confirmed and enhanced existing American tendencies. New England Romanticism took a particularly intellectual bent; the German philosophers, along with Carlyle and Coleridge, best suited the New England sense of moral and intellectual purpose. In the South there was a passion for Sir Walter Scott; his vision of knights, ladies, serfs, and chivalry was easily absorbed and used within the southern plantation tradition. Yet in both North and South, the ideas of Europe grafted onto, and seemingly confirming, American experience helped produce an overriding sense that the triumphant republic gained its inner force from the special inner characteristics of the American people. Even while scientific writers were in the process of defining a variety of human races, the novelists, poets, and historians were beginning to write of the Americans as a dynamic force in world history.

No one phrase was used to describe this "American" race, but everywhere it was linked firmly to its supposed historic roots; these roots were usually thought of as Caucasian, Germanic, and Anglo-Saxon, and the Americans as a race were most often described as the most vigorous branch of the Anglo-Saxon people. Some nationalists, particularly those of Irish origin, preferred to think of the "American" as a distinctive race, a race in which was combined the best elements of the Caucasians. This "American" race, however, was usually given the historical attributes of the Anglo-Saxons. A more uncommon usage was that of Thomas Hart Benton, who in one speech referred to the "Celtic-Anglo-Saxon division" of the Caucasian race.[12]

In the South there was eventually some confusion in terminology as Southerners sought to emphasize their aristocratic origins in contrast to the supposed plebeian ancestry of the Northerners. Southerners became convinced between 1815 and 1850 that they belonged to a superior race emanating from England, but some preferred to use the term *Anglo-Norman* rather than *Anglo-Saxon*. They were describing the same race, the English, but by including Norman they were making sure that their connection to aristocratic forbears was clearly delineated. Carlyle and others had made it quite clear that the Normans, like the Saxons, were a Germanic people, and that whatever the political and class struggles following the Norman Conquest there was no racial split. *Anglo-Norman* became most popular in the South in the years immediately preceding the Civil War.

Before 1850 Southerners were often content to use *Anglo-*

Saxon rather than *Anglo-Norman* when they described the American interaction with other races. As early as 1826 Henry Clay, in discussing the Indians, used Anglo-Saxon in a specifically racial sense. He described the Indians as "essentially inferior to the Anglo-Saxon race, which were now taking their place on this continent."[13] South Carolinian Huge Legaré, disappointed with France, wrote from Paris in 1832 that "I am more than ever inclined to think that liberty is an affair of *idiosyncracy*, and not destined to spread very far beyond the Anglo-Saxon race, if even *they* keep it very much longer."[14] A new generation of Southerners was to keep Legaré's distinction between the Anglo-Saxons and the rest, but were to throw off, or at least hide, his sense of malaise by stressing that the South, the Anglo-Saxons, and liberty could be preserved and enhanced in power by a vigorous policy of racial expansion.

One aspect of this new militancy is illustrated in the prolific and confused career of William Gilmore Simms. Although Simms was a Charlestonian and edited at different times the *Magnolia* and the *Southern Quarterly Review*, his novels found a ready audience in the North. He has been described as "the most prolific novelist, magazine, and newspaper editor of his generation."[15] Like so many southern writers he acknowledged his debt to Scott, arguing that it was Scott who had clothed "the dry bones" of history and furnished it with life and color. "It was . . . only with the publication of Ivanhoe," he wrote, "one of the most perfect specimens of the romance that we possess, that the general reader had any fair idea of the long protracted struggle between the Norman and Saxon people."[16] In 1842 Simms claimed he was "an ultra-American, a born Southron, and a resolute loco-foco."[17] Within ten years he was far more an ultra-Southron than he was an ultra-American.

Although Simms inherited a literary view of the American Indian, at times defended him, and used the tone of literary regret and admiration which continued as one thread in American literature until the middle of the century, in his writings he quickly subordinated this element to a preoccupation with the conquering mission of his race. There was always a streak of violence in Simms's vision of the outward thrust of the United

States. As early as 1835 he wrote in *Yemassee*: "It is in the nature of civilization to own an appetite for dominion and extended sway, which the world that is known will always fail to satisfy. It is for her, then, to seek and to create, and not with the Macedonian madman, to weep for the triumph of the unknown. Conquest and sway are the great leading principles of her existence, and the savage must join in her train, or she rides over him relentlessly in her onward progress." For Simms the mission of his race and his country was dynamic and brutal: "a people once conscious of their superiority, will never be found to hesitate long in its despotic exercise over their neighbours."[18] At an early date in the South, racial assumptions allowed a belief in a survival of the fittest to begin to replace the Enlightenment hope of progress and happiness for all human beings. Within a decade after Simms's comment, Josiah C. Nott was placing this assumption at the heart of his scientific analysis of the characteristics and future of different races.

In the 1840s Simms for a time was aligned with the nationalistic Young America group, but increasingly he became a defender of southern institutions and a promoter of southern nationalism. As he became more southern and less American, he generally preferred to use Anglo-Norman to describe his race rather than Anglo-Saxon. The term was different but the race was the same. Writing in 1849 he commented on the English practice of the "aristocracy marrying the commoner—thus crossing the breed—by which the British nobility has been made the most splendid race of men in the world." This was the same Simms who throughout the late 1830s and 1840s had bitterly attacked the governmental policies of Great Britain.[19] Like so many other Americans he found it easy to praise the English as a race while attacking the policies of the government.

In the era of the Mexican War Simms's espousal of a bellicose racialism became more obvious. The United States was to carry civilization by the sword. Shortly before the war, in February 1846, he published a poem linking American progress to expansion by the "good old Norman stock." He called on Americans to "obey our destiny and blood." Whatever the resistance the

United States should continue to move outward: "The race must have expansion."[20] In 1847 he said Americans would never surrender the land they had won from Mexico, for they were of "the Anglo Norman breed." Simms was fascinated by the idea of the dog-eat-dog nature of the relationships between races and between countries. "You must not dilate against military glory," he told James Henry Hammond. "War is the greatest element of modern civilization, and our destiny is conquest. Indeed the moment a nation ceases to extend its sway it falls a prey to an inferior but more energetic neighbour."[21] In his *Lays of the Palmetto*, written to celebrate the participation of the South Carolinians in the Mexican War, Simms again lauded violence and made quite clear the extent to which Anglo-Saxon and Anglo-Norman merged in his mind. "Never Don or Savage," he wrote, "yet with the Saxon could endure!" And he added that the noble Anglo-Normans would show the mongrel Mexicans that "good blood" had created two mighty nations—England and the United States.[22]

Simms believed that the expansion of the Anglo-Norman race would advance the best interests of the South. He wrote to Hammond that the acquisition of Texas and Mexico would secure the perpetuation of slavery for the next thousand years, and with a phrase that would have delighted George Orwell argued that "slavery will be the medium & great agent for rescuing and recovering to freedom and civilization all the vast tracts of Texas, Mexico &c." Later he told Hammond that his policy was "to use Uncle Sam" and all his resources to acquire Yucatan and Cuba, "which in the event of a dissolution will enure wholly to the South."[23] In editing the *Southern Quarterly Review* from 1849 to 1857, he made it an avowed policy of the journal that 'Negro Slavery is one of the greatest of moral goods & blessings, and that slavery in all ages had been found the greatest and most admirable agent of Civilization."[24] With his faith in the dynamic, violent qualities of the English race, Simms simply discarded any idea of a peaceful American mission and saw the future of the nation and the race in militant conquest. Defending William Walker's efforts in Nicaragua, Simms argued in 1857 that "filibustering is the moral necessity of all of Anglo-Norman breed. It is the necessity of all progressive races."[25] Though of Scotch-Irish and English ancestry, Simms was able to submerge himself within an all-powerful Anglo-Norman or Anglo-Saxon race.

Like Simms, southern novelist William A. Caruthers acknowledged a major debt to Sir Walter Scott, was able to merge his Scotch-Irish ancestry in the dynamic English race, and was a firm believer in American expansion; but unlike Simms he hated slavery.[26] To Caruthers the attraction of extending civilization through expansion was not the simple device of a Southerner to ensure the maintenance of slavery. The destiny of the American or southern people, he believed, lay not in extending any one institution but in the expansive power of the race. "Our western tendency," he said, is irrevocable, and our further progress and future destiny wrapped up in the womb of time."[27] In his *Knights of the Horse-Shoe*, published serially in *Magnolia* in 1841 and as a book in 1845, Caruthers wrote of "that Anglo-Saxon race which was and is destined to appropriate such a large portion of the Globe to themselves, and to disseminate their laws, their language, and their religion, over such countless millions." Governor Alexander Spotswood, in moving west to the Blue Ridge in the early eighteenth century, is described as having begun a march which in little more than a century "would transcend the Rio del Norte, and which, perhaps in half that time may traverse the utmost boundaries of Mexico."[28] Caruthers did not have Simms's joy in conflict and violence, but he believed that the American people were destined to advance indefinitely throughout the world.

While southern novelists celebrated the westward destiny of the race and nation in dramatic form, the South produced more reasoned arguments of the historical world role that the race was to play. General philosophical meanderings on the future of the American people and of the world were popular in the United States in the middle years of the nineteenth century; they were often inspired by European models. Kentucky newspaperman James D. Nourse achieved a national reputation in the late 1840s with his *Remarks on the Past and Its Legacies to American Society*, in which he acknowledged his debt to Thomas Carlyle.

"I confess that I love him so much," wrote Nourse, "that were I to meet him knowingly in the streets of the great Babel, I would certainly astound the Cockneys, by giving him the hearty salutation of the backwoodsman."[29]

To Nourse the two great events in the history of the world were the introduction of Christianity and the birth of American democracy. Nourse wanted world regeneration, but he conceived of this regeneration in racial terms. Progress was not possible without the presence of civilized people, and he saw no reason to believe that certain peoples were ever barbarous. He thought that the idea that men had gradually risen from barbarism into civilization "almost as absurd as the idea that men were originally monkeys, and have gradually ascended in the scale of being."[30] Nourse, unlike many in the 1840s, retained hope that other peoples of the world could be taught the rudiments of civilization, but this was to be achieved by the domination of the world by a superior race.

For Nourse God was bringing civilization to the world through the medium of the Caucasian race and its Anglo-Saxon or Anglo-Norman branch. He accepted the view that the origin of man was in the mountains between the Euphrates and the Indus. This region was the northern edge of a belt of civilization that died away in the south in the sands of Africa. It was the cradle of art, religion, science, and civilization, "of the zone of light, which, shooting westward across Europe and America, will have encircled the globe, when the Anglo-Americans shall have peopled Oregon and California, and the English shall have infused new life and vigor into the ancient civilization of India." The path along which the Caucasian race had girdled the earth was "the illuminated path of the historical Providence of God."[31]

Historically the Romans had laid the foundation for Christianity by combining the religion of the Hebrews with the reason and imagination of the Greeks. To this foundation the Germanic tribes had brought the idea of liberty — "our American liberty," wrote Nourse, "had its origin in the German forests." All of the Germanic nations were remarkable for their free and independent spirit, but "the Anglo Saxons have unquestionably been distinguished by their aptitude for free institutions, their unconquerable love of liberty, and the practical sagacity with which they have detected the enroachments of arbitrary power." The Saxons went to England, almost entirely destroyed the Celts, and laid the basis for free institutions. Other Saxons emigrated to Jutland and Scandinavia and then in concert with the similar inhabitants of those countries scourged Europe as the Danes or Normans. In their conversion to Christianity the Norman knights lost none of their martial qualities, for they "were the flower of European chivalry." After conquering the Saxons in England, these Norman knights eventually combined with the general population to resist arbitrary kings and produce Magna Carta. The Anglo-Saxon or Anglo-Norman race had been given the mission "of reconciling order and liberty, and teaching mankind the science of government."[32]

Although all the Germanic tribes had the spirit of freedom, argued Nourse, the key to the supremacy of England and America was that in those countries there were few Celts. In France, Spain, and Italy the Germanic race comprised a class that ruled over a large Celtic population, but in England the Celts were practically eliminated. In England, wrote Nourse, the population was "wholly Germanic." Given this basic premise, Nourse obviously had to ignore the sizeable Celtic population in America, and he discussed the Americans as essentially unadulterated Anglo-Normans. Between them, Nourse maintained, the English and the Americans were destined to rule the world: "One is tempted to imagine that the Anglo-Norman race has received from Divine Providence a fee-simple conveyance of this planet, with the appurtenances thereunto belonging." The Anglo-Normans had gone all over the world and were to be "the pioneers and teachers of mankind in the science of civil government." Empire was moving westward, and in the Mississippi Valley "perhaps human intelligence is to reach its loftiest earthly manifestations." Everywhere the Anglo-Normans were the bearers of religion, science, and liberty. Napoleon had been unable to arrest "for one hour the march of events which was carrying forward the English race to the dominion of the world."[33]

In viewing the Americans as the supreme manifestation of the English Anglo-Norman race, Nourse offended some who wanted to maintain the uniqueness of America. When he lectured in Cincinnati in 1849 the *Columbian* took him to task for tracing too much in American liberty back to ancient times. Nearly fifty years before Frederick Jackson Turner argued for a distinctive American democracy, the writer in the *Columbian* challenged Nourse's assertion that American liberty had its origin in the woods of Germany, and said that though there had been such a sentiment in Europe the liberty in America was essentially a new liberty.[34]

Nourse's arguments are an excellent example of how the concept of an Anglo-Norman race, although useful as a means of stressing the chivalric origins of the southern aristocracy, was for those who used it only another way of describing the race that had developed in England from the time of the Saxon invasions. As the Civil War approached, some Southerners used *Anglo-Norman* to describe the population of their own region, arguing that the South had received a population blend which contained more Germanic-Norman knights and the North a blend which contained more Germanic-Saxon commoners.[35]

The extent to which even a better mind than that of J. D. Nourse could become imbued with a sense of Germanic-American racial destiny is indicated in the shifting attitudes of German immigrant Francis Lieber. Lieber came to the United States in 1827 as a young man and was a professor at the University of South Carolina from 1836 to 1856 before taking up a post at Columbia. He came to America with a strong predisposition in favor of his adopted country, and he reveals well the extent to which many Europeans concurred in America's estimate of her future world role. "There never has existed, to my knowledge, a government that has been formed so entirely for the good of the people," he wrote while still at sea on the way to the United States. "Never in the history of the world has so much wisdom and humanity been shown as in their civilization."[36] Lieber became vitally interested in the whole problem of nationalism and although in many respects idealistic and humanitarian, he saw the racial element as a vital ingredient in national accomplishment. Where he differed from the mainstream of southern, or even national expansionist, racial ideology was that by 1850 his natural intelligence and common sense was repelled by the extremism of those who defended America's racial mission.[37]

Lieber had a profound faith in the world political mission of what he often called "the Anglican race," particularly in the mission of its American branch. He thought that the greatest contribution of the English (and in this they had an ability above that of any other Germanic people) was in enshrining into government "that whole body of essential principles of civil liberty, representative government, two Houses, parliamentary law, jury (at least, such as they have it in England), responsible ministers, liberty of the press, the taxes belonging to the lower House, most of the choicest fruits of the common law, town, ward, and other primary meetings." The task of this Anglican race, he wrote, was "to rear and spread civil liberty over vast regions in every part of the earth, on continent and isle."[38]

Lieber by 1850 accepted the view that the Negro and Mongolian races were distinct from the white, and that the future of the world lay in the hands of the white race. He also believed that the world mission of the American English race was not simply a peaceful mission of example and education. War was to Lieber a means of giving a new sense of vigor to a nation. Though he condemned unjust wars, he believed that America's destiny was expansionist and that the westward movement of the Americans to and across the Pacific could not and should not be stopped. Where Lieber differed from so many of his contemporaries was in challenging the obvious weaknesses in the more brazen defenses of Caucasian supremacy. In doing so he also testified to the extent to which they had become dominant in American life. He stressed in 1850 that although believing in an original distinction between the white and the black races he was suspicious of the contemporary rampant racial doctrines. He wanted to know why, if the Caucasians were so infinitely superior, they had been so late in producing great nations and why certain groups, such as the Wallachians and the Croatians, "were sheer barbarians to this day." Although Lieber showed the independence of his mind in attacking the most extravagant statements of Caucasian racial supremacy, he also helped to accelerate the process by which even the Caucasian race was divided into superior and inferior divisions—to Lieber "the Anglican race" exhibited special traits that give it the right to control and lead the world.[39]

For the most part, by the 1840s the main southern literary periodicals were unwilling to accept the warnings given by Francis Lieber. While on the one hand they constantly discussed and disseminated the new scientific racism exalting the Caucasians, on the other they accepted in practical form the more general defenses of an aggressive racial mission of the American Anglo-Saxons. Also, as the scientific arguments for racial differences became better known in the late 1840s, these arguments increasingly were used to bolster the more impressionistic views of the destiny of the American Anglo-Saxon race. When in 1843 the American edition of Friedrich von Schlegel's *Philosophy of History* was reviewed in the *Southern Quarterly Review*, the author took the opportunity to challenge the eighteenth-century environmentalist view of racial differences. Rather than climate, he said, the decisive factor was the innate character of the race. The Anglo-Saxon race retained much of its energy and activity in areas of the world where the aborigines were enervated: "The characteristics of particular races remain ineradicable, they undergo slight changes and modifications, according to the admixture of foreign blood, but the original type remains." The characteristics of the Anglo-Saxons at the present day, the reviewer argued, could be seen in the Germanic tribes as described by Tacitus.[40] A similar conclusion was reached in a review of Guizot's works: the Germanic tribes had an ineradicable spirit of liberty, and the Germanic race revivified a worn-out Roman Empire. Where the Germanic tribes had penetrated least—in Greece and Italy—there had been a long sterility. The only vigor in Italy was in the north, where there had been an infusion of German blood.[41] Similar speculations were inspired when Arnold's *Introductory Lectures on Modern History* was reviewed. Arnold's views of the revivifying power of the Germanic peoples fell on ground that had been well prepared, and the reviewer observed how the student could here enter into a field in which he could explore "the greatness and excellence of our race!"[42]

That "our race" was becoming more specifically the Anglo-Saxon or Anglo-Norman rather than the Caucasian was quite apparent in southern periodicals of the 1840s and 1850s. To the general innate superiority of the Caucasians, it was argued, the Anglo-Saxon branch of the Teutons added the inborn talent for political liberty. All the Germanic peoples had this innate sense of liberty, but only the Anglo-Saxons had shown the ability to transform the gift into effective political institutions. These southern periodicals exhibited particular pride that the Anglo-Saxons excelled in the practical skills. "We too are English," wrote a reviewer of the first two volumes of Macaulay's *History of England*, "and all the far-descended honors of the English name are ours by inheritance . . . our race reads lessons to the world in philosophy, in science, in mechanical skill, in the arts of government, in Christian morality . . . we are far behind in the light and frivolous arts." This was "the imperial Anglo-Saxon race, whose mission on earth is like that of the Jews in Canaan, 'to subdue the land and possess it.' "[43] In the following year another writer stated that "the Anglo-Normans" were destined to "attain to universal moral dominion, at least." Other racial stocks in America were discounted. A variety of races had first settled the Western world, but "happily the Anglo-Saxon blood was the fundamental stock, and ideas of religious and civil liberty were imported with it, to expand, and strengthen, and vivify in the pure, free air of this virgin world."[44]

Although in the late 1840s and early 1850s many Southerners were to balk at the prospect of an unrestrained expansion that would bring free "inferior" races within the American union, the rhetoric of racial expansion often operated at a level which ignored such practical problems. The "line of civilization and liberty . . . is constantly being removed westward," wrote B. F. Porter of Alabama in 1847: "The line dividing the civilization of this country from the barbarism of the East, must be farther and farther removed, until it shall throw its reflection across the Pacific." Pride was expressed that the Anglo-Saxon was a militant, even a ferocious race. Though writers might write of the eventual moral triumph of the race, they were more likely to depict it in warlike and heroic terms. The tide of progress, it was said, was rolling westward "like the triumphant Roman chariot."[45]

The increasing acceptance of militant expansionism, which became so rampant in the years of the Mexican War, gave rise to qualms among some writers in the South. Many of them were simply concerned that the new spirit of conquest would create a problem by providing for the absorption of "inferior" peoples, but a few seemed genuinely disturbed at the new bellicose spirit. In an article in 1850 a writer in *De Bow's Review* pointed out how a rampant sense of world destiny was being combined by many with a belief that this would be attained simply by force of arms. The writer argued that in the last half of the century "a *military spirit*" had diffused itself throughout all society, bringing about the establishment of miniature West Points "in every state and on every hill top." There was, said the author, a dream of American destiny carrying national power throughout the world: "The eagle of the republic shall poise itself over the field of Waterloo, after tracing its flight among the gorges of the Himalaya or the Ural mountains, and a successor of Washington ascend the chair of universal empire!"[46]

Some in the South, like many in the North, while subscribing to the idea of the racial destiny of the American people, argued that there was no need to hasten this process by sudden military action. It was clear that Providence intended America to triumph, and that the future was writ large in the whole movement of the Germanic peoples across Europe to the United States. From the Normans, it was argued, the Americans had inherited a passion for the acquisition of territory, and the "more militant aspects of this desire should be curbed." Why hurry the inevitable? — "Cuba will be Americanized — will own the sway of our race, as will St. Domingo, the West India Islands, generally, and all Mexico, in course of time."[47] The belief in racial, expansionist destiny was deeply established in the South by 1850.

The practical difficulties of accomplishing America's racial destiny were more clearly delineated by northern, particularly

New England, writers than those in the South. Northern sentiment, while tending toward the same conclusions on the future role of the American Anglo-Saxon race, was complicated by the persistence of a strong sense of moral, religious mission and by an abolitionist fear that in the short run the expansion of the United States would bring about the extension of slavery rather than simply the extension of Anglo-Saxon liberty. Thus while Northerners, like Southerners, came to believe that the Americans as a race had something special to offer to the world, they had far more qualms about making the mission militant than they did about making it racial. They thought the unique qualities of the Germanic-Anglo-Saxon-American people were what the world needed, but many were unconvinced that conquest was either desirable or necessary. Those Americans whose intellectual home was Boston were by no means immune to the new ideas of race and expansion, but they produced a more complex pattern of thought than those whose intellectual home was Charleston or New Orleans, or even those whose intellectual home was Philadelphia or New York. The moral and religious core that persisted in the New England mind made it more difficult for ideas which totally ignored other peoples to gain acceptance. It may also be that New Englanders, who had no specific stake in the enslavement of blacks, as did the Southerners, or in the removal of Indians, as did the Westerners, felt freer to indulge in mental doubts and humanitarian sentiments.

New England thought was also tempered by strong antislavery feelings in the decades preceding the Civil War. At first, there was a reluctance to admit the permanent inferiority of blacks. In the 1820s Edward Everett, after arguing that the experience of Haiti had demonstrated a Negro capacity for self-government, went on to maintain that there was nothing as far as he knew which would "authorise the conclusion that any one of the several varieties of our race is either intellectually or morally superior or inferior to the rest." Civilization and power, he argued, passed from people to people without regard to color, and the superior of one age might be the inferior of the next.[48] Optimistic views such as Everett's never completely disappeared in New England, but by the 1850s Free-Soilers and even abolitionists were often swept up in the typical racial judgments of the age.

New Englanders were less inclined than Southerners to heap abuse on the innate capacities of other races, and they often asked for less violence and more tolerance in the treatment of other peoples; but from the 1830s on they became interested in, and advocates of, the Germanic and Anglo-Saxon divisions of the white race. The transcendentalists found that the idea of a Teutonic race imbued with the great idea of freedom melded well into their search for a guiding spirit in American democracy and the American nation, and New Englanders in general attacked war and aggression while prophesying the ultimate triumph of an American Anglo-Saxon Christian civilization.

Emerson, although shunning extreme racial arguments, accepted the idea of inequalities among the different races and saw particular merits in the English race. He thought of this race as "Saxon," but he believed it had its origin in a mixture of races and had hybrid strength. The English, he thought, had also gained in stature from their Norse conquerors, for races needed a primitive energy if they were not to be destroyed. Emerson saw the English and their American offspring as having an innate, vital force which drove them on to advance their settlements. Thus though he objected bitterly to the annexation of Texas, with all its implications for the balance of slave and free states, he observed in private that this question was ultimately not a vital one: "It is very certain that the strong British race, which have now overrun so much of this continent, must also overrun that tract, and Mexico and Oregon also, and it will in the course of ages be of small import by what particular occasions and methods it was done. It is a secular question."[49]

In the 1850s, when the new racial doctrines were in full cry, Emerson shaped them to his own needs. Although he found "pungent and unforgettable truths" in the rabid writing of Robert Knox's *Races of Men*, he more often praised the English than he attacked other races.[50] In his *English Traits*, published in 1856, he commented that in England "exists the best stock in the world," and argued that "it is in the deep traits of race that the fortunes of nations are written." The English race had for

Emerson that singleness of purpose, that unified national idea, which made for national greatness. He had spoken in 1847 of "the moral peculiarity of the Saxon race, — its commanding sense of right and wrong." He saw in the rampant expansionism of the 1840s and 1850s immediate ill-effects, such as the extension of slavery, but he was not prepared to condemn the innate drive for dominion which he thought characterized the English and their Germanic ancestors: "The Teutonic tribes," he wrote in *English Traits*, "have a national singleness of heart, which contrasts with the Latin races. The German name has a proverbial significance of sincerity and honest meaning."[51] Emerson wanted to free America from cultural dependence on England, but he believed that the English race and its American counterpart were a major moral force in the world.

Emerson transmuted a variety of philosophical racial ideas through his own genius; Theodore Parker was far more ready to accept a variety of racial doctrines in unadulterated form. Parker not only accepted the superiority of the Anglo-Saxons, he also in private stressed the marked inferiority of the non-Caucasian races of mankind. He combined these racial views with vigorous opposition to the Mexican War, to the extermination of west-coast Indians, and to the extension of slavery.

Parker illustrates well the extent to which Germanic scholarship had penetrated New England thinking by the 1830s. He read widely in German philology and philosophy, studied a whole list of languages (including Icelandic, Swedish, and Anglo-Saxon), and showed enough interest in German thought to buy Herder's complete works — in forty-five volumes. Far more than Emerson, Parker was willing to think in broad terms of superior and inferior races with specific characteristics. For the time being he was willing to accept Blumenbach's division into five races, but he thought this *"provisional."*[52]

Parker had no doubt at all that the Caucasian race was the superior race: "The Caucasian differs from all other races: he is humane, he is civilized, and progresses. He conquers with his head as well as with his hand . . . The Caucasian has been often master of the other races — never their slave. He has carried his religion to other races, but never taken theirs. In history, all religions are of Caucasian origin . . . Republics are Caucasian. All the great sciences are of Caucasian origin; all inventions are Caucasian; . . . all the great poets are of Caucasian origin."[53] But among the Caucasians Parker saw marked distinctions. He believed the Celtic race would "rapidly disappear," and the Italo-Greek would never rise again, for there was no example in history "of an old race becoming young and vigorous again." The future belonged to the Teutonic and Slavic divisions of the Caucasian race. Even beyond this there were divisions, for among the Teutons, the Anglo-Saxons of England and America were supreme. In a hundred years there would be two great powers—the Anglo-Saxon and the Slavonic. It would not be surprising, then, if these two "tribes" should conquer all the world.[54]

Parker looked upon the Anglo-Saxons with particular pride. Although recognizing the English exploitation of India, he commented: "I look with great pride on this Anglo-Saxon people. It has many faults, but I think it is the best specimen of mankind which has ever attained great power in the world."[55] England, to Parker, was a country of "immense practical talent, energy, and materialism." Anglo-Saxon America was just like the mother-country: "the same materialism, the same vulgarity, the same lust for land, and longing for individual freedom."[56]

In spite of his antislavery stance and his condemnation of American policies toward the Indian, Parker was convinced of the inferiority of blacks and Indians: "In respect to *power of civilization*, the African is at the bottom, the American Indian next." This was shown by the whole history of the world.[57] "There are inferior races," he wrote, "which have always borne the same ignoble relation to the rest of men, and *always will*." In two generations there would be a marked change in the Irish in New England: "But, in twenty generations, the negroes will stand just where they are now; that is, if they have not disappeared."[58] Parker wrote in 1859 that the existence of slavery endangered all American democratic institutions. He estimated that by 1900 there would be twenty million slaves: "An Anglo-

Saxon with common sense does not like this Africanization of America; he wishes the superior race to multiply rather than the inferior."[59]

To Parker there was no question that the expansion of Anglo-Saxon America was intimately linked to the progress of the world. He wanted the United States to be "the mother of a thousand Anglo-Saxon states, tropic and temperate on both sides of the equator." If this came to pass, the Mississippi and the Amazon would unite their waters, and America would have a population of hundreds of millions. "The fulfillment of this vision is our province," he wrote; "we are the involuntary instruments of God. Shall America scorn the mission God sends her on?"[60] Parker did not object to Anglo-Saxon expansion — he thought it essential for the future of the world — what he objected to was violent, forcible expansion and the extension of slavery. When in June 1848 he bitterly attacked the Mexican War, with its violent appropriation of territory from Mexico, he made it clear that it was not expansion itself which stimulated his disgust: "Before many years, all of this Northern Continent will doubtless be in the hands of the Anglo-Saxon race. That of itself is not a thing to mourn at. Could we have extended our empire there by trade, by the Christian arts of peace, it would be a blessing to us and to Mexico; a blessing to the world." By taking land by "fraud and blood," however, the United States was forgetting the duties it owed to the world "and to God, who put us here on this new continent."[61] Anglo-Saxon superiority would ensure the ultimate expansion and supremacy of the United States; there was no need for unjust aggression which brought about the extension of the immoral institution of slavery.

While New England as a whole embraced an Anglo-Saxonism which confirmed links with an ancient, free English race, the Norse tradition was somewhat slower to gain acceptance and never had the same pervasive influence as pride in English-Germanic origins. Carlyle helped to inspire pride in the Norse mystique, but it was New Englander George Perkins Marsh who gave the major impetus in the United States to the broadening of the Germanic-Anglo-Saxon theme to include the Norse tradition.

Marsh, who early in his education become acquainted with Coleridge and the German philosophers, in the 1830s turned to the whole subject of Scandinavian antiquity. Corresponding with the Danish linguist Carl Christian Rafn to obtain advice, he gradually gathered a major collection of works on Icelandic and on Scandinavian language and literature generally. In 1838 he published a translation of Rasmus Kristian Rask's Icelandic grammar and followed this with a number of other translations. Marsh was the most prominent of the American Scandinavian scholars, but other New Englanders delved into the northern history and mythology that had fascinated many Europeans since the last half of the eighteenth century. When he was in Copenhagen in 1835, Henry Wadsworth Longfellow took lessons in Icelandic from Rafn, and he was made a member of the Northern Antiquarian Society. Early in the same year he had urged that the Department of Modern Literature at Harvard should be given more money for works in German philology and for the re-publication of old literature.[62]

Marsh, who in 1843 was elected to Congress as a Whig, in the same year published *The Goths in New England*. He revived the old term *Goths* to describe what was in essence the Germanic branch of the Caucasian race. "The Goths, the common ancestors of the inhabitants of North Western Europe," he wrote, "are the noblest branch of the Caucasian race. We are their children. It was the spirit of the Goth, that guided the May-Flower across the trackless ocean; the blood of the Goth that flowed at 'Bunker's Hill." Unlike many who ascribed the violent, restless expansion of the Anglo-Saxons to their Norse forbears, Marsh gave specific credit to the Germanic tribes for all the most desirable attributes of the English and the Americans and blamed Rome for what he found less desirable. Thus, better than most New Englanders, he was able to find racial explanations for what he thought were the contradictions in English and American attitudes and policy: "England is Gothic by birth, Roman by adoption. Whatever she has of true moral grandeur, of higher intellectual power, she owes to her Gothic mother; while her grasping ambition, her material energies, her spirit of exclusive selfishness, are due to the Roman nurse."[63]

For Marsh as for so many others, the love of individual liberty and popular control was an exclusive attribute of the Germanic peoples, and he argued that this had been directly inherited by the Americans. The Gothic was "that great race from which, with little intermixture, we are lineally descended."[64] Although firmly believing in the genius of the Germanic peoples, Marsh retained in his thinking an older environmentalism. The particular guiding spirit and moral and intellectual traits of any nation were imposed by Providence "through the agency of natural causes" — most important among these were "the influence of the climate, soil, and the configuration of the earth's surface." The landing of the Goths in New England had brought about a restoration of primitive vigor by bringing them to a harsher environment.[65]

As a Whig representative Marsh joined his New England colleagues in opposing the violent expansion of the Mexican War. He thought that American aims should be achieved by peace, not war, and that size brought extreme danger to liberty. He expressed in strong words a point of view that was to become extremely important in the political and diplomatic arguments of the late 1840s and early 1850s — the view that other peoples were unfit to share in the representative government developed by the Germanic peoples. In opposing the acquisition of New Mexico and California, he argued that "they are inhabited by a mixed population, of habits, opinions, and characters incapable of sympathy or assimilation with our own; a race, whom the experience of an entire generation has proved to be unfitted for self-government, and unprepared to appreciate, sustain, or enjoy free institutions."[66] As the love of liberty was an innate characteristic only of the Germanic peoples, other races could not be assimilated.

The exaltation of the basic Germanic and Anglo-Saxon character of the American people permeated the writings of New England's Romantic historians, George Bancroft and John Lothrop Motley. It was less dominant, although clearly present, in the writings of William Hickling Prescott and Francis Parkman. They believed that the national character was largely a matter of race, that liberty was the special attribute of the Germanic/Anglo-Saxon peoples, and that Providence had directed human progress westward to America where the United States was engaged in the fulfillment of a divine plan. New England's historians were all influenced by the German thought which saw the present in terms of a complex historical past. Both Bancroft and Motley were inspired by direct contact with German scholarship and thought. They both studied in Germany, developed a great admiration for German ideas, and helped to spread an admiration for Germany in the United States.[67]

Bancroft, while never espousing a virulent racial attitude, saw the Germanic racial origin of the United States as a key determinant in its government. As early as 1824 he wrote that "the child inherits the physical and moral characteristics of the race to which it belongs," and argued that "the descendant of the Pilgrims, whether on the banks of the Detroit, the Iowa, or the Oregon, has the true instinct for liberty."[68] In his *History of the United States* Bancroft stressed the role of the Germanic race as the carrier of the idea of personal liberty, and maintained that through the United States the Anglo-Saxons had a special Providential destiny to fulfill. He wrote from England in 1847 that the English were now beginning to see "the inevitable necessity which appropriates all North America to the Anglo-Saxon Race. They acknowledge our superiority, & the last news from America has compelled them to acknowledge our entire success."[69]

Motley made his own commitment unmistakable in his introduction in 1856 to *The Rise of the Dutch Republic*: "To all who speak the English language, the history of the great agony through which the Republic of Holland was ushered into life must have peculiar interest, for it is a portion of the records of the Anglo-Saxon race — essentially the same whether in Friesland, England, or Massachusetts." The immutable quality of racial inheritance was the rallying cry of those who in the mid-nineteenth century believed that the power of England and the United States would be unaffected by time. Indeed this power would increase as racial superiority brought its inevitable results. The first chapter of Motley's work on the Dutch was largely devoted to a comparison of the Celtic and the Teutonic races. Using Tacitus Motley described the primitive German peoples as believing in popular government, and he contrasted this with the Celtic aristocracies. Motley thought in racial terms. He even used a common southern phrase, and perhaps tacitly admitted the southern belief in their chivalric nature, in describing Sir Philip Sidney as "an Anglo-Norman representative of ancient race." To Motley the Germanic tribesmen were primitive democrats, who showed their essential sense of morality by believing in one God and in having one wife.[70]

William Hickling Prescott was cautious in his racial judgments compared to many of his contemporaries, but even in writing on Spanish themes he at times reflected the pervasive belief in Teutonic excellence. In his *Conquest of Peru*, published in 1847, he compared the Spanish to the Anglo-Saxons: "What a contrast did these children of Southern Europe present to the Anglo-Saxon races who scattered themselves along the great northern division of the western hemisphere!" The spring of action for these Anglo-Saxons was not "the more specious pretext of proselytism; but independence — independence religious and political."[71]

The idea that liberty was the peculiar prerogative of one race — the Anglo-Saxon — was also present in the writings of Francis Parkman. The French and British colonies in North America were not merely divided by political and religious institutions, for the key to these institutions lay in the race: "The Germanic race, and especially the Anglo-Saxon branch of it, is peculiarly masculine, and, therefore, peculiarly fitted for self-government."[72] Parkman, as well as exalting the Anglo-Saxon, rejected the views of those in New England who still clung to the idea of the American Indian as a noble savage. Possibly influenced by his own trip west, he took a view of the Indian that was far more common in the rest of the country than in the environs of Boston. He commented in *The Oregon Trail* that a civilized white could find little sympathy between his own nature and that of the Indian: "With every disposition to do justice to their good qualities, he must be conscious that an impassable gulf lies between him and his red brethren." In writing of a train of emigrants passing an Indian encampment, he commented that the latter were "the people whom they and their descendants, in the space of a century, are to sweep from the face of the earth."[73]

The Romantic historians of New England in general accepted the idea that the concept of liberty and the ability to embody this concept into institutions was a peculiar inheritance of the Anglo-Saxon peoples. They also saw inherent weaknesses in Celts and other races. They generally, however, tempered their racial views with a moral sense which viewed the whole of mankind as awaiting redemption. Bancroft interspersed his praises of the Anglo-Saxon race with hopes for the future of the whole human race and the conviction that "the instinct of Deity" lay within the most diverse human beings. "All are men," he wrote. "When we know the Hottentot better, we shall despise him less."[74] For all his love of the American people, Bancroft still had an optimistic sense of mission. The American race was to carry a message of progress and divine beneficence westward to the rest of the world. Prescott too had a sympathy for the whole human condition and saw the greediness in the rampant spirit of territorial expansion present in the late 1840s. He condemned it, although giving a racial reason for his doubt in the statement that "the Creole blood will not mix well with the Anglo-Saxon."[75]

Although American writers of the years from 1815 to the 1850s were gradually influenced by the new scientific theories on race which in the 1840s became a topic of general discussion, the original impetus for their ideas were the more general theories of Teutonic-Anglo-Saxon greatness which had developed as part of the European Romantic movement, and which in England and America had roots in the sixteenth and seventeenth centuries. They fell heir to the ideas of Anglo-Saxon freedom that had been present in America since the colonial period, and when they sought a guiding principle in their nation's history, they found it in the love of liberty which was characteristic of the Germanic peoples and in the innate ability of the Anglo-Saxons to enshrine liberty in free institutions.

The Americans' response to these ideas was of course shaped by their own heritage and environment. The strong Puritan sense of morality and mission and the lack of any numerous alien race of Indians or blacks tempered in New England the militant racial assumptions which permeated much of American writing in these years. The New Englanders believed passionately in the special Providential mission of the American branch of the Anglo-Saxon race, but they feared the excesses of rampant expansionism, military adventure, and the extension of slavery. They also demonstrated a greater awareness of the practical problems of an expansion which introduced other, supposedly inferior races, within the American republic. Outside New England, however, with the exception of areas in the Old Northwest where New England influence was strong, the new ideas had full reign. They provided a needed rationale for both slavery and the mistreatment of the Indians. Practical difficulties of world domination were played down, and at times the new rhetoric did not merely assume that the American Anglo-Saxons would bring progress to the rest of the races in the world but rather that they would in some mystical manner replace them. These assumptions were made more obvious as American politicians devised policies that would allow none but the American "Anglo-Saxon" population to participate in the American republic and its triumphant advance to world power.

III
AN ANGLO-SAXON POLITICAL IDEOLOGY

10

Racial Destiny and the Indians

> It is impossible to destroy men with more respect to the laws of humanity.
>
> Tocqueville, *Democracy in America* (1835)

Between 1815 and the mid-1850s an American Anglo-Saxon ideology was used internally to bolster the power and protect the status of the existing population and externally to justify American territorial and economic expansion. Internally it was made quite clear that the American republic was a white Anglo-Saxon republic; other white races would be absorbed within the existing racial mass while nonwhite races would be rigorously excluded from any equal participation as citizens. Externally American pressure on adjacent territories was justified by the argument that only the American Anglo-Saxons could bring the political and economic changes that would make possible unlimited world progress. These arguments were used to justify the annexation of sparsely populated areas and the economic penetration of areas that were heavily populated with "inferior" races. The latter were not annexed, because the strong belief that inferior peoples should not be allowed to participate equally in the American system of government was accompanied by a continuing belief that colonial possessions would corrupt the republic. Some in the United States still argued that other peoples could be taught to enjoy republican freedom, but they were outnumbered by those who maintained that many other races were incapable of substantial accomplishments. The United States shaped policies which reflected a belief in the racial inferiority and expendability of Indians, Mexicans, and other inferior races, and which looked forward to a world shaped and dominated by a superior American Anglo-Saxon race.

Between 1815 and 1850 the American Indians were rejected by the white American society. Before 1830 there was a bitter struggle as those who believed in the Enlightenment view of the Indian as an innately equal, improvable being desperately defended the older ideals, but year by year the ideas of those who felt the Indians were expendable were reinforced by a variety of scientific and intellectual arguments. Indian Removal represented a major victory for ideas which, though long latent in American society, became fully explicit only after 1830. Political power was exercised by those who believed the Indians to be inferior, who did not wish them to be accepted as equals within American society, and who expected them ultimately to disappear. In shaping an Indian policy American politicians reflected the new ruthlessness of racial confidence.

The eighteenth-century transatlantic view of the Indian as an innately equal, fully improvable being did not, of course, disappear from American thinking. For two decades after 1815 this view had major defenders. Even after that time missionaries, reformers, and other friends of the Indian hoped for Indian transformation, and the rhetoric of government leaders was frequently couched in terms of improvability. But there is considerable evidence to show that after 1830 neither the mass of the American people nor the political leaders of the country believed that the Indians could be melded into American society.

The eighteenth-century image of the Indian as a "noble savage" also persisted into the middle of the century, though in modified form. Major American writers—Cooper, Hawthorne,

Thoreau, Melville — and their minor followers, while blending harsher tones into their portraits, viewed the Indian as a tragic and in some ways noble figure — and certainly as far more human than the bestial savage portrayed in so many frontier descriptions. Even William Gilmore Simms, for all his rampant expansionism, retained the older literary image of the Indian in much of his writing.[1]

On a popular level, however, this literary image of the Indian as a complex, tragic figure was to a large extent offset by the widespread, horror-laden captivity literature and by the novels of figures such as Robert Montgomery Bird, who depicted the Indian as an expendable wild beast. When Bird published his *Nick of the Woods* in 1837, he admitted that his literary portrait of the Indians was in "hues darker than are usually employed by the painters of such figures. The North American savage has never appeared to us the gallant and heroic personage he seems to others."[2] Yet while the literary view of the Indian was mixed, there was a common assumption that the Indian was doomed to inevitable extinction. A tone of regret for a being who could not be saved permeated creative writing on the Indian in the years until 1850.

The scientific attack on the Indian as inferior and expendable, which burgeoned from 1830 to 1850, gave many Americans the authoritative backing they needed for long-assumed beliefs. Frontiersmen were as pleased to accept the scientific condemnation of the Indians as slaveowners were to accept scientific attacks on the blacks. The dominant scientific position by the 1840s was that the Indians were doomed because of innate inferiority, that they were succumbing to a superior race, and that this was for the good of America and the world. The impotence of the federal government in the face of the massacres of California Indians in the 1850s has to be viewed against the widespread intellectual and popular view that the replacement of an inferior by a superior race was the fulfillment of the laws of science and nature.

Although the idea of removing Indians to distant, unwanted western lands had been suggested after the Louisiana Purchase in 1803, this suggestion originally involved Indians who wished to retain their existing way of life. Indians who resisted assimilation were at times encouraged to remove beyond the Mississippi, but those who were showing signs of accepting the outward forms of white civilization were encouraged to perpetuate themselves upon the land, farm it, bequeath it to their heirs, and transform their way of life. Indian Removal as developed between 1815 and 1830 was a rejection of all Indians as Indians, not simply a rejection of unassimilated Indians who would not accept the American life-style.[3]

The expansion of the United States in the years after 1815 rapidly brought intense pressure on federal commitments to the Indians. As settlers poured into the eastern half of the Mississippi Valley, the demand for land reached unprecedented heights. In the South settlers lured by the rich cotton lands in Georgia, Alabama, and Mississippi spread rapidly over all available areas, and Indian settlements were threatened by white frontiersmen anxious to make their fortunes. The condition of the Indians in the eastern half of the country was disputed at the time and has been disputed since; one reason is the wide variation that existed among tribes from the Great Lakes to the Gulf. The Indians of Ohio, Indiana, and Illinois were in no condition to resist the pressure from white settlers. After decades of war and white contact they were easy to dispossess and to confine on smaller and smaller areas of land. Few Indians were established in successful farming communities on the white pattern; many were demoralized and drifting, with tribal structures shattered, game disappearing, and little hope of survival.

The South was much different. Although there can be considerable disagreement as to the proportion of Indians who had even outwardly conformed to white cultural patterns, and even more difficulty in deciding on the degree of acculturation, there is no doubt that in the states of Georgia, Tennessee, Alabama, and Mississippi there were many Indians who had gone part way in fulfilling Jeffersonian hopes for their transformation. Indeed, until different arguments were needed in the 1820s to justify a different policy, federal officials frequently testified to Indian "progress" in the South, notably among the Cherokees. There were literally thousands of Indians in the southern states who were capable of remaining on the land and even prospering. They were not destitute, they were not disorganized, and they were not doomed to inevitable extinction.[4]

In the years after 1815, even within the context of an Enlightenment Indian policy, a good case could be made for the removal of the remaining Indians from the states of Ohio, Indiana, and Illinois. The assimilation policy had achieved very little success, and it could be argued that the remaining Indians were doomed unless they were removed. This was not the case in the South, and after 1815 the main arguments concerning removal revolved around the states of Tennessee, Georgia, Alabama, and Mississippi. Most white Americans in those areas were simply unwilling to allow Indians, whether transformed or not, to retain land and to achieve equality with white settlers. This accelerated the national process of regarding the Indian simply as an inferior savage who blocked progress. What had been an instinctive reaction of frontiersmen fighting for land was soon to become a majority point of view among Americans and their governmental officials.

When in the years following the War of 1812 Secretary of War William H. Crawford made it clear by word and treaty that the government hoped to keep the Indians on the lands they possessed east of the Mississippi River, and that he wished to assimilate these Indians within American society, he stirred widespread resentment among Tennesseans and other Southerners who wished to obtain all the good land in their region.[5] In 1816 Governor Joseph McMinn of Tennessee indicated that he believed the time was approaching when the federal government should eliminate all general Indian claims within his state by ending tribal ownership. Individual Indians should be able to retain land and pass it on to their heirs. This was not to mean full acceptance into American society, for McMinn suggested that these Indians should be given "all the rights of a free citizen of color of the United States."[6] It soon became apparent that the breaking up of tribal lands was intended to simplify the removal of all Indians from the state, not to promote the assimilation of individuals.

In January 1817 the Senate Committee on Public Lands endorsed the general policy of exchanging Indian lands east of the Mississippi for lands to the west of that river, but insisted that this should be done by the voluntary consent of the tribes. This plan became the cornerstone of Indian policy in the new administration of President James Monroe. His secretary of war, John C. Calhoun, emphasized in the following years that the administration was anxious to effect a voluntary removal of the Indians to the west side of the Mississippi.[7] The policy was a failure because it satisfied neither whites nor Indians. The whites wanted more forceful action by the federal government, and the Indians wanted to stay where they were. Those Indians who had used white "civilization" efforts to expand their own earlier agricultural base had no reason to want to move; they emphasized that they were doing what they had repeatedly been told to do before 1812, and that their lands had been guaranteed to them by the federal government.[8]

Even had the Indians been prepared to cede their tribal lands, the idea of private Indian land ownership was doomed by the unwillingness of the southern whites to accept Indians on a basis of equality. McMinn had suggested giving Indians who remained the rights of "a free citizen of color." Georgia made it clear that she wanted no Indians at all — whether living on tribal land or on private property. In the 1820s the focus of the Indian controversy shifted to Georgia. At the time of the 1802 agreement by which Georgia had ceded her western land claims, the federal government had agreed to extinguish Indian claims within the state.[9] By 1820 Georgia was infuriated that rather than removing the Creeks and the Cherokees the federal government had encouraged permanent occupancy by its civilization program.

In December 1821 the House of Representatives appointed a select committee to consider Georgia's problems under the 1802 agreement. George Gilmer, a representative from that state, proposed this step, resisted efforts to have the question sent to the standing committee on Indian affairs, and chaired the special committee. When the committee reported early in 1822, it argued that the executive had violated the rights of both Georgia and Congress — the former because of the granting of lands in

Georgia to Indians as individuals, the latter because of the agreement that the Indians could become citizens. For the federal government to conform to its 1802 agreement with Georgia, the committee reported, "it will be necessary for the United States to relinquish the policy which they seem to have adopted with regard to civilizing the Indians, and rendering them permanent upon their lands, and changing their title by occupancy into a fee-simple title, at least in respect to the Creek and Cherokee Indians."[10]

The idea of removing most of the Indians by allowing some of them to remain as private property owners was unacceptable to Georgia, and, under pressure from that state, Congress in 1822 and 1823 urged the executive to eliminate not only tribal but also individual Indian land claims within the state. The appropriation of fifty thousand dollars to buy out lands granted to Indians in fee simple since 1814 caused particularly bitter debate, for this was a direct rejection and repudiation of the assimilation and incorporation policies pursued since the 1790s. The total acreage involved was less than twenty-three thousand, but the Indians were not allowed to retain even this tiny portion of the huge Georgia domain. After an initial defeat, the House passed the appropriation by a vote of fifty-eight to thirty; these Indians were to be removed because they were Indians, not because they held huge tribal lands or because they had refused to assume white ways.[11]

In its last two years the Monroe administration was beset by an almost continual crisis in Indian affairs; Tennessee, Georgia, Alabama, and Mississippi were all pressing the federal government to remove the Indians from their states.[12] The Indian tribes for the most part wanted to remain where they were. Those who had achieved the greatest success in assimilation would be the most hurt by removal westward. They had followed Jefferson's injunctions to assume white ways; they were now to be thrown off their land. Faced by the intransigence of the southern states, the executive moved toward the idea of removing all the eastern Indians who were in the path of white settlement.

Sentiment in Georgia became more extreme in these years, particularly after the election of George M. Troup as governor.

When the Cherokees in the fall of 1823 again refused to cede lands, Troup asked the Georgia legislature to demand action by the federal government. This it did, and Troup told Calhoun that the wrongs done to Georgia "must be repaired by an Act of decisive character."[13] The Georgia delegation in Washington attacked the policy of the executive in such violent terms that Monroe in a cabinet meeting said that "he had never received such a paper." It was ruefully asked in the meeting what had kindled "this raging fever for Indian lands."[14]

Governor Troup made it obvious that it was not merely a question of obtaining satisfaction for Georgia under the terms of the 1802 agreement, and that he was not advocating removal from Georgia merely that Indians should be welcomed within the republican fold in a less crowded area. In 1824 he attacked the whole concept of the amalgamation of the Indians within American society: "the utmost of rights and privileges which public opinion would concede to Indians, would fix them in a middle station, between the negro and the white man; and that, as long as they survived this degradation, without the possibility of attaining the elevation of the latter, they would gradually sink to the condition of the former—a point of degeneracy below which they could not fall; it is likely, before they reached this, their wretchedness would find relief in broken hearts."[15]

The extent of the federal dilemma was revealed clearly by the cabinet discussions of February and March 1824. What swayed Monroe and the cabinet was the white unwillingness to have Indians in their states, not any philanthropic aim to save the Indians from degradation and extermination. The situation of the Indians in the Northwest, where some friends of the Indians were suggesting removal to save them, was not a major consideration in the creation of a federal removal policy. The executive and Congress shaped a policy in response to southern pressure. Calhoun made it quite clear in the cabinet at the end of February that the main problem was not those Indians who had failed to respond to white civilization but those who had succeeded. "The great difficulty," he argued, "arises from the progress of the Cherokees in civilization. They are now, within the limits of Georgia, about fifteen thousand, and increasing in equal proportion with the whites; all cultivators, with a representative government, judicial courts, Lancaster schools, and permanent property."[16] The Cherokees were not in danger because they had failed to adapt to white ways; they were in danger because of a Georgian greed for land, the unwillingness of most whites to accept Indians within their society, and the failure of the federal government to honor its previous commitments.

At the end of March Monroe informed Congress of his dilemma. He said he had attempted to fulfill the terms of the 1802 compact with Georgia, but that the Indians were resisting further cessions of land, even though their happiness and security would be promoted if they could be persuaded to move. Congress now joined Georgia in attacking the policy of the executive branch. A select committee appointed to deal with Monroe's message consisted of Georgian John Forsyth as chairman and an additional membership of two other Georgians, one North Carolinian, and one South Carolinian. Not surprisingly the committee urged that Indian claims in Georgia should, if necessary, be extinguished by force.[17]

In January 1825 the executive presented Congress with a comprehensive removal plan. The eastern Indians were to be removed to the region west of Arkansas and Missouri and to the region west of Lake Michigan. The latter suggestion was later abandoned as Wisconsin became more desirable to speculators and settlers. This new land in the West was to be a "permanent" home, and Indian civilization was to be encouraged.[18] Although the federal government had stated what it wanted, dilemmas remained. The question of the use of force had still not been resolved, and the morality of removal was still being questioned in Congress. Congress was badly split on these issues, and in 1825 and 1826 the vague Monroe-Calhoun removal plans could not obtain a general supporting vote in the House.[19]

The new administration of President John Quincy Adams clearly revealed the hardening of attitudes toward the Indians at the national level. Adams himself was not deeply committed on either side of the Indian question, although he was inclined to believe that the Indians could not stay in the East and were probably doomed wherever they were located. James Barbour, his secretary of war until 1828, thought as a Jeffersonian at a time when Jeffersonian dreams were vanishing. His initial and rather naive hope was that the Indians could be given individual plots of land and incorporated as private individuals in the states where they lived. Georgia had already rejected this solution, and in the cabinet in December 1825 Secretary of State Henry Clay candidly told Barbour why any plan for incorporating individual Indians within white society was not acceptable. Clay, who in his public statements often attacked the ruthlessness involved in American expansion, argued that "it was impossible to civilize Indians; that there never was a full-blooded Indian who took to civilization. It was not in their nature. He believed they were destined to extinction, and, although he would never use or countenance inhumanity towards them, he did not think them, as a race, worth preserving. He considered them as essentially inferior to the Anglo-Saxon race, which were now taking their place on this continent. They were not an improvable breed, and their disappearance from the human family will be no great loss to the world. In point of fact they were rapidly disappearing, and he did not believe that in fifty years from this time there would be any of them left." Over the next twenty years American scientists, supposedly on the basis of empirical evidence, resoundingly endorsed Clay's conclusions. John Quincy Adams tells a good deal about his own opinions, as well as those of Barbour, with his comment that "Governor Barbour was somewhat shocked at these opinions, for which I fear there is too much foundation."[20]

Faced by a divided cabinet and intransigent states, Barbour was forced to modify his plans, and he suggested to the cabinet that the Indians should be removed, but that they should be brought to civilization and incorporated into the union by combining them in a separate territory west of the Mississippi. Barbour was to make it quite clear later that he had no real faith in this plan, which had been forced upon him. The cabinet accepted the plan, not out of conviction, but because it was the only politically acceptable one. On the day Barbour reluctantly proposed it to the cabinet, Adams commented about the Indians that "I fear there is no practicable plan by which they can be organized into one civilized, or half-civilized, Government. Mr. Rush, Mr. Southard, and Mr. Wirt all expressed their doubts of the practicability of Governor Barbour's plan; but they had nothing more effective to propose, and I approved it from the same motive."[21] Clay was absent due to illness on this occasion, but his views were already well known to Barbour.

Barbour's experience in dealing with Adams's cabinet makes it quite clear that Indian Removal was not an effort to civilize the Indians under more favorable circumstances, which was how the Jacksonians justified the measure; rather it was an act to allow white Americans to occupy all the lands they wanted east of the Mississippi River. The settlers wanted all of the land and none of the Indians. Many friends of the Indian objected to the new policy, but they were not in sufficient numbers to exert decisive political influence. The only friends of the Indian who supported removal from the beginning were those, like Isaac McCoy, who worked among the demoralized and disorganized northwestern tribes, and who thought removal might save those Indians from simply disappearing under the white advance.[22] Other friends of the Indian eventually supported removal when they had no other choice.

When Barbour in February 1826 sent his plan for an Indian territory beyond the Mississippi to the House Committee on Indian Affairs, he publicly reflected on the inconsistencies of the policy he was proposing. He pointed out that as long as the desire for land "continues to direct our councils" every humane attempt to better the condition of the Indians would fail. After persuading the Indians to farm, he said, the government now desired to expel them: "They see that our professions are insincere; that our promises have been broken; that the happiness of the Indians is a cheap sacrifice to the acquisition of new lands." We tell the Indians they can have new desirable lands, he said, but they ask us "What new pledges can you give us that we shall not again be exiled when it is your wish to possess these lands?" Barbour knew that no honest pledge could be given. The tide of the white population will flow, he wrote, until arrested "by the distant shores of the Pacific."[23]

Barbour found himself in a politically impossible position in the late 1820s. In March 1827 he told Jeremiah Evarts, secretary of the American Board of Commissioners for Foreign Missions, that "one great argument in favor of removal of the Indians is that they *cannot remain where they are*, on account of the determination of the States of Georgia, Alabama, and Mississippi that they *shall not*." Barbour thought that state cupidity would not be resisted permanently by the federal government.[24] He was right. Barbour had no faith in his own plan for a territorial government west of the Mississippi, and even that acknowledgment of possible ultimate Indian equality was to prove unacceptable to Congress.

Support for Indian Removal became broader in the late 1820s as the inability of the federal government to resist southern state pressure became obvious. The only question left was who would grasp the nettle and force the Indians to accept the removal policy. That Thomas A. McKenney, who headed the Office of Indian Affairs within the War Department, and Lewis Cass, of major importance for Indian relations in the Old Northwest, should in the late 1820s have moved from a position of opposing to supporting removal is hardly surprising. They were both servants of a government that for over ten years had urged the necessity of removal and was near the point of abandoning the Indians to the states. The federal government was bowing before southern state pressures, causing confusion and despair among the southern Indians, and then was using this confusion and despair as a justification for removal.[25]

Isaac McCoy, who had long supported removal as in the best interests of the northwestern Indians he served, admitted that general removal "was agitated chiefly for the purpose of obtaining other ends than the welfare of the Indians." Even those politicians who regretted what was happening to the Indians and offered to help McCoy in doing what he could for Indian improvement, had no faith in what they were doing. McCoy later said that they "frankly told me they believed the Indian race was destined to become extinct. It was our duty to adopt all feasible measures for their preservation, but all would fail."[26] Much missionary support for the removal of the southern Indians came when all else had failed and when the federal government had tossed the Indians to the wolves. By that time the missionaries could do little but shepherd their flocks beyond the Mississippi.

The election of Jackson in 1828 sealed the fate of the southern Indians. Since 1814 Jackson had been anxious to clear the Indians from the southern states. After the War of 1812 his presence as a commissioner to negotiate Indian treaties had regularly been requested in the South. The states knew well that he would do all that was possible to obtain land. He was determined to have removal. As president he made it known through Secretary of War John Eaton that he would no longer protect the Indians against the southern states who wanted their lands. Georgia, Alabama, Mississippi, and Tennessee had all given Jackson crushing popular majorities in the 1828 election. Once Jackson was elected the southern states could extend their jurisdiction over the Indian lands within their borders. Neither John Marshall at the Supreme Court nor the missionaries among the Indians could save them.[27]

The general removal bill debated before Congress in the spring of 1830 disavowed the use of force, but it was well understood that the Indians would have no choice. They would either remove or be left to the mercies of the southern states. The bill was bitterly fought, and the opposition repeatedly pointed out the moral failure of federal policy. Edward Everett stated it simply and accurately: *"it is the object of this bill to appropriate a sum of money to cooperate with the States in the compulsory removal of the Indians."*[28] Opposition speaker after speaker pointed out that the southern Indians would now be forced out, that they would suffer in the act of removal, and that the white population would eventually sweep over the new lands that were to be permanently guaranteed. All this was true. When the removal bill passed by a narrow majority, every possible means was used by the Jackson administration to implement the measure. If pressure and bribery would not work, then private allotments were made; it was well understood that the private allotments would pass swiftly into the hands of the whites. Many Indians resisted to the last, citing the earlier federal guarantees of their lands and their progress in civilization. It was of no avail. The southern states got what they wanted—the Indians, civilized or not, were removed.[29]

Lewis Cass, who had long worked among and dealt with the Indians, became under Jackson an ardent advocate of removal. In a long article in 1830 he argued that there seemed to be an insurmountable obstacle in the habits or temperaments of Indians which prevented their adapting to American ways; the differences were such as to designate them "as a distinct variety of the human race." Cass attacked "Rousseau and the disciples of his school," who had persuaded themselves of the inferiority of civilized to savage life. "The Indians," wrote Cass, "are entitled to the enjoyment of all the rights which do not interfere with the obvious designs of Providence, and with the just claims of others." Existing relations with the Indians had "resulted from our superiority in physical and moral power."[30]

Jackson spent no sleepless nights over Indian Removal. He was confident, as those who supported him were confident, that Providence was guiding the hand of the American race, and that the same Providence which had blessed the United States with good government, power, and prosperity had provided that inferior peoples should yield their "unused" domain to those who through its use could benefit themselves and the world. "What good man," asked Jackson in his second annual message in December 1830, "would prefer a country covered with forests and ranged by a few thousand savages to our extensive Republic, studded with cities, towns, and prosperous farms, embellished with all the improvements which art can devise or industry execute, occupied by more than 12,000,000 happy people, and filled with all the blessings of liberty, civilization, and religion?"[31] A member of Congress who supported removal asked, "What is history but the obituary of nations?" He wanted to know if the United States should "check the course of human happiness— obstruct the march of science—stay the works of art, and stop the arm of industry, because they will efface in their progress the wigwam of the red hunter, and put out forever the council fire of his tribe?"[32]

The reality of Indian Removal was seen quite clearly in the 1830s by observers unconcerned with the main Washington debate. Thomas Dew in his 1832 work defending slavery took it for granted that this removal of the Indians was a temporary expedient, and that the American population would soon press once again over the Indian borders. He used the expulsion and assumed future disappearance of the Indians as an argument to defend the expediency and morality of black slavery: more Indians would have been saved, he argued, if they had been enslaved.[33] Tocqueville quickly perceived the shallowness of government promises of a permanent Indian home and future civilization beyond the Mississippi. He said that "the central government, when it promises these unhappy people a permanent asylum in the West, is well aware of its inability to guarantee this." The Creeks and the Cherokees had appealed to the central government against state oppression, Tocqueville said, but the federal government had determined to let a few tribes perish rather than shatter the union. "It is impossible," he said, "to destroy men with more respect to the laws of humanity."[34]

While the eastern Indians moved west beyond the Mississippi, discussions of Indian matters in Congress revealed both the unwillingness of the majority to accept the Indians as equals, and the extent to which a sense of Anglo-Saxon racial destiny and of irreversible distinctions between races was beginning to invade the popular consciousness. James W. Bouldin of Virginia argued that the Indians could not survive in competition with Anglo-Saxons. The Indians, he said, were "a noble, gallant, injured race," which has "suffered nothing but wrong and injury from us, since the Anglo-Saxon race (borrowing an expression of Mr. [John] Randolph, my predecessor, which seems to have become popular) first landed in this country." The solution was to remove them, because otherwise they would disappear. The blacks had grown in number in America only because they were enslaved and under the protection of "the Anglo-Saxons."[35]

The effort to create a formal Indian territory on the usual territorial model, with a degree of self-government and with the purpose of allowing Indians to emerge as equal citizens, was consistently blocked in Congress. The idea particularly stirred the fears of southern Congressmen, who saw the possibility of a dangerous precedent. William Archer of Virginia admitted that it "might be because he was a Southron," but he feared provision for the eventual admission of Indians to the American union would lead to far more serious questions — the possibility of the admission of Cuba, Haiti, and the free colony of blacks in Canada.[36]

As the mistreatment of the Indians was increasingly justified by arguments of their inferiority, some members of Congress, even outside of the Northeast, challenged this new view of Indian deficiencies. Ambrose Sevier of Arkansas said that "there were many individuals of the several tribes, and especially since the establishment of the Choctaw Academy in Kentucky, who were as intelligent as nine tenths of the members of this House."[37] John Tipton of Indiana attacked the whole notion that the Indians were incapable of improvement: "With regard to mental ability, we have no reason to believe they would suffer by a comparison with any other people . . . it would be preposterous to suppose that a whole nation of people were destitute of capacity to improve their condition . . . Are they not human beings, possessing all the passions of rational men, and all the powers of thought which belong to the human mind?" Tipton went to the heart of the matter when he said that it was natural that Americans should look for the causes of Indian disappearance among the Indians rather than among the whites, but this was a false search.[38]

Indian resistance to the rapid appropriation of their lands was used to condemn them further as semihuman savages. Anglo-Saxon aggression was hailed as manly, Indian resistance was condemned as beastly. This was particularly the case in discussing the fighting in Florida in the late 1830s and early 1840s, for here escaped slaves mingled with Indian warriors to complicate the fears of the Southerners. David Levy of Florida argued as the pioneers of western Pennsylvania and Tennessee had argued at the time of the American Revolution. He stressed Indian atrocities, even holding up a barbed spear point taken from the body of a child, and saying, in words reminiscent of Hugh H.

Brackenridge, "let us hear no more, I pray, from any quarter, of sympathy for these Indians. *They* know no mercy. They are demons, not men. They have the human form, but nothing of the human heart. Horror and detestation should follow the thought of them. If they cannot be emigrated, they should be exterminated."[39] The Indian, said William A. Graham of North Carolina, like the wild animals could not be tamed: "You might as well expect the red man to change the color of his skin as his habits and pursuits."[40]

To some southern Congressmen the Florida hostilities, rather than being an effort to dispossess Indians from areas desired by whites, simply became a confrontation between the colored and the white races of the earth. Thomas Hart Benton talked in the Senate of the desolation of forty-one thousand square miles in Florida—"made so by the ravages of the colored races upon the white!" The blacks, he argued, had combined with the Indians to commit wholesale atrocities, and he told a northern senator who had expressed sympathy for the Indians that his sympathy was misplaced—he should realize that "it is his own white race which has been the sufferer in Florida; and that the colored races have exulted in the slaughter and destruction of men, women, and children, descended, like the Senator himself, from the white branch of the human race."[41] The conflict was no longer viewed as that of civilization against savagery, as in the eighteenth century; it was becoming the white race against the colored races.

By the 1840s the friends of the Indian felt overwhelmed by the new tendencies and were very much on the defensive. Daniel Webster had written in 1838 that the Whig members of Congress who had "taken an interest in seeing justice done to the Indians are worn out and exhausted. An Administration man, come from where he will, has no concern for Indian rights."[42] Those friends of the Indian who still believed that the Indians were capable of attaining equality with the white race were in a difficult position in the 1840s and 1850s. Many missionaries were still hopeful that the Indians could be saved by being transformed, and commissioners of Indian affairs often maintained the rhetoric and optimism of an older generation, but most

Americans and their politicians had rejected the Indians as equal fellow citizens.[43]

Faced by unfavorable political realities and by the widespread dissemination of the scientific view that the Indians were inherently inferior, the friends of the Indian spent much of their time trying to defend the Indian capacity for improvement and trying to combat the view that the Indians were doomed to extinction. Isaac McCoy in 1840 attacked the idea that any race of man had been brought into existence with "some innate self-destroying principle," but he acknowledged that "lectures on the manners and customs of the Indians, whether consisting of encomium or censure, usually wind up with a prediction of the utter extinction of the race."[44] Thomas McKenney in 1846 admitted that Indian Removal had not created a haven for the Indians. He said all past experience showed that the United States would seek to dislodge the Indians again unless relations between the United States and the Indian tribes took a new form. His object in asking for a new course of action, he said, was to defend them from adverse judgments and to declare them "*human*." Except for their color and their lack of superior advantages, they were in all respects like white Americans.[45]

When Lewis Henry Morgan in 1851 defended the capacity of the Indians for improvement and argued that education and Christianity would be their only salvation, he was quite frank in admitting the general state of the public mind on this question. "The frequent attempts which have been made to educate the Indian, and the numerous failures in which these attempts have eventuated," he said, "have, to some extent, created a belief in the public mind, that his education and reclamation are both impossible." Morgan stressed that the existing system of federal Indian policy was "evidently temporary in its plans and purposes." It was designed, he argued, for the least possible inconvenience rather than "reclamation" and eventual citizenship: "The sentiment which this system proclaims is not as emphatic as that emblazoned upon the Roman policy towards the Carthaginians — *Carthago est delenda*, — 'Carthage must be destroyed:' but it reads in not less significant characters — *The destiny of the Indian is extermination*. This sentiment, which is so wide-spread as to have become a general theme for school-boy declamation, is not only founded upon erroneous views, but it has been prejudicial to the Indian himself."[46] By 1850 the American public and American politicians had for the most part abandoned any belief in potential Indian equality. They now believed that American Indians were doomed because of their own inferiority and that their extinction would further world progress.

The experience of the United States with the Indians in the first half of the nineteenth century helped to convince many Americans that American expansion might mean the eventual extinction of inferior races that lacked the innate ability to transform their way of life. The American public and American politicians had developed their own racial theories alongside, and even before, those of American intellectuals. They were pleased to gain confirmation of their beliefs from the scientists, but they often articulated ideas about Indian inferiority that received scientific proof only at a later date. As American hopes of creating a policy based on Enlightenment ideals of human equality failed, and as they relentlessly drove the Indians from all areas desired by the whites, Americans transferred their own failure to the Indians and condemned the Indians racially. By 1850 only a minority of Americans believed that transformed Indians would eventually assume a permanent, equal place within American society.

11
Anglo-Saxons and Mexicans

> The Anglo-Saxon blood could never be subdued by anything that claimed Mexican origin.
>
> James Buchanan, February 14, 1845

The decisive years in the creation of a new Anglo-Saxon political ideology were from the mid-1830s to the mid-1840s. In these years American politicians and the American population were overwhelmed by a variety of influences, both practical and theoretical, which inspired a belief that the American Anglo-Saxons were destined to dominate or penetrate the American continents and large areas of the world. Americans had faith that they would increase in such numbers that they would personally shape the destiny of other areas.

The catalyst in the overt adoption of a racial Anglo-Saxonism was the meeting of Americans and Mexicans in the Southwest, the Texas Revolution, and the war with Mexico. In confronting the Mexicans the Americans clearly formulated the idea of themselves as an Anglo-Saxon race. The use of *Anglo-Saxon* in a racial sense, somewhat rare in the political arguments of the early 1830s, increased rapidly later in the decade and became commonplace by the mid-1840s. The manner in which the Anglo-Saxon race was being isolated from other peoples was stated with clarity by Senator Benjamin Leigh of Virginia in January 1836 when opposing the abolitionist petitions. After pointing out that his fellow Congressmen had only to remember how the mobs of Cincinnati, Philadelphia, and New York had dealt with the few free Negroes in their midst to appreciate what would follow general emancipation, he candidly sketched the problem: "It is peculiar to the character of this Anglo-Saxon race of men to which we belong, that it has never been contented to live in the same country with any other distinct race, upon terms of equality; it has, invariably, when placed in that situation, proceeded to exterminate or enslave the other race in some form or other, or, failing in that, to abandon the country."[1]

The idea of the Anglo-Saxon race as a distinct, all-encompassing force was expressed with increasing frequency in the late 1830s. In February 1837 William Gilpin wrote to his father from New Orleans that while the town was still Gallic in character the "Anglo-Saxon is pushing aside the Frenchman and eating him up. The big steamers . . . are Anglo-Saxon, the huge stores and warehouses into which [goods] are piled have an Anglo-Saxon look and an Anglo-Saxon ship bears them hence. [Of] all the new part of the city, the only decent part is English."[2] When Horace Bushnell, in August 1837, delivered an oration on the principles of national greatness, he used old and familiar arguments concerning America as a land saved for events of world significance; however, he used a new precision in writing of the origin of the people for whom the New World had been preserved. "Out of all the inhabitants of the world," he said, ". . . a select stock, the Saxon, and out of this the British family, the noblest of the stock, was chosen to people our country." In contrast, the Mexican state, he said, had started with fundamental disadvantages in the character of its immigrants. If the quality of the British people was changed into that of the Mexican, "five years would make their noble island a seat of poverty and desolation." For Bushnell, God had reserved America for a special people of Saxon blood.[3]

By the 1830s the Americans were eagerly grasping at reasons for their own success and for the failure of others. Although the white Americans of Jacksonian America wanted personal success and wealth, they also wanted a clear conscience. If the United States was to remain in the minds of its people a nation divinely ordained for great deeds, then the fault for the suffering inflicted in the rise to power and prosperity had to lie elsewhere. White Americans could rest easier if the sufferings of other races could be blamed on racial weakness rather than on the whites' relentless search for wealth and power. In the 1830s and 1840s, when it became obvious that American and Mexican interests were incompatible and that the Mexicans would suffer, innate weaknesses were found in the Mexicans. Americans, it was argued, were not to be blamed for forcibly taking the northern provinces of Mexico, for Mexicans, like Indians, were unable to make proper use of the land. The Mexicans had failed because they were a mixed, inferior race with considerable Indian and some black blood. The world would benefit if a superior race shaped the future of the Southwest.

By the time of the Mexican War, America had placed the Mexicans firmly within the rapidly emerging hierarchy of superior and inferior races. While the Anglo-Saxons were depicted as the purest of the pure — the finest Caucasians — the Mexicans who stood in the way of southwestern expansion were depicted as a mongrel race, adulterated by extensive intermarriage with an inferior Indian race. Travelers delighted in depicting the Mexicans as an unimprovable breed and were particularly scathing about the inhabitants of Mexico's northern provinces. T. J. Farnham in 1840 wrote of the Californians as "an imbecile, pusillanimous, race of men, and unfit to control the destinies of that beautiful country." No one who knew "the indolent, mixed race of California," he argued, could believe they would long populate much less govern, the region. The mixed white and Indian races of California and Mexico "must fade away; while the mingling of different branches of the Caucasian family in the States" would produce a race which would expand to cover all the northern provinces of Mexico. "The old Saxon blood must stride the continent," wrote Farnham, "must command all its northern shores . . . and . . . erect the altar of civil and religious freedom on the plains of the Californias."[4]

The Mexican Californians were constantly attacked as shiftless and ineffective. Richard Dana thought them "an idle, thriftless people" and asserted that nothing but the character of the population prevented Monterey from becoming a large town. "In the hands of an enterprising people," he said, "what a country this might be!"[5] Lansford Hastings, in his famous emigrants' guide of 1845, characterized the Mexican inhabitants of California as "scarcely a visible grade, in the scale of intelligence, above the barbarous tribes by whom they are surrounded." This was not surprising, said Hastings. There had been extensive intermarriage and "as most of the lower order of Mexicans, are Indians in fact, whatever is said in reference to the one, will also be applicable to the other." Stereotypes that were to persist in American thinking long after the 1840s were firmly fixed in Hastings's work. A Mexican, he said, "always pursues that method of doing things, which requires the least physical or mental exorcise [sic], unless it involves some danger, in which case, he always adopts some other method." Writing of soldiers who were brought into California in 1842, he commented that they were "mere Indians," and that it was "with these wild, shirtless, earless and heartless creatures, headed by a few timid, soulless, brainless officers, that these semi-barbarians, intend to hold this delightful region, as against the civilized world." The process of dehumanizing those who were to be misused or destroyed proceeded rapidly in the United States in the 1840s. To take lands from inferior barbarians was no crime; it was simply following God's injunctions to make the land fruitful.[6]

In the Southwest there was even a tendency for American travelers to praise the Pueblo Indians in order further to debase the "mongrel" Mexicans. George Kendall, who was on the Texas-Santa Fe expedition, commented in his account of that sorry affair that "the *pueblos,* or town Indians of New Mexico, are by far the better part of the population." Most Mexicans, he said, were content if they could satisfy their animal wants, "and so they will continue to be until the race becomes extinct or amalgamated with Anglo-Saxon stock."[7] Rufus Sage echoed

Kendall: "There are no people on the continent of America, whether civilized or uncivilized, with one or two exceptions, more miserable in condition or despicable in morals than the mongrel race inhabiting New Mexico."[8]

The scathing denunciations of the Mexican race encompassed the inhabitants of central Mexico as well as its outlying provinces, and these denunciations were not confined to writers from any one party or one region in the United States. Waddy Thompson of South Carolina, who went to Mexico in 1842 as minister for the Whig administration, advanced the familiar stereotype in his *Recollections*, which was published in 1847. While condemning aggressive expansionism and the rapacious spirit of acquisition which was developing in the United States, Thompson had no doubt at all of the ultimate result of the meeting of the Anglo-Saxon and the Mexican races. He objected to the means, not to the end. "That our language and laws are destined to pervade this continent," he wrote, "I regard as more certain than any other event which is in the future. Our race has never yet put its foot upon a soil which it has not only kept but has advanced. I mean not our English ancestors only, but that great Teuton race from which we have both descended."[9]

To Thompson an essential element in Mexican weakness was the mixed population. Of seven million inhabitants, he wrote, only one million were white Europeans or their descendants. Of the others there were some four to four and one-half million pure-blooded Indians, and the rest of mixed blood. Thompson, like many others at this time, was easily able to envisage a mysterious disappearance of millions of people. "That the Indian race of Mexico must recede before us," he wrote, "is quite as certain as that that is the destiny of our own Indians." Negroes in Mexico Thompson characterized as "the same lazy, filthy, and vicious creatures that they inevitably become where they are not held in bondage." The general Mexican population Thompson characterized as "lazy, ignorant, and, of course, vicious and dishonest."[10]

The American dismissal of the Mexicans as an inferior, largely-Indian race did not pass unnoticed in Mexico. Mexican ministers in the United States warned their government that the Americans considered the Mexicans an inferior people. The Mexicans realized both that their neighbors to the north were likely to invade their northern provinces, and that they would claim that this was justified because they could make better use of the lands. Mexicans who served as diplomatic representatives in the United States were shocked at the rabid anti-Mexican attitudes and at the manner in which Mexicans were lumped together with Indians and blacks as an inferior race.[11]

The Texas Revolution was from its beginnings interpreted in the United States and among Americans in Texas as a racial clash, not simply a revolt against unjust government or tyranny. Thomas Hart Benton said that the Texas revolt "has illustrated the anglo-Saxon character, and given it new titles to the respect and admiration of the world. It shows that liberty, justice, valour — moral, physical, and intellectual power — discriminate that race wherever it goes." Benton asked "old England" to rejoice that distant Texas streams had seen the exploits of "a people sprung from their loins, and carrying their language, laws, and customs, their *magna charta* and all its glorious privileges, into new regions and far distant climes."[12]

In his two terms as president of Texas, Sam Houston consistently thought of the struggle in his region as one between a glorious Anglo-Saxon race and an inferior Mexican rabble. Victory for the Texans and the Americans in the Southwest would mean that larger areas of the world were to be brought under the rule of a race that could make best use of them. Houston was less imbued with the harsh scientific racial theories that carried most Americans before them in the 1840s than with the romantic exaltation of the Saxons given by Sir Walter Scott and his followers.

Houston's inaugural address in October 1836 contrasted the harsh, uncivilized warfare of the Mexicans with the more humane conduct of the Texans. He conjured up a vision of the civilized world proudly contemplating "conduct which reflected so much glory on the Anglo-Saxon race." The idea of the Anglo-Saxons as the living embodiment of the chivalric ideal always fascinated Houston; the Mexicans were "the base invader" fleeing from "Anglo-Saxon chivalry." In fighting Mexico the Texans were struggling to disarm tyranny, to overthrow oppression, and create representative government: "With these principles we will march across the Rio Grande, and . . . ere the banner of Mexico shall triumphantly float upon the banks of the Sabine, the Texian standard of the single star, borne by the Anglo-Saxon race, shall display its bright folds in Liberty's triumph, on the isthmus of Darien."[13]

While conceiving of the Texas Revolution as that of a freedom-loving Anglo-Saxon race rising up to throw off the bonds of tyranny imposed by a foreign despot, Houston was also fully convinced of the inevitability of general American Anglo-Saxon expansion. To him "the genius as well as the excitability" of the American people impelled them to war. "Their love of dominion," he said, "and the extension of their territorial limits, also, is equal to that of Rome in the last ages of the Commonwealth and the first of the Caesars." The people of the United States, he argued, were convinced that the North American continent had been bestowed on them, and if necessary they would take it by force.[14] He told one correspondent in 1844 that there was no need to be concerned about the population said to occupy the vast area from the 29th to the 46th latitude on the Pacific: "They will, like the Indian race yield to the advance of the North American population."[15]

For the most part Houston was content to exalt the Anglo-Saxons as a chivalric, freedom-loving, and expansionist race without launching bitter attacks on the capacities of other races. But the image he helped to create of a gallant band of Anglo-Saxon freemen struggling to throw off the yoke of Mexican oppression, and the more general image of the Mexicans that was present in the United States from the mid-1830s, helped breed a callousness toward the Mexicans as a people. The Alamo, the massacre at Goliad, and, later, the fate of the Texas-Santa Fe expedition received wide publicity in the United States and increased the venom with which the Mexican race was condemned. Hearing that those on the Texas-Santa Fe expedition had been captured and sent on a long march to Mexico City, the *Mobile Register and Journal* prophesied that a flame of resentment would sweep the United States which "will bring upon that feeble and treacherous race, a dreadful retribution for a long career of perfidy and cruelty."[16] Increasingly Mexicans were lumped with the blacks and the Indians. One man who had been on the Texas-Santa Fe expedition wrote of soon being able to have his turn "with the yellow skins" and said that though he did not think of himself as being much of a soldier he would risk his life in resisting "such beings as the Mexicans."[17] By the early 1840s few were willing to acknowledge that the Mexicans had anything to commend them as a race.

A notable exponent of the argument that Mexicans were worthless was Robert J. Walker, the Pennsylvania-born senator from Mississippi. Walker made the Texas cause his own and for the next thirty years was to be one of the most rampant of expansionists, urging the extension of American power over all North and South America, Iceland, and Greenland, endlessly promoting trade ties to the Pacific, and arguing that ultimately the Anglo-Saxon race would reunite under the American federal system to bring a reign of peace throughout the world. In 1836 he was on the threshold of his career, having just been elected from Mississippi. When urging the recognition of Texas independence, he told the Senate that whether or not the United States extended its jurisdiction over Texas, as he wanted, it should rejoice that American institutions, language, "and our kindred race, predominated over that fair country, instead of the colored mongrel race, and barbarous tyranny, and superstitions of Mexico."[18]

Walker's virulence on racial matters increased with his prominence. By the mid-1840s he had become a leader in the Democratic party, and when in 1845 he became Polk's secretary of the treasury, some of his friends thought that the appointment showed an insufficient recognition of his talents and promise. His annual reports as secretary, in which he urged free trade, were praised in the Democratic press as the finest since Hamilton's.[19] He combined brilliance and an ebullient personality with extravagant racial theories. In 1844, when urging the annexation of Texas, he estimated that five-sixths of the Mexican population were "of the mixed races, speaking more than twenty different languages, composed of every poisonous compound of blood and color." He asked whether such a people could ever subdue and govern the American race in Texas. Even if it could, he argued, it would be folly for the United States to permit the establishment of "this ignorant and fanatical colored population" on the borders of the slave states. If the Mexicans succeeded in retaking Texas, the United States' instinct for self-preservation should force it to act rather than let the region fall again "into the hands of the semi-barbarous hordes of Mexico."[20]

To combat the abolitionists and Whigs who said that the annexation of Texas would mean the expansion of slave power, Walker developed the idea that such an action would both reduce slavery and the number of blacks in the United States. In doing so he increased the gulf between the "Anglo-Saxon" and the "Mexican" races by arguing for a close affinity between Latin Americans and the blacks of the United States. The Mexicans had already been debased in American eyes by being characterized as a race largely intermarried with the Indians; their debasement was now to be completed by the manner in which they were linked to the despised blacks.

In his *Letter on the Annexation of Texas*, which was distributed extensively throughout the country, Walker argued that the annexation of Texas would, by drawing off the slaves to the Southwest, help reduce the number of slaves in the slave states, free the northern states from "the evil" of free blacks, and help the slaves themselves by taking them to a warmer and more hospitable region. Texas would act as a safety valve for the whole union. Slaves siphoned off into Texas would eventually move still farther south into Mexico and Central and South America. Among whites in the United States free blacks would always be a degraded caste, because they were inferior, but blacks would happily move south of the Rio Grande to Mexico and South America where there were so many of their people. In this way the United States, in the course of time, could lose its blacks. With triumphant and specious reasoning Walker concluded that the only way to get rid of slavery was to annex Texas: *"it will certainly disappear if Texas is reannexed to the union."*[21]

Walker's theory of the mass movement of blacks southward was as obviously flawed as the theory that assumed that large populations of non-Anglo-Saxon races would simply recede and disappear before the advance of the Americans, but it immediately found enthusiastic adherents. "Who is there that will object," said Representative John W. Tibbatts of Kentucky, "if all of this unfortunate race shall thus gradually and peaceably finally be withdrawn from our republic?"[22] James Buchanan of Pennsylvania, who was to serve in Polk's cabinet as secretary of state, accepted Walker's contention that slaves would be drawn off into Texas and ultimately across the Rio Grande to mingle with the Mexicans—a nation "composed of Spaniards, Indians, and negroes, blended together in every variety." Texas should be taken, said Buchanan, because "only thus can we fulfill our high destinies, and run the race of greatness for which we are ordained." He thought it impossible that a nation such as Texas, composed chiefly of native-born Americans, could ever remain under the rule of Mexico—"our race of men can never be subjected to the imbecile and indolent Mexican race." Buchanan consistently maintained this position throughout the debates on the annexation of Texas. Texas was free from Mexican rule and could not be retaken: "The Anglo-Saxon blood could never be subdued by anything that claimed Mexican origin." The same blood ran in Texan as in American veins, and both drew courage from the parent stock.[23] As secretary of state under Polk, Buchanan had utter contempt for the Mexicans with whom he had to negotiate.

The racial affinity of Americans and Texans was constantly on the lips of those who favored the annexation of Texas. Levi Woodbury of New Hampshire stated that the Texans had "a body of intelligent and talented men of the true Saxon race. And if all these do not constitute a state, what does?" He thought it was much more the duty of the United States to receive these Saxons into the union than it had been to receive the French of Louisiana or the Spanish of Florida. To Woodbury the Texans had been decoyed to their country by liberal colonization laws, then their rights and privileges invaded, "and their Saxon blood humiliated, and enslaved to Moors, Indians, and mongrels."[24]

David L. Seymour of New York saw annexation as "the easy and natural union of two contiguous nations, both founded by the Anglo-Saxon race, both organized upon the same basis of popular rights and republican equality." The Texans were a superior people. "They are of the Americo-Anglo-Saxon race," said Whig Alexander H. Stephens of Georgia. "They are from us, and of us; bone of our bone, and flesh of our flesh."[25]

Although many southern supporters of the annexation of Texas saw it as a means of protecting slavery and the interests of the slave states, there were supporters of annexation all over the country who saw the slavery question as irrelevant. They believed that the expansion of the Anglo-Americans into Texas was part of an inevitable movement of the American people, and that while the immediate effect might be the extension of slavery, the most important result would be the extension of the progressive power of the American race. As the blacks were more and more viewed as a race apart, whatever the fate of slavery, it was possible to conceive of an expansion which both extended slavery and the current boundaries of American settlement as being for the absolute good of the world. William J. Brown of Indiana was unwilling to accept the argument that the Rio Grande formed the natural boundary between races. To discuss whether or not the American advance should stop there was irrelevant, he argued, for "it *will not*. A half a century will not roll around before it will cover all Mexico; nor a century pass by before it will find its way to Patagonia's snow-invested wilds." He was uncertain how many republics would be carved from this area, but he had no doubt that their destinies "would be guided by Anglo-Saxon hands."[26]

The opponents of the annexation of Texas were unable to prevent it. The measure was firmly supported both in Congress and in the nation, and it was difficult to deny the argument that this was merely a reuniting of Americans who wished to be reunited. Although some objected to expansion that would mean the extension of slavery, practically all viewed the Southwest as an area that eventually would be transformed by Anglo-Saxons. It seemed that no human agency could stop the predestined outward thrust of the American people.

It was in commenting on the annexation of Texas that Democratic politician and publicist John L. O'Sullivan coined the phrase *Manifest Destiny* to describe the process of American expansion. In the early 1840s O'Sullivan, in editing the *Democratic Review*, had not accepted the most virulent of the new racial theories. Although he acknowledged black inferiority, he was generally reluctant to condemn all other races as being incapable of improvement. He had as much in common with the expansionists of the Jeffersonian generation as with those who seized on his phrases at mid-century, and he was more confident of general human improvement than most expansionists of the 1840s. Yet O'Sullivan was convinced that without violence America's population would expand outward in ever-increasing numbers, and though he had at first advised caution on the Texas issue, he was happy to accept the annexation of Texas. His qualms over methods were subsumed in his delight that his vision of American expansion was being realized.

O'Sullivan first used the phrase Manifest Destiny in criticizing other nations for attempting to interfere with a natural process: other nations had intruded, he said, "for the avowed object of thwarting our policy and hampering our power, limiting our greatness and checking the fulfillment of our manifest destiny to overspread the continent allotted by Providence for the free development of our yearly multiplying millions." Slavery had nothing to do with the annexation, he argued, for slaves would be drawn off to the South. Texas had been absorbed as part of the fulfillment of "the general law" which was sending a rapidly increasing American population westward. California would probably soon follow Mexico within the American orbit: "The Anglo-Saxon foot is already on its borders. Already the advance guard of the irresistible army of Anglo-Saxon emigration has begun to pour down upon it, armed with the plough and the rifle, and marking its trail with schools and colleges, courts and representative halls, mills and meeting houses." There was to be no balance of power on the American continent: Spanish America had demonstrated no ability for growth; Canada would break away from England to be annexed by the United States; and no European power could contend "against the simple, solid weight of the two hundred and fifty, or three hundred millions—and American millions—destined to gather beneath the flutter of the stripes and stars in the fast hastening year of the Lord 1945!"[27] In his enthusiasm O'Sullivan had put a touch of Carlyle into his style.

The initial use of the phrase Manifest Destiny in the summer of 1845 attracted no particular attention, but in December of that year O'Sullivan used it again, this time in his newspaper, the *New York Morning News*. O'Sullivan was now concerned with the Oregon question. He maintained that although America's legal title to Oregon was perfect, its better claim was by "the right of our manifest destiny to overspread and to possess the whole of the continent which Providence has given us for the development of the great experiment of liberty and federated self-government entrusted to us." A week later Representative Robert C. Winthrop of Massachusetts referred to the phrase in Congress. It immediately became the subject of debate and inspired both praise and censure. In the following years it was referred to frequently both by advocates and opponents of expansion.[28]

O'Sullivan was able to meld the Texas and Oregon crises in his general assumptions of overriding American destiny, but in Congress discussions of the racial implications of the two controversies differed sharply. In discussing Texas and Mexican rule Congressmen drew few distinctions between Mexicans and their government. It was argued that the instability and ineffectiveness of the Mexican government stemmed from the inadequacies of an inferior population. In discussing Great Britain and Oregon even those Congressmen who were most critical of the British government usually made a clear distinction between the British government and the English race. The English were respected as fellow Anglo-Saxons who were not to be swept out of Oregon as an inferior breed; and those who opposed war with England frequently discussed the disastrous effects of a clash between the two great branches of the Anglo-Saxon race. The sense of Anglo-Saxon racial community, combined with a respect for British power and ability, helped mute the most strident demands for war. While the Texas issue had provided an opportunity for accentuating the differences between superior Americans and inferior Mexicans, the Oregon crisis stimulated a public avowal of the common roots of the American and English peoples.

When in the spring of 1861 the London *Times* correspondent William H. Russell visited Montgomery, Alabama, he said of Georgian Robert Toombs that "he is something of an Anglomaniac, and an Anglo-phobist—a combination not unusual in America."[29] This duality of feeling toward England and the English was a persistent theme in the Oregon debates. In its simplest form it was expressed by Representative Samuel Gordon of New York. He admired the British people as "blood of our blood, bone of our bone, and flesh of our flesh," but he also announced that "I abhor and detest the British Government."[30] Robert J. Walker of Mississippi was able to draw the same distinction. In the 1850s he was to write in grandiloquent terms of plans for a world union of the Anglo-Saxon people, but in the 1840s he attacked British interference on the North American continent and America's abject dependence on the moneyed power of Great Britain: "let us draw nearer and nearer to that happy hour," he said in 1840, "that even our eyes may behold the glorious spectacle when not an acre of American soil shall be polluted by British dominion, or degraded by imperial or despotic power."[31]

Some in the Oregon debates had been so influenced by the surge of Saxonism that they justified a hard line on Oregon with the argument that American Anglo-Saxons were more than a match for English Anglo-Saxons still under an aristocratic government. Representative James B. Bowlin of Missouri argued in January 1845 that destiny had arranged for Americans to check in Oregon England's drive for universal dominion: "she meets those who sprung from a common stock—the same Anglo-Saxon race, and as little accustomed to witness a triumphal march over the ruins of their country, as are the would-be conquerors of the earth." The English were in trouble in Oregon, he believed, because they were meeting free representatives of the same Anglo-Saxon race.[32] Seaborn Jones of Georgia followed a similar line of thought by arguing that the Revolution had "showed that the Anglo-Saxon blood was improved by the spirit of liberty." He then revealed that he had perhaps imbibed a little too much Scott in his youth: "I love a 'foeman worthy of our steel,' " he announced, "and would sooner throw the gage of battle to proud, and haughty, and powerful England, than to bullying, and blustering, and impotent Mexico."[33] Congress generally did not endorse this arrogance of choosing the most difficult opponent.

Although some members of Congress in the mid-1840s were willing, even happy, to talk of a future war with England, most seemed satisfied to believe that a firm American stance would persuade England to yield Oregon to the United States. Most did not want war against a formidable opponent. Representative John S. Pendleton of Virginia thought that though the United States could take Canada the cost would be too heavy. The United States would not have to take it from "the mongrels and hybrids" ("Canadian French and half-breed Indians") that might compose a Canadian army: "we should meet men of our own mettle; it would be Saxon against Saxon; and there is no child's play there."[34]

The desire for firmness, no war, and ultimate American Anglo-Saxon triumph was expressed well in an article in the *Merchants' Magazine* in the spring of 1846. The author asserted that Oregon was the rightful property of the United States, and that English efforts to stop the advance of American pioneers were futile. Yet war should be avoided; it was unnecessary and it would be destructive to commerce. "No power on earth, nor all the powers of the earth, can check the swelling tide of the American population," it was argued, ". . . Every portion of this continent, from the sunny south to the frozen north, will be, in a very few years, filled with industrious and thriving Anglo-Saxons." There need be no war — all could be won by the weight of numbers: "The Oregon country must, all of it, not only up to 54° 40', but beyond it, far up into what is now exclusively Russian, become peopled by the Anglo-Saxon race . . . This is the irresistible flow of our people."[35]

The Oregon debates, while stimulating attacks on British power, also brought out the degree to which many Americans could disregard any immediate differences on the North American continent and see an ultimate compatibility of interests between England and the United States — a compatibility based on the Anglo-Saxon race and on the heritage of democratic institutions that derived from the special abilities of this race. New Englander Caleb Cushing had no doubt about the expansionist destiny of the United States. He believed its destiny was "to people, cultivate, and civilize this Continent."[36] The United States, he thought, should assert its rights to the Oregon country, for this deeply involved the fur trade, the whale fisheries, and trade with Asia. The region would become American if the United States "temperately but firmly" pressed her rights. "The world is wide enough for England and for us," he said. "We have much to gain by a cordial intercourse, conducted as becomes nations of the same blood, and the same tongue, each at the head of civilization in its proper hemisphere . . . Off-shoots of that dominant race, which, starting from the mountains of Caucasus, has proceeded in opposite directions, east and west, encircling the globe."[37] Theodore Parker said that war with England over Oregon would retard the progress of man for half a century.[38]

In an unusual display of agreement, both Daniel Webster and John C. Calhoun opposed any steps that might lead to war and emphasized what they thought to be the underlying compatibility of interests between Great Britain and the United States. Webster said that the likelihood of conflict over Oregon was being overemphasized, and that there could and would be a peaceful solution. Oregon, he added, would be settled mainly by Americans, although with some settlers from England, "but all *Anglo-Saxons;* all men educated in notions of independent government and all self-dependent."[39] This settlement would eventually lead to a great independent power on the Pacific, a republican power of English and American descent. John C. Calhoun told the Senate in March 1846 that he was opposed to war between the United States and Great Britain: "They are the two countries the furthest in advance in this great career of improvement and amelioration of the condition of our race. They are, besides, the two most commercial, and are diffusing, by their widely extended commerce, their blessings over the whole globe. We have been raised up by Providence for these great and noble purposes, and I trust we shall not fail to fulfil our high destiny."[40] In this context "our race" was undoubtedly the white race.

Most members of Congress were content neither to lambast the British government, nor analyze the possibilities of war, but simply to view the American advance to Oregon, for whatever commercial or agrarian reasons, as simply part of America's inevitable western and expansionist destiny. They were confident that this westward movement was one stage in the advance of the American Anglo-Saxons to world power. Senator David R. Atchison of Missouri said there was no way of dissuading the American people from occupying Oregon. Settlers were ready to move in an unbroken column west—"'like the Goths and Huns of old; a nation will emigrate, not for the purpose of destroying, but of building up empires!'" He said nothing could check the westward march of empire. Atchison's predecessor, Lewis F. Linn, had stressed that Americans from the time they had first arrived in Massachusetts had "but obeyed the instinct of our peculiar race—that invincible longing for liberty and space which impels those of Anglo-Saxon descent to trace the rudest tracts, the wildest seas, range the Atlantic and the Indian waste of waters, explore the vast Pacific, and break through the icy barriers of the polar oceans." Rufus Choate of Massachusetts denied that the intense American feeling of nationality involved any deep-seated hatred of England. What it really involved, he said, was a feeling that Americans had "a transcendent destiny to fulfil . . . a career to run, up which we hope to ascend till we stand on the steadfast and glittering summits of the world."[41]

That the Oregon question was settled peacefully and the southwestern problem resulted in war with Mexico stemmed partially from the differences in strength between Great Britain and Mexico. But it also arose from the obvious fact that many American politicians were reluctant to clash with their Anglo-Saxon brethren, whereas they thought as little of clashing with the Mexicans as they did of clashing with the Indians. The Oregon debates revealed the extent to which the British government was hated by some Americans and the extent to which British imperial ambition was feared; but they also revealed a basic admiration for the English people and a pride in belonging to a common Anglo-Saxon stock.

The enthusiasm with which American politicians and publicists sang the praises of the Anglo-Saxon stock was heightened in these years of the mid-1840s by a growing concern about the rapid increase in Irish Catholic and in German immigration. As yet the concern was not general because most Americans had faith that the multiplying Anglo-Saxons could easily absorb other European stocks, particularly those of Teutonic origin; but already some were indicating a desire to preserve their own status and economic interests through a strong emphasis on racial exclusiveness. The prospect of increasing disruptions to society through large-scale immigration, added to the already rapid social and economic change of the 1830s and 1840s, helped encourage many to find security in racial solidarity. The extensive growth in the decades since 1815 had brought widespread opportunities for wealth; yet it had also brought widespread disruption and disappointments. The depression of the late 1830s and early 1840s had increased fears of competition from alien elements. In an age of constant change many were to find security in the certainty of a racial heritage that stretched back into the distant past.[42]

The 1844 election saw the flowering of a vigorous anti-immigrant movement, a movement which hoped to make it more difficult for foreigners (and they were thinking primarily of new non-English immigrants) to achieve the political rights of native-born Americans. In June a large meeting of nativists in Philadelphia praised their congressional supporters as "possessed of some slight recollections of those principles for which our fathers bled—the good old principles of Saxon liberty—the principles which cost to John, his power—to James, his throne—to Charles, his head—to George, his provinces."[43] The Whigs of New York were bitterly disappointed at Clay's loss of the state in 1844. Philip Hone told Clay that though the good, hard-working New York Whigs voted for Clay, "alas! the numerical strength lies not in those classes. Foreigners who have 'no lot or inheritance' in the matter, have robbed us of our birthright, the 'scepter has departed from Israel.' Ireland has reconquered the country which England lost."[44] Although the nativist movement ostensibly supported the native-born against all aliens, in reality nativists were mostly interested in supporting American "Anglo-Saxons" against the rest. Those who thought of the existing American race as "Anglo-Saxon" were able to ignore their own particular origin in assuming that the basic stock should be preserved.

Even those who did not seek to preserve an intact Anglo-American race through specific political action had become convinced by the late 1830s and 1840s that American achievement depended upon more than fortunate institutions and a happy environment; it was a matter of blood. The United States had developed in its own unique manner because it had been settled by members of a particular, superior race, a race with innate attributes making possible the creation of a free, ever-growing government. Robert C. Winthrop of Massachusetts, who opposed militant Manifest Destiny, said in 1839 that "I cannot regard it . . . as a mere lucky accident, that this Atlantic seaboard was settled by colonies of the Anglo-Saxon race!" Providence had arranged for the colonization and civilization of the American continent by *"Englishmen."* One had only to compare American political institutions to the "loathsome and abhorrent" political condition of the French on the North American continent to realize that the superiority sprang from "the comparative capacities for self-improvement of the Races by which they were planted."[45] It was becoming just as important that the Americans were born Anglo-Saxons as that they were bred Americans.

Those who earlier had expressed hope for general human improvement were not immune to the new sense of Anglo-Saxon racial exclusiveness. Edward Everett, speaking in England in 1843, told an audience that "history warrants us in believing in races of men, as well as of inferior animals," and that "the Anglo-Saxon race, from which we Americans trace our descent, is surpassed by none other that ever existed."[46] Daniel Webster, in responding to a toast in 1843, emphasized that even with the separation of New England from Old England, both were proceeding on a mighty career of progress and power; he added that in explaining this, he would not dwell with any particular emphasis on the sentiment "which I nevertheless entertain, with respect to the great diversity in the races of men." Webster went on to point out that "on this continent *all* is to be *Anglo-American* from Plymouth Rock to the Pacific seas, from the north pole to California," and in the eastern world English settlements were everywhere. Webster mused that if there was anything in the idea of the supremacy of races "the experiment now in progress will develop it. If there be any truth in the idea, that those who issued from the great Caucasian fountain, and spread over Europe, are to act on India and on Asia, and to act on the whole Western world, it may not be for us, nor our children, nor our grandchildren to see it, but it will be for our descendants of some generation to see the extent of that progress and dominion of the favored races."[47] The tone of Webster's speech left no doubt as to what he believed, as there was no doubt that the German accounts of the Germanic tribes spreading westward from central Asia to regenerate the world were beginning to gain wide currency in the United States.

Even British imperial power could be viewed in a different light when it involved not resistance to American desires but a general triumph of the Anglo-Saxon race. England's attack on China in the Opium War was celebrated by John Gordon Bennett of the *New York Herald* as "another movement of the Anglo-Saxon spirit in the remotest east, against the barriers of semi-barbarians and a half-civilized race, who have been stationary for twenty centuries or more."[48] This was not a victory for British imperialism, but a triumph for the Anglo-Saxons.

By 1845 many were finding it difficult to believe that free institutions could flourish in any area that did not have a substantial Anglo-Saxon population. Representative Alexander Duncan of Ohio suggested that there "seems to be something in our laws and institutions peculiarly adapted to our Anglo-Saxon-American race, under which they will thrive and prosper, but under which all others wilt and die." Even the French and Spanish whose land had been taken over were not moving away, Duncan said; they were gradually disappearing. Representative James E. Belser of Alabama stated it quite simply when he said it was impossible to limit "the area of freedom — the area of the Anglo-Saxon race."[49]

Along with the exaltation of a particular race came a new sense of urgency and ultimately a willingness to admit the necessity of force — when the ends were so sublime, could one continually quibble about the means? Anglo-Saxons, through the expansion of England and the United States, were visibly taking over the world, and by the 1840s only a few in the United States were prepared to suggest that this was not for the good of the world. Some even began to welcome force rather than regret its necessity. George O. Sanders of Kentucky, later a leader of the political Young America group, wrote in 1844 in regard to the Texas question that "the Americans are everywhere awake. They are booted and spurred, and are panting for the contest."[50] Representative Charles G. Ferris of New York noted that America's "march is *onward, onward.*" The United States was springing forward "to greatness and empire." The imagery of American expansion no longer simply emphasized "spreading"; it stressed "marching." John Reynolds of Illinois thought that the Americans by 1890 would extend through Canada and would have large cities on the Pacific and extensive commerce across that ocean: this was the "onward march of the United States to her high destiny, which no foreign nation can arrest."[51] In this mood the Americans were ready to take what the Mexicans would not sell. Many had convinced themselves that what they wanted was for the good of the world as well as themselves.

12

Race, Expansion, and the Mexican War

> Though the barbarians fall thick as hail, still, as their disposition is warlike and as the slaughter of their armies by the superiority of scientific warfare and the unflinching bravery of men disposed to peace, would teach them helpful lessons, the loss of a few thousand of them would not be so deplorable. The Mexicans will be led by this war to think of their weakness and inferiority.
>
> The *Casket* (Cincinnati), June 10, 1846

The contradictions which had long been implicit in America's sense of mission became explicit at the time of the Mexican War. It became obvious in these years that the United States had now rejected the idea that most other peoples of the world could share in the free government, power, and prosperity of the United States. To sow the seeds of freedom and republicanism over an ever-widening area was not enough to secure world progress, because Americans now believed that these seeds were falling on barren ground. Most peoples, they believed, lacked the innate abilities to take advantage of free institutions. Some races were doomed to permanent inferiority, some to extinction.

While faith in general human improvability was often lost, faith in the expansive power of the American branch of the Anglo-Saxon race increased. The Americans were destined to continue to increase rapidly in numbers and to spread far and wide. But if other peoples could not be instructed in the establishment of free republican states, what would happen to the population in the areas into which the American Anglo-Saxons were expanding? The Americans had two immediate racial models—the Indians and the blacks. Wherever the whites had moved in large numbers the Indians had disappeared, and it was assumed that as the American population expanded its settlements to the Pacific the Indians would be eliminated. The blacks were not disappearing but were increasing in numbers. They were surviving, argued the advocates of slavery, because they had been totally subordinated to a superior race. Even many of those who opposed slavery believed that free blacks could not survive and prosper in close proximity to the white race.

The most irrational American expansionists in the 1840s appeared to believe that the Anglo-Saxons would actually replace numerous world peoples in the course of progress. The practical realities embodied in the idea of "the survival of the fittest" were made use of in America well before they were embodied in a statement of general principle. Some Americans believed that their problems would be solved by having other races, like the Indians, melt away before the American advance. The American Anglo-Saxons would not teach or rule other peoples—they would replace them.

For some, southern slavery taught that another route to a free, prosperous society was the total subordination of the inferior to the superior race. Perhaps this could be the future pattern of the American advance. Mexicans and others might not be enslaved, but they would be subordinated to the rule of a superior people. Military success in Mexico led some Americans to argue that the United States should enforce a military, colonial-style government. They asserted that this would bring prosperity to Mexico, more power and wealth to the United States, and would hasten the time when the whole world would become progressive. The United States would become a colonial power.

This last suggestion brought a crisis in American thinking on expansion. There were many in the United States who believed that the trappings of colonialism would ruin the republic. But they did not want to bring large numbers of non-Anglo-Saxon peoples as equal citizens within the American union. They thought such inferior peoples would also ruin the republic. This dilemma quickly produced strong opposition to immediate expansion. If Americans believed that other peoples would not disappear before the American advance, if they also thought that colonialism would corrupt the nation, and if they believed that other races were incapable of participating in a free government, then opposition to a further extension of territory became their only hope of preserving a free American Anglo-Saxon republic. It meant resisting those who were now convinced that the United States should rapidly assume political control over vast new areas. Yet the expansionists were to be resisted not because this would mean the degradation of other peoples, but because the presence of other races would ruin the society created in the United States.

The general low regard in which the people of Mexico were held by the government and people of the United States helped to precipitate the outbreak of war. Since the time of the Texas Revolution the Mexicans had been repeatedly attacked in the United States as a degenerate, largely Indian race unable to control or improve the territories they owned. Only a minority of Americans felt a sense of guilt in waging war on such a people. Indeed, faced by a people considered so feeble and lacking in self-respect, Polk's administration hoped to achieve the annexation of Texas and the purchase of California without resorting to overt force.

The American minister in Mexico, Wilson Shannon, commented to Calhoun in October 1844 that "I See it is predicted in some of the papers in the U.S. that Mexico will declare war against the U.S.; there is as much probability that the Emperor of China will do so."[1] Because the Mexicans were held in contempt, it was assumed that firmness would force them to yield to American wishes. Unlike the English in Oregon, the Mexicans were neither praised as fellow members of a special race, nor respected as a potentially formidable foe. Before going to Mexico in the fall of 1845 envoy John Slidell told Secretary of State James Buchanan that he did not believe that the Mexicans would go to war: "The truth is that although I have no very exalted idea of Mexican intellect, yet I cannot imagine that any one who could by possibility be elected president, could have so small a modicum of sense as to think seriously of going to war with [the] United States."[2] Secretary of War William L. Marcy as late as July 1845 expressed the opinion that he had at no time felt that war with Mexico was probable "and do not now believe it is."[3] Secretary of State James Buchanan had a particularly low opinion of Mexican character and talents and for much of the war balked at the idea of annexing territory that contained any large number of Mexicans. In his official instructions to Slidell he asked his envoy to be as conciliatory as possible and patiently to endure any unjust reproaches. "It would be difficult," he said, "to raise a point of honor between the United States and so feeble and degraded a Power as Mexico."[4]

The general assumption in the cabinet that Mexico would not fight the United States, or at worst could easily be defeated, was reflected in public opinion throughout the country. Although a few prominent individuals, including Senator Benton, warned that Mexico would fight valiantly to protect its lands, the general assumption was that a weak and degraded Mexico could offer no real resistance to the United States forces. It was even assumed at the beginning of the war that a Mexican population oppressed by the military, the clergy, and a corrupt government would welcome the invading armies. Throughout the conflict some argued that the United States was carrying freedom to the Mexicans, and that a true regeneration of the Mexicans was to take place. But it soon became apparent that most Americans believed that the Mexicans lacked the innate ability to benefit from the opportunity to be given them by liberating American armies.

The older idea of Americans actually carrying the seeds of free institutions to Mexicans who would throw off their bondage and create a sister republic was expressed most often at the beginning of the war in the writings of America's patriotic poets. Many obviously found their inspiration in the older tradition of the widening arc of free institutions. One poet envisioned the stars in America's flag increasing "Till the world shall have welcomed their mission sublime / And the nations of earth shall be one." Another, in leaden verse, sang that "The world is wide, our views are large / We're sailing on in Freedom's barge / Our God is good and we are brave / From tyranny the world we'll save." The sentiment that the United States' flag would be the flag of the world when tyranny had perished was a common one, and many united in conceiving of the invasion as a war of liberation. The inhabitants of Mexico were expected to welcome the Saxons with open arms. A New York poet in May 1846 conjured up an image of Mexicans joyously shouting "The Saxons are coming, our freedom is nigh."[5]

Yet while many poets wrote in an older, idealistic tradition, some reflected the prevailing racial stereotypes of the Mexicans and added sexual overtones to the image of the liberating drive into Mexico. A poem published in Boston in June 1846 and entitled "They Wait for Us" foreshadowed the views of those expansionists who later in the war argued that the American Anglo-Saxons would simply absorb and eliminate what was left of the Mexican population. Neither this poet nor the later politicians had any doubt that extinguishing the remnants of the Mexican race was to be accomplished by a union of American men and Mexican women:

> The Spanish maid, with eye of fire,
> At balmy evening turns her lyre
> And, looking to the Eastern sky,
> Awaits our Yankee chivalry
> Whose purer blood and valiant arms,
> Are fit to clasp her budding charms.
>
> The *man*, her mate, is sunk in sloth —
> To love, his senseless heart is loth:
> The pipe and glass and tinkling lute,
> A sofa, and a dish of fruit;
> A nap, some dozen times by day;
> Sombre and sad, and never gay.[6]

The image of lazy Mexican men and available Mexican women had already been established by the accounts of American travelers. Dana, in his *Two Years before the Mast*, had written of "thriftless, proud, extravagant" California men and of women with "a good deal of beauty" whose morality was "none of the best." Kendall, who was on the Texas-Santa Fe expedition, dismissed Mexican men in the usual fashion, but was obviously fascinated by the women. The "Anglo-Saxon traveler" entering New Mexico, he said, "feels not a little astonished at the Eve-like and scanty garments of the females he meets." He went on to describe the beauty of Mexican women and was obviously delighted that "the forms of the gentler sex obtain a roundness, a fulness, which the divinity of tight lacing never allows her votaries." His general characterization of the women was in striking contrast to his dismissal of Mexican men: the women of northern Mexico "are joyous, sociable, kind-hearted creatures almost universally, liberal to a fault, easy and naturally graceful in their manners." Kendall's distinction between Mexican men and women was commonplace in the travel narratives. "The ladies," Rufus B. Sage wrote, "present a striking contrast to their countrymen in general character, other than morals."[7] The stereotype of exotic, receptive Mexican women and lazy, inept Mexican men was to sink deep into American racial mythology.

The old rhetoric of freeing oppressed peoples and providing for a widening arc of republican institutions, which inspired some of the patriotic poets, was never entirely lacking from more reasoned arguments in the era of the Mexican War. Even the southern *De Bow's Review* published an article explaining the trouble and turmoil of the Mexicans since independence in terms of the paucity of education, the lack of a middle class, and the domination of the people by the clergy and by militarists. "All these causes," it was argued, "must be removed before Mexico can be regenerated; and though difficult, there is no reason to despair of this, for the Mexicans are possessed of great natural capacities, which only require proper cultivation and a favorable field for their development, to enable them to obtain a high grade of intelligence." Although they were not yet ready for republican institutions, this was certainly possible in time.[8]

Expressions of optimism appeared sporadically throughout the war years. John Gordon Bennett's *New York Herald* suggested in the spring of 1847, when arguing that the United States should, if necessary, retain Mexico, that "the universal Yankee nation can regenerate and disenthrall the people of Mexico in a few years."[9] In Congress such sentiments were rare, but emerged in early 1848 among some of those willing to annex the whole of Mexico. Most who favored annexation thought of an Anglo-Saxon elite controlling the Mexicans and their affairs, but there was some sentiment in favor of an older view of regeneration. Senator Sidney Breese of Illinois acknowledged the prevailing view when he said "I have taken a different view of the people of that country, and I think I see in them attributes and elements quite susceptible, by proper appliances, of high improvement."[10]

Some, in the heat and emotion of the conflict, wavered between faith in the improvability of mankind and the new racial pride. Walt Whitman, then editor of the *Brooklyn Daily Eagle*, argued that American expansion was for the good of the whole world: "We pant to see our country and its rule far-reaching," he wrote, "only inasmuch as it will take off the shackles that prevent men the even chance of being happy and good." Yet while Whitman generally attacked the Mexican government rather than the Mexican people, he could not free himself from the prevailing racial interpretation of events. "What has miserable, inefficient Mexico . . . to do," he asked, "with the great mission of peopling the New World with a noble race?" General Zachary Taylor's capture of Monterey in September 1846 was welcomed as "another clinching proof of the indomitable energy of the Anglo-Saxon character." Whitman now wanted peace and the cession of large areas by Mexico. This would be for the good of mankind.[11]

Wartime rhetoric more frequently involved the brutal language of dehumanization. The *Casket*, published in Cincinnati, argued at the beginning of the war that there was "a kind of charm in the thought of 'widening the area of freedom' that is difficult to resist," but discussed the war in terms that would have been completely unacceptable fifty years before. War was to be deplored, the editor argued, but it was sometimes a help to human progress. A war between enlightened nations would shock humanity, "but an occasional conflict with barbarians must be expected." The Mexicans were dismissed as beneath contempt: "Though the barbarians fall thick as hail, still, as their disposition is warlike and as the slaughter of their armies by the superiority of scientific warfare and the unflinching bravery of men disposed to peace, would teach them healthful lessons, the loss of a few thousand of them would not be so deplorable. The Mexicans will be led by this war to think of their weakness and inferiority."[12] Journalists were inspired by the martial spirit of the times to excesses of bombastic pride. The rampantly expansionist *Illinois State Register* in June 1846 contained the comment that the Mexicans "are reptiles in the path of progressive democracy—who, with his bigboots on is bound to travel from Portland to Patagonia—and they must either crawl or be crushed."[13] At times the brutality of thought and language more clearly foreshadows the excesses of twentieth-century racism than it echoes the dreams of Jeffersonian America.

The bitter political dispute concerning the annexation of Mexican territory was primarily an argument not about territory but about Mexicans. Although abolitionists and some Whigs at first opposed any expansion because it involved extending slavery, and though some Southerners eventually opposed expansion because they feared free areas entering the union, most Americans expected and wanted the acquisition of Mexico's sparsely populated northern provinces. Also, many on both sides of the political argument believed that the rest of Mexico was eventually destined to be dominated by the American Anglo-Saxon race. When writing or talking of the indefinite future, rather than the immediate political destiny of Mexico, publicists and politicians argued in simplistic terms of supplanting inferior Mexicans by superior Anglo-Saxons. The antiwar *American Whig Review* summarized well the thinking it said had inspired Polk and impressed the American people: "Mexico was poor, distracted, in anarchy, and almost in ruins—what could she do to stay the hand of our power, to impede the march of our greatness? We are Anglo-Saxon Americans; it was our 'destiny' to possess and to rule this continent—we were *bound* to it! We were a chosen people, and this was our allotted inheritance, and we must drive out all other nations before us!"[14]

The simplistic rhetoric sketched by the *American Whig Review* was reiterated by American politicians throughout the war years. Ignoring the practical problems of the nature of American rule over adjacent areas, they argued that Providence was arranging for an American victory over Mexico in the same manner as she had provided for the vast increase in American power, the disappearance of the Indians, and earlier victories over England. Andrew Johnson of Tennessee both during and after the war argued that Mexico was doomed as a nation; it "had reached its acme, its apex of power under her present rulers." God intended to punish the "perfidious and half-civilized" Mexico, and "the Anglo-Saxon race has been selected as the rod of her retribution."[15]

Though God might be guiding the Americans to the conquest of Mexico, he had not provided a detailed plan for American rule over the Mexican people. American victories in the Mexican War meant that there had to be a practical discussion of the future relationship of the Mexicans to the American federal system. The prophesies of a Manifest Destiny sweeping Americans onward over ever greater areas appeared to be coming true with remarkable rapidity as American armies pressed on into Mexico. To some the northern provinces now seemed only the beginning. Mexico was there for the taking, and it was assumed that the American people, American energy, and American capital could quickly transform the whole region. The stumbling block was the Mexican people. From the very beginning of the war the Whigs had much support among the Democrats in resisting the acquisition of any heavily populated Mexican areas.

The Whigs were, of course, fearful that expansion in the Southwest would mean the extension of slavery, but even after the introduction of the Wilmot Proviso raised fears in the South of large additions of free territory, the Whigs continued to express a bitter opposition to expansion. To the Whig opposition Mexico presented a potential threat to American democratic institutions. They could not accept the idea of United States colonial rule in the area, for this would endanger the republican form of government; the power of the president would be enhanced, militarism would be rife, and corruption would sap the vitals of a free America. But the Whigs also felt that the American political system would be ruined by the participation of millions of "inferior" Mexican citizens. Education was no solution, for most Americans now firmly believed in innate, not simply environmental, inferiority.

Congressional opposition to the possibility of incorporating Mexican people into the union had been expressed even before the war started. Senator Jabez W. Huntington of Connecticut argued that the American constitution was not a constitution "for people of every color, and language, and habits."[16] Democrat William Wick of Indiana said "I do not want any mixed races in our Union, nor men of any color except white, unless they be slaves. Certainly not as voters or legislators." Wick, however, said he would annex any part of the world where American people settled. Generally the Whigs wanted caution and gradualism in expansion, whereas many Democrats were ready for swift action; but neither party wanted other races to participate in the American government.[17]

After the outbreak of war, the Whig press constantly reiterated its fears of racial amalgamation. The *Charleston Mercury* asked if "we expect to melt into our population eight millions of men, at war with us by race, by language, by religion, manners and laws?" The *Richmond Whig* melded condemnation of the Mexican population with criticism of the change in the nature of America's mission, arguing that the United States had "a mission of peace, not of war." Contiguous territory would be annexed by purchase or cession as long as there was any left, but not by conquest. Republican institutions would be threatened by the forceful occupation of an immense territory "occupied by an ignorant, heterogeneous and bigoted population." The *Cincinnati Herald* also wanted no premature, forced extension of America's bounds. What would America do, the editor asked, with eight million Mexicans "with their idol worship, heathen superstition, and degraded mongrel races." They would provide

America with more than twenty new senators and over one hundred representatives. The *Augusta Daily Chronicle*, whose editor balked at swallowing Mexico, went to the heart of the matter: "It would likely prove to be a sickening mixture, consisting of such a conglomeration of Negroes and Rancheros, Mestizoes and Indians, with but a few Castilians."[18] The Whig newspapers condemned the new militarism, but they accepted the new racial theories.

When in the late summer of 1846 the conquest of New Mexico was followed by Colonel Stephen W. Kearny's proclamation announcing America's intention to annex the region, there were immediate protests. "We have far more to dread from the acquisition of the debased population who have been so summarily manufactured into American citizens," said the *Richmond Whig*, "than to hope from the extension of our territorial limits." The *Chicago Daily Journal* expressed a similar objection and commented that these "barbarians will of course be Locofocos — so would an Esquimaux Indian."[19] Consistently, Whig newspapers pointed out that if Mexico, with its "wretched population," were kept, the future alternatives were equally bad: either inferior Mexicans would be incorporated into the union, or the United States would govern by force and weaken its own institutions. The Whigs saw no need for haste in American expansion. Americans were spreading relentlessly outward. Why should the national character be sullied by the use of force or the population diluted by alien ingredients?

Militarism, the extension of slavery, and the forcible addition of a mongrel race dominated the arguments of Whig orators in Congress. The plainest exposition of the problem was given by Representative James Pollock of Pennsylvania, who argued that "the public mind has become diseased" on the subject of territorial aggrandizement. Opposing the taking of any more territory, Pollock asserted that the "Mexican provinces are filled with a population, not only degraded, but of every possible shade and variety of color and complexion, from the deep black of the negro, to the sallow white of the Mexican Indian." Were these to become citizens, he asked, or were the Americans to enslave the colored? If the latter, then nine-tenths of the population of Mexico would have to be enslaved. The Spaniards had a peculiar obstinancy, he maintained, and would fight to the last inch of ground: "Extermination and acquisition must go together. Are we prepared for this? Are we prepared to make the war a war of races, and not stay our hand until every Mexican is driven from the land of his fathers, and the anglo-Saxon race established in the Halls of the Montezumas?"[20] Antislavery Whig Columbus Delano of Ohio condemned the Mexicans as a "sad compound of Spanish, English, Indian, and negro bloods . . . resulting, it is said, in the production of a slothful, indolent, ignorant race of beings," and even Representative Thomas Corwin of Ohio, in his famous speech attacking American aggression, talked of the "half-savage, half-civilized race" of Mexico.[21] The Whigs regularly emphasized what aggression was doing to the United States, not what aggression was doing to Mexico.

The Democrats could agree neither on how much of Mexico should be taken nor on whether the United States should annex territory inhabited by large numbers of Mexicans. Nearly all could agree, however, that Mexicans could not be admitted as equal citizens within the American republic. At the beginning of the war the influential *Democratic Review* said that no period of tutelage would prepare the Mexicans for participation in a free republican system. "*Race,*" wrote the author, "is the key to much that seems obscure in the history of nations," and it explained Mexico's miseries. The largely Indian or half-breed Mexican population lacked the characteristics necessary for the creation and support of free institutions. Throughout the world it was the same — "the whiter race ruling the less white, through all the gradations of color, from the fairest European down to the darkest African." There was no hope for representative, democratic rule in Mexico.[22]

In the cabinet Secretary of State James Buchanan often expressed his fear of the admission of any large number of Mexicans to the union. He argued in the spring of 1847 that the United States should obtain Upper and Lower California, New Mexico, and a Rio Grande boundary, and that the safest way of extending the republic was by the acquisition of areas colonized almost exclusively by Americans. The acquisition of lands southward to the Sierra Madre mountains would raise the question of slavery, but more importantly it would raise basic questions about the nature of the population: "How should we govern the mongrel race which inhabits it? Could we admit them to seats in our Senate & House of Representatives? Are they capable of Self Government as States of this Confederacy?"[23] In the Senate John C. Calhoun strongly opposed expansion into Mexico: "Can we incorporate a people so dissimilar from us in every respect — so little qualified for free and popular government — without certain destruction to our political institutions?"[24] Calhoun was supported by that old warhorse Lewis Cass of Michigan, who said, "We do not want the people of Mexico, either as citizens or subjects. All we want is a portion of territory, which they nominally hold, generally uninhabited, or, where inhabited at all, sparsely so, and with a population, which would soon recede, or identify itself with ours."[25]

Within a year Cass was to modify his stance against expansion into Mexico, but Calhoun remained adamant. In a famous speech in January 1848 Calhoun defended the American government as a government of the white race. In his eagerness to exalt the Caucasians he was even prepared to acknowledge the major role of non-Anglo-Saxon white races. "We have never dreamt of incorporating into our Union any but the Caucasian race — the free white race." To incorporate Mexico would be to incorporate a race largely Indian. "Ours, sir, is the Government of a white race," thundered Calhoun. Although the largest portion of the human family was composed of colored races, he said, these races had never been "found equal to the establishment of free popular government." He admitted that the Mexicans had "Castilian blood in their veins — the old Gothic, quite equal to the Anglo-Saxon in many respects — in some respects superior," but most of the population were either completely or part Indian, "impure races, not as good as the Cherokees or Choctaws." Calhoun specifically rejected the idea that the United States had a mission to spread civil and religious liberty throughout the American continent and the world. Such a mission was impractical because most people lacked the ability to sustain free government.[26]

The fullest discussion of the racial dangers that would be created by Mexican annexation erupted during the late summer of 1847 as an increasing number of Democratic publications discussed the need to annex the whole of Mexico, and, if necessary, to rule it as a colonial possession. There were strong rumors that Polk and his cabinet were preparing at least to annex a considerable area south of the Rio Grande, in addition to New Mexico and California. Late in September Daniel Webster, while bitterly attacking the Mexican War as a Democratic war of aggression, expressed the same disillusionment with the concept of universal mission as Calhoun. Webster announced that he did not want more territory even if it were free territory. He pitied the people of Mexico, he said, but "I should pity them more if they appeared to me to have sense enough to understand the misery of their own condition." Further expansion ran the risk of despotic government in the United States, as it extended the country beyond the area peopled by inhabitants of similar character. Webster trusted that free institutions would eventually spread all over the world, but he said he was "by no means sure that all people are fit for them."[27]

Throughout the winter of 1847–48 the congressional Whigs pointed out the impossibility of integrating the Mexican population within the United States as citizens. Speaker after speaker attacked the Mexicans as unassimilable. In the Senate John M. Clayton of Delaware scoffed at the idea of incorporating eight million people "of a race totally different from ourselves." In the House Jacob Collamer of Vermont said "we should destroy our own nationality by such an act. We shall cease to be the people that we were; we cease to be the Saxon Americanized . . . We shall take in seven or eight millions of people in no way homogenous, incapable of being reduced to common feelings, common interests, common desires with us." Representative Edward C. Cabell of Florida pointed out that "if we annex the land, we must take the *population* along with it. And shall we, . . . by an act of Congress, convert the black, white, red, mongrel, miserable population of Mexico – the Mexicans, Indians, Mulattoes, Mestizos, Chinos, Zambos, Quinteros – into free and enlightened American citizens, entitled to all the privileges which we enjoy?"[28] Whatever the likelihood of replacing Mexicans by Anglo-Saxons in the future, most Americans realized that in practical terms the annexation of the whole of Mexico would mean either that eight million Mexicans would become American citizens or that they would be ruled as colonial subjects.

Even those who in 1847 and 1848 argued that all of Mexico should be annexed gave practically no support to the idea of allowing the Mexicans to enter the union as equal citizens. Some thought that education might ultimately make this possible, but most envisioned a military occupation of the country, an enthusiastic encouragement of commerce and trade with the United States, a rapid influx of American Anglo-Saxons attracted by an enlightened new order and increasing prosperity, a sharp reduction in the Mexican population, and the eventual absorption of a country that had been "Saxonized." The essential ingredients in this general scheme were that Mexico in the immediate future would be administered by the army as a colonial possession, and that the amalgamation of Mexico into the union would be made possible by reducing the Mexican population and gradually replacing Mexicans by Anglo-Saxons.

Most of the arguments claiming that large areas of Mexico could safely be annexed were based on the twin assumptions that the largely Indian Mexicans would fade away, and that the American Anglo-Saxons were destined to outbreed the whole world. "The Mexicans are no better than Indians," said Sam Houston in New York in 1848, "and I see no reason why we should not go in the same course now, and take their land."[29] Two New York senators found no difficulty in envisaging the disappearance of alien peoples before the advance of civilization. John A. Dix thought that the populations of California and New Mexico either would be overwhelmed and eliminated or they would be driven into ever narrower areas. As their usual sources of subsistence diminished, they would ultimately become extinct "by force of an invincible law." Daniel S. Dickinson said that a majority of the Mexican people belonged "to the fated aboriginal races, who can neither uphold government or be restrained by it; who flourish only amid the haunts of savage indolence, and perish under, if they do not recede before, the influences of civilization. Like their doomed brethren, who were once spread over the several States of the Union, they are destined, by laws above human agency, to give way to a stronger race from this continent or another."[30]

Articles in the *Democratic Review* sometimes contradicted each other on the question of just how much of Mexico could safely be taken, but they agreed on the gradual replacement of Mexicans by Anglo-Saxons. Mexico was eventually to be absorbed as part of that movement of the Germanic tribes which had thrust into the Roman Empire, "and which is destined to carry back to Asia the refinement of art and the influences of Christianity, gathered in a journey of two thousand years around the world, from east to west." Was this torrent, which had surged onward for two thousand years, to be "stopped by the theories of the Whig party, the voice of Daniel Webster or the frown of Santa Anna?" The Texas Revolution had been inevitable because the "very virtues of the Anglo-Saxon race made their political union with the degraded Mexican-Spanish impossible."[31] When in the fall of 1847 the magazine defended the occupation of Mexico by an American army, it suggested that the army would initially help instill the commercial principle by supporting free trade and the security of property, but it would eventually provide for a racial change. Soldiers, as they were discharged, would usually remain in Mexico "and gradually infusing vigor into the race, regenerate the whole nation."[32] Earlier the journal had suggested that simple military occupation might be too expensive, but that the Anglo-Saxons would solve the problem by colonization. It did not matter whether a treaty brought more or less territory—it would all be taken in time, "piece by piece."[33]

Although Polk disliked the peace treaty agreed to by Nicholas P. Trist in Mexico, his decision to submit it to Congress was a sensible one. Any attempt to continue the war to obtain substantial areas beyond the Rio Grande would have caused splits among the Democrats as well as incensed the Whig opposition. Polk admitted he would rather have settled for a boundary at the Sierra Madre mountains than at the Rio Grande, but also acknowledged that with Congress and the country reluctant to fight to obtain more territory from Mexico, Congress would probably not give him the men or the money to continue the war. Within the cabinet only Robert J. Walker actively wanted to continue the war to obtain large parts of Mexico, for he was the only member willing to accept a United States colonial domination over the whole area. Buchanan had softened enough to want a Sierra Madre rather than a Rio Grande boundary, but he did not want to annex the most populous areas of Mexico.[34] The Trist Treaty, with a Rio Grande boundary, New Mexico, and California was the most acceptable to the majority of Americans as it obtained the largest possible area from Mexico with the least number of Mexicans. It was not the problem of the extension of slavery but the Hobson's choice of racial amalgamation or imperial dominion that finally frustrated those who were prepared to take most or all of Mexico.

Press comment on the treaty itself echoed the racial arguments of the late stages of the war. The Whigs who wished to assail Polk attacked his militarism, as well as his bringing unsuitable people into the union by annexing the northern provinces of Mexico. The *Richmond Palladium* of Indiana criticized Polk for sacrificing more than twenty thousand lives and spending more than one hundred million dollars "to get hundreds of thousands of a mongrel and debased population upon which to found a representation in Congress."[35] The *American Whig Review* thought the acquisitions would prove to be "the bane and the curse of the country. We may, by these acquisitions of vast regions of territory beyond our lines, with the ignorant and degraded population that belongs to them, convert the Republic which our fathers created for us into an Empire, and our unpretending National Government into a great Power bearing imperial sway over distant provinces and dependencies."[36]

While the Whigs attacked the treaty for the population it had brought into the union, many Democrats prided themselves on obtaining a great dominion comparatively unencumbered by inferior peoples. The *Louisville Democrat* supported the treaty because the United States had obtained "not the best boundary, but all the territory of value that we can get without taking the people. The people of the settled parts of Mexico are a negative quantity. We fear the land, minus the people, is not worth much. We think all Mexico will fall, piece by piece, into this government; but then it must first be settled by a different population, and the union effected by other means than the sword."[37] Some Americans persisted in the belief that seven or eight million Mexicans would somehow disappear or be completely overwhelmed by the all-encompassing American-Anglo-Saxon people.

The total Mexican defeat convinced the Americans that their original judgment of the Mexican race had been correct. The *Southern Quarterly Review* in surveying the causes of the war wrote of the discord that had long existed between the United States and Mexico because of Mexican hatred for their northern neighbor, a hatred "springing from our acknowledged superiority in every thing."[38] Several years later, in 1853, Senator John Clayton spoke of the difficulties this disparity created for further American expansion. He was quite willing to annex more land if, after filling what was available, the United States could honorably obtain contiguous territory (presumably Canada) inhabited by men of our own race and class; but he saw insuperable objections to the future acquisition of Mexico. He did not want imperialism, he did not want an extension of slavery, and he could not quite believe that the numerous Mexican population would simply fade away before Anglo-Saxon pressure. To take Mexico would be to take her people as citizens: "Yes! Aztecs, Creoles, Half-breeds, Quadroons, Samboes, and I know not what else — 'ring-streaked and speckled' — all will come in, and, instead of our governing them, they, by their votes, will govern *us*."[39]

When, in the months after the conclusion of the Mexican War, the possibility arose of intervening in the Mexican province of Yucatan, opponents of intervention again cast their arguments in racial terms. The insurrection in that province brought fears in the American cabinet of English intervention in an area considered essential for future American communications from the Atlantic to the Pacific. Robert J. Walker, thinking primarily of its commercial importance, was in favor of the ultimate annexation of the region to the United States. President

Polk was prepared to support him rather than have the area fall into the hands of England, and in April 1848 the president asked Congress to provide help to stop the area's becoming a European colony. This would also "rescue the white race from extermination or expulsion from their country."[40] Discussions of the question were cast in terms of an uprising of barbarous Mexican Indians against a white ruling class. Representative Joseph R. Ingersoll of Pennsylvania, a Whig, defended intervention on the grounds that the United States would merely be providing aid against "barbarians," but this line of argument met resistance. Another Whig, Joseph M. Root of Ohio, reiterated what had so often been said in previous years — the Spanish-Mexican ruling class were themselves little better than Indians. He thought that the Spaniards in Yucatan "were about equal to the Mexicans; and if there was anything under the face of heaven meaner than a Mexican 'greaser' he should like to know it."[41] His general sympathies, he said, were in favor of the white race, but he would have to be shown better examples of the race than the Spaniards if his feelings were to be stirred.

The United States did not intervene in Yucatan, although the secretary of the navy pointed out in his annual report that American ships had helped white inhabitants fleeing from "a war of races."[42] General intervention in Yucatan, however desirable commercially, posed the same problems for the United States as annexation of large areas of Mexico south of the Rio Grande: there were too many nonwhite, non-Anglo-Saxon people.

After the Mexican War it was clear that if American expansion was to continue into populous areas it either had to be through colonial rule or economic penetration. The American republican government was not a government for all races and all colors — federalism had its limits. Yet Americans were determined to participate fully in shaping the economic future not only of the American continents but also of the world. A search for personal and national wealth was put in terms of world progress under the leadership of a supreme race. In thrusting into the Pacific, Americans revived arguments that the American advance would bring freedom and civilization to all peoples;

but the reality of attitudes toward neighboring peoples in the years of the Mexican War made nonsense of the claims that the American penetration of Asia was intimately connected with the regeneration of other races.

13

A Confused Minority

> If anything was wanting to prove that this age is an age of imbecility and false philosophy, it is furnished in this drivel about races. The Anglo-Saxon race and the Celtic race, and this race and that race, seem to the latest discovery of the present time to account for all moral, social, and political phenomena. This new theory is founded neither on Christianity nor philosophy.
>
> Senator James Shields, February 7, 1852

The Saxonist explanation of the sequence of events on the American continents and in the world did, of course, have its critics and dissenters in the mid-nineteenth century. These dissenters approached the problem from sharply different perspectives, and many of them testified to the pervasive nature of American Anglo-Saxonism. Practically all expansionists enthusiastically endorsed the idea that the future course of American expansion and world history was to be shaped by a superior race imposing its will on a variety of inferior races; not all expansionists, however, were prepared to accept the view that the Americans were simply transplanted Anglo-Saxons. Even the Anglo-Saxonists in America thought of the Americans as a special, progressive branch of the Anglo-Saxon race, but some expansionists went further and argued that the Americans were a separate, superior, unique race.

Among the antiexpansionists there was far more confusion. The most common opposition to expansion was clearly conceived within the prevailing racial theories. Most Whigs who condemned the war with Mexico and the acquisition of new territory believed in the inferiority of the Mexican race. Yet while many Whigs accepted the idea of Americans as a superior branch of the Anglo-Saxon race and agreed that this race was to have a world role, Whigs in general had far less sympathy with American mid-nineteenth-century bellicosity. Most of them thought that the Americans would eventually spread throughout the continent and beyond, but they objected bitterly to what they regarded as an immoral use of force to accelerate this process. They thought it unworthy of a free, republican nation. Even if superior the American people had no divine right to trample on the rights of others; and militarism, like the admission of inferior peoples, would eventually bring ruin on the republic. Much of the opposition to militant expansionism stemmed from concern with what this would do to the United States, not what it would do to other peoples.

Rarest in the opposition to the expansionism of the mid-nineteenth century were those who combined a dislike of military aggression with disbelief in the current racial assumptions. It was unusual by the late 1840s to profess a belief in innate human equality and to challenge the idea that a superior race was about to shape the fates of other races for the future good of the world. To assert this meant challenging not only popular opinion, but also the opinion of most American intellectuals.

The vocal minority who were anxious that the Americans should not be viewed merely as the most talented branch of the Anglo-Saxon race often combined such views with a rejection of other peoples and the advocacy of a vigorous, aggressive foreign policy. Often they were politicians of Irish or Scotch-Irish ancestry. They discussed the future in terms almost identical to the terms of those who used the rhetoric of Anglo-Saxonism; they simply made the American race a distinct race and gave it the characteristics usually given to the Anglo-Saxons, but with the added distinction, from their point of view, that the American was a unique blend of all that was best in the white European races.

James Buchanan, who had frequently expressed his contempt for "the Mexican race" and had stressed its inability to participate in a government of free institutions, thought of the Americans as an ideal mixed blend—always "mixed," not "mongrel"— "mongrel" was reserved for Mexicans and the like. Speaking in Philadelphia in 1851 he praised Pennsylvania as a state settled by immigrants from all the European nations. It was not composed, he said, of "the pure Anglo-Saxon race." English, Germans, Scotch-Irish, Irish, Welsh, French, and a variety of other Europeans had all intermingled in the state: "We are truly a mixed race." Buchanan regarded this as a sign of strength, saying that the intermarriage of close relatives eventually produced puny results, and that this might well apply to nations as well as to families: "May it then not be probable that the intermixture of the natives of the different nations is calculated to produce a race superior to any one of the elements of which it is composed?" Stephen A. Douglas of Illinois agreed with Buchanan. In 1853, in discussing the Clayton-Bulwer Treaty, he challenged South Carolinian Andrew Pickens Butler, who had emphasized America's English heritage. "I cannot recognize England as our mother," said Douglas. "If so, she is and ever has been a cruel and unnatural mother . . . Our ancestry were not all of English origin. They were of Scotch, Irish, German, French, and of Norman descent as well as English. In short, we inherit from every branch of the Caucasian race."[1]

Buchanan and Douglas were not attacking the assumption that there were superior and inferior races, and that the Americans had special abilities even within the superior Caucasian race. They were making the Americans the crème de la crème, a superior blend of all that was best in the white races of Europe. Anglo-Saxonists said that the Americans were Anglo-Saxons, and that Anglo-Saxons were the best endowed of all the Caucasians. Proponents of an American race said the Americans were superior to the English in race as well as in institutions. A writer in the *Democratic Review* in March 1848 defended such a racial hierarchy with great clarity: "As compared with the nations of the continent, the English have far more energy of character, and their advance is proportionately more rapid; but they are, nevertheless, far behind the American race in ceaseless activity and individual vigor."[2] The "American race" was simply the greatest of the white races.

Both Missourian Thomas Hart Benton and New Englander Caleb Cushing were willing to accept a variety of European white races while completely rejecting the races of the rest of the world. Benton wanted American Anglo-Saxonism to be tempered with a sense of its Celtic components, and he was unwilling simply to consign the Mexicans to the realm of the colored inferior races: "We are the first—she the second power of the NEW WORLD. We stand at the head of the anglo-Saxon—she at the head of the south-European race—but we all come from the same branch of the human family—the white branch—which, taking its rise in the Caucasian mountains, and circling Europe by the north and by the south, sent their vanguards to people the two Americas."[3]

Benton coined his own racial designation for the Americans and placed this within a standard mid-century summary of the races of mankind. "Since the dispersion of man upon earth," he said in May 1846, "I know of no human event, past or to come, which promises a greater, and more beneficent change upon earth than the arrival of the van of the Caucasian race (the Celtic-Anglo-Saxon division) upon the border of the sea which washes the shore of the eastern Asia." The Mongolian (or "Yellow" race), argued Benton, had once been the foremost in the arts of civilization, but it had been stationary for thousands of years: "It is a race far above the Ethiopian, or Black—above the Malay, or Brown, (if we must admit five races)—and above the American Indian, or Red: it is a race far above all these, but still, far below the White; and, like all the rest, must receive an impression from the superior race whenever they come in contact." For Benton the "Celtic-Anglo-Saxon" division of the Caucasians was simply a standard-bearer for his beloved white race. One of the few ways in which he was consistent was his arguing repeatedly that the white race alone had followed the divine command to subdue and replenish the earth: "The white race went for land, and they will continue to go for it . . . The principle is founded in their nature, and in God's command; and it will continue to be obeyed."[4]

Caleb Cushing was also quite willing to accept other whites within his superior race. At the end of the 1850s he said: "Whatever we have of great or good in us is the blood of our European fathers. It is the Irish and Scotch and English and German blood of our fathers which constitutes our greatness, our power, and our liberty." He told the members of the Massachusetts Assembly that they all belonged "to the excellent white race, the consummate impersonation of intellect in man and loveliness in woman, whose power and privilege it is, wherever they may go, and wherever they may remain, to Christianize and to civilize, to command and to be obeyed, to conquer and to reign. I admit to an equality with me, sir, the white man, — my blood and race, whether he be a Saxon of England, or the Celtic of Ireland. But I do not admit as my equals either the red man of America, or the yellow man of Asia, or the black man of Africa." Cushing's remarks were reported to have roused the Massachusetts house and galleries to "the wildest enthusiasm."[5]

Though Cushing rejected exclusive Anglo-Saxonism, he accepted fully the idea that in expanding their settlements the Americans were gradually replacing inferior races. In America's relentless expansion, he argued, "men, nations, races, may, must, will, perish before us. That is inevitable. There can be no change for the better save at the expense of that which is. Out of decay springs fresh life." The Indians, like the animals, were retiring before the Americans, and "the Hispano-Americans, wasting away by apparent incapacity of self-government, are suffering one province after another of theirs to relapse into pristine desolation, and thus to become prepared to receive the people and the laws of the United States."[6] It was quite possible to reject exclusive Anglo-Saxonism while maintaining a belief in a superior American race destined to dominate much of the world.

The view that Americans were a distinct race was also expressed by some opponents of immediate expansion, namely, by those who rejected the use of overt force. A striking example of this type of argument was printed in the *American Whig Review* in March 1847. The article began with a balanced and sensible attack on the extreme nationalistic position and on militarism, but finished with a clear assumption of eventual supremacy by white Americans over the other races of the world. There was throughout the nation, said the author, "a very amusing feeling . . . that Americans are a different order of beings from others." In this way an American soldier was worth four Mexicans, three Frenchmen, or two Englishmen. In challenging these assumptions the author at first echoed the arguments of an earlier generation by laying the stress not on the special qualities of the people but on Providence itself; no nation on earth, he said, owed as much to Providence as did the United States, except the Jews.

While rejecting the contention that the Americans were a special, superior people who owed their success simply to their own merits, the author quickly made it apparent that he believed Providence was creating a very special people in America. This population, he said, was made up of all nations, and this in itself was evidence of a providential plan for the benefit of mankind. He argued that for the first time in America "the chief nations of the world are blended in a common fate, in which their individuality is wholly lost. American blood is neither English nor Irish, nor French, nor Spanish, nor German, nor Swiss. But it is all these in large proportions of each, and every day the purely Anglo-Saxon stock is losing its predominancy." The author stated categorically that the Anglo-Saxon stock would be greatly improved by intermixture with other races. The mixture was producing a new race: "the new world was not destined to be a mere extension of British rule, or Saxon blood, or of the characteristic customs and prejudices of one people. It was to be the home of delegates from the race," and "race" was used in such a way as to mean all the people of the world rather than one specific group.

Yet after beginning with a stirring and unusual attack on racial particularism and arrogance, the author quickly elevated his new American race—"this astonishing heterogeneousness of races, perfectly blended into one" — into another superrace, with most of the characteristics of the American Anglo-Saxon race under another guise. The conquest of all of Mexico was unnecessary: "Mexico will ultimately fall a political prey, not to force, but to a superior population, insensibly oozing into her territories, changing her customs, and out-living, out-trading, exterminating her weakest blood." This was as certain, he argued, as the final extinction of the Indian races "to which the mass of the Mexican population seem very little superior." Even this was only the beginning, for South America was to be next. Ironically, at the end of his article, which had already seen a shift from an attack on arrogance to an adoption of it, the author slipped into the literal Anglo-Saxon rhetoric he had begun by attacking. Before America had doubled its three centuries of existence, "South America will speak the English tongue and submit to the civilization, laws and religion of the Anglo-Saxon race." The tide of the American population, with no violence or spirit of conquest, would transform both North and South America.[7]

In a much subtler and gentler form the belief in a unique American people who would eventually transform the world by peaceful means was present in the writings of Herman Melville. Melville had too broad a vision to accept the narrow Anglo-Saxonism with which he was surrounded, and he lauded the variety of strains that was melding to form the new American. The manner in which America had been settled, he said, "should forever extinguish the prejudices of national dislikes. Settled by the people of all nations, all nations may claim her for their own. You cannot spill a drop of American blood without spilling the blood of the whole world."[8] Americans had a great mission to perform, but it was a mission of peace, not war. In *White Jacket* he wrote of the Americans as "the peculiar, chosen people — the Israel of our time; we bear the ark of the liberties of the world." God has given Americans, he said, "the broad domains of the political pagans, that shall yet come and lie down under the shade of our ark, without bloody hands being lifted."[9] In *Mardi*, written during the Mexican War, Melville did not question America's ultimate mission, but he reiterated that it was a peaceful not a warlike mission: "Expand not your area too widely, now. Seek you proselytes? Neighbouring nations may be free, without coming under your banner. And if you cannot lay your ambition, know this: that it is best served by waiting events." In time the United States might cross the equator and have "the Arctic Circles" for boundaries.[10] Melville was still exhibiting a faith in the capacities of other peoples that was being challenged by most Americans. His image of America's role in the world was in many ways more in accord with that of 1800 than that of 1850.

While it was not uncommon for the Americans to be described as a unique and superior blend of Europeans rather than simply as Anglo-Saxons, it was extremely rare for anyone to think of the possibility of Americans ultimately becoming a blend of white and nonwhite races. Miscegenation in the South was almost always ignored in racial considerations, unless it was used to further the arguments for the maintenance of a pure race, as when Josiah Nott argued that mulattoes were less fertile. One of the rare occasions when a different point of view was expressed came, surprisingly, in an article in the *Southern Quarterly Review*. The author wrote of the future extended dominion of the United States — a country, he said, "formed by the admixture and amalgamation of all the races of Europe." This was an acceptable point of view, but in discussing the American advance into California the author went far beyond what was usually acceptable in a northern journal, much less in one published in South Carolina. He suggested that the people of California "promise to exhibit, at no distant day, the fusion of all the European, Asiatic, and American races." Then the author went even further: "The African may be gradually blended with the mass, by uniting with the Asiatics and Indians. In a wide view of human history, this fact is not devoid of deep significance."[11] This was remarkably heady stuff for a southern journal which by 1850 was vigorously defending the innate inferiority of the colored races. It certainly represents no general trend in argument even outside the South.

What perturbed most critics of the new rampant Manifest Destiny was not its racial theories but its bellicosity and arrogance. To be superior, to be a chosen people, meant to many New Englanders, and to some from other parts of the country, the necessity for restrained conduct befitting their high station. Superiority did not confer the right to wage aggressive war, and the opponents of Manifest Destiny had no doubt that the Mexican War was an aggressive war. The Whigs generally opposed taking any territory by force, whether it was inhabited by Mexicans or not. When Julia Webster Appleton heard that her brother, Daniel Webster's son, had died in Mexico she lamented: "He went forth to a wicked & cruel war, & there he has died." Her brother, she said "was a useless sacrifice—to what?—ambition, vain-glory."[12] Governor Mordecai Bartley of Ohio met the federal request for troops, but stated that if the war was declared to acquire territory, it was "a violation of the fundamental principles of our Government and of the spirit and true intent of our national constitution."[13] The idea that using violence to achieve American ends was a betrayal of America's moral position was a consistent argument in Whig criticism of the war. The *Richmond Whig* in January 1848 attacked the view of some expansionists that duty required the United States to keep her troops in Mexico to aid the process of regeneration. It was not America's mission, argued the editor, to wage a series of sanguinary crusades, beginning in Mexico and ending "God knows where" for the purpose of indoctrinating other nations at the point of a bayonet.[14]

The very phrase *Manifest Destiny* infuriated some who saw it as arrogant and impious. Whatever the earthly superiority of the race, it could not take upon itself the interpretation of God's will. Senator James C. Jones of Tennessee said he could not "fall down and worship this blind idol of 'manifest destiny' "[15] Manifest Destiny was seen by some as simply a hypocritical phrase which cloaked naked military aggression. "Away with wretched cant!" said William Duer of New York in February 1848. "If you wish this plunder, this dismemberment of a sister Republic, let us stand forth like other conquerors, and plainly declare our purposes and desires. Let us, like Alexander, who boldly avowed that he went for glory and conquest, declare our objects. Away with this mawkish morality! with this desecration of religion! with this cant about 'manifest destiny,' a DIVINE MISSION, a warrant from the Most High, to civilize, christianize, and democratize our sister republic at the mouth of the cannon! — sentiments which had found their way from dinner-table speeches and club harangues to the mouths of grave Senators."[16] Many objected to "the raw and rampant forms" in which ideas of expansion were often expressed.[17] The population of the United States might well have been chosen for a special role in world history, but this mission, it was argued, would be frustrated and perverted if hastened by force of arms. "Every folly is to be covered by this manifest destiny," said a writer in *De Bow's Review* in 1853. "The thief thinks it is his destiny when he picks your pocket or steals your horse. Others may think it is his destiny to be hung. Our true destiny, we cannot doubt, is to do justice to others, and to see that justice is done to us."[18] Thoreau saw the whole westward drive to the Pacific and Asia as diverting attention from higher matters. "It is perfectly heathenish," he wrote, " — a filibustering *toward* heaven by the great western route. No; they may go their way to their manifest destiny, which I trust is not mine."[19]

Some who attacked "Manifest Destiny" as a justification for armed aggression went out of their way to praise the Americans and condemn other races. Restraint could be a further proof of superiority. The *New Englander* argued that even though great good would come of the war, it should be condemned because war itself was evil. The author had no doubt that the expansion of American settlements was for the good of the world, and that the Americans would make better use of the conquered territory than the original Mexican owners.[20] The first "civilized stock" of Mexico — the Castilian — had much that was noble, but it had been weakened by the admixture of "the effeminate sons and daughters of the land." The Mexicans now presented "a curious compound of pride and self-contempt, idleness and ambition, parsimony with the silliest prodigality, and foul passion with some of the sterner virtues yet remaining." The people of the United States, on the other hand, "sprang from the noblest stock on the earth's face; either of past or present times; a stock the most intellectual, as well as moral, and a stock which in physical qualities had at the time the nation was founded, and yet has no equal. The very best of the nation of this best stock, founded the United States."[21] In spite of all this, argued the *New Englander*, war could not be justified; the end did not justify the means.

The *Massachusetts Quarterly Review* was also able to condemn the Mexicans while condemning the war. It was "a great wrong" for a powerful, civilized people to attack "a nation that is barbarous and feeble." A private company could be raised in Boston which would conquer Mexico in two years, but where would be the glory? Anglo-Saxons could achieve no fame by conquering "the miserable population of Mexico."[22] Many of the New Englanders despised the Mexicans and other races just as much as they despised military violence.

To some the arrogance and violence of the 1840s was seen as an unfortunate inheritance of the Anglo-Saxons, an inheritance which had to be moderated by the many more desirable characteristics of the stock. Anglo-Saxons, it was argued, should not glory in the marauding past of the people from whom they claimed descent. "'The Anglo-Saxon race are destined'—destined to what?" wrote an author in the *American Whig Review* in November 1847, "to re-assert that maxim of tyrants that might is right—that conquest is right—that there are 'rights' of conquest —that the booty belongs to the slayer—that the land is his who can seize and hold it." After attacking the Mexican War as a war of aggression, the author said that if there was to be a destiny for the United States it had to be "by a clear perception of its moral aims." He saw part of the American problem as based on the twin descent from the Normans and the Saxons: the former, although sheltering "under the sanctions of religion and law," were "unscrupulous and lovers of power"; the latter, although having manly virtues, never had "an aspiring and ambitious spirit." From one parent the Americans inherited "the love of liberty and justice" and from the other "the love of foreign dominion." Ultimately, the spirit of aggrandizement had to be tamed, for it led to unjust wars. What was best in American government was traced by the author to the Saxons, and the wild spirit of aggression was viewed as "a taint—a fever—a corruption."[23]

A similar point of view was expressed in the *North American Review*, but the author argued that relentless ambition had always been a characteristic of the American population, and that all the stocks from which the Americans were descended contributed to it. The author took issue with those who thought that the United States was doomed by her "lust of conquest, and the insatiable thirst for the acquisition of territory." He agreed that this was criminal, but he thought it was "the besetting sin" of the stock from which Americans claimed to be descended — the Saxons, the Danes, and the Normans. Americans should not be surprised by the course of events in the 1840s. During the past eight centuries Englishmen, descended from three races with driving ambitions for conquest and territory, had "appropriated to themselves a large share of all the territory inhabited or inhabitable by the human family." Americans had proved themselves true descendants of these Englishmen from the moment they arrived on the continent. Long before the present era of "pride and power," Americans had ridden roughshod over the American Indians and were in the process of exterminating them. The Americans of the 1840s were merely continuing the sins of their forbears.[24]

Attacks on the manner in which Manifest Destiny was used to justify a policy of force were common, but challenges to the assumption that the Anglo-Saxon or American "race" was superior to the people it was overwhelming were rare. Sometimes even this type of challenge had racial overtones, as when critics of the Mexican War argued that the Mexicans were not simply to be dismissed as Indians, but rather should be praised for the European part of their ancestry. The *American Whig Review* in June 1846 attacked the idea of war against a sister republic of the New World, a war with "a people numbering nearly nine millions, a considerable portion of whom rejoice in the pure blood of as gallant and noble a race as belongs to either the New World or the Old."[25] This particular argument, which at its heart accepted the common racial differentiations of the 1840s, was unusual; the Mexicans were generally accepted as a "mongrel," largely Indian race. In the House of Representatives Edwin H. Ewing of Tennessee attempted to move against the tide when he argued that the invasion of Mexico had set on fire "the old Castilian blood." These were not merely the poor Indians who had fled before Cortez: "The best blood of the hidalgos of Spain flows in many of their veins."[26] Representative Thomas Corwin of Ohio asked the members of the House to put themselves in the place of the Mexicans, to imagine that England had taken New York and said to the Americans that "You are not Celts exactly — nor are you quite Anglo-Saxons; but you are a degenerate, an alien, a sort of bastard race," before proceeding to take Massachusetts. But this was the same speech in which Corwin spoke of "the simple, savage mind of the half-civilized Mexicans."[27]

Some, while not prepared to challenge directly the scientifically supported views of human racial differences, became extremely irritated at the sheer extravagance of the claims which were being made on behalf of the Anglo-Saxon race. The *National Intelligencer* in the years of the Mexican War consistently objected to the way in which it was claimed that the Anglo-Saxon race had gained such detailed information on God's intentions for the world, and pointed out that the school of thought which proclaimed the Manifest Destiny of the Anglo-Saxons advocated doctrines that had sent people to prison and the gallows.[28] It attacked such political "Clap-Trap" as "*our Manifest Destiny,*" along with a second word-snare, "*Anglo-Saxonism.*"[29] Even the *Democratic Review*, which after 1846 generally accepted the rampant Anglo-Saxonism, welcomed a new French book on the horrors of English industrialism with the comment that "at this time of unbridled imitation of Anglo-Saxonism, when our most accomplished bon vivants cannot quaff their port save with an Anglo-Saxon smack, it is especially well-timed."[30]

When Francis Lieber came to America from Germany in the 1820s, he was convinced that the Anglo-Saxons in England and America had exhibited unique talents for the enshrinement of freedom in practical political institutions. He never lost this belief, but by 1850 he was shocked by the shallowness of many of the current arguments and was asking for a moderation in tone. "We have nowadays always the Caucasian race in our mouths," he said in that year. "If that *race* is so preeminently superior, how did it happen that civilization flourished on the Ganges thousands of years before the Caucasian race began to work itself out of the mire of barbarism?" Lieber had great hopes for England and the United States, but he simply could not accept the excesses of much of the racial argument: "I believe in races," he said, "as I believe in nations, families, and single brains, but I believe only in certain favorable elements which, under certain circumstances, can produce certain results."[31] Lieber's intelligence was repelled by some of the wilder claims of mid-century.

Occasionally someone went even further and simply pierced the arrant nonsense of much that was being written. Senator James Shields of Illinois, in a speech of sympathy for the Irish, accused the English of wanting to depopulate Ireland and people it with a more serviceable and manageable race. "If anything was wanting to prove that this age is an age of imbecility and false philosophy, it is furnished in this drivel about races," said Shields. "The Anglo-Saxon race and the Celtic race, and this race and that race, seem to be the latest discovery of the present time to account for all moral, social, and political phenomena. This new theory is founded neither on Christianity nor philosophy."[32] Such outbursts against the prevailing beliefs were rare. Most were content to accept the irrationality and the inconsistencies of the racial theories. When Charles Sumner, in *The Law of Human Progress* in 1849, wrote that "man, as an individual, is capable of indefinite improvement. Societies and nations which are but aggregations of men, and, finally, the Human Race, or collective Humanity, are capable of indefinite improvement," his words had a strangely old-fashioned air.[33]

Even those who were strongest in their stand against the extension of slavery found their easiest arguments in opposition to the use of force and violence rather than in declarations of the oneness of mankind. Certainly the powerful Whig movement to stop the annexation of Mexican territory was predicated on a full belief in Mexican inferiority. It was not only that the Whigs generally saw the possibility of admitting large numbers of Mexicans as disastrous to the union—they simply discounted the Mexican abolition of slavery as being of any relevance. Annexation meant to most Whigs the admission of eight million Mexicans unfit to be citizens, not eight million Mexicans as possible recruits for the antislave forces.

Only the extreme abolitionists were prepared as a group to defend Mexican capabilities, and even they thought the American race had a special role in world history. Abolitionist journals, however, went the furthest in combatting those who saw no merit or capacity in the Mexican people. The *National Anti-Slavery Standard* of New York denounced the war as "our first attempt to imitate the grasping monarchies of Europe," urged sympathy for the Mexican cause, and attacked the policies of the Whig leaders. The *National Era*, the organ of the Liberty party, said that the population of Mexico was no more "heterogeneous, ignorant, unfitted for republican institutions" than the immigrants who were pouring into the United States, and argued that any Mexican state that voluntarily wished to enter the union should be allowed to come in. The *Liberator* in January 1848 was extremely critical of Calhoun's speech in which he argued that America was a white man's country, and that the United States could not accept any races with colored blood for entry into the union.[34]

In Congress abolitionist Joshua Giddings of Ohio virulently assailed the Mexican War, but he was unwilling to go the whole way in admitting Mexican equality. He was most intent on using the Mexican War to increase the intensity of his attack on the Southerners and their peculiar institution. "It is true," he said of Mexico, "that their population is less intelligent than that of our free States; and it is equally true that they are more rapidly improving their condition than are our slave States." It is debatable whether he was more desirous of praising the Mexicans or attacking the Southerners when he said that "taking the whole population of our Southern slave States and of Mexico into consideration, I think we shall find the Mexicans the best informed, most intelligent, and most virtuous."[35]

Antislavery writer James Russell Lowell, though himself touched by Anglo-Saxonism, was a particularly shrewd observer of contemporary fashions in rhetoric and an incisive critic of the general tenets of Manifest Destiny. He noted how the Southerners delighted in melding a love of the Norman aristocracy into their overall Anglo-Saxonism, and he called the Norman barons "a race of savages, strong chiefly in their intense and selfish acquisitiveness," who "looked upon their Saxon serfs as mere cattle." These were the serfs, he said, who were "part and parcel of that famous Anglo-Saxon race, concerning whom we have seen so much claptrap in the newspapers for a few years past, especially since the project of extending the area of freedom has been discussed and glorified."[36] Lowell, like other critics of "Manifest Destiny," frequently testified to the pervasive nature of the new Anglo-Saxonism.

Lowell had a common sense about racial matters that was rare in mid-nineteenth-century America. In 1849 he argued that the hopes for liberalism and progress in central Europe had recently been thwarted "in a great measure by foolish disputes about races and nationalities." He emphasized that environment accounted for many of the differences between races, while pointing out that as they had achieved distinction and power, all races had endeavored to account for their preeminence by giving themselves a noble lineage: "we are obliged to content ourselves with vague assertions of our Anglo-Saxon descent," although only the settlers of New England, and only a very few of them, could claim such an origin.[37]

Lowell himself had great admiration for the English and thought that the Anglo-Saxons had very special qualities. He believed that the center of the Anglo-Saxon system was passing from England to the United States, and he supported what he called a "natural" and free American expansion. Canada, he thought, should break away from Great Britain and join the United States: "This is not the manifest destiny of aggressive rapine, as in the case of Texas, but obedience to the attraction of natural laws." Canada, of course, would have added strength to the free states of the union. Lowell's admiration for the basic English stock became even greater later in his life, but in the late 1840s he brought a calm eye and a clear mind to bear on the excesses of the period.[38]

In defending the Negro race Lowell developed the theme that the Africans had much to offer the world in the movement toward a truly Christian civilization. This theme had reoccurred among the abolitionists since the late 1830s, although it had never formed a major part of their arguments. The "gentler and less selfish qualities" of the Negroes, said Lowell, would temper the drive to power of the Caucasians. Caucasian ability to govern and achieve domination at any cost would not create a true civilization without the infusion of humbler qualities.[39]

Earlier defenders of this idea had usually dovetailed it, in some way, within prevailing racial theories. Writing in Cincinnati at the end of the 1830s, Alexander Kinmont suggested that "the whole human family is actually sprung from a single pair, but that this single pair possessed within them the *innate tendency* to give rise, in the progress of generations, to several distinct *origins of races.*" Among these different races Kinmont had no hesitation in selecting the Caucasians as superior in intellect, but he thought that the Negroes might be superior in gentler qualities. He praised the ancient Germans as "a very superior order of men," but he argued that the gentler, moral qualities of the Negroes might lead to the creation of a future glorious civilization in Africa. The deficiency of the blacks in intellect, Kinmont wrote, might not prevent them from building a Christian-based civilization.[40]

The notion of the blacks as natural Christians was also developed, in a somewhat different form, by William E. Channing, and in the late 1840s a number of New Englanders joined Lowell in arguing that the intellectual inferiority of blacks was to some extent compensated for by their possession of more humble qualities. The argument was put in its strongest form in the *North American Review* in April 1849. Africa was discussed as "the home . . . of the mysterious negro races, races yet lying dormant in the germ; destined, perhaps, to rule this earth when our proud Anglo-Saxon blood is as corrupt as that of the descendants of Homer and Pericles." This clearly represents an acceptance of current racial categories, but they are used in a most uncommon sense. "Does the dark race in all its varieties," asked the author, "possess a capacity for understanding and living out the deep meaning of the World's ruler, Christianity, as the offspring of the follower of Odin never did, and never can, understand and act it?" The argument, in essence, was that the Negro was not an inferior being in the eyes of God, even if it were granted that he was "inferior in intellect, energy, and selfishness," for this did not necessarily mean he was "farther from the light and warmth of the gospel."[41] This very suggestion that what the blacks had to offer was not intellect or governing power but humbler, gentler Christian qualities did, of course, reflect the extent to which the general view of innate black inferiority had affected even those who were most anxious to free and elevate the slaves.

Overt, reasoned rejections of the new racial doctrines were rare, and the most searching attacks on the aggressive Anglo-Saxonism of these years were delivered in the late 1840s by an Ohio politician and supporter of black rights—Charles Anderson—and by the distinguished Swiss immigrant and scholar—Albert Gallatin. Both of these men expressed a skepticism which was singularly lacking in most of their contemporaries. In 1849 Charles Anderson delivered an address on Anglo-Saxon destiny at Kenyon College and later to the New England Society of Cincinnati. The next year the talk was published as a pamphlet. Like so many who attacked the "Manifest Destiny" of these years, Anderson in his work testified to the strength of the views he disliked. Where he differed from so many others who disliked "Manifest Destiny" was that, rather than objecting simply to American aggression or to the inherent dangers the expansion presented to the republic, Anderson challenged the whole basis of the prevailing assumptions about the relations between races and what these relations meant for the future course of American and world history.

Anderson admitted that he was challenging "the prevalent and popular notions about *Anglo-Saxon Destiny*," and that the subject he had chosen was "hackneyed by repeated discussions." The errors, he said, were the monopoly of no particular party; it was not a party matter: "I find our whole people, without regard to such distinctions, especially abandoning themselves to a sentiment, which is a fallacy in philosophy, an untruth in history, and a gross impiety in religion." He wished, he said, to arraign the white race to which he belonged for cherishing a dangerous delusion, and he went on to show that he was observing the society around him with a remarkably clear eye. He said it could not have escaped anyone's observation "how decided and how universal is the belief amongst the North Americans and Englishmen of this age, that there is, in . . . the *'Anglo Saxon'* Race, some extraordinary power, or capability of accomplishing greater things, than in any other family of men." Some writers and speakers, he said, described this power by its results and spoke in terms of "Destiny." Anderson challenged the whole argument for Anglo-Saxon supremacy.[42] In turn he attacked the idea that the Anglo-Saxons or any division of "the human race" had any innate superiority, the idea that there even was a specific "Anglo-Saxon race," and the idea that the Americans or any division of the human race had been chosen by God for special works.

In discussing that large group of people who thought that there was a natural Anglo-Saxon supremacy *"in the breed, or the stock, or the blood,"* Anderson pointed out that pride in race had been universal among nations. At times it could be beneficial, but in America it had now assumed absurd proportions. American Anglo-Saxonists were simply ignoring facts in defending their destiny. Anderson had heard the comment that English would soon be the only language spoken in Mexico, the West Indies, and all of South America; he was quick to counter with the point that French was still extensively spoken in Canada (nearly a hundred years after its capture by the British), and German was spoken in areas of the United States. He delighted in quoting some of the more flowery poetry by the patriotic poets of American Anglo-Saxonism. He was particularly amused by the prophecy that the United States and England would "In one tether / of Anglo Saxon might . . . hold the world together / In love, — and peace, — and right." After commenting on England's colonial bloodshed and on the blood spilled by the United States in the Mexican War, Anderson concluded that "whatever good qualities these 'Anglo Saxons' may have, binding up the world with bands of 'peace and love and right,' is not of their number."[43]

In surveying those who had eulogized the Anglo-Saxons, Anderson particularly noted the importance of the English historian Sharon Turner and emphasized that Turner praised the Anglo-Saxons in arguments that were not even sustained by his own detailed researches. The panegyrists of Anglo-Saxon worth in the mid-nineteenth century were, Anderson thought, too numerous to discuss, but he made the shrewd suggestion that the Texas question had done most to give Anglo-Saxonism a contemporary vitality "by connecting the dead idea with a living subject."[44]

After discussing the excesses of the Anglo-Saxon arguments, Anderson dealt with the question, usually ignored in both England and the United States in the mid-nineteenth century, of whether there really was any Anglo-Saxon race. With a critical sense singularly lacking among his contemporaries, Anderson pointed out that Tacitus had not even mentioned the Saxons, and that the Angles and Saxons had never composed most of the population of England. The contemporary British people, he said, were simply not Anglo-Saxons. Even the Anglo-Saxonists, he stressed, often seemed to include Scots, Irish, and Welsh in their depiction of the superior English and American peoples. This British-American people spanning the Atlantic contained a multiplicity of strains: "It is perhaps the most mixed, mongrel and heterogeneous stock of people on earth." He admitted that the British and the Americans had striking achievements to their name, but most of these achievements, he said, stemmed from circumstance, not from some innate superiority or destiny. Even in this, however, he stressed that "superiority" could be judged quite differently in different fields of achievement – the Italians, for example, had supreme achievements in fine arts.[45]

After this refreshing analysis of the Anglo-Saxons and their qualities, Anderson took issue with the idea of special destiny. Here Anderson's solid common sense was on more difficult ground, for one either believed or did not believe in providential destiny. There were few obvious fallacies to be picked apart. Anderson, however, argued that "superiority" was primarily a matter of circumstance. Religion, he said, taught the unity of man and species, even though some areas of the world might allow mankind to develop more fully: "God made of one blood, all the nations of the earth." Anderson quickly surveyed the variety of nations or races that had aspired to universal dominion. These nations attributed their previous success and their confidently expected future "destiny" to "divine appointment" or to a natural superiority of race: the Egyptians believed in both; the Jews began to cherish "this fond delusion of an inbred 'Anglo-Saxon'-like superiority of race as the cause of their great achievements" before they were thrown down and despised; Assyrians, Babylonians, Medeans, and Persians were all convinced of their superiority and their destiny; Romans, Mohammedans, Turks, and a variety of other nations and races had justified their rapacity and bloodshed in terms of their birth and destiny. If America was to pursue a course of conquest and crime, concluded Anderson, then like all deluded nations it would be brought low.[46]

Anderson represents a healthy skepticism and common sense that transcends any particular historical period. He simply took a hard look at the current rhetoric and exposed its shallowness, illogic, and self-serving nature. Albert Gallatin was different. When Gallatin, at well over eighty, coolly analyzed the furor surrounding the Mexican War, he helped reveal the manner in which a great ideal had been corrupted in less than fifty years. This Swiss scholar-politician was a man of the Enlightenment. He believed in progress, he believed that the United States was helping to make the world a better place for human beings, he believed in the special governmental talents of his nation and its people; but he did not believe the bombast, the arrogance, the shallow thought of the rampant forties. In his pamphlets and private letters this old Democratic-Republican opposed the Mexican War and brought a clarity of thought that was sadly lacking in a new breed of politicians.

In his 1847 pamphlet *Peace with Mexico*, Gallatin drew a sharp distinction between a superiority stemming from institutions and a superiority stemming from race. He believed in the first, but not in the second. "Your mission," he told the United States, "is to improve the state of the world, to be the 'model republic,' to show that men are capable of governing themselves, and that this simple and natural form of government is that also which confers most happiness on all, is productive of the greatest development of the intellectual faculties, above all, that which is attended with the highest standard of private and political virtue and morality." The Mexican War he condemned as an act of aggression, and he pointed out that the president and his cabinet would never in their private life have tried to appropriate their neighbor's farm on pretenses similar to those they were using for dismembering Mexico.

Gallatin asserted that in the absence of any real justification for the war with Mexico, the United States had resorted "to a most extraordinary assertion. It is said that the people of the United States have an hereditary superiority of race over the Mexicans, which gives them the right to subjugate and keep in bondage the inferior nation." Gallatin thought it remarkable that a democracy that rejected every hereditary claim of individuals should admit an hereditary superiority of races. Gallatin was puzzled by Anglo-Saxonism. How could a doubtful descent from men who lived a thousand years ago transmit a superiority over one's fellowmen? Even at that time, he said, the Anglo-Saxons were inferior to the Goths (from whom the Spaniards were descended) and in no way superior to the Franks and the Burgundians. The English, he admitted, had superior institutions, but this came not from their Anglo-Saxon descent but from a variety of causes, including a racial mixture of Frenchified Normans, Angevins, and Gascons. The progressive improvement of mankind had stemmed much more from religious and political institutions than from races.[47]

Gallatin in discussing race brought a remembrance of the Enlightenment into the mid-nineteenth century. He simply would not accept a world in which some were doomed to permanent inferiority or extinction and others to worldwide dominion, power, and glory. To Gallatin true morality meant restraint. Even if one admitted a superiority of race, he argued, this meant no superiority of right, any more than a man of superior talents had the right to infringe on a man of inferior talents. Throughout his career Gallatin had seen no need to separate public standards of action and conduct from private standards.

In February 1848 Gallatin was disgusted that even those who

thought the war with Mexico unjust were happy to accept a peace which extorted from Mexico a part of its territory. At the age of eighty-seven Gallatin indicated that this new "Manifest Destiny" was not the dream of republican freedom that had inspired his post-Revolutionary generation: "What shall be said of the notion of an empire extending from the Atlantic to the Pacific, and from the North Pole to the Equator? Of the destiny of the Anglo-Saxon race, of its universal monarchy over the whole of North America?" Asia, he said, had attained "the highest degree of civilization, and even of power" with its empires of Turkey, India, and China. The "allegations of superiority of race and destiny neither require nor deserve any answer; they are but pretences under which to disguise ambition, cupidity, or silly vanity."[48] The clarity of the eighteenth century revealed the tawdriness of much of mid-nineteenth-century nationalistic thought.

Anderson and Gallatin were exceptions. In the mid-nineteenth century opponents of aggressive expansionism for the most part did not object when other races were condemned to permanent inferiority. They were far more concerned with what was to happen to the United States than with what was to happen to the rest of the world. Those who expressed a faith in the innate capacity of other peoples were overwhelmed by a surging tide of arrogant racial theory.

14

Expansion and World Mission

> You talk of carrying to all the races of the world your institutions, your religion, your arts and sciences. You can no more do it than you can give to all the races your color, form, and development.
>
> Senator John Pettit, February 23, 1855

In the years after the Mexican War some questioned the new racial assumptions, many were wary of force, and a majority did not want colonies, but most thought that American commerce could penetrate the world and that the Anglo-Saxons could outbreed other races. This supreme confidence in the racial strength of white America was accompanied by the desire that this special race and its government should not be tainted and weakened by any inferior peoples. What had once been merely felt was now backed by the best scientific evidence — nations and peoples could lose their greatness by mixing with inferior races. Some of these inferior races were destined to serve, others to disappear. For races within the United States the degree to which these special ideas of progress had permeated American thinking was clearly revealed by the debates on slavery and on the status of the areas acquired from Mexico, and for races in the rest of the world by the debates and writings on the nature of American overseas expansion.

In defending slavery Southerners and their friends were able to draw on racial assumptions that were generally accepted throughout the United States. George Fitzhugh, in his *Sociology for the South* and in his earlier newspaper articles, carefully characterized the Anglo-Saxon as well as the African race. At the core of Fitzhugh's argument was the point that blacks freed from slavery would be destroyed by competition with the Anglo-Saxons. "It is the boast of the Anglo-Saxon," wrote Fitzhugh, "that by the arts of peace under the influence of free trade he can march to universal conquest." Whether or not that could be accomplished, it was known by everyone that when Englishmen or Americans settled among "inferior races" they soon became the owners of the soil and "gradually extirpate or reduce to poverty the original owners. They are the wire-grass of nations." The law of nature which "enables and impels the stronger race to oppress and exterminate the weaker" operated between the stronger and weaker members in every society. If the Negro continued to be property he could be saved, for no people on earth loved and cherished property more than the Anglo-Saxons.[1]

Although Fitzhugh's basic purpose was to defend slavery, he was clearly casting his arguments within the framework of the new scientific and political "realism" regarding race. "The Indian, like the savage races of Canaan, is doomed to extermination," he wrote, "and those who most sympathize with his fate would be the first to shoot him if they lived on the frontier." Under God's direction some races were exterminated, some were enslaved: "This is all right, because it is necessary."[2] Southern defenders of slavery were convinced that the free black population was falling prey to disease and mental illness. "Like the aborigines of this country," said Representative Seaborn Jones of Georgia about the free Negroes in 1847, "they will dwindle into numerical nothingness before the onward march of the Anglo-Saxon race."[3]

It was generally agreed that the blacks could be improved only by an admixture of white blood, and this was clearly unthinkable; existing miscegenation in the South was generally ignored. Charles Brown of Pennsylvania said in the House of Representatives that complete equality could be brought about only by amalgamation of the races, but this was not "desired by any sane member of the European branch of the American family. It is too monstrous to think of, and would lead to a degeneracy of the whole people of this country as, in a brief period, to cause them to fall before some invading, superior, and purer northern nation or people, in the same way the Indians have fallen, and the mixed breeds south of us must certainly hereafter fall before us."[4] Representative Orlando B. Ficklin of Illinois discussed the impossibility of a multiracial society's existing without slavery. Free Negroes should be sent to Africa, for in the United States they were overpowered by "a superior race." Ficklin had no hesitation in speaking for his whole region: "The people of my State, (Illinois,) and the people of Indiana, and other of the northwestern States, have no more desire to see the negroes raised to an equality with the whites than have the people of South Carolina, Louisiana, or the most ultra of the slaveholding States."[5]

Since the 1830s the pervasive quality of antiblack feeling had become obvious throughout the free states, even among many people who opposed the institution of slavery. Tocqueville commented that race prejudice appeared stronger in the free than in the slave states and said it was strongest of all in those states where there had never been slavery. "In the United States," he said, "people abolish slavery for the sake not of the Negroes but of the white men."[6] When in the 1830s abolitionists appeared to be advocating both the end of slavery and the incorporation of the blacks into white society, antiabolitionist violence swept the northern cities. Only when it became clear in the 1840s that opposition to slavery and to slave expansion did not have to mean a defense of black equality did the violence die down.[7]

When the Free-Soil party developed in the late 1840s, it included some who wanted an expansion of Negro rights, but it was also strongly influenced by those who thought the blacks inferior and wished to preserve the territories for the free white working man. The Free-Soilers were able to achieve more general support by omitting from their platform planks calling for black equality. Many of the abolitionists within the Free-Soil party were unable to escape the now all-pervasive belief in a superior white race.[8] While the movement opposing the extension of slavery gained ground in the late 1840s and early 1850s, racial discrimination against blacks increased in many northern states; and although the Republican party contained many who defended Negro rights, its general political appeal depended on separating the attack on slave expansion from the equality issue. Debates on slave expansion in the 1850s revolved as much around the issue of preventing blacks from degrading new white areas as they did around the issue of the evils of slavery.[9]

Discussion of slavery and the territories in the 1850s also clearly revealed the extent to which the new scientific "proofs" of racial inequality had permeated the attitudes of members of Congress. They consciously rejected the egalitarianism of the Revolutionary era, used as their authority the findings of the new science, and argued that there was a fixed relationship between the races. Senator John Pettit of Indiana commented that in the Declaration of Independence and other documents it was maintained that all men were created equal: "I hold it to be a self-evident lie." God elected some to everlasting life, some to eternal damnation. This applied to nations and races as well as to individuals: "Let the races have their run. Let them in their turn be swept from the face of the earth." Racial mixture was ruinous to a nation. Other races had to be enslaved, controlled, or exterminated, not regenerated: "You talk of carrying to all the races of the world your institutions, your religion, your arts and sciences. You can no more do it than you can give to all the races your color, form, and development."[10] Representative Thomas L. Clingman of North Carolina told his colleagues that there had been "a prodigious advance in knowledge" since Jefferson's time. The whole doctrine of Negro equality had been exploded, "not merely in the South, but throughout the United States." Almost all "the great men of science" now maintained that the Negro race was distinct. Lemuel D. Evans of Texas demonstrated a knowledge of Nott, Bodichon, Latham, and

Malte-Brun in discussing slavery in America, and Andrew P. Butler of South Carolina told the Senate that "inequality pervades the creation of this universe."[11]

The possibility of black equality or black participation in republican government was rejected by most Northerners as well as Southerners in the 1850s. Only a bloody war, total victory, and the occupation of the defeated South temporarily brought blacks within the political system, and the degradation of the blacks after 1876 stemmed naturally from the assumptions of the prewar years.

The degree to which American republicanism was interpreted as white Anglo-Saxon republicanism was also made clear in the arguments over the territories acquired from Mexico in 1848. The condemnations of the "debased" population of New Mexico, which had been common before 1846, were reiterated after American troops occupied the region. In the Senate in March 1848 Daniel Webster lamented the uselessness of New Mexico and its people—a people "infinitely less elevated in mind and condition than the people of the Sandwich Islands."[12] Senator James D. Westcott of Florida was appalled that some might so interpret the treaty of cession from Mexico, which made the inhabitants of New Mexico and California citizens of the United States, as to include the colored races. Echoing Calhoun he said "our governments were governments of the *white* race," and the political inferiority of blacks and Indians was "a fundamental principle of the Government." He was obviously perturbed, as were many others, that the Mexicans had permitted mixed bloods to participate as citizens in the government of their northern provinces. He objected to the possibility of being "compelled to receive not merely the white citizens of California and New Mexico, but the peons, negroes, and Indians of all sorts, the wild tribe of Camanches, the bug-and-lizard-eating 'Diggers,' and other half-monkey savages in those countries, as *equal citizens of the United States.*"[13] It soon became apparent that many "Anglo-Saxons" were prepared to accept only a few of the inhabitants of the Spanish West and Southwest as white.

The creation in 1850 of the territory of New Mexico as part of the general sectional compromise of that year was regarded with many misgivings. Thomas H. Bayley of Virginia told the House of Representatives in July 1850 that he would never agree to the admission of New Mexico as a state until the character and number of its population made it possible.[14] To many this would happen only when American Anglo-Saxons predominated in the region. Territorial Governor William Carr in December 1852 told the legislative assembly at Sante Fe that it should "obey the obvious dictate of common sense" and not resist American Manifest Destiny. They should "embark upon the Anglo-Saxon wave which is now rolling from East to West, across the Continent, and ultimately prosper, instead of attempting to resist it, and perish."[15] Just how they were to ride the wave was unclear.

Most revealing of the general American attitudes regarding Spanish-American peoples in general were the reactions of Delegate Richard H. Weightman of New Mexico. Weightman, who had been born in Washington, D.C. and who was educated in Virginia and at the United States Military Academy, resented the assertions that non-Anglo-Saxons were unfit to participate in the American government. When President Fillmore pointed out that it would be dangerous to take Cuba because of the differences in the race and character of the inhabitants, Weightman challenged the view that "differences of race, or differences of language, or any other sort of differences, were detrimental to us as a people." He went on to defend his constituents, arguing that though a large majority had Spanish and Indian ancestry mingled generations before, they had no need to be "ashamed of their blood." If he had wanted to convince the people of New Mexico that the government and people of the United States looked upon them with "repugnance and contempt," he said, he would have acted as this administration had acted. Weightman understood well the racial ingredients in the discussions of American expansion, and he said it was worthy of remark that "the argument about 'kindred races,' while it cuts off Cuban and all Mexican annexation, favors Canadian annexation."[16] The American mission was all too clearly restricted to pure Caucasians, preferably Anglo-Saxon.

The early history of California also exhibited to the full the manner in which most Americans were determined that their political system should be reserved for white Anglo-Saxons. The debates in the California constitutional convention in 1849 demonstrated in practical form the nature of the fears surrounding the opposition to the All-Mexico Movement in 1847. A basic problem in the discussion was the question of who could vote, for "Anglo-Saxons" were considerably perturbed at the number of Mexicans with Indian blood who had previously participated as citizens. When it was recommended that all male citizens of Mexico who had elected to become citizens of the United States could vote, this was quickly countered by an amendment which aimed to restrict the suffrage to "white" male citizens. The proposer argued that his object was to exclude "the inferior races of mankind"—particularly blacks and Indians. Blacks had few defenders, there was even an effort to exclude free Negroes from the state, and the problem of which Californians were "white" caused a bitter debate. Some wanted to exclude "wild Indians" but would let mixed Spanish and Indians vote; some even spoke of the Indians as an old noble race and argued in earlier nineteenth-century terms of the desirability of civilization and assimilation. But the eventual compromise left the possibility that in special cases Indians might vote if approved by a two-thirds legislative majority. In practice blacks and obvious Indians were excluded. Spanish-Americans, of whatever blood, usually found themselves grossly discriminated against.[17]

While the ex-Mexicans and their converts were degraded, the "wild" Indians of California were, in the 1850s, treated with an unsurpassed brutality. In the previous twenty years the Indians had been dehumanized. The hunting down and murdering of Indians in California was made easier by the popular assumption that the elimination of the Indians was inevitable. In 1851 United States commissioners met with the Indians and obtained much of the state of California, but left the Indians some eight and one-half million acres in reservations. The Californians bitterly objected to this policy. They wanted more. They wanted everything. The California Assembly asked that the Indians be removed from the state and requested the California senators in Washington to work toward this end. In a minority report of the California Senate, J. J. Warner pointed out that the Indians had nowhere to go, and that the Californians might leave the Indians where they lived "were it not for that spirit of occupation and appropriation so irresistible to our race." If the United States would not seek to elevate the Indians, said Warner, it should at least tolerate their existence: "Has the love of gold blotted from our minds all feelings of compassion or justice?"[18]

It was to no avail. The United States Senate rejected the treaties with the Californian Indians and left the Indians at the mercy of the Californians. Eventually in the 1850s smaller reservations were worked out, but in the meantime the prophecy uttered by California Governor Peter H. Burnett in his annual message of 1851 rapidly became reality: "That a war of extermination will continue to be waged between the two races until the Indian race becomes extinct, must be expected; while we cannot anticipate this result with but painful regret, the inevitable destiny of the race is beyond the power and wisdom of man to avert."[19] In the California of the 1850s the rhetoric of the 1840s became reality: an "inferior" Indian "race" was hastened to its grave as part of the expansive mission of the Anglo-Saxon race.

The rejection of "inferior" races as equal participants in the American republican system, combined with the assumptions of constant Anglo-Saxon growth, permeated American discussions of their world role in the years after the Mexican War. A minority argued that this meant that Americans would have to settle other regions, act as a ruling elite, and create a colonial empire or sister republics, but the majority thought that a vigorous commercial penetration of the globe would create immense wealth while allowing the Anglo-Saxons to outbreed and replace a variety of other races. The most pressing dilemmas existed in regard to those regions that were possible areas for immediate United States expansion. It was much easier to dream of transformation in the distant Pacific, where there was no immediate problem of control, than in Cuba or South America, where the United States might suddenly find itself in the possession of regions heavily populated by "inferior" races.

In the 1850s there were only two main groups that were willing to accept actual American colonial rule over "inferior" populations: the ardent supporters of slave expansion and the Democratic "Young America" group. The colonialists were never in a majority and were badly hurt by the linking of colonialism with the expansion of slavery. The movement promoting expansion in and rule over Central and South America and the whole Caribbean region was seen by some ardent Southerners as a means of giving greater strength to the South within the union or even as the basis for a distinct southern nation. Many of those who advocated such a movement, though willing to accept immediate colonialism, often incorporated the more general idea that the existing mixed races would eventually fade away before the Anglo-Saxons and their black slaves. The whole of Latin America, like Mexico, was viewed as an area that had been ruined by racial mongrelization and by subsequent misrule. "The law of progress—of national growth, of very necessity—that has carried us to the Gulf of Mexico and to the Pacific Ocean, will continue to impel us onward," wrote Northerner John Van Evrie in his defense of slavery in 1853, "and to restore the rapidly perishing civilization of the great tropical center of the continent."[20] Advocates of expansion southward thought of a new civilization emerging, a civilization that in population and culture would recreate the southern plantation states.

As in the case of the annexation of Texas in the 1840s, some Southerners were prepared to argue that expansion to the South would save rather than destroy the union and ultimately would solve the problem of slavery. A key figure in this argument was the naval scientist Matthew F. Maury of the National Observatory in Washington, D.C. Believing that the acquisition of additional contiguous territory from Mexico would break up the union, Maury placed his hopes in the development of a great new republic along the Amazon and its tributaries and on the commercial development of the whole Caribbean region. Maury depicted the Gulf of Mexico as a future Mediterranean clustered about by a white ruling class and an African slave population—and with an isthmian canal and highways linking the oceans and giving the United States the commerce of Europe and Asia. In this scheme the valley of the Amazon would become of vital importance, and Maury asked who would people it: "Shall it be peopled with an imbecile and an indolent people, or by a go ahead race that has energy and enterprise equal to subdue the forest and to develop and bring forth the vast resources that lay hidden there?" When the United States government obtained the right to navigate the Amazon, nothing would prevent "American citizens from the free, as well as from the slave States, from going there with their goods and chattels to settle and to revolutionize and republicanize and Anglo-Saxonize that valley." The new republic would provide a safety valve for southern states overpopulated with slaves.[21]

Maury attempted to promote his Amazon project by arguing that blacks would be siphoned off to the South, but some Southerners in their enthusiasm for expansion into the whole Caribbean region completely forfeited the possibility of general national support by ardently espousing the expansion of the slave system as an end in itself and even by supporting the reopening of the African slave trade. Mexico, Central and South America, Cuba, and the West Indies were all talked of as the likely beneficiaries of an expanding southern slave system, and a variety of southern opportunists either proposed or led filibustering expeditions to take over parts of Latin America for a possible recreation of the southern system.[22]

More than any other area Cuba attracted southern interest in the 1850s, and though the issue of acquiring the island was dominated by the sectional split between North and South, the controversy was also revealing of the constraints placed on American expansion by the new racial ideas. Since early in the century Cuba had been viewed in the United States as the one noncontiguous area that clearly belonged within the American system.[23] Some congressmen had suggested obtaining Cuba even before the Mexican War began, and in the spring of 1848 the cabinet seriously began to discuss the purchase of the island. As in the case of Yucatan, the danger of the island's falling into the possession of England was raised by Polk as a reason for its acquisition. Robert J. Walker, as usual, favored any new increase in territory, but immediately problems arose that went beyond the question of the extension of slavery. Cave Johnson, the postmaster general and a Tennessean, "had objections to incorporating the Spanish population of Cuba into our Union." After considerable discussion the cabinet decided to attempt secret negotiations to buy Cuba for one hundred million dollars. Secretary of State James Buchanan went along with this plan, although he had qualms both about the sectional implications of the purchase and about how the population of the island would be governed. His solution was that the island would have to "be *Americanized*, — as Louisiana has been," but he never explained how he expected to get enough white Anglo-Saxon Americans to Cuba.[24]

Polk's effort to buy Cuba failed — the Spanish did not want to sell — but there was considerable American interest in the acquisition of the island throughout the 1850s. Much of this interest was in the South, particularly after the Kansas-Nebraska Act precipitated vigorous debate on the subject of the expansion of slavery, but there was also northern support. In the North the massive stumbling block to the acquisition of the island was the enhancement of slave power, but in both North and South the presence of a numerous, supposedly unassimilable population brought resistance to expansion in that area. Northern Free-Soiler James Shepherd Pike expressed a common opinion succinctly in 1853 when he wrote that the United States did not want a territory that was filled "with black, mixed, degraded, and ignorant, or inferior races."[25] Northerners did not want a slave empire in Cuba, but they also had no desire to see free Cubans as citizens of the American Republic.

Even in the South, where it could be seen that the acquisition of Cuba would provide a major addition to southern power, considerable doubt was expressed about annexing a free population unfit to enter the American union. It was argued in *De Bow's Review* in 1853 that although it might be necessary to take the island to forestall England or France, annexation should not be eagerly pursued. Cuba, the author said, "is unlike Texas in almost every respect. Texas was in great degree uninhabited. Cuba is densely populated." If Cuba were taken the North would insist on taking Canada. The author also challenged those who believed that the Anglo-Saxons could predominate on the island: "Cuba is now, and will perhaps always be, in the hands of the Spanish race, which can never be assimilated to our own." This last assumption was, in a later article, described as an "insuperable" obstacle to the acquisition of the island. Cuba was too densely populated to be "Americanized," and Americanization consisted not in changing institutions but in changing the racial characteristics of the population.[26] Even if there had been no sectional quarrel in the 1850s, there would have been fundamental objections to the acquisition of Cuba.

In his annual message, submitted in December 1852, President Millard Fillmore summed up the Cuban dilemma. He admitted the grave sectional implications of the acquisition, but he also went to the crux of the racial problem: "Were this Island comparatively destitute of inhabitants, or occupied by a kindred race, I should regard it, if voluntarily ceded by Spain, as a most desirable acquisition. But, under existing circumstances, I should look upon its incorporation into our Union as a very hazardous measure. It would bring into the Confederacy a population of a different national stock, speaking a different language, and not likely to harmonize with the other members."[27]

While expansion to the south and the Caribbean posed questions of racial amalgamation or colonialism that were not solved by the ending of the slavery issue, there were practically no objections on racial grounds to the annexation of Canada. It was clearly understood that Canada could be integrated within the American system, and any undesirable mixed French-Canadian elements would be overwhelmed by Americans who would move in to join their Anglo-Saxon brethren. Any drive to obtain Canada in the 1850s was, of course, slowed by southern fears of additions to the free states, but the ultimate problem was British power. Unfortunately for the Americans in the second half of the nineteenth century, the area that best fitted their ideal for future expansion — sparsely populated with an existing Anglo-Saxon influence — was held by the strongest power in the world. Here they had to put their faith in the inevitability of American progress and success and in the growth of the American population.

Representative Hiram Bell of Ohio stated the case for Canada in 1853 when he opposed the annexation of Cuba. After pointing out the deficiencies of the Cuban population, he said that there "is a country and there is a people competent for self-government." This was Canada, an area of 2,652,000 people, "bone, as it were, of our bone, flesh of our flesh, deriving their origin from the same Anglo-Saxon source." Even *De Bow's Review* admitted that Canada offered much more for the United States than areas occupied by less desirable populations. One writer in the review in 1850 admitted that there would be a sectional problem if Canada were annexed for "free soilism," but he said that in general the South would support the measure if it were simply to extend our territory. "Aside from slavery and protection," he said, "we believe that a majority of the American people would be in favor of the annexation of Canada."[28]

The Young Americans would have been happy to take Canada, but unlike most other Americans they would also have been happy to take a variety of other areas. In the early 1850s the Young Americans became a contentious group within the Democratic party. They poured scorn on "the old fogies" and stressed "sympathy for the liberals of Europe, the expansion of the American republic southward and westward, and the grasping of the magnificent purse of the commerce of the Pacific."[29] Their main spokesmen were George O. Sanders of Kentucky and William Corry of Ohio, but the group also enlisted support from more prominent politicians, including Stephen A. Douglas of Illinois. Sanders, who ardently defended a militant expansionist position, took over the *Democratic Review* in 1852 and turned it into the organ of Young America. In the presidential race of that year the Young Americans placed their hopes in Stephen A. Douglas. They were sadly disappointed that Douglas did not win the Democratic nomination, and that they received no significant recognition after the Democratic victory.[30]

The leaders of the Young Americans did not think of themselves as Anglo-Saxonists. They delighted in twisting the lion's tail and argued that British power should be reduced and that the United States should resist British pretensions. They did not want the Americans to be the supreme Anglo-Saxons, but rather a unique blend of European Caucasians; the Caucasus, said a writer in the *Democratic Review* in October 1852, was the "land of heroism and adventurous spirit, where man has attained the highest degree of external perfection, and whence the principal nations of Europe are supposed to derive their descent."[31] Yet like others who defended a distinct "American" race while finding it difficult to accept pure Anglo-Saxonism, the Young Americans gave to the American race all the attributes usually given to the Anglo-Saxons. George Fitzhugh saw the Young Americans, for all their talk of universal regeneration, as part of the Anglo-Saxon movement. He said that the congressional members of Young America "boast that the Anglo-Saxon race is manifestly destined to eat out all other races, as the wire-grass destroys and takes the place of other grasses. Nay, they allege this competitive process is going on throughout all nature, the strong are everywhere devouring the weak; the hardier plants and animals destroying the weaker, and the superior races of man exterminating the inferior."[32]

The Young Americans often used a rhetoric of republicanism and world freedom, but the general tone of the *Democratic Review* while it was under their influence revealed the extent to which they envisaged a world dominated by the white American race. Lip service was paid to old ideas of regeneration, but the arguments were blended with a hard-core belief in innate superiority and future American world dominance. That Americans needed to be fully aware of their strength was the theme of an article on Central America in the spring of 1853, for "it depends on them and them alone, whether the tide of Christianity, civilization and Liberty continues to advance on this great continent, or again recedes before the reaction of barbarism." Savages were fighting for dominion in Yucatan, and Indian and mongrel races greatly outnumbered the whites in the whole of Central and South America. These whites badly needed protection; such was their imbecility . . . such their indolence, weakness and degeneracy" that they needed to be shielded by "a more wise and energetic race." The key to the relative vigor and resources of nations, argued the author, was in their populations, not simply in numbers, but in "the moral, physical and intellectual qualities of a people that form the basis of their superiority." The British Empire was taken to task in the article because it was not "one people, of one race, one language and one God." The United States had the strength of racial, political, and religious unity: "they conquer to set free, and every accession of territory is only an extension of civilization and liberty."[33]

Young America was, of course, a minority and extreme movement within the Democratic party, and its influence faded rapidly after the 1852 election, but many of its underlying assumptions received general support in the 1850s. The members of the movement were unusual in that they accepted a whole variety of the current expansionist ideas in exaggerated form, were anxious to intervene all over the world, and looked forward to the rapid acquisition of territory in North and South America.

More typical of the 1850s was the belief that commercial penetration and population growth were the keys to future American relations with the rest of the world. American economic growth and the new technology would prepare the way for the ever-increasing American population to thrust outward into the most distant regions. The problems that had shattered hopes of territorial expansion into Latin America and the Caribbean could be delayed. The penetration of distant regions could even be justified by the optimistic rhetoric of an earlier generation, and the harsh language used when discussing adjacent peoples could be modified, for there was no immediate prospect of adding large areas with vast populations of "inferior" races.

Asia became of particular interest to the expansionists because it appeared to offer limitless commercial opportunity while fulfilling the age-old dream of the westward movement of civilization. The American thrust into the Pacific was to be the grand culmination of the movement that had begun so long ago in the highlands of central Asia. Those Aryan tribesmen who had begun their march with the sun thousands of years before were now to return home. What had so long been prophesied was to come to pass: arts, sciences, religion, the whole of civilization were to return to their original birthplace after completing a circuit of the globe.

The manner in which the old dreams of the westward movement of civilization had merged with the newer German-influenced ideas of the westward movement of a superior people became obvious in the writings and speeches of the decade from 1845 to 1855, though at times the racial implications were cloaked in a rhetoric of universal progress. It was assumed that the arrival of Americans on the shores of the Pacific would lead to an immediate drive into Asia. The supreme benefits arising from the occupation of Oregon, said the *Daily Ohio Statesman* in 1845, had long been anticipated "by those who have cast their mind before the onward march of civilization west."[34] Early in the following year Representative Henry W. Hilliard of Alabama said he was awed by the vast possibilities opened up by the expansion to the Pacific of a nation living under the laws of Alfred and speaking the language of Shakespeare and Milton. The destiny of the United States was clear. "Civilization and intelligence started in the East," he said; "they have travelled and are still travelling westward; but when they shall have completed the circuit of the earth, and reached the extremest verge of the Pacific shores . . . then shall we enjoy the sublime destiny of returning these blessings to their ancient seat." Hilliard talked of taking free institutions and the Gospel back to "the dark family." Representative Cornelius Darragh of Pennsylvania stressed that with title to Oregon "we shall be neighbours of the Chinese," and that the improved arts and sciences would soon be handed back to the East along with republicanism and Christianity.[35]

A discussion of boundaries in the California constitutional convention of 1849 led H. W. Halleck to urge that the state should not be made too small, for "no other portion of the globe will exercise a greater influence upon the civilization and commerce of the world. The people of California will penetrate the hitherto inaccessible portions of Asia, carrying with them not only the arts and sciences, but the refining and purifying influence of civilization and Christianity; they will unlock the vast resources of the East, and, by reversing the commerce of the world, pour the riches of India into the metropolis of the new State."[36] California in these years demonstrated in microcosm the strengths and the dilemmas of American expansion: boundless confidence in the prospects of future wealth; dreams of casting a beneficent light on the darkest recesses of Asia; supreme confidence in the abilities of the American Anglo-Saxon people; and the actual rejection and oppression of non-Anglo-Saxon races.

Politicians and writers took a particular delight in the early 1850s in embellishing their defenses of commerce, Christianity, and racial destiny with this theme of the westward movement of civilization. Presley Ewing of Kentucky avowed his faith in the westward course of progress in 1852 and caused laughter in the House by saying that if he were not a Whig he would call himself a Young American. "The march of civilization," he said, "like the march of christianity has been, from the days of the wise men of Chaldea down to the present time, from East to West. You might as well attempt to turn back the natural sun in its course, as to revert the sun of civilization in its westward way."[37] In a long, strange book on the westward movement of civilization, E. L. Magoon argued that the "travels of men, and the trade-currents of God, move spontaneously and perpetually toward the West." For Magoon even the west end of every great town was the section of growth and expansion.[38] The emphasis now was not so much on the transfer of civilization—from Greece to Rome, to England, to America, to Asia—but rather on its ever wider dissemination. The United States, unlike other empires, would not pass into oblivion. America was to break the pattern of the rise and fall of empires, said a writer in the *North American Review* in 1846, for "with every stage of progress, civilization embraces more and more individuals, extends to a larger and larger portion of the community, and of course it is less liable to be exterminated or transferred."[39]

There was never any doubt that civilization was to be carried into Asia along the paths of commerce. Most enthusiasts for the penetration of the Pacific region believed that commercial and technological progress would do just as much as Christianity to bring civilization and progress to backward regions. "Civilization, which formerly only progressed by conquest," said Gilbert Dean of New York in the House, "now follows in the peaceful track of the merchant ship." In discussing Hawaii one author suggested that the "steamboat or locomotive are the knight-errants of the present day." Secretary of the Treasury Robert J. Walker in his annual report, submitted in December 1848, discussed the use of steamships for Asian trade and wrote that "the light of Christianity, following the path of commerce, would return with all its blessings to the East, from which it rose." Commerce, he said, was the precursor of Christianity, teaching peace and intercourse among all nations and fostering the mutual interests of mankind. Walker made it clear in his other writings in the 1850s that he believed this reign of free trade and peace was to arrive under the world rule of the Anglo-Saxon race.[40]

But what if there were resistance to commercial penetration? It was made clear that such obscurantism would not be tolerated. When Secretary of the Navy John P. Kennedy in his annual report, submitted in December 1852, defended the American thrust into Asia, the attempt to establish commercial relations with Japan, and the "enforcement of a more liberal system of intercourse upon China," he said no country had the right to refuse their ports to those Europeans and Americans who pursued trade and exploration throughout the globe. In writing of future Asian progress he let an iron fist be glimpsed through the soft trappings of civilization. "Christendom is constrained," he wrote, "by the pressure of an increasing necessity, to publish its wants and declare its rights to the heathen, and in making its power felt will bring innumerable blessings to every race which shall acknowledge its mastery."[41]

Commerce and civilization were inextricably entwined, but essential to their progress was the constant presence of the Anglo-Saxon race, a race that even in Asia would ultimately replace inferior peoples. The Anglo-Saxons, said Simeon North at New Haven in 1847, were the men "whose enterprise explores every land, and whose commerce whitens every sea." The course of the Anglo-Saxon race "had been steadily onward, to empire and greatness."[42] A writer in the *Southern Literary Messenger* in 1852 noted that "the Anglo-Saxon branch of the Germanic race" had most of the commerce of the world in its hands. Now its impact was to be felt throughout Africa, eastern Asia, and Japan. As the "multiplying millions of the Anglo-Germanic race" surged onward, "every ocean will swarm with their ships; every coast and island will be occupied with their establishments; their language, their science, their literature and their religion, will pervade all the kindreds and tribes of Heathendom."[43] Senator Augustus Dodge of Iowa said in the Senate in 1853 that the Anglo-Saxon race was the largest in number and the most energetic in the world. "It is gradually taking possession of all the ports and coasts of the world, and its language superseding almost every other." In passing he said that he thought "American" would be a better name for the race than "Anglo-Saxon."[44] "The superior races of the great cradles of western Asia have spread," said a writer in *Putnam's*, "pursuing the paths of the sun, until they now quite circle the globe." Americans, in expanding their settlements, carried "the best blood of time" in their veins—the Anglo-Saxon.[45]

Assumptions of overwhelming growth in population and power were a commonplace of expansionist writers in the 1850s. William H. Seward of New York prophesied an American population of two hundred million by 1950 and thought that the sheer mass of white Americans would grow so large that it would swallow alien elements without a trace. In time Americans would settle in great numbers in the valley of Mexico, Yucatan, and Central America. Only the "inferior masses" of Africans and Indians would remain unassimilated; the Indians would ultimately disappear. Seward believed in a distinct American race—a race composed of the best elements of the Caucasians. This race was using the sea to create the greatest commercial empire the world had ever seen. "The world," he said, "contains no seat of empire so magnificent as this."[46] William Gilpin, who was an impassioned believer in the westward movement of civilization, argued that "*our* North America will rapidly attain to a population equalling that of the rest of the world combined." Commodore Robert F. Stockton, who after his service in the navy and in California flirted with a number of political movements including Young America and the American party, said that even within its existing boundaries the United States would within fifty years "acquire more wealth and power than any sovereign potentate or dominion which now sways or ever before swayed any portion of the destiny of mankind." But he was unwilling that the "Anglo-American race" should recoil from any boundary.[47]

Ultimately, as the Anglo-Saxons multiplied, many inferior races would disappear. As early as 1843 a writer in the *Merchants' Magazine* suggested that the name *Hawaii* should be retained — "the indigenous population, after they may have disappeared before, or become absorbed in, the tide of western civilization, should still yield a trace of their former existence, though it be but a name."[48] The superior American race, said a writer in *De Bow's Review* in 1852, was to achieve world dominance through replacing other peoples. Already, by rapid colonization, the United States had supplanted the "inferior" race on the Pacific coast. The same process would take place in Mexico, South America, Asia, and the Pacific as the American race advanced: "wherever they go, this inferior native population, as a result of amalgamation, and that great law of contact between a higher and a lower race, by which the latter gives way to the former, must be gradually supplanted, and its place occupied by this highest of races." Eventually, without wars of conquest, but through the laws of contact between superior and inferior races, the United States in all probability "will occupy the entire extent of America, the rich and fertile plains of Asia, together with the intermediate isles of the sea, in fulfilment of the great purpose of heaven, of the ultimate enlightenment of the whole earth, and the gradual elevation of man to the dignity and glory of the promised millenial day." This, of course, was not the regeneration of the peoples of the world, but the creation of a better world by the replacement of a variety of other races by a superior race.[49]

Most writers were unclear as to the process by which this replacement of other races would occur, but a writer in the *Merchants' Magazine* in 1855 was more explicit. Wars of extermination were not needed, he wrote, because superior races simply had the commercial power to secure for themselves the largest share of the means of subsistence. This would bring about "the extinction in future times of all the barbarous races." It was likely that the Mexicans were already doomed, and other races that could not adapt would also disappear. "It is better that an inferior race should thus become extinct, the author argued, "than that the development of a superior race should be prevented."[50]

Most were willing to tighten the general bonds of Caucasian unity when confronted by nonwhite races, but there were also indications that some would like to foster more exclusive Anglo-Saxon unity by ending the traditional rivalry with the government of Great Britain. If only England would change her policies, Representative Lemuel Evans of Texas said in 1856, then "the two grand branches of the Anglo-Saxon stock, the one pressing from the bay of Bengal, and the other from the golden gulf of California, would meet in some beautiful group of sunny isles in the Pacific ocean, and together clasp their united hands in love and peace around the globe."[51] The same thought had been expressed in 1850 by the American minister in England, Abbot Lawrence. "If the Anglo-Saxons of Great Britain and the United States are true to each other, and to the cause of human freedom," he wrote, "they may not only give their language, but their laws to the world, and defy the power of all *despots* on the face of the Globe."[52]

The hope that an Anglo-Saxon union would bring a new Roman age to the world was expressed regularly from the middle of the nineteenth century on. It never overcame the idea that the American Anglo-Saxon race would triumph over all other peoples, nor did it end the attacks on the British abuse of power, but many Americans took pride in English success as reinforcing the belief that race was all-important. One writer in 1850 defended the importance of a strong American navy and conjured up a dream of the "ANGLO NORMAN RACE . . . , with its transatlantic millions coming to the rescue of its German kindred and European liberty." In this dream the combined Anglo-Norman fleets swept the French and the Russians from the ocean and based peace on the principle "that no power on earth should build dock-yards or support navies, except the Anglo-Norman Race, its kindred and allies." This vision of an Anglo-American future did not prevent the writer from suggesting that the United States should eliminate British influence in the Caribbean by taking Cuba.[53]

The most influential politican to discuss a future triumph of the combined English races at any length was Polk's ex-secretary of the treasury, Robert J. Walker, who in the 1850s still thought of himself as a possible future president. Walker visited England in the early 1850s and discussed the whole matter of Anglo-Saxon destiny in a series of letters with British imperialist Arthur Davies, who had become interested in the possible union of the United States and the British Empire. The correspondence was published as a pamphlet in London in 1852. Davies said that he firmly believed in the sentiment that Walker had expressed in their conversations: "That a time shall come when the human race shall become as one family, and that the predominance of our Anglo-Celt-Sax-Norman stock shall guide the nations to that result." In his letters Walker quickly moved the center of power from Europe to the New World. There should be no question of the United States becoming part of the British Empire — if an amalgamation took place it would be by the British becoming part of the American union. Such a merging "would unite in one confederacy, more than two hundred millions of people, each State by separate State legislation taking charge of its own local concerns, governed by a race speaking the same language, of superior intellect and energy, covering now nearly one half the territory of the globe, and diffusing itself gradually over the remainder." He quickly pointed out that such a country would secure the commerce as well as the peace of the world. In time "this great confederacy would ultimately embrace the globe we inhabit." Walker's tone in these letters was that of the Christian regeneration of the world, but what he was actually describing was the expansion and rise to supreme power of the Anglo-Saxons.[54]

The idea of an Anglo-Saxon United States of the world was not a passing fancy dreamed up by Walker as a diversion for his English trip. During the Mexican War Walker had looked forward to the time "foretold in Holy Writ — When the world shall be United States, with one commerce, one language, and one confederacy."[55] Typically Walker thought of commerce as the first result of his great racial triumph. Walker's private secretary, J. Ross Browne, while on the way to California in the spring of 1849, revealed the thinking of his employer. At Lima, Peru he was shocked to hear that thousands of people from Peru and Chile were on their way to San Francisco. "It is monstrous to take such villains into our confederacy," he wrote to his wife, "to make them swear allegiance to our government. I see clearly now the splendid destiny of the Anglo-Saxons. They are absorbing, overhauling all other races. Their destiny is supremacy. I believe with Mr. Walker in the only true millennium—a world of United States, bound together by mutual interests, by one language, and one confederacy."[56]

When an American politician of the stature of Robert J. Walker could indulge in the dream of a millennium brought about by the extension of the Anglo-Saxon race throughout the world, it is not surprising that less responsible figures would draw from current ideas even more grandiose world plans for the superior American Anglo-Saxon race. In January 1852 a congress of German immigrants at Philadelphia founded the American Revolutionary League for Europe with the avowed object of assisting in the liberation of European nations. At the first meeting a motion to encourage all people to throw off tyranny, apply for admission to the union, and become the nucleus for "the World's Republic" failed, but the same proposal passed at a tiny meeting at Wheeling, Virginia in the fall of that year. The group was never anything more than an impotent fringe organization, but two of its supporters—Theodore Poesche and Charles Goepp—in 1853 published a work that starkly revealed the direction that racial Anglo-Saxon expansionism had taken in the previous twenty years. In *The New Rome* they pointed out that the new league had "inscribed universal annexation on its banners" and prophesied that when the Anglo-Saxons won control of the countries of the Germanic confederation there would be a death struggle between the United States and Russia.[57]

The New Rome was a work of the wildest speculation, but in many respects it merely put into direct and more extravagant language what was being suggested as the inevitable wave of the future by a variety of respectable politicians and periodicals. Poesche and Goepp were thoroughgoing defenders of the idea that much of what was best in the world had stemmed from the efforts of the Anglo-Saxon branch of the Teutonic people. The authors lauded the German instinct for freedom, which they said had been perpetuated institutionally by the Anglo-Saxons, but much of their analysis consisted of crude racial theory. They were willing to accept man as a single species consisting of separate varieties, but these varieties had been produced not environmentally but genetically. Inferior varieties were "multifarious" in the world; the superior races were few. The authors were not content to accept the idea of a single Caucasian race embracing all whites; they said philological studies had shown that the Caucasians had two separate origins: the Abyssinian race had originated in the highlands of Abyssinia, had scattered outward to create Egypt, Nineveh, and Babylon, and had given rise to the Hebrews and the Phoenicians; the "Indo-Germanic" or "Arian" race had originated in the Hindu Kush of central Asia, had spread outward into India and Persia and eventually into Greece and Italy. In Greece and Italy this "Indo-Germanic" branch had "established the undoubted superiority of the race over every other." The "Arians" had split to create the Celts, the Germans, and the Slavs.[58]

The Germans in general, but specifically the Anglo-Saxons, had contributed most to the liberty of the world. Although all the nations of Europe had helped "to raise the edifice of human freedom," the chief credit was due to the Anglo-Saxons. The Germanic spirit—which embodied the right of the individual to be left alone—was to be realized in the universality of the American union. The Puritans, they said, had first sheltered "the Germanic principle" in America.[59]

Like so many propounders of racial Anglo-Saxonism, Poesche and Goepp had boundless faith in the reproductive capacity of the white American people. "Arians" and "Blacks" could not remain as they were in America. Nature would not permit "the most perfect and the most gross examples of the same species long to continue side by side." Expatriation of the blacks was unworkable. They had to stay in America, but there would be no deterioration of the white race. This would happen only, the authors argued, if males of the lower race cohabitated with females of the higher—"the ovum of the latter being thus tainted." But with the cohabitation of the white male and the black female, "the ovum is improved." Such interbreeding was now gaining ground in America, Poesche and Goepp argued, and it was resulting in a " 'white washing' process." This would eventually erase "all traces of the black race not capable of advantageous admixture with the white."[60]

As the white gradually eliminated all other races from America, the new Roman age would be brought about by rapid expansion. Canada and everything down to the isthmus of Panama should be annexed quickly, although the non-Teutonic descent of some of the inhabitants of the former and the mostly Indian population of the latter would present problems. This expansion was, however, only the beginning. Hawaii would soon be American, and the authors thought that Australia should be encouraged to become independent of England and enter the union by a "little stretch of the Monroe Doctrine." England and her colonies would also eventually be annexed to the United States, for the Anglican empire was essentially oceanic and America its natural center. Thus England, though she did not know it, was busily engaged in extending America's Anglo-Saxon empire. With the American continent and Australia united, the "annexation of the remaining countries will be a question of time, regulated by American convenience." English was to be the universal tongue: *"Nothing is more certain than that the English language will extend over all the earth, and will very shortly become the common medium of thought — the language of the world."*[61]

Poesche and Goepp were two justly obscure writers and dreamers, but in *The New Rome* they inadvertently caricatured the thought of their expansionist generation. Their scientific racial theories on black and white ova were absurd, but were they much more absurd than the eminent physician Josiah Nott's theories on sterile mulattoes? Their image of slightly extending the Monroe Doctrine to cover Australia was ludicrous, but was it much more ludicrous than the eminent politician Robert J. Walker's suggestion of a United States of the world? Nearly all the ideas in Poesche and Goepp's work could be found one way or another in a variety of respectable sources.

By the 1850s the American sense of idealistic mission had been corrupted, and most of the world's peoples were condemned to permanent inferiority or even to extinction. General world progress was to be accomplished only by the dominating power of a superior race, and a variety of lesser races were accused of retarding rather than furthering world progress. A traditional colonial empire had been rejected, but it was believed that the expansion of a federal system might ultimately prove possible as American Anglo-Saxons outbred, overwhelmed, and replaced "inferior" races. This time was to be hastened by commercial penetration of the most distant regions of the earth. The commercial endeavors of a superior people were confidently expected to transform the world while bringing unprecedented power and prosperity to the United States.

Conclusion

In the three quarters of a century after the American Revolution, Americans rethought their relationships with other peoples of the world. By the 1850s two ideas were firmly engrained in American thinking: that the peoples of large parts of the world were incapable of creating efficient, democratic, and prosperous governments; and that American and world economic growth, the triumph of Western Christian civilization, and a stable world order could be achieved by American commercial penetration of supposedly backward areas.

It is not difficult to find the seeds of this rejection of non-American, non-Anglo-Saxon peoples in the eighteenth century at the time of the greatest optimism concerning the ameliorating effects of American republicanism. The prevailing eighteenth-century intellectual belief in an innate general human capacity for progress had never convinced whites in close proximity to large numbers of black slaves or frontiersmen clashing with Indians that those they dominated or destroyed were fully their equals. At that time the possibility of the United States inspiring republican progress across Latin America and large areas of the globe undoubtedly seemed more likely because the peoples who were to be involved in this transformation were largely unknown and distant, and because they appeared to have no basic interests which clashed with those of the United States. The peoples of Mexico, Central America, and the Caribbean could still be viewed benignly in the late eighteenth century, for the United States had seemingly limitless horizons of opportunity stretching westward across the Mississippi Valley. The latent racialism which permeated southern plantation society or the western frontiers could be ignored when talking or writing of transformations that were to occur among distant peoples. Even in the 1850s, when the racialism was no longer latent, the peoples of the distant Pacific were often written or talked of in the vague language of regeneration and redemption, because, in the immediate future, it seemed impossible that the United States would have to work out specific relationships with such peoples.

Yet while there were potential problems with eighteenth-century attitudes, the change from the time of the Revolution to the mid-nineteenth century is still striking. At the time of the Revolution America's leaders sincerely believed that they could teach the peoples of the rest of the world to govern themselves in happiness and prosperity; they did not believe that the majority of other peoples were unteachable or expendable. The doubts that already existed about the innate capacity of America's black slaves were not allowed to overshadow the belief that ultimately most of the peoples of the world could be taught to share in the republican system of the new nation. America's leaders were able to envision an expansion across the North American continent that would quickly transform the lives of America's Indians for the better and would, by enhancing the power and prosperity of the United States, demonstrate to the world that the Americans had found in their federal republicanism a way to ensure the happiness as well as the security of their citizens. The incipient racialism which frequently shaped the acts of southern slaveowners or western frontiersmen had no coherent body of thought to justify and enlarge it. The Americans of the Revolutionary generation were ethnocentric, and in their attitudes to other peoples it is possible to perceive a nascent racialism, but their dominant mood in approaching other peoples of the world was optimistic. They thought of them as fellow human beings, not as members of inferior races. Even in considering black slaves they readily conceded the possibility of some transformation, some solution, that would end the dilemma of slavery. In the dawn of republicanism, when hope was high, everything seemed possible.

The remarkable outward thrust, economic growth, and rise to power of the United States in the seventy-five years after 1783 not only turned optimism into arrogance but also brought obvious conflicts of interest with other peoples. At the heart of the American and western European consignment of other races to an inferior, lesser human status was the need to justify exploitation and destruction. This need was particularly pressing in countries that prided themselves on their democratic ideals. The rhetoric of freedom could not countenance the mistreatment, exploitation, or destruction of equals. It took only a few years for it to become obvious that the creation of a new American republican government would neither make the Indians happy to yield their lands for the benefit of world civilization nor in some magic manner cause slavery and the slaves to disappear. Governmental dreams of an Indian policy based on Enlightenment ideals were in disarray by 1815 and were shattered by 1830. It was easier to blame Indian incapacity for this failure than it was to condemn the American desire for lands and profit. It was similarly convenient for Southerners to deny the innate potential of blacks when they realized fully that continuing slavery suited them much better than abolishing it. By the 1830s pro-Indian and antislavery spokesmen were drawn almost exclusively from areas in which there were few blacks and fewer Indians. It was much easier to take a high moral tone in Boston than in Nashville or Mobile. When basic interests were involved intellectuals thought hard to discover why blacks should be enslaved or Indians dispossessed.

America's racial theorists in these years have to be considered as an integral part of the society in which they lived. They cannot simply be discussed as part of an intellectual tradition that stretched from the rethinking of attitudes toward human beings in the sixteenth and seventeenth centuries through the Enlightenment and into the nineteenth century. Their prejudices helped shape their research, and their research helped give society the justifications it needed for its actions. They obviously drew heavily on a transatlantic intellectual tradition, but they also drew on American experience with blacks and Indians and European experience with their colonial peoples to explain the apparent wide discrepancies between the achievements of different races. Scientific discussions of race were hopelessly confused in the first half of the nineteenth century. Race, culture, language, nationality were jumbled together in even the most respected works. Physical scientists bolstered their theories of racial differentiation with cultural observations and apparent historical evidence. In effect, by mid-century, America's racial theorists were explaining the enslavement of blacks, the disappearance of Indians, and the defeat of the Mexicans in a manner that reflected no discredit on the people of the United States.

Scientific theories of superior and inferior races were eagerly grasped by an American society undergoing complex changes. As Jacksonian America brought at least a much greater expectation, if not always the reality, of social mobility, and as the old order began to crumble, the elaborate racial hierarchies provided a new certainty and created a new aristocracy, an aristocracy of race. There was no logic in the way this new superior race was defined. By the late 1840s most Americans either thought of themselves as the descendants of English immigrants, speaking English, bound together by a common culture and a talent for government, or they thought of themselves as a superior, distant "American" race, drawn from the very best of the stocks of western and northern Europe. The former argument was clearly in the ascendancy, but there were indications by the early 1850s that the idea of the Americans as a distinct race might challenge the Anglo-Saxon theorists. This potential challenge never developed, mainly because of the increasing fear of mass immigration by non-Teutonic peoples.

A professed dislike of the English aristocratic government and a commercial rivalry with Great Britain were not enough to drive the American political and cultural establishment into a fervent kinship with the rapidly increasing immigrant masses. Even those who had been attracted by the idea of a superior "American" race balked at the idea of the creation of a "mongrel" America with traits drawn from a mass of new immigrants. The established basis of society might be changing, but it was still possible to cling to the continuity of a special heritage that stretched back across the Atlantic to England and then across the North Sea to Germany. Immigrants could not be made to change their own racial heritage, but they could be forced to conform to prevailing standards in language and culture and could be absorbed as quickly as possible within the main Anglo-Saxon tradition. In the later years of the century, as the new immigration threatened to become overwhelming, many argued that the entrance of the new stocks should be checked before the American Anglo-Saxon race was polluted by the presence of inferior strains.

The acceptance of "Anglo-Saxon" as the prevailing type in America in the latter part of the century was made easier by the continuing confusion over race, language, culture, and nationality. Many who were not of exclusively English origin had already found it easy to slip into the prevailing Anglo-Saxon rhetoric and beliefs, and Theodore Roosevelt was to see his heritage and name as no obstacle in defending a full-scale Anglo-Saxon interpretation of American and world history. The American Anglo-Saxonists reached new heights of confidence in the last years of the nineteenth century.

Many Americans continued to reject a formal imperial system as well as the admission of inferior peoples into the union, but practically all were able to support American world trade and the economic penetration of distant lands. The transformation of other areas by American enterprise was repeatedly defended as a moral as well as a commercial good; it was the means by which the superior Anglo-Saxon race could bring Christian civilization and progress to the world as well as infinite prosperity to the United States. Without taking on the dangerous burdens of a formal empire, the United States could obtain the markets and raw materials its ever-expanding economy needed. American and world economic growth, the triumph of Western Christian civilization, and a stable world order could be achieved by the American economic penetration of underdeveloped areas. And as Anglo-Saxons sought out the most distant corners of the globe, they could ultimately replace a variety of inferior races. The Anglo-Saxonism of the last half of the century was no benign expansionism, though it used the rhetoric of redemption, for it assumed that one race was destined to lead, others to serve—one race to flourish, many to die. The world was to be transformed not by the strength of better ideas but by the power of a superior race.

Notes

Introduction

1. In discussing aspects of racial thought in the first half of the nineteenth century, I have used the terms *racialism* and *racialist* rather than the terms *racism* and *racist*. This is meant to draw some distinction between *racist* thought in the context of present knowledge of racial matters and *racialist* thought in the context of nineteenth-century knowledge. The terms *racism* and *racist* are charged with meanings that can cause confusion when applied to the thought of the first half of the nineteenth century.

1 Liberty and the Anglo-Saxons

1. Thomas D. Kendrick, *British Antiquity* (London: Methuen, 1950), p. 115; Fred J. Levy, *Tudor Historical Thought* (San Marino,

Calif.: Huntington Library, 1967), p. 79; Eleanor N. Adams, *Old English Scholarship in England from 1566-1800* (New Haven: Yale University Press, 1917), p. 11.

2. Adams, *Old English Scholarship*, pp. 16-23, 33-41; May McKisack, *Medieval History in the Tudor Age* (Oxford: Oxford University Press, Clarendon Press, 1971), pp. 26-49; Levy, *Tudor Historical Thought*, pp. 115-122; Kendrick, *British Antiquity*, pp. 115-116.

3. Adams, *Old English Scholarship*, p. 31; Levy, *Tudor Historical Thought*, pp. 95-101; Richard T. Vann, "The Free Anglo-Saxons: A Historical Myth," *Journal of the History of Ideas*, 19 (April 1958): 261-262.

4. "The Trojans in Britain," in George S. Gordon, *The Discipline of Letters* (Oxford: Oxford University Press, Clarendon Press, 1946), pp. 37-49; Kendrick, *British Antiquity*, pp. 3-14, 37; Levy, *Tudor Historical Thought*, pp. 53-68, 133; McKisack, *Medieval History*, pp. 98-103; Antonia Gransden, *Historical Writing in England, c. 550 to c. 1307* (London: Routledge & Kegan Paul, 1974), pp. 201-209.

5. Samuel Kliger, *The Goths in England: A Study in Seventeenth and Eighteenth Century Thought* (Cambridge, Mass.: Harvard University Press, 1952), pp. 33-66; Léon Poliakov, *The Aryan Myth: A History of Racist and Nationalist Ideas in Europe*, trans. Edmund Howard (New York: Basic Books, 1974), pp. 79-90.

6. Poliakov, *Aryan Myth*, pp. 90-91; Richard Foster Jones, *The Triumph of the English Language: A Survey of Opinions concerning the Vernacular from the Introduction of Printing to the Restoration* (Stanford, Calif.: Stanford University Press, 1953), pp. 215-218, 269-270.

7. Kendrick, *British Antiquity*, pp. 116-118; Levy, *Tudor Historical Thought*, p. 143; Jones, *Triumph of the English Language*, p. 220; Adams, *Old English Scholarship*, pp. 43-44; Kliger, *Goths in England*, pp. 115-119; Frank Edgar Farley, *Scandinavian Influences in the English Romantic Movement* (Boston: Ginn, 1903), pp. 8-9; Stuart Piggott, *Celts, Saxons, and the Early Antiquaries* (Edinburgh: Edinburgh University Press, 1967), pp. 12-13.

8. McKisack, *Medieval History*, pp. 150-153; Kendrick, *British Antiquity*, pp. 119-120; Piggott, *Celts, Saxons*, pp. 17-18. Verstegen's book went through five editions by 1673, Kliger, *Goths in England*, p. 115.

9. Jones, *Triumph of the English Language*, pp. 222-236; Kliger, *Goths in England*, pp. 1-2, 114-197.

10. Tacitus, *Dialogus, Agricola, Germania* (1914; reprint ed., Lon-

don: W. Heinemann, 1963), pp. 269, 275, 277, 281, 289; Jones, *Triumph of the English Language*, pp. 214-215; Kliger, *Goths in England*, pp. 112-113, quotation (1689) from an English pamphleteer.

11. Levy, *Tudor Historical Thought*, pp. 137-138; Adams, *Old English Scholarship*, pp. 27-30. As early as 1568 William Lambarde had issued a collection of Anglo-Saxon laws, but much of the most influential work was published in the fifty years after 1590. For a discussion of the role of the Anglo-Saxons in seventeenth-century political controversy, see "The Norman Yoke," in Christopher Hill, *Puritanism and Revolution: Studies in Interpretation of the English Revolution of the 17th Century* (London: Secker & Warburg, 1958), pp. 50-122; J. G. A. Pocock, *The Ancient Constitution and the Feudal Law: A Study of English Historical Thought in the Seventeenth Century* (1957; reprint ed., New York: W. W. Norton, 1967), pp. 16-17, 92-123. Also Adams, *Old English Scholarship*, pp. 42, 47-53, 67; McKisack, *Medieval History*, pp. 155-169; Herbert Butterfield, *The Englishman and His History* (1944; reprint ed., n.p.: Archon Books, 1970), pp. 31-38; Roberta F. Brinkley, *Arthurian Legend in the Seventeenth Century* (Baltimore: Johns Hopkins University Press, 1932), pp. 26-33.

12. Butterfield, *Englishman and His History*, pp. 29-30, 41; Hill, "Norman Yoke," pp. 58-59; Vann, "Free Anglo-Saxons," pp. 265-266.

13. Hill, "Norman Yoke," pp. 60-87; Vann, "Free Anglo-Saxons," pp. 265-272; Butterfield, *Englishman and His History*, pp. 49-50, 69-73, 80-81; Pocock, *Ancient Constitution*, pp. 56-58, 125-136; Christopher Hill, *Intellectual Origins of the English Revolution* (Oxford: Oxford University Press, Clarendon Press, 1965), p. 257; Kliger, *Goths in England*, pp. 137-141.

14. See Caroline Robbins, *The Eighteenth-Century Commonwealthman: Studies in the Transmission, Development, and Circumstance of English Thought from the Restoration of Charles II until the War with the Thirteen Colonies* (Cambridge, Mass.: Harvard University Press, 1959), pp. 91-94, 98-102, and passim.

15. David C. Douglas, *English Scholars, 1660-1730*, 2nd ed. rev. (London: Eyre & Spottiswoode, 1951), passim; Adams, *Old English Scholarship*, pp. 70-81, 86-88; Farley, *Scandinavian Influences*, pp. 12-14.

16. The standard work concerning the impact of the Whig view of the Anglo-Saxons on eighteenth-century America is H. Trevor Colbourn, *The Lamp of Experience: Whig History and the Intellectual Origins of the American Revolution* (Chapel Hill: University of North

Carolina Press, 1965). See also Gordon S. Wood, *The Creation of the American Republic, 1776-1787* (Chapel Hill: University of North Carolina Press, 1969), pp. 11-23; Bernard Bailyn, *The Ideological Origins of the American Revolution* (Cambridge, Mass.: Harvard University Press, Belknap Press, 1967); Henry F. May, *The Enlightenment in America* (New York: Oxford University Press, 1976), pp. 155-157; Lance Banning, *The Jeffersonian Persuasion: Evolution of a Party Ideology* (Ithaca, N.Y.: Cornell University Press, 1978), pp. 13-90.

17. See Colbourn, *Lamp of Experience*, pp. 3-56, for the colonial view of history and colonial reading. For Jefferson and Coke see Jefferson to John Page, Dec. 25, 1762, in Julian P. Boyd, ed., *The Papers of Thomas Jefferson* (Princeton: Princeton University Press, 1950-), I, 5; Jefferson to James Madison, Feb. 17, 1826, in Andrew A. Lipscomb and Albert E. Bergh, eds., *The Writings of Thomas Jefferson*, 20 vols. (Washington, D. C.: Thomas Jefferson Memorial Association, 1905), XVI, 156.

18. Bernard Bailyn, ed., *Pamphlets of the American Revolution, 1750-1776*, vol. 1, *1750-1765* (Cambridge, Mass.: Harvard University Press, Belknap Press, 1965), p. 25; Colbourn, *Lamp of Experience*, pp. 25, 55.

19. Colbourn, *Lamp of Experience*, pp. 8, 31-32.

20. Ibid., p. 26; Paul Merrill Spurlin, *Montesquieu in America, 1760-1801* (University: Louisiana State University Press, 1940), pp. 88-89, 258-262.

21. Jacques Barzun, *The French Race: Theories of Its Origins and Their Social and Political Implications Prior to the Revolution* (1932; reprint ed., Port Washington, N.Y.: Kennikat Press, 1966), pp. 151-152, 251; Colbourn, *Lamp of Experience*, pp. 27, 43; Thomas Preston Peardon, *The Transition in English Historical Writing, 1760-1830* (New York: Columbia University Press, 1933), pp. 79-81.

22. Quotation in Asa Briggs, *Saxons, Normans and Victorians* (London: Historical Association, 1966), p. 6. Also Hill, "Norman Yoke," pp. 95-96; Colbourn, *Lamp of Experience*, pp. 30-31. Colbourn accepts Obadiah Hulme as the author of the *Historical Essay*.

23. Demophilus, *The Genuine Principles of the Ancient Saxon, or English Constitution* (Philadelphia, 1776), p. 17; Colbourn, *Lamp of Experience*, pp. 190-191; Wood, *Creation of the American Republic*, pp. 227-229.

24. Bailyn, ed., *Pamphlets of the American Revolution*, I, 52-53; Colbourn, *Lamp of Experience*, pp. 74-76, 78-79, 129-130, 143-146.

25. For Henry see Jay B. Hubbell, *The South in American Literature, 1607-1900* (Durham, N.C.: Duke University Press, 1954), pp. 117-118. For Washington and Macaulay see Colbourn, *Lamp of Experience*, pp. 153-154.

26. For Jefferson and the Anglo-Saxons see Colbourn, *Lamp of Experience*, pp. 158-184; H. Trevor Colbourn, "Thomas Jefferson's Use of the Past," *William and Mary Quarterly*, 3rd ser., 15 (Jan. 1958): 56-70; Merrill D. Peterson, *Thomas Jefferson and the New Nation: A Biography* (New York: Oxford University Press, 1970), pp. 57-61; Gilbert Chinard, ed., *The Commonplace Book of Thomas Jefferson : A Repertory of His Ideas on Government* (Baltimore: Johns Hopkins University Press, 1926), pp. 212-229, 297.

27. For Jefferson's Anglo-Saxon grammar see "Essay on the Anglo-Saxon Language," in Lipscomb and Bergh, eds., *Writings of Jefferson*, XVIII, 365-411. For the quotations see Jefferson to John Cartwright, June 5, 1824; to Hon. J. Evelyn Denison, Nov. 9, 1825, in ibid., XVI, 51, 135.

28. Chinard, ed., *Commonplace Book*, pp. 21-22, 206-212; Colbourn, *Lamp of Experience*, pp. 26 (quotation), 159-162.

29. Chinard, ed., *Commonplace Book*, pp. 206-207; Boyd, ed., *Papers of Jefferson*, VI, 604.

30. See the discussion in Gilbert Chinard, *Thomas Jefferson: The Apostle of Americanism*, 2nd ed. rev. (Boston: Little, Brown, 1948), pp. 49-51; Peterson, *Thomas Jefferson*, pp. 57-61.

31. Colbourn, *Lamp of Experience*, pp. 29, 158-161; Peterson, *Thomas Jefferson*, pp. 57-61; letter of Oct. 25, 1825, in Lipscomb and Bergh, eds., *Writings of Jefferson*, XVI, 125; Harold T. Colbourn, "The Saxon Heritage: Thomas Jefferson Looks at English History" (Ph.D. diss., Johns Hopkins, 1953), pp. 70-126; Chinard, ed., *Commonplace Book*, pp. 19, 135-162, 186-193; Nathan Schachner, *Thomas Jefferson: A Biography* (New York: T. Yoseloff, 1957), pp. 32-77.

32. Letter of Oct. 25, 1825, in Lipscomb and Bergh, eds. *Writings of Jefferson*, XVI, 127.

33. *A Summary View of the Rights of British America* (1774), original text in Boyd, ed., *Papers of Jefferson*, I, 121-137.

34. Charles Francis Adams, ed., *Familiar Letters of John Adams and His Wife Abigail Adams, during the Revolution* (Boston, 1875), p. 211; Jefferson to Edmund Pendleton, Aug. 13, 1776, in Boyd, ed., *Papers of Jefferson*, I, 492.

35. Peterson, *Thomas Jefferson*, pp. 113-116; Colbourn, *Lamp of Experience*, pp. 169-171.

36. Jefferson to John Cartwright, June 5, 1824; to Hon. J. Evelyn Denison, Nov. 9, 1825, in Lipscomb and Bergh, eds., *Writings of Jefferson*, XVI, 42-46, 130.

37. James Wilson, "Lectures on Law," in Robert Green McCloskey, ed., *The Works of James Wilson*, 2 vols. (Cambridge, Mass.: Harvard University Press, Belknap Press, 1967), I, 348-352, 356-357, 400, 437; II, 515-518, 550; Colbourn, *Lamp of Experience*, pp. 125-127.

2 Aryans Follow the Sun

1. There is a discussion of the Romantic emphasis on uniqueness in Hans G. Schenk, *The Mind of the European Romantics: An Essay in Cultural History* (New York: F. Ungar, 1967), pp. 14-18. See also Hoxie Neale Fairchild, *The Romantic Quest* (New York: Columbia University Press, 1931), pp. 1-21; George L. Mosse, *The Crisis of German Ideology: Intellectual Origins of the Third Reich* (New York: Grosset & Dunlap, 1964), pp. 13-17; Hans Kohn, *Prelude to Nation-States: The French and German Experience, 1789-1815* (Princeton: Van Nostrand, 1967), pp. 168-169, 187.

2. Poliakov, *Aryan Myth*, pp. 80-85; Hans Kohn, *The Idea of Nationalism: A Study in Its Origin and Background* (New York: Macmillan, 1951), pp. 142-146.

3. Charles E. McClelland, *The German Historians and England: A Study in Nineteenth-Century Views* (Cambridge: Cambridge University Press, 1971), pp. 16-20; Henry A. Beers, *A History of English Romanticism in the Eighteenth Century* (New York, 1898), p. 380; Reinhold Aris, *History of Political Thought in Germany from 1789 to 1815* (1936; reprint ed., New York: Russell & Russell, 1965), pp. 222-231.

4. Hans S. Reiss, ed., *The Political Thought of the German Romantics, 1793-1815* (New York: Macmillan, 1955), pp. 2-3; Cedric Dover, "The Racial Philosophy of Johann Herder," *British Journal of Sociology*, 3 (June 1952): 124-133; James S. Slotkin, ed., *Readings in Early Anthropology* (Chicago: Aldine, 1965), p. 214; Théophile Simar, *Etude critique sur la formation de la doctrine des races aux XVIII siècle et son expansion aux XIX siècle* (Brussels: M. Lamertin, 1922), pp. 91-100; Rohan D'O. Butler, *The Roots of National Socialism* (New York: E. P. Dutton, 1942), pp. 23-28; Robert Reinhold Ergang, *Herder and the Foundations of German Nationalism* (New York: Columbia University Press, 1931), pp. 88-249.

5. Friedrich Meinecke, *Cosmopolitanism and the National State*, trans. Robert B. Kimber (Princeton: Princeton University Press,

1970), pp. 9-159; Butler, *Roots of National Socialism*, pp. 35-56, 73-77; Hannah Arendt, *The Origins of Totalitarianism* (New York: Harcourt, Brace, 1951), pp. 165-170; F. H. Hankins, *The Racial Basis of Civilization: A Critique of the Nordic Doctrine* (New York: Knopf, 1926), pp. 60-61; McClelland, *German Historians*, pp. 28-29; Poliakov, *Aryan Myth*, pp. 97-101; Kohn, *Prelude to Nation-States*, pp. 229-251.

6. Simar, *Etude critique*, pp. 16-20; Barzun, *French Race*, pp. 76-84; Poliakov, *Aryan Myth*, pp. 17-24.

7. Barzun, *French Race*, pp. 18-19; Arendt, *Origins of Totalitarianism*, pp. 162-163. Robert Molesworth, who wrote *An Account of Denmark*, published an English translation of *Francogallia* in 1711; see Kliger, *Goths in England*, pp. 197-199.

8. Baron de Montesquieu (Charles de Secondat), *The Spirit of the Laws*, trans. Thomas Nugent, rev. ed., 2 vols. (New York, 1899), I, 161, 163; Simar, *Etude critique*, pp. 30-31, 51-52; M. Seliger, "Race-Thinking during the Restoration," *Journal of the History of Ideas*, 19 (April 1958): 275; Thor J. Beck, *Northern Antiquities in French Learning and Literature (1755-1855): A Study in Preromantic Ideas* (New York: Columbia University Press, 1934), pp. 20-23, 78; Barzun, *French Race*, pp. 200-204. Montesquieu's compatriot Mably subscribed to similar ideas in the 1760s and though less well known in England and America was praised extensively in France in the last decades of the eighteenth century.

9. Piggott, *Celts, Saxons*, p. 9; Farley, *Scandinavian Influences*, pp. 202-203; John Pinkerton, *A Dissertation on the Origin and Progress of the Scythians or Goths* (London, 1787), pp. 99-100.

10. Farley, *Scandinavian Influences*, pp. 43, 190-194; Edward D. Snyder, *The Celtic Revival in English Literature, 1760-1800* (1923; reprint ed., Gloucester, Mass.: Peter Smith, 1965), p. 192.

11. Beers, *English Romanticism in the Eighteenth Century*, pp. 190-196; Beck, *Northern Antiquities*, pp. 9-13, 23-26, 73; Farley, *Scandinavian Influences*, p. 30; Peardon, *Transition in English Historical Writing*, p. 106.

12. Paul H. Mallet, *Northern Antiquities*, intro. Burton Feldman, 2 vols. (1770; reprint ed., New York, 1979), I, xiii, Bishop Percy's preface; Hans Aarsleff, *The Study of Language in England, 1780-1860* (Princeton: Princeton University Press, 1967), pp. 166-167.

13. Fairchild, *Romantic Quest*, pp. 259, 278; Alice Chandler, *A Dream of Order: The Medieval Ideal in Nineteenth-Century English Literature* (Lincoln: University of Nebraska Press, 1970), pp. 26-27;

Beers, *English Romanticism in the Eighteenth Century*, pp. 264-265.

14. Thomas Percy, *Reliques of Ancient English Poetry*, ed. Henry B. Wheatley, 3 vols. (1765; London, 1887), III, 341.

15. Peardon, *Transition in English Historical Writing*, pp. 108-112, 130-138; Farley, *Scandinavian Influences*, pp. 34-38, 195.

16. Pinkerton, *Dissertation*, pp. 24-35, 42-69. See also Peardon, *Transition in English Historical Writing*, pp. 114-117, 141-147; Farley, *Scandinavian Influences*, pp. 196-198; Beck, *Northern Antiquities*, pp. 121-122.

17. Pinkerton, *Dissertation*, pp. 33-34.

18. Ibid., p. 91.

19. Poliakov, *Aryan Myth*, pp. 186-188; Viktor Rydberg, *Teutonic Mythology: Gods and Goddesses of the Northland*, trans. Rasmus B. Anderson, 3 vols. (London: Norrena Society, 1906), I, 5; Slotkin, ed., *Readings in Early Anthropology*, pp. 100-101; Aarsleff, *Study of Language*, pp. 143-153; Isaac Taylor, *The Origin of the Aryans: An Account of the Prehistoric Ethnology and Civilisation of Europe*, 2nd ed. (London, 1892), p. 17. For the various traditions of attributing an Oriental origin to the German peoples, see Kliger, *Goths in England*, pp. 210-215, 288-298.

20. Winfred P. Lehmann, ed., *A Reader in Nineteenth-Century Historical Indo-European Linguistics* (Bloomington: Indiana University Press, 1967), pp. 7-20; Aarsleff, *Study of Language*, pp. 115-136; Taylor, *Origin of the Aryans*, p. 1; Harold Peake, *The Bronze Age and the Celtic World* (London: Benn Bros., 1922), p. 132.

21. Otto Schrader, *Prehistoric Antiquities of the Aryan Peoples: A Manual of Comparative Philology and the Earliest Culture, Being the "Sprachvergleichung und Urgeschichte,"* trans. Frank Byron Jevons (London, 1890), p. 5; Aarsleff, *Study of Language*, pp. 159-160; Salomon Reinach, *L'Origine des Aryens: histoire d'une controverse* (Paris, 1892), p. 8.

22. Rydberg, *Teutonic Mythology*, I, 11-17; Louis L. Snyder, *Race: A History of Modern Ethnic Theories* (New York: Longmans, Green, 1939), pp. 60-62.

23. Aarsleff, *Study of Language*, pp. 154-159; Henry A. Beers, *A History of English Romanticism in the Nineteenth Century* (New York: Henry Holt, 1901), pp. 157-158; Hankins, *Racial Basis of Civilization*, pp. 15, 61; Poliakov, *Aryan Myth*, pp. 190-192; Rydberg, *Teutonic Mythology*, I, 6-7; Kohn, *Prelude to Nation States*, pp. 180-186; Meinecke, *Cosmopolitanism*, p. 64-70.

24. Schrader, *Prehistoric Antiquities*, p. 5; Aarsleff, *Study of Lan-*

guage, pp. 159-160; Reinach, *L'Origine des Aryens*, p. 15; Taylor, *Origins of the Aryans*, pp. 2-3.

25. Hankins, *Racial Basis of Civilization*, p. 15; Taylor, *Origin of the Aryans*, pp. 9-10; Reinach, *L'Origine des Aryens*, pp. 11-12; Schrader, *Prehistoric Antiquities*, p. 6.

26. Quoted in Poliakov, *Aryan Myth*, p. 197; see also Reinach, *L'Origine des Aryens*, pp. 12-13; Hankins, *Racial Basis of Civilization*, pp. 16-17; Schrader, *Prehistoric Antiquities*, p. 7; Rydberg, *Teutonic Mythology*, I, 11-17.

27. Quoted in Butler, *Roots of National Socialism*, p. 103; see also Hankins, *Racial Basis of Civilization*, p. 62; Simar, *Etude critique*, pp. 120-123.

28. Poliakov, *Aryan Myth*, pp. 196-198; Taylor, *Origin of the Aryans*, pp. 10-13; Hankins, *Racial Basis of Civilization*, p. 16; Reinach, *L'Origine des Aryens*, pp. 13-15; Holger Pedersen, *The Discovery of Language: Linguistic Science in the Nineteenth Century*, trans. John Webster Spargo (1924; Bloomington: Indiana University Press, 1962), pp. 37-43; Schrader, *Prehistoric Antiquities*, pp. 8-11; Rydberg, *Teutonic Mythology*, I, 11-17; Thomas Huxley, "The Aryan Question and Pre-Historic Man," *Collected Essays, 1893-1894*, 9 vols. (reprint ed., Hildesheim: G. Olms, 1970), VII, 271-328.

29. Quoted in Poliakov, *Aryan Myth*, p. 199. See also Simar, *Etude critique*, p. 78.

30. "Origin and Affinities of Language," *Edinburgh Review*, 51 (July 1830): 531-533, 537, 562.

31. Aarsleff, *Study of Language*, p. 208. See the introductory essay in James Cowles Prichard, *Researches into the Physical History of Man*, ed. George W. Stocking, Jr. (Chicago: University of Chicago Press, 1973), pp. lxxiii-lxxiv.

32. Aarsleff, *Study of Language*, pp. 161, 182-203.

33. Sharon Turner, *The History of the Anglo-Saxons from the Earliest Period to the Norman Conquest*, 5th ed., 3 vols. (London, 1828), I, 2-5, 88; III, 1-2. The old view of the free Anglo-Saxons continued to appear in a variety of writings in the late eighteenth century; see Peardon, *Transition in English Historical Writing*, pp. 82, 84-89, 101; Hill, "Norman Yoke," pp. 94-104.

34. Thomas Carlyle, "Sir Walter Scott," *Critical and Miscellaneous Essays*, IV (London, 1899), 77. See also Chandler, *Dream of Order*, pp. 25-51; Peardon, *Transition in English Historical Writing*, pp. 214-217; Beers, *English Romanticism in the Nineteenth Century*, pp. 1-44.

35. Quoted in George P. Gooch, *History and Historians in the Nineteenth Century* (1913; reprint ed., New York: Peter Smith, 1949), p. 170.

36. Quoted in C. V. Wedgwood, *The Sense of the Past* (New York: Collier Books, 1967), p. 27.

37. Quoted in Beers, *English Romanticism in the Nineteenth Century*, p. 37.

38. *Ivanhoe* (Boston: Houghton Mifflin, 1913), chaps. 1 and 20; Schenk, *Mind of the European Romantics*, pp. 34-36.

39. Augustin Thierry, *History of the Conquest of England by the Normans*, 3 vols. (London, 1825); Seliger, "Race Thinking during the Restoration," pp. 275-281; Simar, *Etude critique*, pp. 74-75.

3 Science and Inequality

1. For this subject see John S. Haller, *Outcasts from Evolution: Scientific Attitudes of Racial Inferiority, 1859-1900* (Urbana: University of Illinois Press, 1971); John C. Greene, *The Death of Adam: Evolution and Its Impact on Western Thought* (Ames: Iowa State University Press, 1959); George W. Stocking, Jr., *Race, Culture, and Evolution: Essays in the History of Anthropology* (New York: Free Press, 1968); Herbert H. Odom, "Generalizations on Race in Nineteenth-Century Physical Anthropology," *Isis*, 58 (spring 1967): 5-18; Francis C. Haber, *The Age of the World: Moses to Darwin* (Baltimore: Johns Hopkins University Press, 1959), pp. 1-2; John C. Greene, "Some Early Speculations on the Origin of Human Races," *American Anthropologist*, 56 (Jan. 1954): 31-41; Eric Voegelin, "The Growth of the Race Idea," *Review of Politics*, 2 (July 1940): 283-317.

2. Slotkin, ed., *Readings in Early Anthropology*, pp. 42-43, 81-82, 96-97; Margaret T. Hodgen, *Early Anthropology in the Sixteenth and Seventeenth Centuries* (Philadelphia: University of Pennsylvania Press, 1964); Poliakov, *Aryan Myth*, p. 133; Thomas K. Penniman, *A Hundred Years of Anthropology*, 2nd ed. rev. (London: Duckworth, 1952), pp. 44-47; Greene, *Death of Adam*, p. 221.

3. See Arthur O. Lovejoy, *The Great Chain of Being: A Study of the History of an Idea* (1936; reprint ed., Cambridge, Mass.: Harvard University Press, 1971); Anthony J. Barker, *The African Link: British Attitudes to the Negro in the Era of the Atlantic Slave Trade, 1550-1807* (London: Frank Cass, 1978); Greene, *Death of Adam*, pp. 201-202; Poliakov, *Aryan Myth*, pp. 144-145; Dante A. Puzzo, "Rac-

ism and the Western Tradition," *Journal of the History of Ideas*, 25 (Oct.-Dec. 1964): 579-586.

4. David B. Davis, *The Problem of Slavery in Western Culture* (Ithaca, N.Y.: Cornell University Press, 1966), p. 446; Greene, *Death of Adam*, pp. 175-176; Winthrop D. Jordan, *White over Black: American Attitudes toward the Negro, 1550-1812* (Chapel Hill: University of North Carolina Press, 1968), pp. 216-217. See also Richard H. Popkin, "The Philosophical Basis of Eighteenth-Century Racism," in Harold E. Pagliaro, ed., *Racism in the Eighteenth Century*, Studies in Eighteenth-Century Culture, vol. 3 (Cleveland: Case Western Reserve University Press, 1973), pp. 245-262.

5. Slotkin, ed., *Readings in Early Anthropology*, pp. x, 94-95, 176-177, 185-186; Jordan, *White over Black*, pp. 217-222, 234; Arthur O. Lovejoy, "Buffon and the Problem of Species," in Bentley Glass, Owsei Temkin, and William L. Strauss, Jr., eds., *Forerunners of Darwin, 1745-1859* (Baltimore: Johns Hopkins University Press, 1959), pp. 93-95; also Lovejoy, "The Argument for Organic Evolution before the Origin of Species, 1830-1858," in ibid., pp. 394-395; Greene, *Death of Adam*, pp. 131-155.

6. Slotkin, ed., *Readings in Early Anthropology*, p. 190; Greene, *Death of Adam*, pp. 222-226; John R. Baker, *Race* (New York: Oxford University Press, 1974); Haller, *Outcasts from Evolution*, pp. 4-6.

7. Greene, *Death of Adam*, pp. 218-219, 235-238; L. Perry Curtis, *Apes and Angels: The Irishman in Victorian Caricature* (Washington, D.C.: Smithsonian Institution Press, 1971), pp. 8-9; Philip D. Curtin, *The Image of Africa: British Ideas and Action, 1780-1850* (Madison: University of Wisconsin Press, 1964), pp. 230-236.

8. Quoted in Jordan, *White over Black*, p. 17; see also Hodgen, *Early Anthropology*, pp. 407-426.

9. Jordan, *White over Black*, pp. 251-253; Poliakov, *Aryan Myth*, p. 176; Greene, *Death of Adam*, p. 221; Davis, *Problem of Slavery in Western Culture*, p. 477.

10. Poliakov, *Aryan Myth*, pp. 178-180.

11. Quotation in ibid., pp. 180-181; Curtin, *Image of Africa*, p. 371.

12. Pinkerton, *Dissertation*, pp. 33-34.

13. Slotkin, ed., *Readings in Early Anthropology*, pp. 208-211; Davis, *Problem of Slavery in Western Culture*, pp. 459-463; Jordan, *White over Black*, pp. 491-494.

14. Charles White, *An Account of the Regular Gradation in Man, and in Different Animals and Vegetables* (London, 1799), pp. 80, 124, 131-135; Jordan, *White over Black*, pp. 499-502.

15. Henry Home, Lord Kames, *Sketches of the History of Man*, 2nd ed. (1778; reprint ed., Hildesheim: G. Olms, 1968), I, 20, 50, 72-84.

16. Ibid., I, 46, 75. See also Gladys Bryson, *Man and Society: The Scottish Inquiry of the Eighteenth Century* (Princeton: Princeton University Press, 1945), pp. 64-66.

17. Bernard Romans, *A Concise Natural History of East and West Florida*, intro. Rembert W. Patrick (1775; reprint ed., Gainesville: University of Florida Press, 1962), pp. 38, 39, 55. See also Daniel J. Boorstin, *The Lost World of Thomas Jefferson* (New York: Henry Holt, 1948), pp. 68-69.

18. For Prichard see George F. Stocking, Jr., intro., Prichard, *Researches into the Physical History of Man* (Chicago: University of Chicago Press, 1973), pp. ix-cx; Penniman, *Hundred Years of Anthropology*, pp. 77-81.

19. Prichard, *Researches into the Physical History of Man*, 3rd ed., 5 vols. (London, 1836-1847), I (1836), 105-109, V (1847), 548, 550; also Prichard, *The Natural History of Man*, ed. Edwin Norris, 4th ed., 2 vols. (London, 1855), I, 10, 68-69.

20. Prichard, *Researches*, III (1841), 342, 377-378. See also Greene, *Death of Adam*, pp. 238-244.

21. *Lectures on Comparative Anatomy, Physiology, Zoology, and the Natural History of Man*, 9th ed. (London, 1848), pp. 328-330; Kentwood D. Wells, "Sir William Lawrence (1783-1867): A Study of Pre-Darwinian Ideas on Heredity and Variation," *Journal of the History of Biology*, 4 (fall 1971): 319-361.

22. For anthropometry and the work of Lavater and Camper, see Haller, *Outcasts from Evolution*, pp. 9-11; Curtis, *Apes and Angels*, pp. 7-8; Greene, *Death of Adam*, pp. 188-192; Slotkin, ed., *Readings in Early Anthropology*, pp. 197-199; Jordan, *White over Black*, pp. 224-226.

23. Curtis, *Apes and Angels*, pp. 8-9, 110; Penniman, *Hundred Years of Anthropology*, p. 55.

24. Earl W. Count, "The Evolution of the Race Idea in Modern Western Culture during the Period of the Pre-Darwinian Nineteenth Century," *Transactions of the New York Academy of Sciences*, 2nd ser., 8 (Feb. 1946): 161; Jacques Barzun, *Race: A Study in Superstition*, rev. ed. (New York: Harper & Row, 1965), pp. 36-38; Curtin, *Image of Africa*, pp. 363-364; Frederic E. Faverty, *Matthew Arnold: The Ethnologist* (Evanston: Northwestern University Press, 1951), pp. 36-37; Penniman, *Hundred Years of Anthropology*, pp. 65-66.

25. Count, "Evolution of the Race Idea," pp. 150-151; Haller, *Outcasts from Evolution*, p. 11; Curtis, *Apes and Angels*, p. 11; Penniman, *Hundred Years of Anthropology*, p. 76.

26. Erwin H. Ackerknecht, *Medicine at the Paris Hospital, 1794-1848* (Baltimore: John Hopkins University Press, 1967), p. 172.

27. There is a convenient short summary of Spurzheim's views in his *Outlines of Phrenology* (Boston, 1832). See also John D. Davies, *Phrenology: Fad and Science; A Nineteenth-Century American Crusade* (New Haven: Yale University Press, 1955), p. 6-11.

28. See David A. De Giustino, "Phrenology in Britain, 1815-1855: A Study of George Combe and His Circle" (Ph.D. diss., University of Wisconsin, 1969).

29. Robert E. Riegel, "Early Phrenology in the United States," *Medical Life*, 37 (July 1930): 361-363, 369-371; Davies, *Phrenology*, p. 80; De Giustino, "Phrenology in Britain," pp. 79-91.

30. *The Constitution of Man considered in Relation to External Objects* (1828; Hartford, Conn., 1844), p. 28.

31. Combe, "Phrenological Remarks on the Relation between the Natural Talents and Dispositions of Nations, and the Development of Their Brains," in Samuel G. Morton, *Crania Americana* (Philadelphia, 1839), p. 276.

32. George Combe, *A System of Phrenology*, 5th ed., 2 vols. (Edinburgh, 1843), II, 328.

33. Ibid., II, 329.

34. George Combe, *Notes on the United States of North America during a Phrenological Visit in 1838-1840*, 2 vols. (Philadelphia, 1841), I, 92-93.

35. George Combe, *Lectures on Phrenology*, ed. Andrew Boardman, 3rd ed. rev. (New York, 1840), p. 110.

36. *Phrenological Journal*, 19 (July 1846): 214.

37. Loren Eiseley, *Darwin's Century: Evolution and the Men Who Discovered It* (Garden City, N.Y.: Doubleday, 1958), pp. 132-133; *Edinburgh Review*, 82 (July 1845): 6.

38. Haber, *Age of the World*, pp. 1-2, 192, 218-219, 264, 268-269.

39. *Edinburgh Review*, 79 (Jan. 1844): 9. See also ibid., 69 (April 1839): 26-35; 74 (Jan. 1842): 221-230; 83 (April 1846): 226-237.

4 Racial Anglo-Saxonism in England

1. Apart from L. P. Curtis, *Anglo-Saxons and Celts: A Study of Anti-Irish Prejudice in Victorian England* (Bridgeport, Conn.: Confer-

ence on British Studies, 1968), which concentrates on the years after 1850, nineteenth-century Anglo-Saxonism in England has been neglected by historians. There is useful information on racial attitudes in Douglas A. Lorimer, *Colour, Class and the Victorians: English Attitudes to the Negro in the Mid-Nineteenth Century* (Leicester: University of Leicester Press, 1978), and Christine Bolt, *Victorian Attitudes to Race* (London: Routledge & Kegan Paul, 1971). Poliakov, *Aryan Myth* in part deals with England.

2. Carlyle, *On Heroes and Hero Worship* (London, 1897), pp. 19, 189; cf. ibid., p. 144.

3. Charles Frederick Harrold, *Carlyle and German Thought: 1819-1834* (1934; reprint ed., Hamden, Conn.: Archon Books, 1963) surveys the main influences on Carlyle. See also Faverty, *Matthew Arnold*, pp. 14-15.

4. Carlyle, *On Heroes and Hero Worship*, pp. 19, 28, 29, 32.

5. Carlyle, "Chartism," in *Critical and Miscellaneous Essays*, IV, 200.

6. Ibid., pp. 171-172, 175.

7. Carlyle to Emerson, June 24, 1839, in Charles Eliot Norton, ed., *The Correspondence of Thomas Carlyle and Ralph Waldo Emerson, 1834-1872*, 2 vols. (Boston, 1883), I, 247.

8. Carlyle, "Occasional Discourse on the Nigger Question," *Critical and Miscellaneous Essays*, IV, 350, 376-377.

9. Thomas Arnold, *Introductory Lectures on Modern History Delivered in Lent Term MDCCCLII, with the Inaugural Lecture Delivered in December MDCCCXLI*, 5th ed. (London, 1860), p. 158.

10. Ibid., pp. 26-28.

11. Arthur Penryhn Stanley, *The Life and Correspondence of Thomas Arnold, D.D.*, 12th ed. (London, 1881), II, 324.

12. *Edinburgh Review*, 82 (Oct. 1845): 142-143.

13. Ibid., pp. 164-165.

14. I. A. Blackwell, intro., Mallet, *Northern Antiquities*, trans. Bishop Percy, rev. ed. (London, 1847), pp. 28 note, 44-45.

15. *Edinburgh Review*, 94 (Oct. 1851): 167.

16. John Mitchell Kemble, *The Saxons in England: A History of the English Commonwealth till the Period of the Norman Conquest*, 2 vols. (London, 1849), I, 5.

17. *Edinburgh Review*, 84 (Jan. 1849): 82.

18. Racial writer Robert Knox claimed that the word *Caucasian* had risen to such popularity because of its use by Disraeli in his novels; see Henry Lonsdale, *A Sketch of the Life and Writings of Robert Knox, the Anatomist* (London, 1870) p. 380.

19. Quoted in William F. Monypenny and George F. Buckle, *The*

Life of Benjamin Disraeli, Earl of Beaconsfield, rev. ed., 2 vols. (New York: Macmillan, 1929), I, 871.

20. *Coningsby* (1844; New York: M. W. Dunne, 1904), chaps. 32 and 37.

21. Ibid., chap. 37.

22. *Tancred* (1847; New York: M. W. Dunne, 1904), chap. 20.

23. Robert G. Latham, *The Natural History of the Varieties of Man* (London, 1850), pp. 13-14, 107-108.

24. Latham, *The Germania of Tacitus* (London, 1851), Epilegomena, pp. cxxix-cxlii.

25. For his life see Lonsdale, *Life of Knox.*

26. Robert Knox, M.D., *The Races of Men: A Philosophical Enquiry into the Influence of Race over the Destinies of Nations,* 2nd ed. (London, 1862), pp. v, 23-24, 341.

27. Ibid., pp. 36, 44, 89, 107, 156, 380-381, 488.

28. Ibid., pp. 9-10, 46, 59.

29. Ibid., pp. 57, 131, 135, 370-371, 374.

30. Ibid., pp. 26, 194-195, 208, 379.

31. Ibid., pp. 224-226, 450, 456, 598-599.

32. *Anglo-Saxon* (London, 1849-1850). *Non Angli Sed Angeli* were also the first words of the lead article in the first issue. The comment on Knox is in ibid., 1 (April 1849): 163. For the purpose of the *Anglo-Saxon* see Derek Hudson, *Martin Tupper: His Rise and Fall* (London: Constable, 1949), pp. 90-91. When its first numbers were reviewed in America, the *Democratic Review,* 25 (Oct. 1849): 383, said of the new periodical: "It recognises no distinctions, except those of race."

33. *Anglo-Saxon,* 1 (April 1849): 144, 205.

34. Ibid., 1 (Jan. 1849): 3-4; 1 (July 1849): 5-16.

35. Ibid., 2 (1850): 6-14, 39, 453, 467. The *Edinburgh Review,* 88 (July 1848): 49, also praised Brooke, commenting: "Would that the cause of commerce and civilization might always in this manner go hand in hand!"

36. William R. W. Stephens, *The Life and Letters of Edward A. Freeman,* 2 vols. (London, 1895), I, 108, 120, 126.

37. Margaret Farrand Thorp, *Charles Kingsley, 1819-1875* (Princeton: Princeton University Press, 1937), p. 1. There is a revealing account of Kingsley in Susan Chitty, *The Beast and the Monk: A Life of Charles Kingsley* (London: Hodder and Stoughton, 1974).

38. Kingsley to his wife, Fanny Kingsley, Jan. 26, 1851, in *Charles Kingsley: His Letters and Memories of His Life,* ed. Fanny Kingsley, 2 vols. (London, 1877), I, 253.

39. Kingsley to the Rev. Alfred Strettell, April 17, 1849, ibid., I,

201. The idea of active (male) races and passive (female) races was most fully developed by Gustav Klemm in his *Allgemeine kulturgeschichte der Menschheit*, 10 vols. (Leipzig, 1843–1852); see Michael D. Biddiss, *Father of Racist Ideology: The Social and Political Thought of Count Gobineau* (New York: Weybright and Talley, 1970), p. 110.

40. Kingsley, *Hypatia*, 2 vols. (1853; New York, 1899), preface, p. xviii.

41. Kingsley, *The Roman and the Teuton: A Series of Lectures Delivered before the University of Cambridge* (1864; London, 1891), pp. 305-306.

42. Kingsley to J. M. Ludlow, Dec. 1849, in Kingsley, *Letters and Memories*, I, 222-223.

5 Providential Nation

1. See Ernest Lee Tuveson, *Redeemer Nation: The Idea of America's Millennial Role* (Chicago: University of Chicago Press, 1968), pp. 140-142; May, *Enlightenment in America*; Loren Baritz, *Sources of the American Mind: A Collection of Documents and Texts in American Intellectual History*, 2 vols. (New York: Wiley, 1966), I, 11; Loren Baritz, *City on a Hill: A History of Ideas and Myths in America* (New York: Wiley, 1964), pp. 3, 98; John R. Bodo, *The Protestant Clergy and Public Issues, 1812-1848* (Princeton: Princeton University Press, 1954), pp. 5-6.

2. S. B. Liljegren, ed., *James Harringtons Oceana* (Heidelberg: C. Winter, 1924), pp. 185, 187. Zera S. Fink, *The Classical Republicans* (Evanston, Illinois: Northwestern University Press, 1945), pp. 81-83, discusses those who argued that the English Commonwealth should strive for world empire. See also Caroline Robbins, ed., *Two English Republican Tracts* (London: Cambridge University Press, 1969), pp. 42-43.

3. John Milton, "The Ready and Easy Way to Establish a Free Commonwealth," in J. A. St. John, ed., *The Prose Works of John Milton*, 5 vols. (London, 1848–1853), II, 114.

4. Conrad Cherry, ed., *God's New Israel: Religious Interpretations of American Destiny* (Englewood Cliffs, N.J.: Prentice-Hall, 1971), pp. 22-23.

5. From Bulkeley, *The Gospel Covenant* (1651), quoted in Baritz, ed., *Sources*, I, 37.

6. See Baritz, *City on a Hill*, pp. 64-65; Cherry, ed., *God's New Israel*, pp. 55-59.

7. See Loren Baritz, "The Idea of the West," *American Historical*

Review, 66 (April 1961): 618-640. See also Davis, *Problem of Slavery in Western Culture*, pp. 4-6.

8. Alexander C. Fraser, ed., *The Works of George Berkeley*, 3 vols. (Oxford, 1871), III, 232.

9. Jefferson to William Ludlow, Sept. 6, 1824, in Lipscomb and Bergh, eds., *Writings of Jefferson*, XVI, 74-75.

10. Quoted in Tuveson, *Redeemer Nation*, p. 101; Baritz, *City on a Hill*, p. 94. See also Henry Steele Commager, *Jefferson, Nationalism, and the Enlightenment* (New York: G. Braziller, 1975).

11. Gerald Stourzh, *Benjamin Franklin and American Foreign Policy*, 2nd ed. (Chicago: University of Chicago Press, 1969), pp. 54-65; Fred Lewis Pattee, *The Poems of Philip Freneau*, 3 vols. (Princeton: The University Library, 1902-1907), I, 73; Claude Milton Newlin, *The Life and Writings of Hugh Henry Brackenridge* (Princeton: Princeton University Press, 1932), p. 23; Philip S. Foner, ed., *The Complete Writings of Thomas Paine*, 2 vols. (New York, 1945), I, 17.

12. Timothy Dwight, "America: or, a Poem on the Settlement of the British Colonies," in William J. McTaggart and William K. Bottorff, eds., *The Major Poems of Timothy Dwight* (Gainesville, Fla.: Scholars' Facsimiles & Reprints, 1969), p. 11.

13. Adams's comment is quoted in Edward McNall Burns, *The American Idea of Mission: Concepts of National Purpose and Destiny* (New Brunswick, N.J.: Rutgers University Press, 1957), p. 65. Jefferson's statement is in Boyd, ed., *Papers of Jefferson*, IX, 218.

14. Jedidiah Morse, *The American Geography; or, A View of the Present Situation of the United States of America* (1789; reprint ed., New York: Arno, 1970), p. 469.

15. Quoted in Baritz, *City on a Hill*, p. 107. Much of the material in the preceding nine paragraphs was first used in a Louis Martin Sears lecture by this writer at Purdue University on February 1, 1978.

16. *Annals of Congress*, 12th Cong., 1st sess., p. 657, Jan. 4, 1812.

17. Ibid., p. 458, Dec. 11, 1811.

18. Jefferson to John Jacob Astor, Nov. 9, 1813, in Lipscomb and Bergh, eds., *Writings of Jefferson*, XIII, 432. See also Frederick Merk, *Manifest Destiny and Mission in American History: A Reinterpretation* (New York: Knopf, 1963), pp. 8-14.

19. See Samuel Flagg Bemis, *John Quincy Adams and the Foundations of American Foreign Policy* (New York: Knopf, 1949), p. 529; *Register of Debates*, 18th Cong., 2nd sess., pp. 711-713; Clay to J. Q. Adams, Aug. 30, 1827, in Calvin Colton, ed., *The Works of Henry Clay*, 10 vols. (New York: G. P. Putnam's Sons, 1904), IV, 172.

20. Judge David Campbell to Governor Richard Caswell, Nov. 30,

1786, in James G. M. Ramsey, *The Annals of Tennessee to the End of the Eighteenth Century* (1853; reprint ed., Knoxville: East Tennessee Historical Society, 1967), p. 350.

21. Quoted in Bemis, *John Quincy Adams and the Foundations of American Foreign Policy*, p. 182.

22. Colton, ed., *Works of Clay*, VI, 147, 203.

23. *Annals of Congress*, 15th Cong., 1st sess., p. 98, Jan. 12, 1818.

24. Quoted in Fred Somkin, *Unquiet Eagle: Memory and Desire in the Idea of American Freedom, 1815-1860* (Ithaca, N.Y.: Cornell University Press, 1967), p. 97.

25. *American State Papers, Indian Affairs*, II (Washington, 1834), 853.

26. *Annals of Congress*, 17th Cong., 1st sess., p. 1391, March 23, 1822.

27. Ibid., 20th Cong., 2nd sess., p. 141, Dec. 30, 1828.

28. Hall J. Kelley, *A Geographical Sketch of That Part of North America Called Oregon* (1830), in Fred Wilbur Powell, ed., *Hall J. Kelley on Oregon* (1932; reprint ed., New York: Da Capo, 1972), p. 67. Kelley is discussed in Powell's introduction, pp. vii-xxi.

29. Thomas Hart Benton, *Selections of Editorial Articles from the St. Louis Enquirer on the Subject of Oregon and Texas, as Originally Published in That Paper in the Years 1818-19* (St. Louis, 1844), p. 20. See also the discussion of Benton in Henry Nash Smith, *Virgin Land: The American West as Symbol and Myth* (Cambridge, Mass.: Harvard University Press, 1950), pp. 23-24.

30. Benton, *Selections*, p. 5; also ibid., pp. 13-27.

31. *Congressional Globe*, 29th Cong., 1st sess., pp. 917-918, June 3, 1846.

32. Benton, *Selections*, pp. 8, 24.

33. *Register of Debates*, 18th Cong., 2nd sess., pp. 711-713, March 1, 1825.

34. Charles F. Adams, ed., *Memoirs of John Quincy Adams*, 12 vols. (Philadelphia, 1874-1877), VIII, 186.

35. See John H. Schroeder, "Rep. John Floyd, 1817-1829: Harbinger of Oregon Territory," *Oregon Historical Quarterly*, 70 (Dec. 1969): 339-341.

36. Boyd, ed., *Papers of Jefferson*, IX, 218; Jefferson to James Monroe, Nov. 24, 1801, in Lipscomb and Bergh, eds., *Writings of Jefferson*, X, 296.

37. *Annals of Congress*, 16th Cong., 1st sess., pp. 1729-1730, April 3, 1820.

38. Monroe to Jefferson, Aug. 23, 1820, in Stanislaus M. Hamilton, ed., *The Writings of James Monroe*, 7 vols. (1898–1903; reprint ed., New York: AMS Press, 1969), VI, 152.

39. Schachner, *Thomas Jefferson*, p. 1.

40. Morse, *American Geography*, pp. 63, 68. See also Jordan, *White over Black*, pp. 336-339.

41. *Annals of Congress*, 12th Cong., 1st sess., p. 452, Dec. 10, 1811. The comment from 1815 is quoted in William C. Bruce, *John Randolph of Roanoke, 1773-1833*, 2 vols. (New York: G. P. Putnam's Sons, 1922), I, 426.

42. *Annals of Congress*, 18th Cong., 1st sess., p. 1187, Jan. 24, 1824. Randolph was referred to as helping to popularize the term *Anglo-Saxon* in a speech by Representative James W. Bouldin of Virginia, *Register of Debates*, 24th Cong., 1st sess., p. 4551, June 29, 1836.

43. Edward Everett, *Orations and Speeches on Various Occasions*, 2nd ed., 4 vols. (Boston, 1850–1868), I, 62-63, 382, 529.

44. Ibid., pp. 27, 33, 38.

45. *Register of Debates*, 18th Cong., 2nd sess., p. 689, Feb. 26, 1825.

46. Ibid., 19th Cong., 1st sess., p. 342, March 14, 1826.

6 The Other Americans

1. Boorstin, *Lost World of Thomas Jefferson*, pp. 59-65; Bernard W. Sheehan, *Seeds of Extinction: Jeffersonian Philanthropy and the American Indian* (Chapel Hill: University of North Carolina Press, 1973), pp. 3-44; William R. Stanton, *The Leopard's Spots: Scientific Attitudes toward Race in America, 1815–1859* (Chicago: University of Chicago Press, 1960), pp. 3-15; William M. Smallwood and Mabel S. C. Smallwood, *Natural History and the American Mind* (New York: Columbia University Press, 1941), pp. 289-292.

2. There is an excellent discussion of Smith in Samuel Stanhope Smith, *An Essay on the Causes of the Variety of Complexion and Figure in the Human Species*, ed. Winthrop D. Jordan (Cambridge, Mass.: Harvard University Press, Belknap Press, 1965), pp. vii-liii.

3. John Drayton, *A View of South-Carolina* (1802), in Thomas D. Clark, ed., *South Carolina: The Grand Tour, 1780–1865* (Columbia: University of South Carolina Press, 1973), pp. 25-26.

4. Hugh Williamson, *Observations on the Climate in Different Parts of America* (New York, 1811), pp. 32, 35, 41-43, 47, 57, 95.

5. The basic work is Jordan, *White over Black*. See also A. Leon Higginbotham, Jr., *Race and the American Legal Process: The Colonial Period* (New York: Oxford University Press, 1978); Ronald Sanders, *Lost Tribes and Promised Lands: The Origin of American Racism* (Boston: Little, Brown, 1978). Ronald T. Takaki, *Iron Cages: Race and Culture in Nineteenth-Century America* (New York: Knopf, 1979), emphasizes the cultural and economic bases of racism in the years after the Revolution and throughout the nineteenth century.

6. Jordan, *White over Black*, pp. 269-304, 441-451.

7. See Fredrika Teute Schmidt and Barbara Ripel Wilhelm, "Early Proslavery Petitions in Virginia," *William and Mary Quarterly*, 3rd ser., 30 (Jan. 1973): 133-146. For a general discussion of the impact of the Revolution on the proslavery argument, see Duncan J. MacLeod, *Slavery, Race, and the American Revolution* (London: Cambridge University Press, 1974).

8. For Jefferson, blacks, and slavery see Thomas Jefferson, *Notes on the State of Virginia*, ed. William Peden (1787; reprint ed., Chapel Hill: University of North Carolina Press, 1955), pp. 138-143; John Chester Miller, *The Wolf by the Ears: Thomas Jefferson and Slavery* (New York: Free Press, 1977); Jordan, *White over Black*, pp. 429-458; David Brion Davis, *The Problem of Slavery in the Age of Revolution, 1770-1823* (Ithaca, N.Y.: Cornell University Press, 1975), pp. 171-184; William Cohen, "Thomas Jefferson and the Problem of Slavery," *Journal of American History*, 56 (Dec. 1969): 503-526; William W. Freehling, "The Founding Fathers and Slavery," *American Historical Review*, 77 (Feb. 1972): 81-93.

9. St. George Tucker, *A Dissertation on Slavery: With a Proposal for the Gradual Abolition of It in the State of Virginia* (1796; reprint of 1861 ed., Westport, Conn.: Negro Universities Press, 1970), pp. 84-93.

10. See Roy Harvey Pearce, *Savagism and Civilization: A Study of the Indian and the American Mind* (Baltimore: Johns Hopkins University Press, 1967); Robert F. Berkhofer, *The White Man's Indian: Images of the American Indian from Columbus to the Present* (New York: Knopf, 1978); Gary B. Nash, "The Image of the Indian in the Southern Colonial Mind," in Edward Dudley and Maximillian E. Novak, eds., *The Wild Man Within: An Image in Western Thought from the Renaissance to Romanticism* (Pittsburgh: University of Pittsburgh Press, 1972), pp. 55-57, 63-73; Richard Slotkin, *Regeneration through Violence: The Mythology of the American Frontier, 1600-1860* (Middletown, Conn.: Wesleyan University Press, 1973), pp. 3-179; Rich-

ard Drinnon, *Facing West: The Metaphysics of Indian-Hating and Empire-Building* (Minneapolis: University of Minnesota Press, 1980), pp. 3-61; G. E. Thomas, "Puritans, Indians, and the Concept of Race," *New England Quarterly*, 48 (March 1975): 3-27.

11. Slotkin, *Regeneration through Violence*, p. 153; Sheehan, *Seeds of Extinction*, pp. 19-21.

12. Geoffrey Symcox, "The Wild Man's Return: The Enclosed Vision of Rousseau's Discourses," in Dudley and Novak, *The Wild Man Within*, pp. 229-234; Hoxie N. Fairchild, *The Noble Savage: A Study in Romantic Naturalism* (New York: Columbia University Press, 1928); Albert Keiser, *The Indian in American Literature* (New York: Oxford University Press, 1933).

13. Antonello Gerbi, *The Dispute of the New World: The History of a Polemic, 1750-1900*, trans. Jeremy Moyle, rev. ed. (Pittsburgh: University of Pittsburgh Press, 1973). Also Slotkin, *Regeneration through Violence*, pp. 202-205.

14. Knox to Wayne, Jan. 5, 1793, in Richard C. Knopf, ed., *Anthony Wayne: A Name in Arms* (Pittsburgh: University of Pittsburgh Press, 1960), p. 165; Knox report of Dec. 29, 1794, *American State Papers, Indian Affairs*, I (Washington, 1832), 544.

15. Speech of the Secretary of War, April 4, 1792, *American State Papers, Indian Affairs*, I, 230. See also Reginald Horsman, *Expansion and American Indian Policy, 1783-1812* (East Lansing: Michigan State University Press, 1967), pp. 54-65.

16. Jefferson to Chastellux, June 7, 1785, in Boyd, ed., *Papers of Jefferson*, VIII, 185; Jefferson to a delegation of Delaware, Mohicans, and Munsees, Dec. 1808, War Department, Secretary's Office, Letters Sent, Indian Affairs, B: 395, National Archives, Washington, D.C.

17. Jefferson, addresses, Dec. 1808, Jan. 1809, War Department, Secretary's Office, Letters Sent, Indian Affairs, B: 395-396, 412-413; Dearborn to Hawkins, May 24, 1803, ibid., A: 349-351.

18. Crawford report of March 13, 1816, *American State Papers, Indian Affairs*, II, 28; ibid., II, 151, Jan. 22, 1818.

19. The degree to which the image of the Indian as a "violent savage" affected thinking at all levels of American society is discussed in Sheehan, *Seeds of Extinction*, pp. 185-212.

20. Quoted in Ramsey, *Annals of Tennessee*, p. 622.

21. St. Clair to Governor Penn, May 29, 1774, to the Secretary of War, July 5, 1788, in William Henry Smith, ed., *The St. Clair Papers*, 2 vols. (1882; reprint ed., Freeport, N.Y.: Books for Libraries, 1971), I, 301, II, 48-49.

22. Extract from Morgan to John Hancock, March 15, 1777, in Samuel P. Hildreth, *Pioneer History* (1848; reprint ed., New York: Arno, 1971), pp. 114-115. See also William Irvine to Mrs. Irvine, April 12, 1782, in Mary C. Darlington, ed., *Fort Pitt and Letters from the Frontier* (1892; reprint ed., New York: Arno, 1971), pp. 239-240.

23. Craig to General Knox, March 6, 1791, in Smith, ed., *St. Clair Papers*, II, 202.

24. Josiah Harmar to the Secretary of War, Nov. 15, 1786, ibid., II, 19.

25. Hamtramck to St. Clair, Dec. 2, 1790, ibid., II, 198.

26. Sevier to Governor Richard Caswell, May 14, 1785, in Ramsey, *Annals of Tennessee*, p. 315.

27. David Campbell to Governor Richard Caswell, March 18, 1787, ibid., p. 355.

28. John F. D. Smyth, *A Tour in the United States of America*, 2 vols. (London, 1784), I, 345-346; Marquis de Chastellux, *Travels in North America, in the Years 1780, 1781 and 1782*, trans. Howard C. Rice, Jr., 2 vols. (Chapel Hill: University of North Carolina Press, 1963), II, 436.

29. See Daniel Marder, ed., *A Hugh Henry Brackenridge Reader, 1770-1815* (Pittsburgh: University of Pittsburgh Press, 1970), p. 98; also Claude Milton Newlin, *The Life and Writings of Hugh Henry Brackenridge* (Princeton: Princeton University Press, 1932).

30. From the *United States Magazine*, April 1779, reprinted in Marder, ed., *Brackenridge Reader*, p. 100.

31. Quoted in Newlin, *Life and Writings of Brackenridge*, p. 60.

32. *Narratives of the Perils and Sufferings of Dr. Knight and John Slover* (1782; reprint ed., Cincinnati, 1867), pp. 5-6.

33. *Pittsburgh Gazette*, Sept. 20, 1786, reprinted in Marder, ed., *Brackenridge Reader*, p. 120.

34. From the *National Gazette*, Feb 6, 1792, May 15, 1793, in Newlin, ed., *Life and Writings of Brackenridge*, pp. 127, 128, 131-132.

35. Archibald Loudon, *A Selection of Some of the Most Interesting Narratives of Outrages Committed by the Indians in Their Wars with the White People*, 2 vols. in 1 (1808-1811; reprint of 1888 ed., New York: Arno, 1971), p. iv.

7 Superior and Inferior Races

1. See Stanton, *Leopard's Spots*, p. 18.

2. Harriot W. Warner, ed., *Autobiography of Charles Caldwell*,

M.D. (Philadelphia, 1855).

3. Ibid., p. 269; Caldwell, "An Essay on the Causes of the Variety of Complexion and Figure in the Human Species," *American Review of History and Politics*, 2 (July 1811): 128-166; also ibid., in *Port-Folio*, 3rd ser., 4 (July-Nov. 1814): 8-33. 148-163, 252-271, 362-382, 447-457; Stanton, *Leopard's Spots*, pp. 19-23; George M. Fredrickson, *The Black Image in the White Mind: The Debate on Afro-American Character and Destiny, 1817–1914* (New York: Harper & Row, 1971), pp. 71-73.

4. Warner, ed., *Autobiography of Caldwell*, pp. 270-273.

5. Ibid., pp. 333, 390; Thomas Cary Johnson, Jr., *Scientific Interests in the Old South* (New York: D. Appleton Century, 1936), pp. 37-38; *Phrenological Journal*, 14 (1841): 283-284; R. W. Haskins, *History and Progress of Phrenology* (Buffalo, 1839), pp. 105-107; Combe, *Lectures on Phrenology*, intro. Boardman, pp. 79-81; Davies, *Phrenology*, p. 13; Combe, *Notes on the United States*, II, 293.

6. Quoted in Haskins, *Phrenology*, pp. 110-111.

7. Charles Caldwell, *Thoughts on the Original Unity of the Human Race* (New York, 1830), pp. iii, vi-vii, 1-2, 173.

8. Ibid., pp. 72-73.

9. Ibid., pp. 88, 134-135.

10. Ibid., pp. 141-142, 144, 146, 151.

11. Ibid., p. 136.

12. See Robert E. Riegel, "Early Phrenology in the United States," *Medical Life*, 37 (July 1930): 361-376; Riegel, "The Introduction of Phrenology to the United States," *American Historical Review*, 39 (Oct. 1933): 73-78; Davies, *Phrenology*, pp. 6-11, 16-29, 37.

13. George H. Calvert, ed., *Illustrations of Phrenology: Being a Selection of Articles from the Edinburgh Phrenological Journal, and the Transactions of the Edinburg Phrenological Society* (Baltimore, 1832), pp. 29, 30, 32-36.

14. Amariah Brigham, M.D., *Observations on the Influence of Religion upon the Health and Physical Welfare of Mankind* (Boston, 1835), pp. 300-302.

15. See Fredrickson, *Black Image*, pp. 43-46, for a discussion of the impact of the abolitionists. The various historical explanations advanced to account for the rise of proslavery thought are discussed in David Donald, "The Proslavery Argument Reconsidered," *Journal of Southern History*, 37 (Feb. 1971): 3-18. Donald sees the proslavery argument as a "search for social stability in a rapidly changing world," ibid., p. 18. See also William Sumner Jenkins, *Pro-Slavery Thought in*

the Old South (1935; reprint ed., Gloucester, Mass.: Peter Smith, 1960); Arthur Young Lloyd, *The Slavery Controversy, 1831-1860* (Chapel Hill: University of North Carolina Press, 1939).

16. Cooper's letter is quoted in Jenkins, *Pro-Slavery Thought*, p. 252; *Carolina Law Journal* (Columbia, S.C., 1831), 1 (1830): 100. See also MacLeod, *Slavery, Race, and the American Revolution*, pp. 86-88, 106.

17. For the Virginia debates see Joseph Clarke Robert, *The Road from Monticello: A Study of the Virginia Slavery Debate of 1832* (1941; reprint ed., New York: AMS Press, 1970). Roane's speech is quoted in ibid., p. 81. See also Clement Eaton, *The Mind of the Old South*, rev. ed. (Baton Rouge: Louisiana State University Press, 1967), pp. 8-13.

18. Thomas R. Dew, *Review of the Debate in the Virginia Legislature of 1831 and 1832* (Richmond, 1832), pp. 8, 87, 103.

19. Richard H. Colfax, *Evidence against the Views of the Abolitionists, Consisting of Physical and Moral Proofs, of the Natural Inferiority of the Negroes* (New York, 1833), p. 29.

20. Fredrickson, *Black Image*, p. 74; Philip D. Curtin, *The Image of Africa: British Ideas and Action, 1780-1850* (Madison: University of Wisconsin Press, 1964), p. 371. Some Northerners also joined in this early defense of slavery. The most influential of the early publications by Northerners was James Kirke Paulding, *Slavery in the United States* (New York, 1836).

21. J. Jacobus Flournoy, *An Essay on the Origins, Habits, &c. of the Negro Race: Incidental to the Propriety of Having Nothing to do with Negroes* (New York, 1835), pp. 4-5, 10, 17, 21, 22.

22. James H. Hammond, "Slavery in the Light of Political Science," (1845), in E. N. Elliott, ed., *Cotton is King and Pro-Slavery Arguments* (1860; reprint ed., New York: Negro Universities Press, 1969), pp. 637-638; see also Fredrickson, *Black Image*, pp. 46-48; Lloyd, *Slavery Controversy*, p. 227.

23. The standard work on the American school of ethnology is Stanton, *Leopard's Spots*. The book is of great value concerning the scientific work of the school, but Stanton also argues that such work did not have a widespread popular impact. There is considerable evidence to the contrary. Fredrickson suggests this in his *Black Image*, pp. 46-48. See also A. Irving Hallowell, "The Beginnings of Anthropology in America," in Frederica De Laguna, ed., *Selected Papers from the American Anthropologist, 1888-1920* (Evanston, Ill.: Row, Peterson, 1960), pp. 58-67; Stuart Creighton Miller, *The Unwelcome*

Immigrant: The American Image of the Chinese, 1785–1882 (Berkeley and Los Angeles: University of California Press, 1969), pp. 154-157; John S. Haller, Jr., *Outcasts from Evolution: Scientific Attitudes of Racial Inferiority, 1859–1900* (Urbana: University of Illinois Press, 1971), pp. 74-78.

24. See Stanton, *Leopard's Spots*, pp. 23-41; Harry L. Shapiro, "The Direction of Physical Anthropology," in Jacob W. Gruber, ed., *The Philadelphia Anthropological Society: Papers Presented on Its Golden Anniversary* (New York: Distributed by Columbia University Press, 1967), pp. 47-49; Ales Hrdlicka, "Physical Anthropology in America," in De Laguna, *Selected Papers*, pp. 314-319; Elizabeth Cary Agassiz, ed., *Louis Agassiz: His Life and Correspondence* (Boston, 1885), p. 417.

25. Samuel George Morton, *Crania Americana; or, A Comparative View of the Skulls of Various Aboriginal Nations of North and South America. To Which is Prefixed an Essay on the Varieties of the Human Species* (Philadelphia, 1839), pp. 1-44, 88.

26. Ibid., pp. 1-4.

27. Ibid., pp. 4-6, 17.

28. Ibid., pp. 6, 81-82. In a footnote to his remarks on pp. 81-82 Morton quoted William Lawrence to the effect that it was useless to expect Indians to achieve equality with Europeans.

29. Combe, *Notes on the U.S.*, I, 307-308; Davies, *Phrenology*, pp. 20-22, 146-147; Stanton, *Leopard's Spots*, pp. 35-37; Charles Gibbon, *The Life of George Combe*, 2 vols. (London, 1878), II, 53.

30. *American Journal of Science and Arts*, 38 (Jan.–March 1840): 341.

31. Combe, "Phrenological Remarks on the Relation between the Natural Talents and Dispositions of Nations, and the Development of Their Brains," in Morton, *Crania Americana*, pp. 271-272, 275.

32. Silliman's review is reprinted in *American Phrenological Journal*, 2 (June 1840): 385-396, and Caldwell's review, which originally appeared in the *Western Journal of Medicine and Surgery*, is reprinted in extract in ibid., 3 (Dec. 1840): 124-126.

33. Morton, *An Inquiry into the Distinctive Characteristics of the Aboriginal Race of America*, 2nd ed. (Philadelphia, 1844), pp. 4, 12, 36. See also Morton, *Some Observations on the Ethnography and Archaeology of the American Aborigines* (New Haven, Conn., 1846), p. 9.

34. Morton, *Crania Ægyptiaca; or, Observations on Egyptian Ethnography, Derived from Anatomy, History and the Monuments* (Philadelphia, 1844), pp. 1-3, 8, 15.

35. There is considerable information on Nott in Stanton's *Leopard's Spots*. See also William H. Anderson, M.D., *Biographical Sketch of Dr. J. C. Nott* (Mobile, 1877), and Kenneth R. H. Mackenzie, "The Life and Anthropological Labours of Dr. Nott of Mobile, Hon. F.A.S.L.," *Anthropological Review* (London), 6 (1868): lxxix-lxxxi, 450-452.

36. Nott, *Two Lectures on the Connection between the Biblical and Physical History of Man* (New York, 1849), p. 5.

37. Nott, *Two Lectures, on the Natural History of the Caucasian and Negro Races* (Mobile, 1844), pp. 16, 28-35.

38. Ibid, pp. 36-38.

39. Nott, *Two Lectures on the Connection between the Biblical and Physical History of Man*, pp. 36-37. For Morton's encouragement of Nott, see *Southern Quarterly Review*, 8 (July 1845): 160.

40. Quoted in Edward Lurie, *Louis Agassiz: A Life in Science* (Chicago: University of Chicago Press, 1960), p. 257. For Agassiz, Morton, and Nott see Asa Gray to Morton, Oct. 13, 1846, in Samuel G. Morton Papers, Historical Society of Pennsylvania; Nott to Joseph Leidy, Oct. 4, 1854, March 15, 1856, in Joseph Leidy Papers, Academy of Natural Sciences of Philadelphia.

41. Agassiz, "The Diversity of Origin of the Human Races," *Christian Examiner*, 49 (July 1850): 110, 111, 142-145; also "Geographical Distribution of Animals," ibid., 48 (March 1850): 181-204.

42. Nott to Morton, May 4, 1850, quoted in Lurie, *Louis Agassiz*, p. 261. See also Lurie, "Louis Agassiz and the Races of Man," *Isis*, 45 (Sept. 1954): 227-242.

43. Bachman, *The Doctrine of the Unity of the Human Race Examined on the Principles of Science* (Charleston, S.C., 1850). There is a good discussion of Bachman's work in Stanton, *Leopard's Spots*, pp. 123-136, 170-173.

44. William Frederick Van Amringe, *An Investigation of the Theories of the Natural History of Man* (New York, 1848), pp. 157, 205, 213, 217. In this same year Charles Pickering, who had accompanied the Wilkes exploring expedition to the Pacific, published *The Races of Man* (Boston, 1848). Pickering described eleven separate races. To avoid controversy he simply ignored the question of whether these races constituted separate species, but he insisted that the races existed independently of climate.

45. Lieut.-Col. Charles Hamilton Smith, *The Natural History of the Human Species*, intro. S. Kneeland (Boston, 1852), pp. 15, 94-95.

46. John H. Van Evrie, *Negroes and Negro "Slavery": The First an*

Inferior Race: The Latter Its Normal Condition, 3rd ed. (1853; New York, 1863), pp. 44, 47, 80. See also Fredrickson, *Black Image*, pp. 91-95.

47. Gliddon to Squier, June 24, 1851, in The Papers of Ephraim Squier, Library of Congress, Washington, D.C. See also the discussion of Gliddon in Stanton, *Leopard's Spots*, pp. 49-50.

48. Gliddon to Squier, March 7, April 6, 10, 23, June 4, July 14, 1854, in Squier Papers, Library of Congress; Lurie, *Louis Agassiz*, p. 264.

49. Nott and Gliddon, *Types of Mankind* (Philadelphia, 1854), p. xxxviii, footnote.

50. Ibid., pp. xlvi, 56, 69, 72, 82, 95.

51. Ibid., pp. 53, 77, 79.

8 The Dissemination of Scientific Racialism

1. *American Whig Review*, 9 (April 1849): 386; 12 (Dec. 1850): 567; also *Massachusetts Quarterly Review*, 2 (Sept. 1849): 428.

2. *Farmer's Register*, 1 (1834): 665, quoted in Weymouth T. Jordan, *Ante-Bellum Alabama: Town and Country* (Tallahassee: Florida State University, 1957), p. 86.

3. *Southern Literary Journal*, 1 (Nov. 1835): 192.

4. Ibid., n.s., 3 (March 1838): 168. In 1838 Harper's *Memoir on Slavery* was published as a pamphlet as well as being issued in several numbers of the *Southern Literary Journal*.

5. *Southern Agriculturalist*, 12 (June and Aug. 1839): 289, 290-294, 411-418.

6. *Southern Literary Messenger*, 5 (Sept. 1839): 616-620.

7. *Southern Quarterly Review*, 2 (Oct. 1842): 327.

8. *Magnolia*, 4 (Nov. 1842): 265-270; ibid., 4 (June 1842): 366.

9. *American Whig Review*, 12 (Dec. 1850): 577.

10. Combe, *Notes on the United States*, I, 84, II, 17-18; Madeleine Stern, *Heads and Headliners: The Phrenological Fowlers* (Norman: University of Oklahoma Press, 1971) discusses the popularization of phrenology.

11. Orson S. Fowler and Lorenzo N. Fowler, *Phrenology Proved, Illustrated, and Applied*, 35th ed. enl. (New York, 1846), p. 26; Orson S. Fowler, *Phrenological Chart* (Baltimore, 1836), p. 3.

12. Combe, *Notes on the United States*, I, 259-260; cf. ibid., II, 192-193.

13. Fowler and Fowler, *Phrenology Proved*, pp. 31-32.

14. Ibid., pp. 29-31.
15. *Democratic Review*, 11 (Aug. 1842): 113-139; see also ibid., 9 (Oct. 1841): 401-402 (the full title of the magazine was *The United States Magazine and Democratic Review*).
16. Ibid., 11 (Dec. 1842): 603-621.
17. Ibid., 3 (Oct. 1838): 115, 129; 11 (July 1842): 45, 52. See also ibid., 12 (Dec. 1842): 630-644; 12 (April 1843): 401; 14 (Feb. 1844): 169-184.
18. *Southern Quarterly Review*, 3 (April 1843): 290.
19. Ibid., 5 (Jan. 1844): 148, 156.
20. *Democratic Review*, 19 (Oct. 1846): 243, 247, 254.
21. Ibid., 26 (April 1850): 328. See also ibid., 27 (Aug. 1850): 133-146, and 27 (Sept. 1850): 209-220.
22. Ibid., 26 (June 1850): 570-571. Smyth's book was *The Unity of the Human Races Proved to Be the Doctrine of Scripture, Reason, and Science* (New York, 1850).
23. *Democratic Review*, 27 (Sept. 1850): 213-214.
24. Ibid., 27 (July 1850): 48; see also ibid., 29 (Sept. 1851): 246-257.
25. Ibid., 27 (Dec. 1850): 496.
26. Ibid., 29 (Dec. 1851): 571.
27. *American Whig Review*, 1 (May 1845): 525. See also ibid., 3 (April 1846): 383-396, and *North American Review*, 55 (April 1845): 426-478, and 57 (April 1846): 465-506.
28. *American Whig Review*, 10 (Oct. 1849): 440.
29. Ibid., 12 (Nov. 1850): 446.
30. *New Englander*, 8 (Nov. 1850): 546-548, 580-584.
31. *Southern Literary Messenger*, 20 (Nov. 1854): 661.
32. *American Whig Review*, 9 (April 1849): 386-396, 398.
33. Ibid., 12 (Dec. 1850): 567-586.
34. *Massachusetts Quarterly Review*, 2 (Sept. 1849): 438-440.
35. *New Englander*, 8 (Aug. 1850): 370-377.
36. *Southern Quarterly Review*, 7 (April 1845): 372-448; ibid., 8 (July 1845): 148-190.
37. Ibid., 9 (Jan. 1846): 7.
38. Ibid.
39. Ibid., 17 (July 1850): 426-451; 18 (Nov. 1850): 385-426.
40. *Southern Quarterly Review*, 18 (Nov. 1850): 392.
41. Ibid., 18 (April 1851): 392-419; 20 (July 1851): 118-132, 206-238; 20 (Oct. 1851): 458-480; 23 (April 1853): 422-445; 24 (July 1853): 59-92.

42. Ibid., 26 (Oct. 1854): 304.
43. Ibid., 27 (Jan. 1855): 116-174.
44. Ibid., 21 (Jan. 1852): 175.
45. Ibid., p. 161.
46. Ibid., p. 87.
47. *De Bow's Review*, 17 (July 1854): 69.
48. Ibid., pp. 25-39.
49. Ibid., 11 (July 1851): 65-69. See also ibid., 3 (May 1847): 419-422; 4 (Nov. 1847): 275-289; 5 (May-June 1848): 455-499; 7 (Sept. 1849): 206-225; 11 (Oct. 1851): 403-405; 11 (Dec. 1851): 630-634. The *Southern Quarterly Review* was more skeptical about the quality of Cartwright's work, 22 (July 1852): 49-63.
50. *De Bow's Review*, 10 (Feb. 1851): 119-128, 128 (quotation). Also Samuel G. Morton, "Hybridity in Animals, Considered in Reference to the Question of the Unity of the Human Species," *American Journal of Science*, 2nd ser., 3 (Jan.-Feb. 1847): 39-50, 203-212. There is a good discussion of the hybridity argument in Stanton, *Leopard's Spots*, pp. 113-117, 131-135.
51. *De Bow's Review*, 10 (March 1851): 331.
52. Ibid., 4 (Nov. 1847): 280. Nott had earlier argued that all the Indians were of one race.
53. Ibid., 16 (Feb. 1854): 147-148.
54. Ibid., 12 (May 1852): 508-515, 520; *Southern Quarterly Review*, 24 (July 1853): 71.
55. *Democratic Review*, 26 (April 1850): 345.
56. *Southern Quarterly Review*, 28 (April 1851): 345.
57. See Ruth Miller Elson, *Guardians of Tradition: Schoolbooks of the Nineteenth Century* (Lincoln: University of Nebraska Press, 1964), pp. 62-89. Elson has the best discussion of race in the schoolbooks, although she does little to indicate changes in attitude in the course of the nineteenth century.
58. *Putnam's Monthly Magazine*, 4 (July 1854): 2, 13-14; 5 (Jan. 1855): 79-88. The magazine quickly printed an article defending unity, but the total effect was to emphasize the diversity of races.

9 Romantic Racial Nationalism

1. Jay B. Hubbell, *The South in American Literature, 1607-1900* (Durham, N.C.: Duke University Press, 1954), pp. 186-187; Howard Mumford Jones, *Ideas in America* (Cambridge, Mass.: Harvard University Press, 1944), pp. 107-112; Benjamin T. Spencer, *The Quest*

for Nationality: An American Literary Campaign (Syracuse, N.Y.: Syracuse University Press, 1957), pp. 74, 90-95.

2. Rollin G. Osterweis, *Romanticism and Nationalism in the Old South* (New Haven: Yale University Press, 1949), pp. 41-53; Eaton, *Mind of the Old South* (1967 ed.), pp. 246-248; Burns, *American Idea of Mission*, pp. 41-46; Frank Luther Mott, *A History of American Magazines, 1741-1850* (Cambridge, Mass.: Harvard University Press, 1938), p. 415; Carl Bode, *The Anatomy of American Popular Culture, 1840-61* (Berkeley and Los Angeles: University of California Press), pp. 149-154.

3. Quoted in Frank Luther Mott, *Golden Multitudes: The Story of Best Sellers in the United States* (New York: Macmillan, 1947), pp. 68, also ibid., pp. 65-69; William E. Dodd, *The Cotton Kingdom: A Chronicle of the Old South* (New Haven: Yale University Press, 1919), pp. 62-63; Osterweis, *Romanticism and Nationalism*, pp. 44-49; Hubbell, *South in Literature*, pp. 188-192.

4. Osterweis, *Romanticism and Nationalism*, p. 203.

5. *Mobile Daily Commercial Register*, Oct. 28, 1839.

6. Marshall T. Polk to James K. Polk, Dec. 19, 1830, in Herbert Weaver, ed., *Correspondence of James K. Polk*, I, 1817-1832 (Nashville: Vanderbilt University Press, 1969), p. 363.

7. Francis O. Matthiessen, *American Renaissance: Art and Expression in the Age of Emerson and Whitman* (London: Oxford University Press, 1941), p. 6; Henry A. Pochmann, *German Culture in America: Philosophical and Literary Influences, 1600-1900* (Madison: University of Wisconsin Press, 1957), pp. 88-95; Hubbell, *South in Literature*, p. 425; G. Harrison Orians, "The Rise of Romanticism, 1805-1855," in Harry Hayden Clark, ed., *Transitions in American Literary History* (Durham, N.C.: Duke University Press, 1953), pp. 227-229.

8. Trist to Jesse Burton Harrison, Aug. 1, 1839, quoted in John T. Krumpelmann, *Southern Scholars in Goethe's Germany* (Chapel Hill: University of North Carolina Press, 1965), p. 72.

9. *Democratic Review*, 8 (July 1840): 13; *North American Review*, 62 (April 1846): 382; *Southern Quarterly Review*, 14 (July 1848): 77.

10. Pochmann, *German Culture in America*, pp. 19-20, 59-78; Scott Holland Goodnight, *German Literature in American Magazines Prior to 1846* (Madison: University of Wisconsin Press, 1907), pp. 16-17, 34; Spencer, *Quest for Nationality*, pp. 35-36; Orians, "Rise of Romanticism," p. 208; Krumpelmann, *Southern Scholars*, pp. 34, 77-78, 159; William R. Taylor, *Cavalier and Yankee: The Old South*

and American National Character (1961; New York: Harper & Row, 1969), pp. 41-43; Osterweis, *Romanticism and Nationalism*, p. 35. The quotation from Ticknor is in Orie William Long, *Literary Pioneers: Early American Explorers of German Culture* (Cambridge, Mass.: Harvard University Press, 1935), p. 16.

11. Pochmann, *German Culture in America*, p. 63; David Lowenthal, *George Perkins Marsh: Versatile Vermonter* (New York: Columbia University Press, 1958); René Wellek, "Minor Transcendentalists," in *Confrontations: Studies in the Intellectual and Literary Relations between Germany, England, and the United States during the Nineteenth Century* (Princeton: Princeton University Press, 1965), pp. 154-160.

12. *Congressional Globe*, 29th Cong., 1st sess., p. 917, May 28, 1846.

13. Adams, ed., *Memoirs of John Quincy Adams*, VII, 90.

14. H. S. Legaré to I. E. Holmes, Oct. 2, 1832, in *Writings of Hugh Swinton Legaré*, 2 vols. (1846; reprint ed., New York: Da Capo, 1970), I, 204. See also Taylor, *Cavalier and Yankee*, pp. 15, 53-61, 203-205.

15. Jon L. Wakelyn, *The Politics of a Literary Man: William Gilmore Simms* (Westport, Conn.: Greenwood, 1973), pp. xi-xii. Also Taylor, *Cavalier and Yankee*, pp. 268-297; Eaton, *Mind of the Old South* (1967 ed.), pp. 254-263; Osterweis, *Romanticism and Nationalism*, pp. 113-115.

16. William Gilmore Simms, *Views and Reviews in American Literature, History and Fiction: First Series*, ed. C. Hugh Holman (1845; Cambridge, Mass.: Harvard University Press, Belknap Press, 1962), pp. 45-46.

17. Simms to George F. Holmes, Aug. 15 [1842], in Mary C. Simms Oliphant et al., eds., *The Letters of William Gilmore Simms*, 5 vols. (Columbia: University of South Carolina Press), I, 319; Perry Miller, *The Raven and the Whale: The War of Words and Wits in the Era of Poe and Melville* (New York: Harcourt, Brace & World, 1956), pp. 104-109.

18. Simms, *The Yemassee*, ed. Alexander Cole (1835; reprint ed., New York: American Book Company, 1937), pp. 22, 76.

19. Simms to William Elliott, March 7 [1849], in Oliphant, ed., *Letters of Simms*, II, 493. See also John W. Higham, "The Changing Loyalties of William Gilmore Simms," *Journal of Southern History*, 9 (May 1943): 210-223; Jay B. Hubbell, "Literary Nationalism in the Old South," in David Kelly Jackson, ed., *American Studies in Honor*

of *William Kenneth Boyd* (Durham, N.C.: Duke University Press, 1940), pp. 178-179.

20. *Democratic Review*, 18 (Feb. 1846): 91-94.

21. Simms to Hammond, June 4, 1847, in Oliphant, ed., *Letters of Simms*, II, 322; also Simms to Hammond, March 29, 1847, ibid., II, 289. Also William P. Trent, *William Gilmore Simms* (Boston, 1892), pp. 123-124.

22. Quoted in Aaron Kramer, *The Prophetic Tradition in American Poetry, 1835-1900* (Rutherford, N.J.: Fairleigh Dickinson University Press, 1968), pp. 57-58.

23. Simms to Hammond, July 15, 1847, May 20 [1848], in Oliphant, ed., *Letters of Simms*, II, 330-333, 411-412.

24. Simms to John P. Kennedy, April 5, 1852, in ibid., III, 174. Also Wakelyn, *Politics of a Literary Man*, pp. 188-189.

25. Quoted in Eaton, *Mind of the Old South* (1967 ed.), p. 255.

26. Hubbell, *South in American Literature*, pp. 334, 495-502; Taylor, *Cavalier and Yankee*, pp. 205-224.

27. From Caruthers, *A Lecture* . . . , March 14, 1843, quoted in Curtis Carroll Davis, *Chronicler of the Cavaliers: A Life of the Virginia Novelist, Dr. William A. Caruthers* (Richmond, Va.: Dietz Press, 1953), p. 233.

28. Caruthers, *The Knights of the Horse-Shoe* (Wetumpka, Ala., 1845), p. 161.

29. James D. Nourse, *Remarks on the Past and Its Legacies to American Society* (Louisville, 1847), p. vi.

30. Ibid., pp. v, 26-27, 36.

31. Ibid., pp. 35-36.

32. Ibid., pp. 39, 71-72, 176-178, 182-185, 206-207.

33. Ibid., pp. 174-175, 215-217, 218, 223.

34. *Columbian* (Cincinnati), Dec. 8, 1849. Nourse gave a course of lectures in Cincinnati and also lectured in Boston and New York.

35. See the discussion of the Southerners as Normans in Osterweis, *Romanticism and Nationalism*, pp. 78-79.

36. Letter of June 10, 1827, Thomas Sergeant Perry, ed., *The Life and Letters of Francis Lieber* (Boston, 1882), p. 70. For the life of Lieber see Merle Curti, "Francis Lieber and Nationalism," in *Probing Our Past* (New York, 1955), pp. 119-151; Philip S. Paludan, *A Covenant with Death: The Constitution, Law, and Equality in the Civil War Era* (Urbana: University of Illinois Press, 1975), pp. 62-65.

37. See Paludan, *Covenant*, pp. 61-108, for a discussion of Lieber's nationalism. Paludan underestimate the extent to which Lieber believed in the special destiny of "the Anglican race."

38. Lieber to George S. Hillard, Feb. 25, 1847, in Perry, ed., *Life and Letters of Lieber*, p. 207; also quotation in Burns, *American Idea of Mission*, pp. 41-42.

39. Lieber to George S. Hillard, April 1850, to Charles Sumner, Feb. 22, 1851, in Perry, ed., *Life and Letters of Lieber*, pp. 245-246; Curti, "Francis Lieber," pp. 134-140.

40. *Southern Quarterly Review*, 3 (April 1843): 310-311.

41. Ibid., 4 (July 1843): 157.

42. Ibid., 10 (July 1846): 147.

43. Ibid., 15 (July 1849): 399-400.

44. Ibid., 17 (April 1850): 27; *De Bow's Review*, 17 (Oct. 1854): 363.

45. *De Bow's Review*, 4 (Sept. 1847): 122; ibid., p. 31.

46. Ibid., 11 (Aug. 1850): 165-168.

47. *Southern Quarterly Review*, 21 (Jan. 1852): 4.

48. [Alexander H. Everett], *America: or a General Survey of the Political Situation of the Several Powers of the Western Continent, with Conjectures on Their Future Prospects* (Philadelphia, 1827), pp. 212-213, 217.

49. Quoted in Philip L. Nicoloff, *Emerson on Race and History: An Examination of English Traits* (New York: Columbia University Press, 1961), pp. 119-120. See also ibid., pp. 48-96; Burns, *American Idea*, pp. 190-191; Samuel Kliger, "Emerson and the Usable Saxon Past," *Journal of the History of Ideas*, 16 (Oct. 1955): 476-493.

50. Quoted in Frederic E. Faverty, *Matthew Arnold: The Ethnologist* (Evanston, Ill.: Northwestern University Press, 1951), p. 17.

51. Emerson, *English Traits*, ed. Howard Mumford Jones (Cambridge, Mass.: Harvard University Press, Belknap Press, 1966), pp. 75, 86. His statement in 1847 is from a speech at Manchester; see ibid., p. 201.

52. Parker to David A. Wasson, Dec. 12, 1857, in Octavius B. Frothingham, *Theodore Parker: A Biography* (Boston, 1874), p. 327; also Harold C. Goddard, *Studies in New England Transcendentalism* (1908; reprint ed., New York: Hillary House, 1960), p. 85; Wellek, "Minor Transcendentalists," pp. 172-174; Fredrickson, *Black Image*, p. 120; John Weiss, *Life and Correspondence of Theodore Parker*, 2 vols. (New York, 1864), I, 48, 72-73, 77-78; Burns, *American Idea*, p. 191; Parker to David A. Wasson, Dec. 12, 1857, in Frothingham, *Theodore Parker*, p. 327.

53. Quoted in Josiah C. Nott and George R. Gliddon, *Types of Mankind* (Philadelphia, 1854), p. 462.

54. Parker to Professor E. Desor, Aug. 9, 1852, in Frothingham, *Theodore Parker*, pp. 318-320.

55. Parker to Miss Cobbe, Dec. 4, 1857, in Weiss, *Life and Correspondence of Parker*, I, 463.

56. Frothingham, *Theodore Parker*, p. 319.

57. Parker to David A. Wasson, Dec. 12, 1857, ibid., p. 327.

58. Parker to Miss Hunt, Nov. 16, 1857, ibid., p. 467.

59. Parker to Francis Jackson, Nov. 24, 1859, in Weiss, *Life and Correspondence of Parker*, II, 176.

60. Quoted in Burns, *American Idea*, pp. 260-261.

61. Parker, Second Sermon on the Mexican War, June 25, 1848, in Weiss, *Life and Correspondence of Parker*, II, 90.

62. Lowenthal, *George Perkins Marsh*, pp. 49-59; also Oscar J. Falnes, "New England Interest in Scandinavian Culture and the Norsemen," *New England Quarterly*, 10 (June 1937): 211-242; Long, *Literary Pioneers*, pp. 161-192; Longfellow to Stephen Longfellow, Sept. 20, 1835, to Thomas Wren Ward, July 23, 1835, in Andrew Hilen, ed., *The Letters of Henry Wadsworth Longfellow* (Cambridge, Mass.: Harvard University Press, Belknap Press, 1966-), I, 500-501, 514-516.

63. George P. Marsh, *The Goths in New England: A Discourse Delivered at the Anniversary of the Philomathesian Society of Middlebury College, Aug. 15, 1843* (Middlebury, Vt., 1843), pp. 13-14.

64. Ibid., p. 21.

65. Marsh, "Address," 1844, in Cephas Brainerd and Eveline W. Brainerd, eds., *The New England Society Orations: Addresses, Sermons and Poems Delivered before the New England Society in the City of New York, 1820-1885*, 2 vols. (New York: Century, 1901), I 382, 389.

66. Lowenthal, *George Perkins Marsh*, pp. 69-71, 104-107; speech of Marsh in the House of Representatives, Feb. 10, 1848, in Caroline Crane Marsh, *Life and Letters of George Perkins Marsh* (New York, 1888), p. 464.

67. David Levin, *History as Romantic Art: Bancroft, Prescott, Motley, and Parkman* (1959; New York: Harcourt, Brace & World, 1963). Also Thomas F. Gossett, *Race: The History of an Idea in America* (1963; New York: Schocken, 1965), pp. 88-93, 94-95; Philip Wayne Powell, *Tree of Hate: Propaganda and Prejudices Affecting United States Relations with the Hispanic World* (New York: Basic Books, 1971), pp. 119-122; Long, *Literary Pioneers*, pp. 108, 110, 146, 204, 208; George W. Curtis, *The Correspondence of John Lothrop Motley*, 2 vols. (New York, 1889), I, 13, 18-21, 37.

68. "The Doctrine of Temperaments" (1824), in George Bancroft, *Literary and Historical Miscellanies* (New York, 1855), pp. 2-4.

69. Bancroft to Buchanan, May 18, 1847, in John B. Moore, ed., *The Works of James Buchanan*, 12 vols. (1908-1911; reprint ed., New York: Antiquarian Press, 1960), VII, 309; Levin, *History as Romantic Art*, pp. 79-82.

70. Motley, *The Rise of the Dutch Republic* (1856; New York: Harper, 1900), introduction, chapter 1; Levin, *History as Romantic Art*, pp. 86-91.

71. Quoted in Gossett, *Race*, p. 91; Levin, *History as Romantic Art*, pp. 75-76; Bode, *Anatomy of American Popular Culture*, pp. 242-245.

72. Quoted in Gossett, *Race*, p. 95; Levin, *History as Romantic Art*, pp. 91-92.

73. Parkman, *The Oregon Trail*, ed. E. N. Feltskog (Madison: University of Wisconsin Press, 1969), pp. 96, 292-293; also ibid., introduction, p. 45a.

74. "The Office of the People" (1835), in Bancroft, *Literary and Historical Miscellanies*, pp. 413, 414-415.

75. Prescott to Robert C. Winthrop, May 30, 1847, in Roger Wolcott, ed., *The Correspondence of William Hickling Prescott, 1833-1847* (Boston: Houghton Mifflin, 1925), p. 642; also Prescott to Lord Morpeth, Nov. 30, 1844, ibid., p. 520.

10 Racial Destiny and the Indians

1. See Edwin S. Fussell, *Frontier: American Literature and the American West* (Princeton: Princeton University Press, 1965); Pearce, *Savagism and Civilization*; Berkhofer, *White Man's Indian*, pp. 71-96; Kay Seymour House, *Cooper's Americans* (Columbus: Ohio State University Press, 1965), pp. 47-71; Keiser, *Indian in American Literature*; Davis, *Chronicler of the Cavaliers*, p. 165; Simms, *Views and Reviews*, ed. Holman, pp. 128-147.

2. Robert Montgomery Bird, *Nick of the Woods, or The Jibbenainosay: A Tale of Kentucky*, ed. Cecil B. Williams (1837; reprint ed., New York: American Book Co., 1939), preface to 1st ed., p. 5.

3. Annie H. Abel, "The History of Events Resulting in Indian Consolidation West of the Mississippi River," American Historical Association, *Annual Report*, 1906, I (Washington, 1908), 241-259, discusses the details of Jefferson's plans. For the arguments after 1815 see Reginald Horsman, *The Origins of Indian Removal*, The Clarence

M. Burton Memorial Lecture, 1969 (East Lansing: Michigan State University Press, 1970).

4. Evidence of this can be found in Henry Thompson Malone, *Cherokees of the Old South: A People in Transition* (Athens: University of Georgia Press, 1956); Arthur H. De Rosier, *The Removal of the Choctaw Indians* (Knoxville: University of Tennessee Press, 1970).

5. See Crawford report, March 13, 1816, *American State Papers, Indian Affairs*, II, 26-28. In March 1816 a federal treaty with the Cherokee acknowledged their right to lands south of the Tennessee River. This produced extensive protests from Tennessee; see ibid., pp. 88-91, 99, 110-115.

6. McMinn to Crawford, Oct. 25, 1816, ibid., II, 115. Jackson also protested; see Jackson to Thomas Pinckney, May 18, 1814, to Crawford, June 10, 13, 1816, in John S. Bassett, ed., *Correspondence of Andrew Jackson*, 7 vols. (Washington, D.C.: Carnegie Institution, 1926-1935), II, 3, 243-249.

7. Report of Senate Committee, Jan. 9, 1817, *American State Papers, Indian Affairs*, II, 123-124; War Department, Secretary's Office, Letters Sent, Indian Affairs, D: 154, 168, 176, 204-205, National Archives, Washington, D.C.

8. Cherokee chiefs and headmen to the U.S. Commissioners, July 2, 1817, *American State Papers, Indian Affairs*, II, 142-143.

9. Clarence E. Carter, ed., *The Territorial Papers of the United States* (Washington, D.C., 1934-), V, 142-146.

10. *Annals of Congress*, 17th Cong., 1st sess., p. 555; *American State Papers, Indian Affairs*, II, 259-260. In a treaty early in 1821 the federal government had failed to obtain enough land to satisfy Georgia, 7 *U.S. Stats.*, pp. 215-218.

11. *Annals of Congress*, 17th Cong., 2nd sess., pp. 318, 391-395, 487, 1087-89, 1093-94, 1168, 1372-73.

12. The Mississippi pressures can be followed in De Rosier, *Removal of the Choctaw Indians*, pp. 48-80. For Alabama see *Annals of Congress*, 17th Cong., 2nd sess., 224, 793, 1056-57. Also War Department, Letters Sent, Indians Affairs, E: 387-388.

13. War Department, Secretary's Office, Letters Received, Indian Affairs, 1822-1823, letter of George M. Troup, Dec. 22, 1823, and enclosures.

14. Adams, ed., *Memoirs of John Quincy Adams*, VI, 255-256; also, ibid., p. 262; Edward J. Harden, *The Life of George M. Troup* (Savannah, Ga., 1859), pp. 216-218.

15. Troup to Calhoun, Feb. 28, 1824, in *American State Papers, Indian Affairs*, II, 475-476.

16. Adams, ed., *Memoirs of John Quincy Adams*, VI, 267-268, 271-272.

17. *Annals of Congress*, 18th Cong., 1st sess., pp. 462-471, 1961, 2151, 2695, 3266; *American State Papers, Indian Affairs*, II, 495-498.

18. *American State Papers, Indian Affairs*, II, 541-544.

19. See Francis P. Prucha, *American Indian Policy in the Formative Years: The Indian Trade and Intercourse Acts, 1790-1834* (Cambridge, Mass.: Harvard University Press, 1962), pp. 229-231.

20. Adams, ed., *Memoirs of John Quincy Adams*, VII, 89-90, 92.

21. Ibid., VII, 113.

22. See George A. Schultz, *An Indian Canaan: Isaac McCoy and the Vision of an Indian State* (Norman: University of Oklahoma Press, 1972).

23. *American State Papers, Indians Affairs*, II, 646-649.

24. Ebenezer C. Tracy, *Memoir of the Life of Jeremiah Evarts* (Boston, 1845), p. 271.

25. McKenney in 1827 was sent to visit the southern tribes to help persuade them to move; it was at this time that he determined that this was for the good of the Indians; Thomas L. McKenney, *Memoirs, Official and Personal: With Sketches of Travels among the Northern and Southern Indians*, 2 vols. in 1, 2nd ed. (New York, 1846), I, 60-61, 159-161, 167, 315-317.

26. Isaac McCoy, *History of the Baptist Indian Missions* (New York, 1840), p. 399.

27. See McKenney, *Memoirs*, pp. 349-351; [Jeremiah Evarts], *Essays on the Present Crisis in the Condition of the Indians* (Boston, 1829), pp. 102-103; W. David Baird, *Peter Pitchlynn: Chief of the Choctaws* (Norman: University of Oklahoma Press, 1972); De Rosier, *Removal of the Choctaw*, pp. 98-112; Mary Elizabeth Young, *Redskins, Ruffleshirts and Rednecks: Indian Allotments in Alabama and Mississippi, 1830-1860* (Norman: University of Oklahoma Press, 1961), pp. 14-20; Michael P. Rogin, *Fathers and Children: Andrew Jackson and the Subjugation of the American Indian* (New York: Knopf, 1975), pp. 206-248; Ronald N. Satz, *American Indian Policy in the Jacksonian Era* (Lincoln: University of Nebraska Press, 1975).

28. *Speeches on the Passage of the Bill for the Removal of the Indians, Delivered in the Congress of the United States, April and May, 1830* (1830; reprint ed., Millwood, N.Y.: Kraus, 1973), p. 265, May 19, 1830.

29. Ibid., passim; Young, *Redskins, Ruffleshirts and Rednecks*, pp. 44-74, 192; De Rosier, *Removal of the Choctaw*, pp. 100-167; Satz, *American Indian Policy*, pp. 64-125.

30. "Removal of the Indians," *North American Review*, 30 (1830): 69-73, 76, 79.

31. James D. Richardson, *A Compilation of the Messages and Papers of the Presidents*, 20 vols. (New York, 1897-1917), III, 1084.

32. *Register of Debates*, 21st Cong., 1st sess., p. 1083, Richard H. Wilde of Georgia, May 19, 1830.

33. Thomas R. Dew, *Review of the Debate in the Virginia Legislature of 1831 and 1832* (Richmond, 1832), pp. 32-34.

34. Alexis de Tocqueville, *Democracy in America*, ed. J. P. Mayer and Max Lerner, 2 vols. in 1 (1835; reprint ed., New York: Harper & Row, 1966), I, 308-312.

35. *Congressional Globe*, 24th Cong., 1st sess., appendix, p. 486. June 29, 1836.

36. *Register of Debates*, 23rd Cong., 1st sess., pp. 4776-77, June 25, 1834.

37. Ibid., 23rd Cong., 2nd sess., p. 1461, Feb. 23, 1835.

38. *Congressional Globe*, 25th Cong., 2nd sess., appendix, p. 269, April 18, 1838.

39. Ibid., 27th Cong., 2nd sess., appendix, p. 503, June 12, 1842.

40. Ibid., 25th Cong., 2nd sess., appendix, p. 470, May 24, 1838.

41. Ibid., 25th Cong., 3rd sess., appendix, p. 162, Feb. 1839.

42. Webster to Hiram Ketchum, May 12, 1838, in *The Writings and Speeches of Daniel Webster*, 18 vols. (Boston: Little, Brown, 1903), XVI, 297.

43. See Michael C. Coleman, "Not Race but Grace: Presbyterian Missionaries and American Indians, 1837-1893," *Journal of American History*, 67 (June 1980): 41-60; Francis P. Prucha, "American Indian Policy in the 1840's: Visions of Reform," in John G. Clark, ed., *The Frontier Challenge: Responses to the Trans-Mississippi West* (Lawrence: University Press of Kansas, 1971), pp. 81-110. Prucha argues in "The Image of the Indian in Pre-Civil War America," *Indiana Historical Society Lectures, 1970-1971: American Indian Policy* (Indianapolis: Indiana Historical Society, 1971), pp. 3-19, that the prevailing opinion was that the Indian was equal and improvable.

44. McCoy, *History of Baptist Indian Missions*, pp. 577-587.

45. McKenney, *Memoirs*, II, 80, 128. See also *North American Review*, 63 (Oct. 1846): 481-496; 64 (April 1847): 292-314; *American Whig Review*, 1 (May 1845): 502-510; 5 (June 1847): 614-629; 9 (April 1849): 385-398; 9 (June 1849): 631-637; Henry R. Schoolcraft, *Notes on the Iroquois* (Albany, 1847); Schoolcraft, *Information Respecting the History, Condition and Prospects of the Indian Tribes of the United States*, 6 vols. (Philadelphia, 1851-1857).

46. Lewis H. Morgan, *League of the Ho-de-no-sau-nee or Iroquois*, ed. Herbert M. Lloyd, 2 vols. (1851; reprint ed., New York: Dodd, Mead, 1901), II, 108-111, 117, 120-121.

11 Anglo-Saxons and Mexicans

1. *Register of Debates*, 24th Cong., 1st sess., p. 201, Jan. 19, 1836.
2. Quoted in Thomas L. Karnes, *William Gilpin: Western Nationalist* (Austin: University of Texas Press, 1970), p. 39.
3. Horace Bushnell, *An Oration, Pronounced before the Society of Phi Beta Kappa, at New Haven, on the Principles of National Greatness*, (August 15, 1837), pp. 5, 9, 11, 16.
4. Quoted in Robert F. Heizer and Alan M. Almquist, *The Other Californians: Prejudice and Discrimination under Spain, Mexico, and the United States to 1920* (Berkeley and Los Angeles: University of California Press, 1971), p. 140.
5. Richard Henry Dana, *Two Years before the Mast*, intro. Charles Warren Stoddard (1840; New York, 1899), chaps. 13 and 21.
6. Lansford Hastings, *The Emigrants' Guide to Oregon and California* (1845; reprint ed., New York, Da Capo, 1969), chaps. 13 and 21.
7. George Wilkins Kendall, *Narrative of the Texan Santa Fé Expedition*, intro. Milo M. Quaife (Chicago: R. R. Donnelley & Sons, 1929), p. 512.
8. David J. Weber, ed., *Foreigners in Their Native Land: Historical Roots of the Mexican Americans* (Albuquerque: University of New Mexico Press, 1973), p. 72.
9. Waddy Thompson, *Recollections of Mexico* (New York, 1847), pp. 204, 239.
10. Ibid., pp. 6, 23, 187, 239.
11. See Gene M. Brack, *Mexico Views Manifest Destiny, 1821-1846: An Essay on the Origins of the Mexican War* (Albuquerque: University of New Mexico Press, 1975), pp. 46, 104, 120, 169-181; Glenn W. Price, *Origins of the War with Mexico: The Polk-Stockton Intrigue* (Austin: University of Texas Press, 1967), p. 17; Weber, ed., *Foreigners in Their Native Land*, pp. 59-60.
12. *Congressional Globe*, 24th Cong., 1st sess., appendix, p. 512, July 1, 1836.
13. Inaugural, Oct. 22, 1836, Houston to Anna Raguet, New Year 1837, Houston to Santa Anna, March 21, 1842, in Amelia W. Williams and Eugene C. Barker, eds., *The Writings of Sam Houston, 1813-1863*, 8 vols. (Austin: University of Texas Press, 1938-1943), I, 450, II, 31, 526-527.

14. Houston to Capt. Charles Elliot, May 13, 1843, ibid., III, 386.
15. Houston to William S. Murphy, May 6, 1844, ibid., IV, 324, 403.
16. *Mobile Register and Journal,* Jan. 4, 1842.
17. S. P. Griswold to R. W. Griswold, Sept. 29, 1842, in *Passages from the Correspondence and Other Papers of Rufus W. Griswold* (Cambridge, Mass., 1898), pp. 124-125.
18. *Congressional Globe,* 24th Cong., 1st sess., p. 394, May 23, 1836.
19. See James P. Shenton, *Robert John Walker: A Politician from Jackson to Lincoln* (New York: Columbia University Press, 1961). Also "Memoirs of Robert J. Walker by Mrs. M. W. Cook (1873)," Robert J. Walker Papers, Library of Congress, Washington, D.C.; "Robert J. Walker," *Democratic Review,* 16 (Feb. 1845): 157-164.
20. *Congressional Globe,* 28th Cong., 1st sess., appendix, p. 557, May 20 and 21, 1844.
21. *Letter of Mr. Walker, of Mississippi, Relative to the Reannexation of Texas: In Reply to the Call of the People of Carroll County, Kentucky to Communicate His Views on That Subject* (Philadelphia 1844), pp. 13-15. See also Frederick Merk, *Fruits of Propaganda in the Tyler Administration* (Cambridge, Mass.: Harvard University Press, 1971), pp. 21-26. Walker's general argument, without the racial overtones regarding Latin Americans, had been used as early as the first decade of the nineteenth century by those who maintained that the Louisiana Purchase would encourage the wide dispersal of slaves and the eventual eradication of slavery; see MacLeod, *Slavery, Race, and the American Revolution,* pp. 57-58.
22. *Congressional Globe,* 28th Cong., 1st sess., appendix, p. 450, May 7, 1844. See also *Democratic Review,* 15 (July 1844): 3-16; *Southern Quarterly Review,* 6 (Oct. 1844): 483-520; *Southern Literary Messenger,* 10 (May 1844): 315-326.
23. Buchanan, speeches, June 8, 1844, Feb. 14, 1845, in Moore, ed., *Works of Buchanan,* V, 11-12, 15-16, 40-41, 100, 106.
24. *Congressional Globe,* 28th Cong., 1st sess., appendix, pp. 764, 766, 771, June 4, 1844.
25. Ibid., 28th Cong., 2nd sess., appendix, pp. 212, 313, Jan. 23, 25, 1845.
26. Ibid., appendix, pp. 96-97, Jan. 14, 1845. See also ibid., appendix, p. 43, Jan. 3, 1845 (James Belser of Alabama).
27. *Democratic Review,* 17 (July-Aug. 1845): 5-10.
28. See Julius W. Pratt, "The Origin of Manifest Destiny," *Amer-*

ican Historical Review, 32 (July 1927): 795-798, 796 (quotation); Pratt, "John L. O'Sullivan and Manifest Destiny," *New York History*, 14 (July 1933): 213-234.

29. William Howard Russell, *My Diary North and South*, ed. Fletcher Pratt (New York: Harper, 1954), p. 101.

30. *Congressional Globe*, 29th Cong., 1st sess., appendix, p. 116, Jan. 14, 1846.

31. *Speech of Mr. Walker, of Mississippi, on the Bill to Provide for Collection, Safe-Keeping and Disbursement of the Public Monies.* Senate, Jan. 21, 1840 (Baltimore, 1840).

32. *Congressional Globe*, 28th Cong., 2nd sess., appendix, p. 163, Jan. 29, 1845.

33. Ibid., 29th Cong., 1st sess., appendix, p. 177, Jan. 15, 1846.

34. Ibid., appendix, p. 143, Jan. 26, 1846.

35. *Merchants' Magazine and Commercial Review*, 14 (May 1846): 435-439.

36. Speech of July 4, 1839, quoted in Fred Somkin, *Unquiet Eagle: Memory and Desire in the Idea of American Freedom, 1815-1860* (Ithaca, N.Y.: Cornell University Press, 1967), p. 64.

37. *Congressional Globe*, 25th Cong., 2nd sess., appendix, pp. 569-570, May 17 and 22, 1838.

38. See Parker to George Bancroft, Nov. 18, 1845, in Frothingham, *Theodore Parker*, p. 382. The *Casket* (Cincinnati), April 22, 1846, said that war between England and America would be "the most direful catastrophe that could befal humanity." (p. 11)

39. Speech on the Oregon question at Faneuil Hall, Boston, Nov. 7, 1845, in *Writings and Speeches of Daniel Webster*, XVI, 314-315.

40. *Congressional Globe*, 29th Cong., 1st sess., appendix, p. 475, March 16, 1846.

41. Ibid., 28th Cong., 1st sess., appendix, pp. 239-240 (Atchison, Feb 22, 1844); ibid., 27th Cong., 3rd sess., appendix, pp. 152, 154 (Linn, Jan. 26, 1843); ibid., 28th Cong., 1st sess., appendix, pp. 585, 588 (Choate, March 21, 1844).

42. See Sam Bass Warner, Jr., *The Private City: Philadelphia in Three Periods of Its Growth* (Philadelphia: University of Pennsylvania Press, 1968), pp. 125-157; David Brion Davis, *The Slave Power Conspiracy and the Paranoid Style* (Baton Rouge: Louisiana State University Press, 1969), pp. 26-28; Seymour Martin Lipset and Earl Raab, *The Politics of Unreason: Right Wing Extremism in America, 1790-1877*, 2nd ed. (Chicago: University of Chicago Press, 1978), pp. 47-67; Ray A. Billington, *The Protestant Crusade, 1800–*

1860: A Study of the Origins of American Nativism (New York: Macmillan, 1938).

43. Quoted in Billington, *Protestant Crusade,* p. 205.
44. Hone to Clay, Nov. 28, 1844, in *Works of Clay,* V, 509.
45. Winthrop, "Address to the New England Society of New York, 1839," in Brainerd and Brainerd, *New England Society Orations,* I, 240, 244, 248-250.
46. Everett, reply to a toast at Derby, July 13, 1843, in Everett, *Orations and Speeches,* II, 466.
47. Webster, reply to a toast, 1843, in Brainerd and Brainerd, eds., *New England Society Orations,* I, 364-370.
48. *New York Herald,* Nov. 24, 1840, quoted in Stuart Creighton Miller, *The Unwelcome Immigrant: The American Image of the Chinese, 1785-1882* (Berkeley and Los Angeles: University of California Press, 1969), p. 96; also ibid., pp. 104-106.
49. *Congressional Globe,* 28th Cong., 2nd sess., p. 88 (Belser, Jan. 3, 1845), appendix, p. 178 (Duncan, Jan. 29, 1845).
50. Sanders to R. J. Walker, March 17, 1844, in Robert J. Walker Papers, Library of Congress.
51. *Congressional Globe,* 27th Cong., 1st sess., appendix, p. 227 (Ferris, July 17, 1841); ibid., 27th Cong., 3rd sess., appendix, p. 111 (Reynolds, Jan. 30, 1843).

12 Race, Expansion, and the Mexican War

1. Shannon to Calhoun, Oct. 29, 1844, "Correspondence of John C. Calhoun," ed. by Franklin Jameson, American Historical Association, *Annual Report,* 1899, II (Washington, D.C., 1900), 981.
2. Slidell to Buchanan, Sept. 25, 1845, in John B. Moore, ed., *The Works of James Buchanan,* 12 vols. (1908-1911; reprint ed., New York: Antiquarian Press, 1960), VI, 264.
3. Marcy to Prosper Wetmore, July 6, 1845, June 13, 1846, in William L. Marcy Papers, Library of Congress.
4. Buchanan to Slidell, Nov. 10, 1845, in Moore, ed., *Works of Buchanan,* VI, 305.
5. William M'Carty, comp., *National Songs, Ballads, and Other Patriotic Poetry, Chiefly Relating to the War of 1846* (Philadelphia, 1846), pp. 12, 22, 37.
6. Ibid., p. 45.
7. Dana, *Two Years before the Mast,* intro. Stoddard, chap. 21; Kendall, *Narrative of the Texan Santa Fé Expedition* (1929 ed.), pp. 428, 432-433; Weber, ed., *Foreigners in Their Native Land,* p. 174.

8. *De Bow's Review*, 1 (Feb. 1846): 130-131; also ibid., 2 (July 1846): 21-24.

9. *New York Herald*, May 15, 1847, quoted in John D. P. Fuller, *The Movement for the Acquisition of All Mexico, 1846-1848* (Baltimore: Johns Hopkins University Press, 1936), pp. 62-63.

10. *Congressional Globe*, 30th Cong., 1st sess., appendix, p. 349, Feb. 14, 1848.

11. *Brooklyn Daily Eagle*, June 6, July 7, Oct. 13, 1846, Dec. 2, 1847, in Walt Whitman, *The Gathering of the Forces*, ed. by Cleveland Rodgers and John Black, 2 vols. (New York: G. P. Putnam's Sons, 1920), I, 242-244, 246-248, 264-266. See also Kramer, *Prophetic Tradition in American Poetry*, pp. 60-62.

12. *Casket*, May 13, 1846, p. 37, June 10, 1846, p. 69.

13. *Illinois State Register*, July 17, 1846, quoted in Fuller, *Movement for the Acquisition of All Mexico*, p. 41.

14. *American Whig Review*, 4 (July 1846): 14.

15. LeRoy P. Graf and Ralph W. Haskins, eds., *The Papers of Andrew Johnson* (Knoxville: University of Tennessee Press, 1967-), I, 312, 366, 456, May 29-30, 1846, Jan. 5, 1847, Aug. 2, 1848.

16. *Congressional Globe*, 28th Cong., 2nd sess., appendix, p. 397, Feb. 21 and 22, 1845; see also ibid., pp. 353, 354.

17. Ibid., 29th Cong., 1st sess., appendix, p. 201, Jan. 30, 1846; also ibid., p. 184. There is an extensive discussion of Whig opposition to the war in John H. Schroeder, *Mr. Polk's War: American Opposition and Dissent, 1846-1848* (Madison; University of Wisconsin Press, 1973).

18. *Charleston Mercury*, May 25, 1846; *Richmond Whig*, June 10, 1846; *Cincinnati Herald and Philanthropist*, June 17, 1846; *Augusta Daily Chronicle and Sentinel*, July 31, 1846. I would like to thank Professor John H. Schroeder of the University of Wisconsin-Milwaukee for allowing me to use his extensive collection of extracts from Whig newspapers.

19. *Richmond Whig*, Oct. 9, 1846; *Chicago Daily Journal*, Oct. 30, 1846.

20. *Congressional Globe*, 29th Cong., 2nd sess., appendix, pp. 131, 133, Jan. 26, 1847; also ibid., p. 339.

21. Ibid., p. 281, Feb. 2, 1847; Joseph Morrow, *Life and Speeches of Thomas Corwin* (Cincinnati, 1896), p. 289, Feb. 11, 1847.

22. *Democratic Review*, 18 (June 1846): 434, 477.

23. Buchanan to General James Shields, April 23, 1847, in Moore, ed., *Works of Buchanan*, VII, 286-287.

24. *Congressional Globe*, 29th Cong., 2nd sess., appendix, p. 327, Feb. 9, 1847.

25. Ibid., p. 191, Feb. 10, 1847.

26. Ibid., 30th Cong., 1st sess., pp. 98-99, Jan. 4, 1848.

27. Webster, speech on the Mexican War, Springfield, Mass., Sept. 29, 1847, in *Writings and Speeches of Daniel Webster*, XVI, 351, 360.

28. *Congressional Globe*, 30th Cong., 1st sess., p. 162 (Clayton, Jan. 12, 1848); p. 283 (Collamer, Feb. 1, 1848); p. 299 (Bell, Feb. 3, 1848); p. 429 (Cabell, March 4, 1848).

29. Williams and Barker *Writings of Sam Houston*, V, 34-35.

30. *Congressional Globe*, 30th Cong., 1st sess., p. 256 (Dix, Jan. 26, 1848); p. 158 (Dickinson, Jan. 12, 1848).

31. *Democratic Review*, 20 (Feb. 1847): 99-100.

32. Ibid., 21 (Nov. 1847): 381-382, 388-390.

33. Ibid., 20 (June 1847): 484-485; 21 (Oct. 1847): 291.

34. James K. Polk, *The Diary of James K. Polk during His Presidency, 1845-1849*, ed. Milo M. Quaife, 4 vols. (Chicago: A. C. McClurg, 1910), II, 159-161, 162-165, 217, 276-277, 347-349.

35. *Richmond Palladium*, March 8, 1848.

36. *American Whig Review*, 7 (May 1848): 448.

37. *Louisville Democrat*, March 9, 1848, quoted in Merk, *Manifest Destiny and Mission*, pp. 151-152.

38. *Southern Quarterly Review*, 18 (Nov. 1850): 428.

39. *Congressional Globe*, 32nd Cong., 3rd sess., appendix, p. 270, March 15, 1853.

40. Polk to Senate and House of Representatives, April 29, 1848, in *Congressional Globe*, 30th Cong., 1st sess., p. 709; Quaife, ed., *Diary of Polk*, III, 444-445.

41. *Congressional Globe*, 30th Cong., 1st sess., p. 711 (Ingersoll, April 29, 1848); p. 712 (Root, April 29, 1848).

42. Report of the Secretary of the Navy, Dec. 4, 1848, ibid., 30th Cong., 2nd sess., appendix, p. 23.

13 A Confused Minority

1. Moore, ed., *Works of Buchanan*, VIII, 409, Jan. 11, 1851; *Congressional Globe*, 32nd Cong., 2nd sess., appendix, p. 275 (Douglas, March 16, 1853).

2. *Democratic Review*, 22 (March 1848): 207.

3. *Congressional Globe*, 28th Cong., 1st sess., appendix, p. 576, June 12, 1844.

4. Ibid., 29th Cong., 1st sess., pp. 917-918, May 28, 1846; ibid., 27th Cong., 3rd sess., appendix, p. 74, Jan. 12, 1843.

5. Claude M. Fuess, *Life of Caleb Cushing*, 2 vols. (New York: Harcourt, Brace & Company, 1923), II, 230-231, Feb. 1859.

6. Ibid., II, 194-195, speech at Newburyport, April 23, 1857.

7. *American Whig Review*, 5 (March 1847): 231-233, 239.

8. Melville, *Redburn: His First Voyage* (1849), quoted in Hans Kohn, *American Nationalism: An Interpretive Essay* (New York: Macmillan, 1957), p. 148.

9. *White Jacket* ("The Works of Herman Melville," 16 vols., London, 1922-1924; reprint ed., New York: Russell & Russell, 1963), p. 189.

10. *Mardi* (reprint ed., New York: Russell & Russell, 1963), II, 245. See also Louise K. Barnett, *The Ignoble Savage: American Literary Racism, 1790-1890* (Westport, Conn.: Greenwood, 1975), p. 166-184; Carolyn L. Karcher, "Melville's 'The 'Gees': A Forgotten Satire on Scientific Racism," *American Quarterly*, 27 (Oct. 1975): 421-442.

11. *Southern Quarterly Review*, 17 (July 1850): 312.

12. Julia Webster Appleton to Daniel Webster, Feb. 23, 1848, in C. H. Van Tyne, ed., *The Letters of Daniel Webster from Documents Owned Principally by the New Hampshire Historical Society* (1902; reprint ed., New York: Greenwood, 1968), p. 604. See also Merk, *Manifest Destiny and Mission*, pp. 153-156; Schroeder, *Mr. Polk's War*.

13. Quoted in Edgar A. Holt, *Party Politics in Ohio, 1840-1850* (Columbus, Ohio: F. J. Heer Printing Co., 1931), p. 283.

14. *Richmond Whig*, Jan. 7, 1848.

15. *Congressional Globe*, 32nd Cong., 1st sess., appendix, p. 304, March 18, 1852.

16. Ibid., 30th Cong., 1st sess., p. 347, Feb. 14, 1848.

17. Ibid., 33rd Cong., 1st sess., appendix, p. 55 (Israel Washburn of Maine, Jan. 4, 1854).

18. *De Bow's Review*, 15 (Dec. 1853): 590.

19. Thoreau to H. Blake, Feb. 27, 1853, quoted in Arthur A. Ekirch, Jr., *The Idea of Progress in America, 1815-1860* (1944; reprint ed., New York: Peter Smith, 1951), pp. 163-164. See also William W. Greenough, *The Conquering Republic: An Oration Delivered before the Municipal Authorities of Boston, July 4, 1849* (Boston, 1849), p. 33; *National Intelligencer*, Dec. 15, 1846.

20. *New Englander*, 5 (Jan. 1847): 140-142.

21. Ibid., 4 (July 1846): 428-430.

22. *Massachusetts Quarterly Review*, 1 (Dec. 1847): 10, 11, 51.

23. *American Whig Review*, 6 (Nov. 1847): 441, 444, 451.

24. *North American Review*, 56 (April 1848): 426, 430-431.

25. *American Whig Review*, 3 (June 1846): 565.

26. *Congressional Globe*, 29th Cong., 2nd sess., appendix, p. 272, Jan. 28, 1847.

27. Ibid., pp. 214, 216, Feb. 11, 1847.

28. *National Intelligencer*, Dec. 25, 1846, June 8, Dec. 18, 1847.

29. Ibid., Jan. 15, 1848.

30. *Democratic Review*, 28, (March 1851): 242.

31. Lieber to George S. Hillard, in Perry, ed., *Life and Letters of Lieber*, pp. 245-246.

32. *Congressional Globe*, 32nd Cong., 1st sess., appendix, p. 178, Feb. 7, 1852.

33. Sumner, *The Law of Human Progress* (1849), quoted in Ekirch, *Idea of Progress*, p. 258.

34. *National Anti-Slavery Standard*, June 4, 1846; *National Era*, Aug. 19, 1847; *Liberator*, Jan. 21, 1848.

35. *Congressional Globe*, 29th Cong., 1st sess., appendix, p. 644, May 12, 1846.

36. James Russell Lowell, *The Anti-Slavery Papers of James Russell Lowell*, 2 vols. (Boston: Houghton Mifflin, 1902), I, 19-20, Feb. 13, 1845.

37. Ibid., I, 25, Feb. 1849.

38. Ibid., II, 142-146, Nov. 1849. See also Barbara Miller Solomon, *Ancestors and Immigrants: A Changing New England Tradition* (Cambridge, Mass.: Harvard University Press, 1956), pp. 8-9.

39. Lowell, *Anti-Slavery Papers*, I, 22, 1845.

40. Alexander Kinmont, *Twelve Lectures on the Natural History of Man and the Rise and Progress of Philosophy* (Cincinnati, 1839), pp. 172, 188, 190-193, 215, 221, 241, 245. See also Fredrickson, *Black Image*, pp. 101-112; Ronald G. Walters, *The Anti-Slavery Appeal: American Abolitionism after 1830* (Baltimore: Johns Hopkins University Press, 1976), pp. 57-60.

41. *North American Review*, 68 (April 1849): 265, 267. For a discussion of the extent to which abolitionists accepted the idea of innate black inferiority, see William H. Pease and Jane H. Pease, "Antislavery Ambivalence: Immediatism, Expediency, Race," *American Quarterly*, 17 (Winter 1965): 682-695.

42. Charles Anderson, *An Address on Anglo-Saxon Destiny: Delivered before the Philomathesian Society of Kenyon College, Ohio, August 8, 1849 and Repeated before the New England Society of Cincinnati: December 20, 1849* (Cincinnati, 1850), pp. 3-4.

43. Ibid., pp. 4-5, 8-10.

44. Ibid., pp. 10-11.

45. Ibid., pp. 12-26. Ohio physician Daniel Drake also pointed out that "Anglo-Saxon" was not an accurate description of the existing English race but rather "an arbitrary epithet for a compound of Celts, Romans, Angles, Saxons, Jutes or Danes, and Normans," in *Systematic Treatise* (1850), quoted in Henry D. Shapiro and Zane L. Miller, eds., *Physician to the West: Selected Writings of Daniel Drake on Science and Society* (Lexington: University Press of Kentucky, 1970), p. 346.

46. Anderson, *An Address on Anglo-Saxon Destiny*, pp. 29-45.

47. Gallatin, "Peace with Mexico" (1847), in Henry Adams, ed., *The Writings of Albert Gallatin*, 3 vols. (1879; reprint ed., New York: Antiquarian Press, 1960), III, 581-586.

48. Gallatin to Garrett Davis, Feb. 16, 1848, in ibid., II, 661-662.

14 Expansion and World Mission

1. George Fitzhugh, *Sociology for the South, or, the Failure of Free Society* (1854; reprint ed., New York: Burt Franklin, n.d.), pp. 231, 266-267.

2. Ibid., p. 287.

3. *Congressional Globe*, 29th Cong., 2nd sess., appendix, p. 363, Feb. 13, 1847.

4. Ibid., 30th Cong., 2nd sess., appendix, p. 118, Feb. 3, 1849.

5. Ibid., appendix, p. 156, Feb. 17, 1849.

6. Tocqueville, *Democracy in America*, ed. Mayer and Lerner, I, 315-316.

7. Leonard L. Richards, *Gentlemen of Property and Standing: Anti-Abolition Mobs in Jacksonian America* (New York: Oxford University Press, 1970), pp. 3-19, 31, 45-46, 155, 157-164; also Lorman Ratner, *Powder Keg: Northern Opposition to the Antislavery Movement, 1831-1840* (New York: Basic Books, 1968), pp. 4-5.

8. Eric Foner, "Racial Attitudes of the New York Free Soilers," *New York History*, 46 (Oct. 1965): 311-329; Foner, "Politics and Prejudice: The Free Soil Party and the Negro, 1849-1852," *Journal of Negro History*, 50 (Oct. 1967): 239-256; James A. Rawley, *Race and Politics: "Bleeding Kansas" and the Coming of the Civil War* (Philadelphia: Lippincott, 1969), pp. 12-13.

9. Eugene H. Berwanger, *The Frontier against Slavery: Western Anti-Negro Prejudice and the Slavery Extension Controversy* (Urbana: University of Illinois Press, 1967), pp. 4-5, 22, 32-40, 78-84,

91-95, 101-102, 127, 136; Rawley, *Race and Politics*, pp. x-xi, 50-51, 194-198, 258-272; Litwack, *North of Slavery*, pp. 14-15, 24-27, 31, 46-47, 91, 276-277; Eric Foner, *Free Soil, Free Labor, Free Men: The Ideology of the Republican Party before the Civil War* (New York: Oxford University Press, 1970), pp. 261-295; Robert F. Durden, "Ambiguities in the Antislavery Campaign of the Republican Party," in Martin Duberman, ed., *The Antislavery Vanguard: New Essays on the Abolitionists* (Princeton: Princeton University Press, 1965), pp. 363-381; Durden, *James Shepherd Pike: Republicans and the American Negro, 1850-1882* (Durham, N.C.: Duke University Press, 1957), pp. vii-viii, 31-34; cf. the discussion in Richard H. Sewell, *Ballots for Freedom: Antislavery Politics in the United States, 1837-1860* (New York: Oxford University Press, 1976). This is less critical of the antislavery spokesmen.

10. *Congressional Globe*, 33rd Cong., 1st sess., appendix, pp. 212-214, Feb. 20, 1854; 33rd Cong., 2nd sess., appendix, pp. 235-237, Feb. 23, 1855.

11. Ibid., 33rd Cong., 1st sess., appendix, p. 233 (Butler, Feb. 24, 1854), p. 491 (Clingman, April 4, 1854); 34th Cong., 3rd sess., appendix, pp. 228-247 (Evans, Feb. 4, 1857).

12. Ibid., 30th Cong., 1st sess., p. 535, March 23, 1848.

13. Ibid., 30th Cong., 1st sess., appendix, pp. 48-49, July 25, 1848.

14. Ibid., 31st Cong., 1st sess., appendix, p. 1137, July 17, 1850.

15. Quoted in Robert W. Larson, *New Mexico's Quest for Statehood, 1846-1912* (Albuquerque: University of New Mexico Press, 1968), p. 77.

16. *Congressional Globe*, 32nd Cong., 2nd sess., appendix, pp. 103-108, Jan. 10, 1853.

17. J. Ross Browne, *Report of the Debates in the Convention of California, on the Formation of the State Constitution, in September and October, 1849* (Washington, D.C., 1850), p. 63 (quotation), also pp. 7-38, 48-50, 61-74, 137-141, 305-307, 331-341; Berwanger, *Frontier against Slavery*, pp. 65-74; Weber, ed., *Foreigners in Their Native Land*, pp. 148-151.

18. Minority Report of a Special Committee of the California Senate, written by J. J. Walker, quoted in Heizer and Almquist, *The Other Californians*, pp. 74-76, and ibid., pp. 67-74.

19. Quoted in Heizer and Almquist, *The Other Californians*, p. 26. See also Sherburne F. Cook, *The Conflict between the California Indian and White Civilizations*, 4 vols. (Berkeley and Los Angeles: University of California Press, 1943), I, 3, 5, III, 4-5, 92-94; Cook, *The*

Population of the California Indians, 1769-1970 (Berkeley and Los Angeles: University of California Press, 1976), pp. xv, xvi, 43-44.

20. John H. Van Evrie, *Negroes and Negro "Slavery": The First an Inferior Race: The Latter Its Normal Condition*, 3rd ed. (1853; New York, 1863), p. 334.

21. Maury to Herndon, April 20, 1850, in J. G. de Roulhac Hamilton, ed., *The Papers of William Alexander Graham*, 4 vols. (Raleigh, N.C.: State Department of Archives and History, 1957-1961), III, 433-435; Maury to Wm. Blackford, Sept. 24, 1852, in Matthew M. Maury Papers, Library of Congress; Maury, *The Amazon, and Atlantic Slopes of South America* (Washington, D.C., 1853), pp. 49, 63.

22. See Robert E. May, *The Southern Dream of a Caribbean Empire, 1854-1861* (Baton Rouge: Louisiana State University Press, 1973); Ronald T. Takaki, *A Pro-Slavery Crusade: The Agitation to Reopen the African Slave Trade* (New York: Free Press, 1971), pp. 1-6.

23. See Basil Rauch, *American Interest in Cuba, 1848-1855* (New York: Columbia University Press, 1948), pp. 11-30.

24. Quaife, ed., *Diary of Polk*, III, 446, 469, 475-487, 493; Buchanan to Saunders, June 17, 1848, in Moore, ed., *Works of Buchanan*, VIII, 99.

25. Quoted in Durden, *James Shepherd Pike*, p. 31.

26. *De Bow's Review*, 14 (Jan. 1853): 64-66; 14 (May 1853): 421. See also Ottis C. Skipper, *J. D. B. De Bow: Magazinist of the Old South* (Athens: University of Georgia Press, 1958), p. 65.

27. *Congressional Globe*, 32nd Cong., 2nd sess., appendix, p. 1.

28. Ibid., p. 59, Jan. 10, 1853; *De Bow's Review*, 9 (Oct. 1850): 405-412. See also Donald F. Warner, *The Idea of Continental Union: Agitation for the Annexation of Canada to the United States, 1849-1893* (Lexington: University of Kentucky Press, 1960).

29. Quoted in Merle E. Curti, *Probing Our Past* (New York: Harper, 1955), p. 232.

30. For the Young Americans see Siert F. Riepma, " 'Young America': A Study in American Nationalism before the Civil War" (Ph.D. diss., Western Reserve University, 1939); Donald L. Spencer, *Louis Kossuth and Young America: A Study of Sectionalism and Foreign Policy* (Columbia: University of Missouri Press, 1977); Curti, "Young America," in *Probing Our Past*, pp. 219-245; Curti, "George N. Sanders: American Patriot of the Fifties," *South Atlantic Quarterly*, 27 (Jan. 1928): 79-87. See also Corry to Joseph Holt, March 10, Aug. 16, 1852, in Joseph Holt Papers, Library of Congress.

31. *Democratic Review,* 31 (Oct. 1852): 301.
32. Fitzhugh, *Sociology for the South,* pp. 31-32.
33. *Democratic Review,* 32 (May 1853): 395-397, 399, 413-414.
34. *Daily Ohio Statesman* (Columbus), Jan. 15, 1845, clipping in Robert J. Walker Papers, Library of Congress.
35. *Congressional Globe,* 29th Cong., 1st sess., appendix, p. 115 (Hilliard, Jan. 6, 1846); p. 171 (Darragh, Feb. 9, 1846).
36. J. Ross Browne, *Report of the Debates in the Convention of California,* pp. 433-434.
37. *Congressional Globe,* 32nd Cong., 1st sess., appendix, p. 532, April 24, 1852.
38. Elias L. Magoon, *Westward Empire; or, The Great Drama of Human Progress* (New York, 1856), p. vi.
39. *North American Review,* 63 (Oct. 1846): 337, 352-353.
40. Congressional Globe, 32nd Cong., 1st sess., appendix, p. 814 (Dean, July 9, 1852); *Merchants' Magazine and Commercial Review,* 9 (July 1843): 16; *Congressional Globe,* 30th Cong., 2nd sess., appendix, pp. 14-15, Dec. 9, 1848.
41. *Congressional Globe,* 32nd Cong., 2nd sess., appendix, p. 9, Dec. 4, 1852.
42. Simeon North, *Anglo-Saxon Literature: An Oration Delivered before the Connecticut Alpha of the Phi, Beta, Kappa, at New Haven, August 18th, 1847* (Utica, 1847), pp. 5, 7.
43. *Southern Literary Messenger,* 18 (July 1852): 410-411. See also *Democratic Review,* 26 (April 1850): 345.
44. *Congressional Globe,* 32nd Cong., 2nd sess., appendix, p. 238, Feb. 18, 1853.
45. *Putnam's Monthly Review,* 3 (Feb. 1854): 183-184, 191-193.
46. George E. Baker, ed., *The Works of William H. Seward,* new ed., 5 vols. (Boston, 1887-1889), I, 56-58, 103, 248-249; *Congressional Globe,* 32nd Cong., 2nd sess., appendix, p. 147, Feb. 8, 1853. See also Ernest N. Paolino, *The Foundations of the American Empire: William H. Seward and U.S. Foreign Policy* (Ithaca, N.Y.: Cornell University Press, 1973), pp. 25-38.
47. William Gilpin, *The Central Gold Region: The Grain, Pastoral, and Gold Regions of North America, with Some New Views of Its Physical Geography; and Observations on the Pacific Railroad* (Philadelphia, 1860), appendix, speech of Nov. 5, 1849; [Samuel John Bayard], *A Sketch of the Life of Com. Robert F. Stockton* (New York, 1856), appendix, p. 83, speech of July 4, 1851.
48. *Merchants' Magazine and Commercial Review,* 9 (July 1843): 15.

49. *De Bow's Review*, 12 (June 1852): 614-631.
50. *Merchants' Magazine and Commercial Review*, 32 (June 1855): 706-708.
51. *Congressional Globe*, 34th Cong., 1st sess., appendix, p. 1306, July 24, 1856.
52. Quoted in Derek Hudson, *Martin Tupper: His Rise and Fall* (London: Constable, 1949), p. 107.
53. *Southern Literary Messenger*, 16 (Jan. 1850): 1-6.
54. *An Outline of the Empire of the West . . . Shadowed in Correspondence between the Hon. R. J. Walker, Late Secretary of the Treasury of the United States, and Arthur Davies, Commander, R.N.* (London, 1852), pp. 13, 21-22.
55. Walker, toast at a Philadelphia dinner, in the *Buffalo Commercial Advertiser*, Aug. 3, 1847, clipping in Robert J. Walker Papers, Library of Congress.
56. Browne to Lucy Browne, June 5, 1849, in Lina Fergusson Browne, ed., *J. Ross Browne: His Letters, Journals and Writings* (Albuquerque: University of New Mexico Press, 1969), p. 112.
57. Theodore Poesche and Charles Goepp, *The New Rome; or, The United States of the World* (New York, 1853), pp. 99-100, 105. See also Spencer, *Louis Kossuth and Young America*, pp. 11-12, 170; Eitel W. Dobert, "The Radicals," in Adolf E. Zucker, ed., *The Forty-Eighters: Political Refugees of the German Revolution of 1848* (New York: Columbia University Press, 1950), pp. 156-167.
58. Poesche and Goepp, *New Rome*, pp. 48-55.
59. Ibid., pp. 27, 46.
60. Ibid., pp. 55-57.
61. Ibid., pp. 13-14, 16, 20-22, 76-77, 81, 87, 88, 177-178.

Index

Adams, John, 16, 22, 86, 87
Adams, John Quincy, 92, 197, 198
Adams, Sam, 18
Adelung, Johann Christoph, 33, 37
Agassiz, Louis, 125, 132, 133, 134, 147, 149
Alabama: and the Indians, 192-201 *passim*
Amazon, valley of the, 180, 280-281
American Board of Commissioners for Foreign Missions, 200
American Party, 290
American race: distinct from all others, 4, 164, 249, 250-256, 285, 290, 301-302
American Revolutionary League for Europe, 294
American school of ethnology, 102, 125-133, 146, 151
American Whig Review: and ethnology, 139; and phrenology, 142; and Indians, 150; and Mexican War, 236-237, 245, 260; and American race, 254-255; and American aggression, 259; mentioned, 149
Anderson, Charles, 266-269
Anglo-Norman race, 164-171 *passim*, 292
Anglo-Saxon, The, 74-75
Anglo-Saxon England, myth of: in colonial America, 3-4, 9, 15-17, 81; in England, 10-15, 63-77; in American Revolution, 17-18, 23, 81; Thomas Jefferson and, 18-23; Romantic movement and, 38-41; Scott and, in America, 160-161; and Anglo-Normans, 164-165, 166-168, 171
Anglo-Saxon race: Americans as

Anglo-Saxons, 1-2, 4, 94-96, 97, 128, 170-171, 177-178, 183, 198, 213-214, 217-218, 221-228, 243-244, 302-303; definitions of, 4, 268; and the Germanic tribes, 11-12, 14-15, 19-20, 37-39, 63-69, 74, 75-77, 154, 169-171, 173-174, 183-184, 289-290; as Caucasians, 44, 58-59, 69-71, 156, 159-160, 178-179, 210; and the Norse peoples, 63-64, 72, 76, 177, 180-182; and world mission, 74-75, 172, 230, 243, 267, 292-296, 302-303; origins of use as a racial term, 94-95, 208-209; and Anglo-Norman myth, 164-165, 166-168, 171
Anthropometry; and race, 54-56
Antislavery movement, 176-177, 263-265, 274, 275
Appleton, Julia Webster, 257
Archer, William, 204
Arnold, Thomas, 65-66, 173
Arthurian legends, 10-11
Aryanism: and American racialism, 5; development of myth of, 24, 32, 36, 295; popularization of term, 34; in *Edinburgh Review*, 68; Latham and, 71; mentioned, 1. *See also* Germanic peoples; Teutonism
Asia: peoples of, 4, 253, 256; as origin of races, 33-34, 35, 36, 37; American interest in, 86, 90, 91, 92, 286-290, 291; civilization of, 91, 271, 286-287
Asiatic Researches, 33
Astor, John Jacob, 87
Atchison, David R., 224
Atkins, John, 48
Augusta Daily Chronicle, 239
Australia, 45, 296

Bachman, John, 133
Bancroft, George, 162, 163, 182-183
Barbour, James, 88, 96-97, 197-200
Bartley, Mordecai, 257
Bayley, Thomas H., 277
Becamus, Goropius, 11

Bell, Hiram, 283
Bell, John, 118
Belser, James E., 228
Bennett, John Gordon, 227, 234
Benton, Thomas Hart: and expansion, 87, 91; and westward movement of civilization, 89-90, 91-92, 252-253; racial views, 90-91, 164, 205, 213, 252-253; and Asian trade, 90, 92; and Texas Revolution, 213; and Mexican War, 232
Berkeley, George, 83
Bernier, François, 46
Bible: and unity of man, 45, 117, 124, 126, 132, 133, 148, 149; challenged, 119, 136, 140; flippant tone toward, 152. *See also* Christianity; Religion
Bigelow, John, 148
Bird, Robert Montgomery, 191
Blacks: eighteenth century condemnations of, 48, 49-50, 51; attitude toward in early national period, 100-103; science and, 119-120, 122, 130-131, 132, 153-154; phrenologists and, 121-122, 144-145; southern view of, 122-125, 140-142, 153-154, 300; Theodore Parker on, 178-180; in Mexico, 212, 216; as natural Christians, 264-266; antagonism to, in North, 274-275. *See also* Slavery
Blackwell, I. A., 67-68
Bland, Richard, 18
Blumenbach, Johann Friedrich: classification of mankind, 47; and anthropometry, 54, 55; challenged, 71, 124; in American thought, 98, 126; mentioned, 49, 52, 54, 69, 141, 142
Bodichon, Eugène, 275
Bopp, Franz, 34-35
Boulainvilliers, Henri, comte de, 28
Bouldin, James W., 203
Bowlin, James B., 221
Brackenridge, Hugh Henry, 85, 98, 112-114, 204-205
Breese, Sidney, 235

Brigham, Amariah, 121
Brooke, James, 77, 319
Brooklyn Daily Eagle, 235
Brown, Charles, 274
Brown, William J., 218
Browne, J. Ross, 293-294
Bruno, Giordano, 45
Buchanan, James, 208, 217, 232, 240-241, 251, 282
Buffon, Georges Louis Leclerc, comte de, 47, 49, 52, 105, 154
Bulkeley, Peter, 82-83
Burgh, James, 21
Burnaby, Andrew, 84
Burnett, Peter H., 279
Burns, Robert, 63
Bushnell, Horace, 209
Butler, Andrew Pickens, 251, 276

Cabell, Edward C., 242
Caldwell, Charles, 117-120, 128, 143
Calhoun, John C., 194, 196-197, 223-224, 241
California: people of, 182, 210-211, 243, 256, 276, 287; constitutional convention, 278, 287; Indian policy in, 278-279; mentioned, 4, 6, 169, 245, 293
Calvert, George Henry, 121, 163
Camden, William, 11, 12
Camper, Pieter, 54, 55, 141, 142
Canada: annexation of, 219, 222, 228, 264, 277, 283-284, 295; mentioned, 6
Care, Henry, 21
Caribbean, 280-283, 286, 299
Carlyle, Thomas: and Germanic-Norse mystique, 38, 63-65; on Sir Walter Scott, 40; influence in America, 162,163, 180; mentioned, 220
Carr, William, 277
Carroll, Charles, 18
Cartwright, John, 23
Cartwright, Samuel A., 153-154
Caruthers, William A., 168
Casket (Cincinnati), 229, 235-236
Cass, Lewis, 200, 202, 241
Caucasians: Anglo-Saxons and, 1, 4, 43-44, 58, 69-70, 71-72, 126-127, 150, 159, 179, 252; and expansion, 1, 90-91, 136-137, 156, 252-253; and American race, 4, 251, 252, 284-285; and Indo-Europeans, 33; science and, 33, 43-44, 47, 67, 126-127, 130, 135, 136-137, 141, 159-160; phrenologists and, 58, 128; Disraeli on, 69-70, 318; Robert Knox on, 71-72; New England attitudes regarding, 150-151, 284-285; superiority questioned, 172-173, 261-262
Celts, 4, 30, 31-32, 49, 74, 131, 170, 253, 262, 295
Central America, 6, 216, 280, 281, 285, 290, 299
Chambers, Robert, 59, 149
Channing, William E., 265
Charleston Mercury, 238
Chastellux, François Jean, marquis de, 112
Chicago Daily Journal, 239
China, 91, 92, 156, 227, 271, 287, 289
Choate, Rufus, 224
Choctaw Academy, Ky., 204
Christianity: and origins of mankind, 2, 44-45; and expansion, 2, 89, 169, 288-289; English church, 9, 10, 14, 22, 76; and Teutonic nations, 67, 76; and commerce, 89, 288-289. *See also* Bible; Religion
Cincinnati, 171, 266
Cincinnati Herald, 239
Civilization, westward movement of: and American expansion, 5, 83, 84, 169, 170, 290; John Adams and, 86; T. H. Benton and, 89-90, 91-92, 252-253; James Barbour and, 96; William A. Caruthers and, 168; and drive to Asia, 286-289
Clay, Henry: and expansion, 87, 93; and South America, 87-88; and American mission, 88; on Anglo-Saxon race, 165; on Indian inferiority, 198; ill, 199; and 1844 election, 225

Clayton, John M., 242, 246
Clayton-Bulwer Treaty, 251
Clingman, Thomas L., 275
Cluverius, Philippus, 28-29
Coates, B. H., 118
Coke, Sir Edward, 12, 13, 16, 18, 20
Coleridge, Samuel Taylor, 162, 163, 181
Colfax, Richard H., 124
Collamer, Jacob, 242
Colonial America: and Anglo-Saxon England, 3-4, 15-17; and westward movement of civilization, 5, 83; reading in, 16-17; sense of mission, 82-83
Colonialism, American: dilemma of, 230-231, 247-248; Whigs and, 238; and Mexico, 243; Robert J. Walker and, 245; proponents, 279-280
Columbian, 171
Combe, Andrew, 57
Combe, George, 57, 58, 118, 120, 127-128, 143, 144
Commerce, American: and Asia, 90, 92, 288-290; as civilizing force, 223-224, 319; and world dominance, 286-290; and Christianity, 288-289, and world progress, 297, 298, 302-303
Commonwealthmen, 14-15
Congress, U.S.: and Indian Removal, 193-195, 197, 201, 202; on the nature of the Indian, 203-205; and Texas annexation, 217-218; and Manifest Destiny, 220, 257-258; and Oregon, 221-224; and Mexican War, 235, 237-238, 239-241, 242-244; and Yucatan, 247; and racial arrogance, 262, 263; and the territories, 275-277; and Canadian annexation, 283-284; and westward movement of civilization, 288
Cook, James, 45
Cooper, Thomas, 122, 140-141
Corry, William, 284
Corwin, Thomas, 240, 261
Cotton, Sir Robert, 13
Craig, Isaac, 111

Crawford, Colonel William, 112
Crawford, William Harris, 108, 193
Crèvecoeur, Michel Guillaume St. Jean de, 93
Cuba: W. G. Simms on, 167; Americanization of, 175; fears regarding, 204; Fillmore and, 277, 281; dilemma of, 281-283; mentioned, 6, 292
Cushing, Caleb, 223, 253
Cuvier, Georges, 47

Daily Ohio Statesman, 287
Dalrymple, Sir John, 16, 21
Dana, Richard, 211, 234
Darragh, Cornelius, 287
Darwin, Charles, 125
Davies, Arthur, 293
Dean, Gilbert, 288
Dearborn, Henry, 108
De Bow's Review: extinction of inferior races, 139, 155-156, 291; J. C. Nott and, 151, 153-155; and American militancy, 175; and regeneration of Mexico, 234; and Manifest Destiny, 258; and Cuba, 282-283; and Canada, 284
Declaration of Independence, 17, 22, 125, 275
Delano, Columbus, 240
Democratic Party: and Mexican War, 240-242, 245-246; Young America, 284-286; in 1852 election, 284; mentioned, 215, 219
Democratic Review: and Van Amringe, 134; and polygenesis, 145-146, 147-148; and Indians, 146; and blacks, 147, 148; and Carlyle, 162; O'Sullivan as editor, 219-220; and Mexican annexation, 240, 244; and American race, 251-252; on Anglo-Saxonism, 261; on the Caucasus, 284-285; and Young Americans, 285-286; mentioned, 149
"Demophilus," 17
De Pauw, Cornelius, 105
Dew, Thomas R., 123, 124, 203
Dickinson, Daniel S., 243

Disraeli, Benjamin, 62, 69-70, 71, 318
Dix, John A., 243
Dodge, Augustus, 290
Douglas, Stephen A., 251, 284
Drayton, John, 99
Duer, William, 257
Duncan, Alexander, 227-228
Dwight, Timothy, 86

Eaton, John, 201
Edda, 29
Edinburgh Review: and philology, 36-37; and race, 43, 60; on Robert Chambers, 59; and Teutonic peoples, 67, 68-69; in America, 160
Edwards, Jonathan, 83
Edwards, William F., 55
Egypt, 119, 126, 129, 130, 135, 142
Election of 1844, 225-226
Ellis, Anthony, 21
Emerson, Ralph Waldo, 65, 177-178
England. *See* Great Britain; Anglo-Saxon England, myth of
Enlightenment: and Revolutionary generation, 24, 82, 98, 298-299; and race, 44-46; and American progress, 84; and Indians, 104-105, 106, 107, 114, 193, 207; Gallatin as man of, 269, 270
Evans, Lemuel D., 275-276, 292
Evarts, Jeremiah, 200
Everett, Edward: and expansion, 88; and English origins, 95-96, 97; and human equality, 96-97, 176; and German thought, 162; on Indian Removal, 201; and Anglo-Saxon race, 226; mentioned, 161
Ewing, Presley, 288

Farmer's Register, 140
Farnham, T. J., 210
Ferris, Charles G., 228
Fichte, Johann Gottlieb, 27, 63
Ficklin, Orlando B., 274
Fillmore, Millard, 277, 283
Fitzhugh, George, 273, 285
Florida: Indian wars in, 204-205
Flournoy, J. J., 124

Floyd, John, 92
Follen, Carl, 163
Forsyth, John, 197
Foster, Georg, 48
Fowler, Charlotte, 143
Fowler, Lorenzo, 143, 144, 145
Fowler, Orson, 143, 144, 145
Foxe, John, 10
France: Teutonism in, 27-28, 36; and American thought, 160
Franklin, Benjamin, 18, 85
Franklin, state of, 87, 111-112
Freeman, E. A., 66, 75
Free Soil Party, 176, 274-275, 282

Gaines, Edmund P., 88
Gall, Franz Joseph, 56-57, 118
Gallatin, Albert, 266, 269-271
Geoffrey of Monmouth, 11
Georgia: and the Indians, 192, 193, 194-196, 198, 200, 201
Germanic peoples: and philology, 5, 32-38; and expansion, 5, 34-36, 37-38, 63-64, 74, 76-77, 170, 289-290; laudation of, in Germany, 11, 26-28; Anglo-Saxons and, 11-12, 14-15, 16, 17, 18, 19-20, 37, 39, 63-69, 74, 75-77, 131, 169-171, 173-174, 181-182, 183-184, 289-290; Tacitus on, 12; French and, 27-28, 36; and regeneration of Roman Empire, 36, 39, 66, 68-69, 76, 173, 244. *See also* Aryanism, Teutonism
Germany: Romantic movement in, 25-27; philology in, 32-36; and American thought, 160, 162-164, 178, 183
Gibbon, Edward, 29
Giddings, Joshua, 263
Gilmer, George, 194
Gilpin, William, 209, 210
Girty, Simon, 113
Gliddon, George R., 125, 135, 136-137, 152, 153, 157
Glorious Revolution of 1688, 14, 15
Gobineau, Joseph Arthur, comte de, 2
Goepp, Charles, 294, 295, 296

Goethe, Johann Wolfgang von, 63, 121, 162
Gordon, Samuel, 221
Graham, William A., 205
Gray, Asa, 132
Great Britain: development of Anglo-Saxon myth in, 10-15; Parliament of, 12, 13, 23, 172; philology in, 36-37; Romantic movement in, 38-42; scientific racialism in, 49-51, 52-54, 59-61; phrenology in, 57-59; racial Anglo-Saxonism in, 62-67; American criticisms of, 220, 221, 222, 284, 285-286; and Opium War, 227; as natural ally of the United States, 267, 292-294. *See also* Anglo-Saxon England, myth of
Greek revolutionaries, 95
Grimm, Jakob, 35-36
Guenebault, J. H., 124
Guizot, François, 173

Haiti, 97, 204
Halleck, H. W., 287
Hammond, James Henry, 125, 167
Hamtramck, John, 111
Hancock, John, 110
Harper, John A., 86
Harper, Robert G., 141
Harrington, James, 82
Harrison, William Henry, 115
Hastings, Hansford, 211
Hawaii, 288, 291, 296
Hay, John, 161
Hegel, Georg W. F., 27
Heine, Heinrich, 40
Henry, Patrick, 18
Herder, Johann Gottfried von, 27, 30, 63, 178
Hickes, George, 15
Hilliard, Henry W., 287
Historical Essay on the English Constitution, 17
Hobbes, Thomas, 14
Hone, Philip, 225
Hotman, François, 28
Houston, Sam, 213-214, 243

Hume, David, 48
Huntington, Jabez W., 238
Hutten, Ulrich von, 26

Illinois State Register, 236
Immigration: American fears of, 225-226, 302
India, 32, 36, 90, 169, 179, 271, 287, 295
Indians, American: as a race, 51-52, 118, 119-120, 130-131, 179; phrenology and, 58-59, 121, 127-128, 144-145; expendability of, 76-77, 155, 156, 198; colonial and early national attitudes toward, 103-115; science and, 118, 120, 127, 129, 130-131, 136, 191; periodicals and, 146-150, 155, 156; defense of, 150, 205-207; Parkman on, 184-185; Indian Removal, 190, 191-192, 193-194, 197-203; literary view of, 190-191; civilization of, 192-193, 196-197; Congressional discussion of, 193, 194-195, 197, 201, 203-205; southern states and, 193, 194-196, 198; John Quincy Adams administration, 197-201; in California, 278-279; failure of U.S. policy, 300-301
Ingersoll, Joseph R., 247
Irish, 4, 164, 226, 250. *See also* Celts

Jackson, Andrew, 88, 201, 202
Jamaica, 148
Japan, 91, 289
Jefferson, Thomas: and Anglo-Saxon England, 9, 18-23, 93; and English lawyers, 16; on Tacitus, 16; and idea of progress, 84; and American expansion, 86-87, 92-93; and Enlightenment, 98; and blacks, 101, 102; defends America, 105; and Indians, 107-108, 114-115; attacked, 125; mentioned, 123
Jews: as a race, 70-71, 73
Johnson, Andrew, 237
Johnson, Cave, 281
Johnson, Richard M., 86-87
Jones, James C., 257

Index

Jones, Seaborn, 221, 273
Jones, Sir William, 33
Jordan, Winthrop, 100
Joscelyn, John, 10
Junius, Francis, 15

Kames, Henry Home, Lord, 20-21, 48, 51, 99, 124
Kansas-Nebraska Act, 282
Kant, Immanuel, 63
Kashmir, vale of, 33
Kearny, Stephen W., 239
Kelley, Hall J., 89
Kemble, John M., 37, 68
Kendall, George, 211, 212, 234
Kennedy, John P., 289
Kentucky, 111
Kern, Richard H., 135
Kingsley, Charles, 75-77
Kinmont, Alexander, 265
Klaproth, Julius von, 35, 37
Kneeland, S., 134
Knox, Henry, 106-107, 108, 111
Knox, Robert, 71-73, 155, 156, 177, 318
Kuhn, A., 35

Laing, Samuel, 67
Lambarde, William, 307
Lassen, Christian, 35
Latham, R. G., 71, 275
Latin America, 255, 280-281, 285-286, 291, 299
Lavater, Johann Kaspar, 54-55
Lawrence, Abbot, 292
Lawrence, William, 53-54, 124, 141, 329
Legaré, Hugh, 165
Leigh, Benjamin, 209
Levellers, 13
Levy, David, 204
Liberator, 263
Lieber, Francis, 163, 171-173, 261-262, 336
Link, H. F., 34
Linn, Lewis F., 224
Linnaeus, Carolus, 46-47, 52, 98
List, Friedrich, 35
Logan, Benjamin, 111

Long, Edward, 49-50
Longfellow, Henry Wadsworth, 162, 163, 181
Louisiana Purchase, 344
Louisville Democrat, 245
Lowell, James Russell, 263-265
Lyell, Charles, 60

Mably, Gabriel Bonnot de, 311
Macaulay, Catherine, 17, 18, 20
Macaulay, Thomas Babington, 174
McCoy, Isaac, 199, 200, 206
McKenney, Thomas A., 200, 206, 341
McMinn, Joseph, 193, 194
Magna Carta, 14
Magnolia, 141-142, 165, 168
Magoon, E. L., 288
Mallet, Paul Henri, 19, 29, 30, 67
Malte-Brun, Conrad, 276
Mangum, Willie P., 161
Manifest Destiny: origin of phrase, 219-220; criticisms of, 256-264, 266-271; mentioned, 226, 237, 277. *See also* Mission, American
Marcy, William L., 232
Marsh, George Perkins, 163, 180-182
Marshall, John, 201
Massachusetts Quarterly Review, 139, 150, 259
Maury, Matthew F., 280
Meiners, Christoph, 48, 49
Melville, Herman, 255-256
Merchants' Magazine, 222, 291-292
Mexicans: low estimates of, 130-131, 209, 210-213, 215-216, 217, 233, 238-239, 240-241, 242-243, 245; as Indians, 210, 211, 212, 216, 231, 239-240, 243-244, 247; women, 223-224; U.S. officials and, 231-232; defense of, 234-235, 252, 260-261, 263; late eighteenth century view of, 299
Mexican War: and bellicose racialism, 166-167; opposition to, 180, 182, 237-240; racial factors leading to, 231-232; as war of liberation, 232-233; and regeneration of Mexico, 234-235; peace

treaty, 244-246; mentioned, 1, 6, 175
Mexico: future American expansion over, 167, 168, 175, 177, 180, 219, 237, 255, 281, 290, 291; problems of annexation, 242-244, 262-263
Michelet, Jules, 36, 60, 160
Milton, John, 82
Mirror of Justices, 13
Mission, American: "chosen people," 3, 5; colonial, 82-83; Revolutionary, 84-85, 115; early national, 86-88, 96-97, 115; W. G. Simms on, 168; increasing bellicosity, 175, 228, 235-236, 257-260; Parker on, 180; Bancroft on, 185; contradictions in, 186, 229-230; world scope, 224; Calhoun on, 241; Melville on, 255-256; Gallatin on, 269-270. *See also* Manifest Destiny
Missionaries: and Indians, 205-206
Mississippi, 192, 193, 200, 201
Mobile Register and Journal, 214-215
Modus Tenendi Parliamentum, 13
Molesworth, Robert, 14-15, 19, 29
Moluntha, Shawnee chief, 111
Monogenesis, 44-45, 48, 52, 99, 133, 145
Monroe, James, 87, 93, 194, 195, 196, 197
Monroe Doctrine, 296
Montesquieu, Charles Louis de Secondat, baron de, 16, 28
Morgan, George, 110
Morgan, Lewis Henry, 206-207
Morse, Jedediah, 86, 94
Morton, Samuel George: and skull capacity, 56; and American school of ethnology, 125; *Crania Americana*, 125, 126-127, 145; on Indian inferiority, 127, 150; *Crania Ægyptica*, 129; impact of work, 131-132; death of, 135; mentioned, 119, 128, 133, 134, 142, 146, 147
Möser, Justus, 26-27
Motley, John L., 162, 182, 183-184

Napoleon, 95, 170
National Anti-Slavery Standard, 263
National Era, 263

National Intelligencer, 261
Nativism, 225-226
New England: Puritan thought in, 3, 82-83; periodicals and race, 148-151; Coleridge and, 162; Romanticism in, 163-164; and American racial destiny, 175-185; and Manifest Destiny, 256-257; and blacks as natural Christians, 265
New Englander, 150, 258-259
New England Society of Cincinnati, 266
New Mexico, 182, 211-212, 239, 243, 245, 276-277
New Orleans, 209
Newspapers, Whig: and Mexican War, 238-239, 245
New York Herald, 227, 234
New York Morning News, 220
Nicaragua, 167
Norman Conquest: and reuniting of northern peoples, 11, 32, 64; and English loss of liberties, 13-14, 16-23 *passim*, 38
Norse tradition, 14-15, 29-30, 32, 38, 63-65, 67, 72, 75-76, 162, 180-182
North, Simeon, 289
North American Review, 162, 163, 260, 265-266, 288
North Carolina, 109, 112
Nott, Josiah C.: racial views, 116, 129-131, 151-155, 166; and American school of ethnology, 125; and mulattoes, 130, 256; and Agassiz, 132, 133; *Types of Mankind*, 135, 136-137, 153, 157; attacked, 149; mentioned, 147, 275, 296
Nourse, James D., 168-171
Novalis, 63

Opium War, 227
Oregon, 6, 89, 96, 169, 177, 220-225
O'Sullivan, John L., 219-220

Paine, Thomas, 81, 85
Panama Congress, 97
Paracelsus, 45
Parker, Matthew, 10
Parker, Theodore, 163, 178-180, 223

Parkman, Francis, 182, 184-185
Patterson, Henry S., 135-136
Pelloutier, Simon, 19, 29
Pendleton, John S., 222
Pennsylvania, 17-18, 23, 109, 110, 112, 113, 251
Percy, Thomas, 30, 39, 67
Periodicals: New England, 139, 148-151; Southern, 140-142. *See also* individual periodicals by name
Pettit, John, 272, 275
Peyrère, Isaac de la, 45
Philology: German, 5, 32-36; in England, 36-38
Phrenological Journal, 57
Phrenology: and race, 56-59, 120-122, 143-145; practical phrenology, 120, 142-145; S. G. Morton and, 127-128; mentioned, 54
Pickering, Charles, 330
Pike, James Shepherd, 282
Pinkerton, John, 31-32, 39, 48, 49
Poesche, Theodore, 294, 295, 296
Polk, James K.: and Mexican War, 231; and Mexican annexation, 242; and Trist Treaty, 244; Whigs and, 245; and Cuba, 281-282; mentioned, 217, 231, 293
Pollock, James, 239
Polygenesis: early defenses of, 45; in eighteenth century, 48-52; in mid-nineteenth century, 60; J. C. Nott and, 129-130; degree of acceptance in America, 132-133, 140, 145-146, 147, 152, 153
Pontiac, 109
Porter, B. F., 174
Pott, Augustus Friedrich, 25, 35
Prescott, William Hickling, 150, 182, 184
Prichard, James C., 37, 52-53, 71, 118, 150
Puritans: thought of, 3, 82-83; and Indians, 103
Putnam's, 157, 290

Quarterly Review, 160
Quetelet, L. A. J., 55
Quincy, Jr., Josiah, 18

Races: early classifications of, 43-44, 46-48; Enlightenment and, 45-46; J. C. Prichard and, 52-53; anthropometry and, 54-56; and environment, 98-99, 116; extinction of inferior, 73, 77, 139, 155-156, 291-292, 303
Racialism, scientific: and Romantic movement, 4-5, 44; polygenetic arguments, 45, 48-52, 60; phrenology and, 56-59, 120-122, 127-128, 142-145; early development in America, 117-120; S. G. Morton and, 125-129, 131-132; J. C. Nott and, 129-131, 135-137, 154-155; Agassiz and, 132-133; at mid-century, 133-135, 156-157; dissemination of, in America, 139-157
Rafn, Carl Christian, 181
Ramsay, W. G., 141
Randolph, John, 94, 95, 203
Ranke, Leopold von, 40
Rapin-Thoyras, Paul de, 17, 20
Rask, Rasmus Kristian, 37, 181
Real Whigs, 14-15, 18-19, 20-21
Reed, Thomas B., 97
Reformation, 10, 26
Religion: and origin of mankind, 44-45; challenged by racial theories, 117, 119, 132, 149, 152; caution of racial theorists toward, 126, 139-140; attempts to reconcile science and religion, 133, 147. *See also* Christianity; Bible
Republican Party, 275
Retzius, Anders, 56
Revolution, American: and sense of mission, 3, 82, 84-85; myth of Anglo-Saxon England and, 4, 9, 13, 15, 16, 17-18, 21-22, 81; impact on view of blacks, 100-101
Reynolds, John, 228
Reynolds, Thomas C., 163
Rhode, J. G., 35
Richardson, Joseph, 88
Richmond Palladium, 245
Richmond Whig, 238, 239, 257
Roane, William H., 123
Roman Empire: regeneration of, 36,

39, 66, 68-69, 76, 173, 244; influence of, 181
Romans, Bernard, 48, 51-52, 104
Romantic movement: and race, 5, 25-26; in America, 5, 158-159; and primitive peoples of Europe, 30-31; German, 32-33; in England, 38-41; and individualism, 41-42
Root, Joseph M., 247
Rousseau, Jean-Jacques, 202
Rush, Richard, 199
Russell, William H., 221

Sage, Rufus, 211-212, 234
St. Clair, Arthur, 110
St. Domingo, 175
Sanders, George O., 228, 284
Sarawak, 75, 77
Schlegel, Friedrich von, 34, 63, 173
Schleiermacher, Friedrich, 27
Schoolbooks, American: and race, 157
Scientific racialism. *See* Racialism, scientific
Scott, Sir Walter: influence of T. Percy on, 30; impact on Anglo-Saxonism, 38, 39-41; *Ivanhoe*, 40-41, 161, 165; influence in America, 160-161, 164, 165, 213, 222; mentioned, 75
Selden, John, 13
Sevier, Ambrose, 204
Sevier, John, 111
Seward, William H., 290
Seymour, David L., 218
Shannon, Wilson, 231
Shields, James, 249, 262
Sidney, Sir Philip, 184
Silliman, Benjamin, 127, 128
Simms, William Gilmore, 165-168, 191
Slavery: defense of, 101, 122-124, 140, 167, 273-274; and Texas annexation, 216-218; and Mexican War, 237; proposed expansion in 1850s, 280-283. *See also* Blacks
Slidell, John, 232
Smith, John Augustine, 116

Smith, Samuel Stanhope, 99, 116-117, 124
Smyth, John, 112
Smyth, Thomas, 147, 148, 149
Societé Ethnologique de Paris, 55
Society of Antiquaries, 12-13
South: and black inferiority, 122-125, 140-142; and American racial destiny, 164-175; and Indian Removal, 192-197, 200, 201; and Florida Indian war, 205; and a Caribbean empire, 280-283
South America, 216, 255, 281, 285
Southard, Henry, 108
Southard, Samuel L., 199
Southern Agriculturalist, 141
Southern Literary Journal, 140
Southern Literary Messenger, 141, 163, 289-290
Southern Quarterly Review: and the Indians, 146; J. C. Nott and, 151-152; racial views of, 152-153, 156; and Carlyle, 162; W. G. Simms as editor, 165, 167; and Anglo-Saxon race, 173, 174; and Mexicans, 246; and racial amalgamation, 256
Spelman, Sir Henry, 13, 16, 21
Spotswood, Alexander, 168
Spurzheim, Johann Gaspar, 56-57, 118, 120
Squier, Ephraim G., 125, 135
Staël, Madame de, 160
Stephens, Alexander H., 218
Stockton, Robert F., 290
Sumner, Charles, 262

Tacitus: and Germanic tribes, 10, 11, 12, 15, 17, 26, 27, 29; American interest in, 16; Jefferson on, 19; Montesquieu and, 28
Tennessee, 109, 110, 111-112, 192, 193, 195, 201
Teutonism: and American racialism, 3, 5, 154, 178, 212; origins of, 11, 27-29; in England, 63-65, 67-68, 75, 76. *See also* Aryanism; Germanic peoples

Texas: Revolution in, 213-215, 231, 244, 268; annexation of, 216-219; mentioned, 6, 93, 167
Texas-Santa Fe expedition, 211, 214-215, 234
Thierry, Augustin, 38-39, 40, 41, 160
Thompson, Waddy, 212
Thoreau, Henry David, 258
Thorpe, Benjamin, 37
Thwaites, Edward, 15
Tibbats, John W., 217
Ticknor, George, 162, 163
Tidyman, Philip, 163
Tiedemann, Friedrich, 56
Times (London), 221
Tipton, John, 204
Tocqueville, Alexis de, 189, 203, 274
Toombs, Robert, 221
Transcendentalists, 177
Transylvania University, 117, 118
Trimble, David, 88
Trist, Nicholas P., 162, 244, 245
Troup, George M., 88, 195, 196
Tucker, St. George, 102
Turner, Frederick Jackson, 171
Turner, Sharon, 39, 268

Ussher, James, 45

Van Amringe, William Frederick, 133-134, 147
Van Evrie, John H., 135, 280
Verstegen, Richard, 11, 13, 29
Virey, Jean-Joseph, 48, 49, 50, 124
Virginia, 22, 101, 102, 122-123
Voltaire, 48, 124

Walker, Robert J.: sketch of, 215; on Texas annexation, 215-217; racial views, 215-216, 293-294, 296; and Great Britain, 221, 293-294, 296; and colonialism, 245, 246-247, 281; and commercial expansion, 289
Walker, William, 167
Wanley, Humphrey, 15
Warner, J. J., 279
Washington, George, 18, 111, 114
Wayne, Anthony, 109
Webster, Daniel: and Indians, 205; and Oregon, 223; and race, 226-227, 276; on American mission, 242; son of, 257; mentioned, 143, 244
Weightman, Richard H., 277
Westcott, James D., 276
West Indies, 65, 175, 281
Whig history: classic Whig view of the past, 14-15; in America, 15-17, 18, 18-19, 20-21. *See also* Real Whigs
Whig Party: and 1844 election, 225-226; and Mexican War, 237-240, 245; and Mexican inferiority, 242-243, 250, 262-263; and American bellicosity, 250
White, Charles, 48, 50-51, 99, 141
Whitman, Walt, 235
Wick, William, 238
William the Conqueror, 22. *See also* Norman Conquest
Williamson, Hugh, 99
Wilson, James, 23-24
Winthrop, Robert C., 220, 226
Wirt, William, 199
Woodbury, Levi, 217
Wyclif, John, 10

Young America, 166, 228, 280, 284-286, 288, 290
Yucatan, 167, 246-247, 281, 285, 290